The Illusion of Full Inclusion

A Comprehensive
Critique of a Current
Special Education Bandwagon

SECOND EDITION

Edited by
James M. Kauffman
and
Daniel P. Hallahan

pro·ed
An International Publisher

8700 Shoal Creek Boulevard
Austin, Texas 78757-6897
800/897-3202   Fax 800/397-7633
www.proedinc.com

© 1995, 2005 by PRO-ED, Inc.
8700 Shoal Creek Boulevard
Austin, Texas 78757-6897
800/897-3202   Fax 800/397-7633
www.proedinc.com

Library of Congress Cataloging-in-Publication Data

The illusion of full inclusion : a comprehensive critique of a current special education
    bandwagon / edited by James M. Kauffman, Daniel P. Hallahan.—2nd ed.
    p. cm.
    Includes bibliographical references and index.
    ISBN 0-89079-995-4
    1. Mainstreaming in education—United States.   2. People with
disabilities—Education—United States.   3. Special education—United States.
4. Inclusive education—United States.   I. Kauffman, James M.   II. Hallahan,
Daniel P., 1944–

LC4031.I45 2004
371.9'046'0973—dc22

2004050359

Art Director: Jason Crosier
Designer: Nancy McKinney-Point
This book is designed in Minion and Gill Sans.

Printed in the United States of America

1 2 3 4 5 6 7 8 9 10   08 07 06 05 04

Contents

Preface

What may be special education's largest bandwagon ever, one having gathered such great mass and momentum that it seems to many unstoppable, began its roll almost imperceptibly in the mid-1980s. Astute observers immediately warned that this bandwagon, although just forming, had all the potential for mischief of a loose cannon (Lieberman, 1985; Mesinger, 1985). Within 10 years, its size, velocity, and direction became potentially fatal not only to those on board but to the entire special education community through which it was traveling. Two decades later, the devastation of the full inclusion movement (FIM) is apparent, and the struggle to preserve special education's historic mission is even more critical (Kauffman & Hallahan, 2005). Thus, this second edition includes readings that are nearly two decades old as well as those written recently.

The FIM bandwagon offers an attractive platform—the merger of special and general education into a seamless and supple system that will support all students adequately in general schools and general education classrooms, regardless of any student's characteristics. Those offering cautions warn that this platform, although having an appealing sheen, is not sufficiently substantial for students who make particularly heavy demands on any system of education. A single structure, critics of the FIM argue, can be made sufficiently strong to support some students with disabilities in regular schools and classes, but it cannot offer equally effective support in the same place at the same time for all students; a special, supplementary structure is required to keep many students with special needs from dropping through the floor of public education.

This book is intended to show why full inclusion can provide only an illusion of support for all students—an illusion that may trick many into jumping on the bandwagon but is sure to produce disappointment, if not outrage, in its riders when the juggernaut crushes the students it was supposed to defend. The growth and increasing momentum of the full inclusion bandwagon have been due in part to the ready availability of books providing a rationale for scrapping the present special education structure altogether. Many of us who take a cautious deliberative approach to special education reform saw a need for a book warning of the dangers of embracing the illusory rhetoric of full inclusion. Now, we see a need for a second edition of a book that many have found useful.

As in the first edition, we have organized the essays comprising this book into three major sections. Part I provides context and historical perspective. Part II is a series of critiques of the FIM, with particular attention paid to conceptual and policy issues. Part III takes up various issues from the perspective of concern for groups with specific disabilities.

Although many more cautionary writings are available than those we have been able to include in this second edition, we believe these selections provide a good beginning for helping individuals interested in the full inclusion controversy weigh alternatives to what has become increasingly popular but misguided rhetoric in school reform. We certainly do not believe that any of the readings included in the first edition, but not the second, should be ignored. Simply, we had to make difficult choices about what to include and what not to include, given the necessity of keeping the length of the book reasonable. We encourage readers of this edition to delve into the references cited, some of which are references to chapters included in the first edition.

Together, these essays and organizational statements, we hope, will be an effective tool for informing educators, advocates for students with disabilities, and policymakers of the obliteration of special education that we can still avoid—but only if we quickly, forcefully, and effectively unite to steer the full inclusion bandwagon away from its collision with the realities of childhood, schooling, disabilities, teaching, and parenting.

We thank the copyright holders of the works that are reprinted in this volume for their permission to use their material. We are grateful also to Don Hammill and Lee Wiederholt for suggesting that we collect essays for such a volume and for giving us the go-ahead for a second edition. We also thank the personnel at PRO-ED for publishing them in a timely fashion.

Finally, we note that all royalty earnings from the sale of this book are assigned to the Eli M. Bower Endowed Fellowship Fund at the University of Virginia. This fund provides an annual stipend to a graduate student in the Curry School of Education who is preparing to work with children with emotional or behavioral disorders.

J. M. K.
D. P. H.
Charlottesville, VA

REFERENCES

Lieberman, L. M. (1985). Special education and regular education: A merger made in heaven? *Exceptional Children, 51,* 513–516.

Kauffman, J. M., & Hallahan, D. P. (2005). *Special education: What it is and why we need it.* Boston: Allyn & Bacon.

Mesinger, J. F. (1985). Commentary on "A rationale for the merger of special and regular education" or, Is it now time for the lamb to lie down with the lion? *Exceptional Children, 51,* 510–512.

Contributors

Barbara D. Bateman, PhD
University of Oregon
Eugene, Oregon

Michael Bina, PhD
The Hadley School for
the Blind
Winnetka, Illinois

Michele Brigham, MEd
Albemarle County Public
Schools
Charlottesville, Virginia

Margaret N. Carr, MEd
Woodway Elementary School
Fort Worth, Texas

Jean B. Crockett, PhD
Virginia Polytechnic Institute
and State University
Blacksburg, Virginia

Steven R. Forness, EdD
University of California at
Los Angeles
Los Angeles, California

James J. Gallagher, PhD
University of North Carolina
Chapel Hill, North Carolina

Michael M. Gerber, PhD
University of California at
Santa Barbara
Santa Barbara, California

Michael F. Gliona, BA
Save Our Special Schools
(SOSS)
Los Angeles, California

Alexandra K. Gonzales
Save Our Special Schools
(SOSS)
Los Angeles, California

Frank M. Gresham, PhD
University of California at
Riverside
Riverside, California

Daniel P. Hallahan, PhD
University of Virginia
Charlottesville, Virginia

Eric S. Jacobson, JD
Save Our Special Schools
(SOSS)
Los Angeles, California

James M. Kauffman, EdD
University of Virginia
Charlottesville, Virginia

Kenneth A. Kavale, PhD
Regent University
Virginia Beach, Virginia

Harlan Lane, PhD
Northeastern University
Boston, Massachusetts

Sandra Lewis, PhD
Florida State University
Tallahassee, Florida

Donald L. MacMillan, PhD
University of California at
Riverside
Riverside, California

Kathleen McGee, PhD
Westerville Public Schools
Westerville, Ohio

Devery R. Mock, PhD
University of Iowa
Iowa City, Iowa

William C. Morse, PhD
University of South Florida
Tampa, Florida

Bernard Rimland, PhD
Autism Research Institute
San Diego, California

Melvyn I. Semmel, PhD
University of California at
Santa Barbara
Santa Barbara, California

Judith D. Singer, PhD
Harvard University
Cambridge, Massachusetts

PART I

Full Inclusion in Historical Context

For at least 5 decades, many special educators have called for the inclusion of students with disabilities in general education schools and classrooms to the extent that such inclusion is appropriate for individual children. The idea of appropriate inclusion has not been questioned for decades, if ever, by special educators. The Full Inclusion Movement (FIM) is of comparatively recent vintage (Crockett & Kauffman, 1999; Fuchs & Fuchs, 1994; Lloyd & Gambatese, 1991).

In the mid-1970s, the consensus of advocates for children and youth with disabilities, including special educators, was that students with disabilities should be a part of mainstream classes, when their special educational needs could be met there. The mandate for education in the "least restrictive environment" (LRE) was incorporated into the Education for All Handicapped Children Act of 1975 (better known as Public Law 94-142, and later known as IDEA, the Individuals with Disabilities Education Act). Like P.L. 94-142, IDEA (in its 1990 and 1997 reauthorizations) also mandated that a continuum of alternative placements (CAP) be available to students with

1

disabilities, under the assumption that an array of options ranging from full-time placement in general classrooms to placement in special residential schools or hospitals is necessary to meet the needs of individual students. Furthermore, since 1975 federal law has mandated that appropriate education and related services and the least restrictive placement be determined on an individual basis; it has proscribed decisions based on diagnostic categories of students (e.g., categories such as learning disability, emotional disturbance, mental retardation, deafness, and autism).

Beginning in 1975, federal special education law prescribed, first, the determination of appropriate education and related services and, only subsequently, that the least restrictive environment for delivery of those services be determined—in all instances, on a case-by-case basis. Contrary to this idea, advocates of full inclusion call for a uniform placement decision first, followed by consideration of what might constitute an appropriate education and related services that could be delivered in that placement. Full inclusion makes placement the prepotent issue in special education; it defines as appropriate only that which can be delivered in the general school or general classroom, assuming that any service that can be delivered in a special class or special school can be delivered at least as effectively in a neighborhood school and regular classroom.

In the early 1980s, some individuals and advocacy groups began challenging the concepts of LRE and CAP, arguing that the LRE—for all students—is the general school and general classroom and that a CAP is unworkable and unnecessary for providing appropriate education and related services. In essence, the argument of these advocates of full inclusion was that students with disabilities should no longer be included in a general classroom with duration of placement and extent of inclusion based on case-by-case evaluation; rather, they argued that students with disabilities should be treated, for purposes of placement, as a single category or class. All individual consideration was to be constrained by universal placement of stu-

dents with disabilities in general schools and classes. This argument is a radical break with the history of special education, which recognizes the need for a diversity of environments in response to a diversity of student characteristics (see Crockett & Kauffman, 1999).

The current full inclusion thrust has roots in the civil rights, deinstitutionalization, and educational reform movements of the late 1960s and early 1970s (see Crockett & Kauffman, 1999; Kauffman & Lloyd, 1995; Lloyd & Gambatese, 1991). Around that time, two articles that were particularly influential in shaping advocacy for mainstreaming in that era and setting the course toward full inclusion in the subsequent decades appeared in Exceptional Children, the primary journal of the Council for Exceptional Children. Those articles included Lloyd Dunn's suggestion that special education for mildly retarded students was segregationist (Dunn, 1968) and Evelyn Deno's suggestion that special education could become unnecessary by giving its expertise to general education (Deno, 1970). The articles provided impetus for the mainstreaming movement of the 1970s, which saw the rise of the resource room model as a means to the end of including students in more general classroom activities. In the 1990s, however, the resource model was decried as "segregationist" by advocates of full inclusion, who urged its abandonment in favor of a model of collaborative consultation between general and special educators. The idea of merging general and special education began gaining momentum in the 1980s with other publications in Exceptional Children, specifically calls by special educators William Stainback and Susan Stainback (Stainback & Stainback, 1984) for a merger of general and special education and the assertion of Madeline Will, then head of the federal special education agency, that regular education should take the initiative in serving most students with disabilities with consultation from special educators (Will, 1986). This movement to merge general and special education and educate most students with disabilities in regular classes through consultation or collaboration of general and special educators became *known as the Regular Education Initiative, or REI (see Lloyd, Singh, & Repp, 1991).*

The opening chapter in Part I of this book, among the first extended responses to the idea of merging general and special education, was written by educational researcher, Judith Singer. Singer's essay remains one of the most incisive analyses of the issues. In the second chapter, special educator and attorney Barbara Bateman notes that some controversial issues in special education are perpetual, including the issue of where students should be taught. The next three chapters in Part I (by MacMillan, Semmel, & Gerber; Gallagher; and Morse, respectively) are from a series of 25-year retrospectives on the articles by Dunn and Deno, including evaluations of their historical significance and continuing legacy. Chapter 6 is an essay about the meaning of restriction and the relationship of the current FIM to the notion of what is restricted in teaching and for what reason. Chapter 7 is about how the purposes of special education have changed with the FIM and how students suffer from the idea that remaining in the regular classroom is more important than effective instruction. Part I ends with a chapter calling for new ways of conceptualizing and talking about the LRE. It questions the depiction of restrictiveness as a cascade and offers an alternative to talk of "segregation" in special placements.

REFERENCES

Americans with Disabilities Act of 1990, 42 U.S.C. § 12101 *et seq.*

Crockett, J. B., & Kauffman, J. M. (1999). *The least restrictive environment: Its origins and interpretations in special education.* Mahwah, NJ: Erlbaum.

Deno, E. (1970). Special education as developmental capital. *Exceptional Children, 37,* 229–237.

Dunn, L. M. (1968). Special education for the mildly retarded—Is much of it justifiable? *Exceptional Children, 35,* 5–22.

Education for All Handicapped Children Act of 1975, 20 U.S.C. § 1400 *et seq.*

Fuchs, D., & Fuchs, L. S. (1994). Inclusive schools movement and the radicalization of special education reform. *Exceptional Children, 60,* 294–309.

Individuals with Disabilities Education Act of 1990, 20 U.S.C. § 1400 *et seq.*

Individuals with Disabilities Education Act Amendments of 1997, 20 U.S.C. § 1401 (26b).

Kauffman, J. M., & Lloyd, J. W. (1995). A sense of place: The importance of placement issues in contemporary special education. In J. M. Kauffman, J. W. Lloyd, D. P. Hallahan, & T. A. Astuto (Eds.), *Issues in educational placement: Students with emotional and behavioral disorders* (pp. 3–19). Hillsdale, NJ: Erlbaum.

Lloyd, J. W., & Gambatese, C. (1991). Reforming the relationship between regular and special education: Background and issues. In J. W. Lloyd, A. C. Repp, & N. N. Singh (Eds.), *The regular education initiative: Alternative perspectives on concepts, issues, and methods* (pp. 3–13). Dekalb, IL: Sycamore.

Lloyd, J. W., Singh, N. N., & Repp, A. C. (Eds.). (1991). *The regular education initiative: Alternative perspectives on concepts, issues, and methods.* Dekalb, IL: Sycamore.

Stainback, W., & Stainback, S. (1984). A rationale for the merger of special and regular education. *Exceptional Children, 51,* 102–111.

Will, M. C. (1986). Educating children with learning problems: A shared responsibility. *Exceptional Children, 52,* 411–416.

CHAPTER I

Should Special Education Merge with Regular Education?

Judith D. Singer

This chapter is from "Should Special Education Merge with Regular Education?" by J. D. Singer, 1988, *Educational Policy*, 2, pp. 409–424. Copyright 1988 by Sage Publications. Reprinted with permission.

Eleven years ago, the United States began implementation of P.L. 94-142, the Education for All Handicapped Children Act [now called the Individuals with Disabilities Education Act, or IDEA], requiring the public schools to identify and then to provide special education services to all youngsters with educational, emotional, developmental, or physical disabilities. Hailed as a "Bill of Rights" for children with handicaps, the law outlined a process whereby all children, regardless of the severity of their handicap, were to be guaranteed the same educational rights and privileges accorded to their nonhandicapped peers: "a free appropriate public education."

P.L. 94-142 has been remarkably successful in influencing state and local educational policy and practice. Between the 1976–1977 and 1986–1987 school years, the number of special education students increased by 19% to 4.4 million and the number of special education teachers increased by 63% to 292,000 (Office of Special Education and Rehabilitative Services [OSERS], 1988, pp. 4, 34). Eleven percent of all elementary and secondary school students now receive specialized instruction or services under the law, including thousands of severely handicapped children who previously would have been denied any education and many more mildly handicapped children who previously would have received no supplemental curricula or assistance. Special education enjoys bipartisan support in Congress, and local programs are a source of pride in many school districts across the country (for an overview of the implementation of P.L. 94-142, see Clune & Van Pelt, 1985; Singer & Butler, 1987).

Despite these successes, all is not well within special education. P.L. 94-142's provisions for individualized learning goals, curricula, and services have made it intrinsically difficult (if not virtually impossible) to evaluate educational outcomes for groups of children (see Bryk & Light, 1981; Kennedy, 1978). In the absence of documented improvements, critics argue that the special education system established under P.L. 94-142 has failed to help children with mild and moderate handicaps, especially youngsters with learning disabilities, emotional disturbances, and mental retardation. They maintain that many of the students being served are not "truly" handicapped, that the individualized educational programs being used are ineffective, and that one major intent of the law—placement in the "least restrictive environment" commensurate with the child's needs—is being subverted. They conclude that the existing special education system should be dismantled and the regular education system should reassume responsibility for mildly and moderately handicapped students (Gartner & Lipsky, 1987; Lytle, 1988; Reynolds, Wang, & Walberg, 1987; Will, 1986).

Ironically, this proposal comes not from regular educators seeking to reclaim lost resources, but from special educators criticizing their own profession. Indeed, regular educators have not even been asked whether they are willing to reassume responsibility for these children. First outlined in the early 1980s, the proposal has been gaining momentum, especially since Madeleine Will, Assistant Secretary of the Office of Special Education and Rehabilitative Services, expressed her support for a variant of it, which has come to be known as the Regular Education Initiative.[1]

Should special education transfer responsibility for mildly and moderately handicapped children back to regular education? Would this change improve the educational experiences and outcomes of special needs students in a way that cannot be done under the present system? In this paper, I use evidence gathered during a decade of research on P.L. 94-142 to demonstrate that, however well-intentioned, the Regular Education Initiative is a deeply flawed proposal with substantial downside risks. Many of its supporting assumptions are refuted by recent research, and others are simply naive. Full-time regular class placement is not necessarily better for all students with mild and moderate handicaps, and even if it were, it is unlikely that regular education is willing or even able to serve many of these students.

Moreover, the potential risks associated with the Regular Education Initiative far outweigh any potential gains. Shifting responsibility for mildly and moderately handicapped children to regular education will not produce the improved educational outcomes that have remained elusive to date. Eliminating labels does not eliminate problems. Children with special needs will continue to be with us and they will continue to need services. The difference that the Regular Education Initiative would make is that individualization of placement and curricula, now mandated by law, would no longer be guaranteed.

But proponents of the initiative are correct when they argue that the educational programs being delivered to students with mild and moderate handicaps could be (and should be) improved. Despite years of research, we still do not know which curricula and services are most effective for teaching children with different types of problems. Special education practices vary widely across states and school districts. To improve educational outcomes for handicapped children, however, we should not simply transfer responsibility for these children to regular education; rather, we should work within the present combined system towards developing and disseminating effective instructional techniques, curricula, and service options.

ASSUMPTIONS UNDERLYING THE REGULAR EDUCATION INITIATIVE

Proponents of the Regular Education Initiative present a simple and compelling argument: Current special education programs have failed to serve mildly and moderately handicapped students adequately; therefore, the programs should be dismantled, and primary responsibility for these students should be given back to regular education. To support their view, proponents have argued that:

1. school districts are overidentifying special needs students;
2. special needs students are being segregated in separate settings;
3. special education students rarely return to regular education;
4. regular class placements would produce better educational outcomes for all these students;
5. regular educators would willingly serve mildly and moderately handicapped students full-time;
6. special needs students would continue to receive specialized services within regular education; and
7. the due process guarantees established under P.L. 94-142 would not be affected. (Gartner & Lipsky, 1987; Lilly, 1986; Lipsky & Gartner, 1987; Reynolds et al., 1987; Stainback & Stainback, 1984; Stainback, Stainback, Courtnage, & Jaben, 1985; Will, 1986)

Let us examine the evidence concerning each of these points.

Are School Districts Overidentifying Special Needs Students?

As a percentage of total public school enrollment, the proportion of students receiving special education services grew rapidly after implementation of P.L. 94-142, from approximately 8% to 11%. Since the early 1980s, the rate of growth has slowed, however, so that the 11% figure has been reasonably stable for several years and has always fallen well below the 12% cap proposed in the law's regulations. Moreover, despite an initial congressional estimate of 1.75 million unserved children, the total number of children served has increased by less than 700,000.[2]

But there has been dramatic growth in one group of children—those classified as learning disabled. As a proportion of total enrollment, the learning disabled population grew from 1.8% in 1976–1977 to 4.7% in 1986–1987; this group now represents 44% of special education students nationally (OSERS, 1988). This growth has been attributed to many factors, including increasing public awareness of learning disabilities; the desire not to stigmatize children with more traditional labels; the need for a convenient category for those reclassified from the mentally retarded category in the wake of court action discouraging this designation; the need for supplemental services for children at a time when other sources of support, such as Title I and funding for bilingual education, have been drying up; the hope of improving state and school district standardized test results at a time when scores are being so closely scrutinized; and the unintended financial incentives created by the uniform reimbursement formulae used in some states allowing part of the allocation for learning disabled children to be used as a cross-subsidy for services for other special education groups.[3]

The preference for classifying students as learning disabled, drawing from other categories within special education and from the general education population, may be the biggest change in education practice brought about by P.L. 94-142. At issue, however, is not the increase per se, but whether the increase indicates that school districts are serving students who are not "truly" handicapped. Learning disabled is a "soft" category subject to variable interpretation. Experts in the field concede that there are definitional difficulties in identifying these students and that, using existing measurement techniques, some of the students identified as learning disabled are indistinguishable from low-achieving regular education students (see, e.g., Algozzine & Ysseldyke, 1986).

But definitional difficulties aside, these youngsters do exist, and they do need help in school (see Keogh, 1988; Shepard, 1987). The learning disabled label did not create their problem: they were given the label because of their problem. By extension, taking away the label will not make their problem disappear. Clearly, improved measurement technology is needed. Until such technology is developed, however, the evidence of a handicap must be gathered by teachers and parents using the available imperfect techniques. For professionals who deal with these children on a day-in and day-out basis, the fact that some students are having problems in school is all the evidence required to document the need for supplemental services (see Bryan, Bay, & Donahue, 1988).

Are Special Needs Students Being Segregated?

Many proponents of the Regular Education Initiative incorrectly argue that the overwhelming majority of students with special needs are being educated in substantially separate placements. During the 1986–87 school year, 68% of all students with special needs received all or most of their education in regular classrooms, including 77% of students classified as learning disabled, 46% of students classified as emotionally disturbed, and 33% of students classified as mentally retarded (OSERS, 1988, p. 30). Although some states and school districts still prefer separate class placements for some groups of students, most mildly and moderately handicapped children actually are substantially mainstreamed.

Nor is there evidence to suggest that the regular education classes attended by special education students are "second-class" regular classes, disproportionately filled with special needs students. As part of the Collaborative Study of Children with Special Needs, my colleagues and I examined the classroom placements of over 950 elementary school students with special needs in five major metropolitan school districts and found that the regular classes that they attended did not look at all unusual (Singer, Butler, Palfrey, & Walker, 1986). In fact, their classes were quite similar to other regular classes in the districts we studied—relatively homogeneous with respect to age, with an average of 27–28 students of whom only three or four had special needs. Moreover, regular class time was not restricted to nonacademic subjects such as music, art, and gym; across all of the special needs students we studied, 58% spent all or most of their *academic* instructional time in regular classes. If a major goal of the Regular Education Initiative is to ensure that special needs students are placed in regular education classes, that goal is already being attained in many school districts across the country.

Do Special Education Students Ever Leave Special Education?

Some proponents of the initiative have argued that special education is a one-way street: Once a child enters, he is unlikely ever to leave. Regrettably, the federal government does not collect national data on the length of time that children receive special education services, nor on the proportion of students who are "decertified" each year. The failure to collect this information has led Alan Gartner and Dorothy Kerzner Lipsky to speculate that "decertification data ... most likely would show an embarrassingly low level of return to general education" (Gartner & Lipsky, 1987, p. 367).

But some empirical evidence is available on this topic, and it suggests that the level of return is not "embarrassingly low" at all. In a 2-year study of over 1,000 elementary school students in three major metropolitan school districts that had received special education services for at least 6 months in 1982, my colleagues and I found that 17% had returned to regular education by 1984 (Walker et al., 1988). Not surprisingly, the decertification rates varied by the child's handicap. The rates were highest for those classified as speech impaired (33%), but 15% of those classified as learning disabled and 9% of those classified as emotionally disturbed also returned to regular education during the 2-year study period. If these rates of return still seem low, it is important to remember that they are only biennial estimates: The probability that a special education student will *eventually* return to regular education is much higher. Although these results cannot be generalized to all school districts across the country, it seems that, for many children, special education is not a one-way street.

Are Regular Classes Better?

The Regular Education Initiative is predicated on the assumption that regular classes are better for *all* students with mild to moderate handicaps. But a review of the research on the efficacy of regular class placements reveals serious methodological flaws and much conflicting evidence.

Numerous researchers have compared the effects of regular and special class placement on student learning: One meta-analysis found 264 studies published between 1975 and 1984.[4] Few studies have involved the random assignment of students to placement, however, and only weak conclusions can be drawn from the large number of studies not based on random assignment, because such studies suffer from an incurable selection bias. Under P.L. 94-142, special needs students are placed in classroom settings commensurate with their functional abilities. As a result, mainstream settings tend to be populated with less impaired students and separate settings tend to be populated with more impaired students. When nonexperimental studies find, as many do, that students in mainstream settings perform better than students in separate settings, we cannot determine whether the differential is attributable to the mainstream setting or to the fact that these students were less impaired to begin with.

Aware of these methodological problems, several teams of researchers have synthesized the results of the highest quality studies comparing regular and special class placements. Unfortunately, these teams have reached conflicting conclusions. For example, the two major meta-analyses found that although regular classes were marginally better for mentally retarded children (mean effect sizes of .14 and .22), special classes were marginally better for learning disabled children (mean effect sizes of .29 and .39) (Carlberg & Kavale, 1980; Wang & Baker, 1985–1986). In a third research synthesis, Nancy Madden and Robert Slavin concluded that "for most students with mild academic handicaps, the best placement is in a regular class using individualized instruction or in a regular class supplemented by well-designed resource support" (Madden & Slavin, 1983, p. 554). Note that Madden and Slavin are not advocating just any type of regular placement, but rather regular placement with specific modes of supplemental instruction and support, given in *either* the regular classroom or the resource room. Thus, the safest generalization is that *some* types of regular class placement, especially ones that involve supplemental support services, are better for *some* mildly handicapped children.

Is this sufficient evidence to warrant a major policy shift requiring regular class placement for *all* mildly and moderately handicapped students? Probably not, for after all, regular class placement is commonplace under the present special education system. The difference is that the present system mandates that placement and service decisions be made on a case-by-case basis. This individualization of placement and services would be at serious risk if primary responsibility for all mildly and moderately handicapped students was returned to regular education.

A more general problem with the initiative is that placement per se may not be the most important issue. When a panel of the National Academy of Sciences examined the overrepresentation of minority youngsters in programs for the mildly mentally retarded, for example, they concluded that placement was not the issue at all:

> On the whole we are forced to conclude that administrative setting, in and of itself, does not determine whether an educational program is effective or appropriate. Rather it is the things that go on in that setting that matter. (Heller, Holtzman, & Messick, 1982, p. 85)

Decades of research on educational effectiveness tell us that it is what actually happens in a class that makes the difference. Proponents of the initiative turn the clocks back by emphasizing issues of administration and placement over issues of instructional techniques and personnel. Thus, we should be asking questions such as: Which instructional strategies and supplemental curricula are most likely to be effective for the child? What type of training and credentials will the best teacher for this child have? How can we balance the costs and benefits to the child of being pulled out of the usual classroom? (Will being pulled out create discontinuities in peer friendships and informal learning? Will the child gain in those areas emphasized in the pullout session only to fall behind in areas covered in the base classroom?) Only when we begin to address these questions will we begin to understand how to improve educational outcomes for children with special needs (for a more detailed explication of these issues, see Lloyd, Crowley, Kohler, & Strain, 1988).

Would Regular Education Reassume Responsibility for These Children?

Most mildly and moderately handicapped children receiving special education services were referred for services either because they were performing poorly in regular education or because they were disruptive (see, e.g., Applied Management Sciences, 1983; Bickel, 1982; Mehan, Meihls, Hertweck, & Crowdes, 1981). Special education was the solution to the regular educator's thorny problem of how to provide supplemental resources to children in need while not shortchanging other students in the class (see, e.g., Gans, 1987; Gerber & Semmel, 1984; Weatherley, 1979). Nothing else has happened within regular education to solve this problem. What leads special educators to believe that regular educators are willing to take back responsibility for special needs children?

Regular education is in the midst of its own crisis, fueled by the national reform movement. Calls for excellence have taken precedence over calls for equity. Some special educators have taken the reform movement's omission of special education as a snub, reflecting regular education's belief that "special education students are not considered worthy or needy of educational attention" (Sapon-Shevin, 1987, p. 305). But consider a different interpretation: Regular education is already so overburdened that it can hardly handle its own problems; it is not in a position even to conceive of handling problems that it has traditionally delegated to special education. In the current educational climate, which seems unlikely to change in the foreseeable future, regular educators simply will not accept the dissolution of over half of the special education program.

Laurence Lieberman used the metaphor of marriage to describe the proposed merger:

> We [special education] have thrown a wedding and neglected to invite the bride [regular education]. If this is that invitation to holy matrimony, it was clearly written by the groom, for the groom, and the groom's family. (Lieberman, 1985, pp. 513–514)

Special educators would do well to put themselves in regular educators' shoes. The Regular Education Initiative offers regular educators little incentive to participate. One powerful incentive would be money. Since the education of a special education student costs an average of twice as much as the education of a regular student, some observers have suggested that regular education would welcome the additional resources.[5] But the extra dollars currently allocated to the relatively small number of mildly and moderately handicapped students would not go very far when spread across *all* students in a district. Regular education administrators would question whether the extra dollars were worth the extra effort, and it is likely that many would forego the limited additional dollars rather than take on the potentially unlimited additional responsibility.

How Could Resources Be Targeted?

The philosophy of the Regular Education Initiative has been compared to that of the Civil Rights movement: There is no such thing as separate but equal (Gartner & Lipsky, 1987). Although this may ring true, note that special needs students do not require equal treatment under the law, but *preferred* treatment. And to receive preferred treatment, it is necessary to have some means of identifying those eligible to receive the supplemental services as well as some description of what those services are. As James Kauffman, Michael Gerber, and Melvyn Semmel point out:

> If low performing and mildly handicapped students are to be served well, then resources for their instruction must be protected. Effective protection of these resources may be achievable, in many cases, for instruction within regular education. Nevertheless, they must be identified as "special," "additional," "remedial," "compensatory," or by some other label that clearly sets them aside. The necessity for this identification is as

obvious to us as the necessity for budget lines for "national defense" and "education." (Kauffman, Gerber, & Semmel, 1988, p. 10)

Thus, Regular Education Initiative or not, identification of children as handicapped and classification of them according to their needs will remain with us as two-edged swords. On the one hand, most of us would agree that if a child has special needs, it is advantageous to find the child as early as possible, evaluate the child's problem, and develop a strategy for ensuring that the child receives the best education we can deliver. On the other hand, most of us also recognize that identification and classification can produce unintended negative effects in the form of stigmatizing labels, inferior tracking, and inappropriate placement, that may establish artificially low educational expectations and may fundamentally alter life chances for the child.

So we are left with a conundrum: How can we ensure that children with special needs receive the necessary supplemental services but not the potential negative consequences? Hence the need for a designation that has as few negative connotations as possible and a method for ensuring that children so designated actually get the necessary services.

Given these constraints, the learning disabled designation may be about as flexible and nonstigmatizing as any means yet devised for targeting compensatory education to slow learners of many kinds. Consider that most parents and children would prefer being called learning disabled rather than being incorrectly labeled mentally retarded or stupid or being allowed to fail repeatedly in school without any specialized help.[6] Note, too, that in much diversity is much protective coloring; it may be a decided advantage that the learning disabled designation masks sizable differences in ability and performance. Under this label, special educators have been able to target differentiated services to individual children's needs at a time when other sources of support within regular education have been unable to do so.

It is also important to note that previous attempts to "delabel" children generally have failed. Although this failure is partly because national accountability requirements and some state reimbursement formulae have remained linked to diagnostic categories, the bigger problem has been that administrators, parents, teachers, and children invent new labels as fast as old ones are proscribed (Coles, 1987; Weatherley & Lipsky, 1977). The new labels tend to be more euphemistic and less derogatory (e.g., "resource room child" rather than "learning disabled child," or "minimally brain damaged child" rather than "educably mentally retarded child"), but the labeling of children continues to be functional, for all its positive and negative consequences.

Indeed, one positive effect of P.L. 94-142 has been to reduce the impulse to label, but to effect something more subtle. Because more children than ever are now identified as having special needs and the climate of belief regarding the acceptability of handicapped children in mainstream settings has fundamentally changed, it has become easier for children to be called "handicapped" in general and "learning disabled" in particular. The social stigma associated with labels has diminished somewhat and become more diffuse, even to the point that some middle-class parents are now relieved to be able to call their child learning disabled, because this label reduces to a specific syndrome what previously had been called general and unaccountable failure on the part of the child.

What Effect Would a Merger Have on Handicapped Children's Rights?

P.L. 94-142 was initiated to guarantee a broad set of educational rights for all children with special needs. The guarantee did not take the form of specific curricula and services, but rather specific *procedures,* ranging from the development of an individualized educational program to the implementation of a due process system, whereby parents could contest a placement decision made by school district staff and administrators.

The law's emphasis on procedures, not curriculum, enabled advocacy to flourish. Although a learning disabled child, a hearing impaired child, and a paraplegic child may not share specific educational *needs,* P.L. 94-142 established that they do share specific educational *rights.* This allowed a diverse set of special interest groups, including parent associations, children's rights activists, legal aid organizations, disease-specific philanthropies, and medical societies to join together to secure these shared procedural rights for all handicapped children.[7] In unity, these groups found strength.

If responsibility for mildly and moderately handicapped youngsters were returned to regular education, the rights of all children with handicaps—not just those who were being decertified—could be affected.[8] Children classified as learning disabled, emotionally disturbed, and mentally retarded comprise two-thirds of the special education population nationally. Without this constituency, advocates for the physically, hearing, vision, and health impaired students would represent a much smaller proportion of the population. The smaller the constituency, the less influential the group can be. To continue to be heard, special education must remain united.

Two solutions to the potential advocacy gap have been proposed. Secretary Will has suggested that each school district should create a parent advisory board. But research on the effectiveness of similar groups established under P.L. 94-142 suggests that they are ineffective watchdogs when under the control of an effective administrator. The other suggestion has been to extend the due process guarantees currently available to special education students to all students in the schools (Reynolds et al., 1987; Singer & Butler, 1987; Will, 1986). But consider the irony that this proposal comes from critics who argue that the due process guarantees have not ensured quality education for special needs students. If these critics believe that the due process guarantees have failed within special education, why do they believe that the guarantees will work within general education? It therefore seems likely that under the proposed changes, a sizable advocacy gap would remain.

WHERE SHOULD SPECIAL EDUCATION GO FROM HERE?

Although the Regular Education Initiative is deeply flawed, it is important to recognize that there are serious problems with the existing special education system. We still do not know which combinations of curriculum and support services produce the best outcomes for different types of children. Classification practices differ widely among states and school districts. A child with academic and behavior problems may be called learning disabled in one district, emotionally disturbed in another district, and ineligible for special education services in a third (Singer, Palfrey, Butler, & Walker, 1989; see also Heller et al., 1982). Because these designations are a major determinant of a child's classroom placement and related services, the type of education a special needs child receives ends up depending, in large part, on nothing more than where he happens to live.

The policy question for the 1990s is how to address these problems. Proponents of the Regular Education Initiative argue that the best solution is to abandon the current system, but in doing so, I fear that we would be throwing out the baby with the bath water. Individualized planning and placement in the least restrictive environment are now guaranteed under the law and should remain so. However, thoughtful experimentation with alternative service delivery models is called for, and thus I support the recommendations of Margaret Wang and Maynard Reynolds, two of the proponents of the initiative, who are calling for randomized experiments comparing instructional modalities (Wang, Reynolds, & Walberg, 1986). The funding of such research deserves high priority. But experimentation should be conducted within the present system; we should not abandon the system until we identify a better alternative.

For if we do go forth with the initiative, we run the risk of losing sight of the children themselves, most of whom desperately need some type of supplemental service. Giving regular education responsibility for mildly and moderately handicapped children will not only fail to solve the students' problems, it may create new ones. These children will remain with us, and they will continue to need services. The Regular Education Initiative would simply place a greater burden on the already beleaguered regular education teacher. To the extent that special education has become a surrogate compensatory education program for some students, this may be appropriate in a period of fiscal austerity when other sources of federal and state support are no longer able to meet these students' educational needs.[9] The inclusion of many mildly handicapped children may be the most fundamental and significant entitlement granted by P.L. 94-142, and it should not be rescinded.

Thus, the biggest risk with the Regular Education Initiative is that it gives ammunition to the naysayers who would do nothing at all for children with mild to moderate handicaps.[10] For many of these people, the real intent of the merger is to eliminate or reallocate supplemental funds from children with mild and remediable problems and return to a pre–P.L. 94-142 world. Some of these same individuals would also be in favor of returning the most severely impaired children to separate institutional settings, simply to get these students out of the way of what they regard as the main business of schooling. It is this risk that is most threatening, not only because individualized instruction for children with special needs deserves supplemental support but also because appropriate services are being delivered to many handicapped children. If the implementation of P.L. 94-142 has been so subverted in some school districts that some children are being segregated in special classes and are being denied an appropriate education, this is a serious distortion of the intent of the law and a departure from what is found in many school systems nationwide.

ENDNOTES

1. One of the earliest proposals of this type was written by Reynolds and Wang (1981). More recent proposals include those by Gartner and Lipsky (1987); Reynolds, Wang, and Walberg (1987); and Stainback and Stainback (1984). Secretary Will's proposal is outlined in "Educating Children with Learning Problems: A Shared Responsibility" (Will, 1986).

2. See, for example, Zill (1985) and OSERS (1988). During the 1975 hearings before the U.S. Senate Subcommittee on the Handicapped and U.S. House Subcommittee on Select Education, participants agreed on an estimate of 1.75 million unserved children (94th Cong., 1st Sess., 2 June 1975, Rep. No. 94-168).

3. The growth in the size of the learning disabled category received attention from the U.S. General Accounting Office (1981) and the National Association of State Directors of Special Education (NASDSE; 1983).

4. The meta-analysis is reported in Wang and Baker (1985–1986). For a review of this literature in regard to the Regular Education Initiative, see Hallahan, Keller, McKinney, Lloyd, and Bryan (1988).

5. The 2:1 ratio of special education costs to regular education costs has been documented independently in several studies (e.g., Kakalik, Furry, Thomas, & Carney, 1981; Raphael, Singer, & Walker, 1985).

6. A similar point is made by Lieberman (1980).

7. McLaughlin (1987) discusses the need for grass-roots advocacy to effect policy change.

8. A similar point is raised by Mesinger (1985).

9. The overlap between compensatory and special education is discussed in Birman (1981).

10. For critiques that argue that special education has assumed unwarranted priority over regular education, see, for example, Pittenger and Kuriloff (1982) and Vernon (1981).

REFERENCES

Algozzine, B., & Ysseldyke, J. E. (1986). The future of the LD field: Screening and diagnosis. *Journal of Learning Disabilities, 19,* 394–398.

Applied Management Sciences. (1983). *A study to evaluate procedures undertaken to prevent erroneous classification of handicapped children.* (Executive summary II; Department of Education Contract Number 300-79-0669).

Bickel, W. E. (1982). Classifying mentally retarded students: A review of placement practices in special education. In K. A. Heller, W. H. Holtzman, & S. Messick (Eds.), *Placing children in special education: A strategy for equity* (pp. 182–229). Washington, DC: National Academy Press.

Birman, B. F. (1981). Problems of overlap between Title I and P.L. 94-142: Implications for the federal role in education. *Educational Evaluation and Policy Analysis, 3,* 5–19.

Bryan, T., Bay, M., & Donahue, M. (1988). Implications of the learning disabilities definition for the Regular Education Initiative. *Journal of Learning Disabilities, 21,* 23–28.

Bryk, A. S., & Light, R. J. (1981). Designing evaluations for different environments. In R. A. Berk (Ed.), *Educational evaluation methodology: The state of the art* (pp. 11–31). Baltimore: Johns Hopkins University Press.

Carlberg, C. & Kavale, K. (1980). The efficacy of special versus regular class placement for exceptional children: A meta-analysis. *The Journal of Special Education, 14,* 295–309.

Clune, W. H., & Van Pelt, M. H. (1985). A political method of evaluating the Education for All Handicapped Children Act of 1975 and the several gaps of gap analysis. *Law and Contemporary Problems, 48,* 7–62.

Coles, G. (1987). *The learning mystique: A critical look at learning disabilities.* New York: Pantheon.

Education for all Handicapped Children Act of 1975, 20 U.S.C. § 1400 *et seq.*

Gans, K. D. (1987). Willingness of regular and special educators to teach students with handicaps. *Exceptional Children, 54,* 41–45.

Gartner, A., & Lipsky, D. K. (1987). Beyond special education: Toward a quality system for all students. *Harvard Educational Review, 57,* 367–395.

Gerber, M. M., & Semmel, M. I. (1984). Teacher as imperfect test: Reconceptualizing the referral process. *Educational Psychologist, 19,* 137–148.

Hallahan, D. P., Keller, C. E., McKinney, J. D., Lloyd, J. W., & Bryan, T. (1988). Examining the research base of the Regular Education Initiative: Efficacy studies and the adaptive learning environments model. *Journal of Learning Disabilities, 21,* 29–35.

Heller, K. A., Holtzman, W. A., & Messick, S. (Eds.). (1982). *Placing children in special education: A strategy for equity.* Washington, DC: National Academy Press.

Individuals with Disabilities Education Act of 1990, 20 U.S.C. § 1400 *et seq.*

Kakalik, J., Furry, W., Thomas, M. A., & Carney, M. F. (1981). *The cost of special education.* Santa Monica, CA: Rand.

Kauffman, J. M., Gerber, M. M., & Semmel, M. I. (1988). Arguable assumptions underlying the Regular Education Initiative. *Journal of Learning Disabilities, 21,* 6–11.

Kennedy, M. M. (1978). Developing an evaluation plan for P.L. 94-142. In C. C. Rentz & R. R. Rentz (Eds.), *New directions for program evaluation* (Series no. 2, pp. 19–38). San Francisco: Jossey-Bass.

Keogh, B. K. (1988). Improving services for problem learners: Rethinking and restructuring. *Journal of Learning Disabilities, 21,* 19–22.

Lieberman, L. M. (1980). The implications of noncategorical special education. *Journal of Learning Disabilities, 13,* 14–17.

Lieberman, L. M. (1985). Special education and regular education: A merger made in heaven? *Exceptional Children, 52,* 513–516.

Lilly, M. S. (1986). The relationship between general and special education: A new face on an old issue. *Counterpoint, 6,* 10.

Lipsky, D. K., & Gartner, A. (1987). Capable of achievement and worthy of respect: Education for handicapped students as if they were full-fledged human beings. *Exceptional Children, 53,* 69–74.

Lloyd, J. W., Crowley, E. P., Kohler, F. W., & Strain, P. S. (1988). Redefining the applied research agenda: Cooperative learning, prereferral, teacher consultation and peer mediated interventions. *Journal of Learning Disabilities, 21,* 43–52.

Lytle, J. H. (1988). Is special education serving minority students? *Harvard Educational Review, 58,* 120–126.

Madden, N. A., & Slavin, R. E. (1983). Mainstreaming students with mild handicaps: Academic and social outcomes. *Review of Educational Research, 53,* 519–569.

McLaughlin, M. W. (1987). Learning from experience: Lessons from policy implementation. *Educational Evaluation and Policy Analysis, 9,* 171–178.

Mehan, H., Meihls, J. L., Hertweck, A., & Crowdes, M. S. (1981). Identifying handicapped students. In S. B. Bacharich (Ed.), *Organizational behavior in schools and school districts* (pp. 381–428). New York: Praeger.

Mesinger, J. F. (1985). Commentary on "A rationale for the merger of special and regular education" or, Is it now time for the lamb to lie down with the lion? *Exceptional Children, 51,* 510–512.

National Association of State Directors of Special Education (NASDSE). (1983). *State/local communications forum for exploring issues related to P.L. 94-142.* Washington, DC: Author.

Office of Special Education and Rehabilitative Services (OSERS). (1988). *Tenth annual report to Congress on the implementation of the Education of the Handicapped Act.* Washington, DC: U.S. Department of Education.

Pittenger, J. C., & Kuriloff, P. (1982). Educating the handicapped: Reforming a radical law. *The Public Interest, 66,* 72–96.

Raphael, E. S., Singer, J. D., & Walker, D. K. (1985). Per pupil expenditures on special education in three metropolitan school districts. *Journal of Education Finance, 11,* 69–88.

Reynolds, M. C., & Wang, M. C. (1981, September). *Restructuring "special" school programs: A position paper.* Paper presented at the National Invitational Conference on Public Policy and the Special Education Task Force of the 1980s, Racine, WI.

Reynolds, M. C., Wang, M. C., & Walberg, H. J. (1987). The necessary restructuring of special and regular education. *Exceptional Children, 53,* 391–398.

Sapon-Shevin, M. (1987). The national education reports and special education: Implications for students. *Exceptional Children, 53,* 300–306.

Shepard, L. A. (1987). The new push for excellence: Widening the schism between regular and special education. *Exceptional Children, 53,* 327–329.

Singer, J. D., & Butler, J. A. (1987). The Education for All Handicapped Children Act: Schools as agents of social reform. *Harvard Educational Review, 57,* 125–152.

Singer, J. D., Butler, J. A., Palfrey, J. S., & Walker, D. K. (1986). Characteristics of special education placements: Findings from probability samples in five metropolitan school districts. *The Journal of Special Education, 20,* 319–337.

Singer, J. D., Palfrey, J. S., Butler, J. A., & Walker, D. K. (1989). Variation in special education classification across school districts: How does where you live affect what you are labeled? *American Educational Research Journal, 26,* 261–281.

Stainback, W., & Stainback, S. (1984). A rationale for the merger of special and regular education. *Exceptional Children, 51,* 102–111.

Stainback, W., Stainback, S., Courtnage, L., & Jaben, T. (1985). Facilitating mainstreaming by modifying the mainstream. *Exceptional Children, 52,* 144–152.

U.S. General Accounting Office. (1981, September). *Disparities still exist in who gets special education* (IPE-81-1). Washington, DC: Author.

Vernon, M. (1981). Education's "Three Mile Island": P.L. 94-142. *Peabody Journal of Education, 59,* 24–29.

Walker, D. K., Singer, J. D., Palfrey, J. S., Orza, M., Wenger, M., & Butler, J. A. (1988). Who leaves and who stays in special education: A 2-year follow-up study. *Exceptional Children, 54,* 393–402.

Wang, M. C., & Baker, E. T. (1985–1986). Mainstreaming programs: Design features and effects. *The Journal of Special Education, 19,* 503–521.

Wang, M. C., Reynolds, M. C., & Walberg, H. J. (1986). Rethinking special education. *Educational Leadership, 44,* 26–31.

Weatherley, R. A. (1979). *Reforming special education: Policy implementation from state level to street level.* Cambridge, MA: MIT Press.

Weatherley, R., & Lipsky, M. (1977). Street-level bureaucrats and institutional innovation: Implementing special education reform. *Harvard Educational Review, 47,* 171–197.

Will, M. C. (1986). Educating children with learning problems: A shared responsibility. *Exceptional Children, 52,* 411–415.

Zill, N. (1985). *The school-age handicapped.* Washington, DC: National Center for Education Statistics.

CHAPTER 2

Who, How, and Where: Special Education's Issues in Perpetuity

Barbara D. Bateman

This chapter is reprinted, with changes, from "Who, How, and Where: Special Education's Issues in Perpetuity," by B. D. Bateman, 1994, *The Journal of Special Education, 27,* pp. 509–520. Copyright 1994 by PRO-ED, Inc. Reprinted with permission.

Major themes seen often in this retrospective include who we are as special educators and how we practice our profession, who should be served by special education, individualization of services, and special education placements. These same issues were central in special education before Dunn (1968) and Deno (1970) and appear destined to remain with us, even though they are potentially solved by the Individuals with Disabilities Education Act (IDEA). The IDEA addresses eligibility, individualization, and placement squarely and reasonably. It is an ironic tribute to the parents and special educators of the 1960s and 1970s who foresaw and addressed these issues that they are nevertheless still tearing at the fabric of special education in the 1990s.

Perhaps it is no surprise that the old-timers in special education know that many of the issues haven't changed in an even longer time, as illustrated by a personal example. As a woefully undereducated, naive, and not-yet-certified special education teacher in the mid-1950s, I went to a state residential school for the blind to teach a class of eight children who were blind, multiply handicapped, and, except for Jerry, functioning at a severely or profoundly retarded level. They ranged from 6 years to 12 years old. Two were not toilet trained, two were nonambulatory, and only Jerry had language beyond echolalia. Jerry was the youngest in the class, very verbal and very bright, and his only disability was congenital blindness. He was mobile, curious, and courageous. With little education, a bare classroom devoid of equipment or supplies, no budget, no aide, and one bathroom at the far end of the wing, this "teacher" could not begin to serve that class of children appropriately, and it was clear that Jerry was being served the least well of all. Without consultation or permission, I naively suggested to Jerry's mother that she place him immediately in a public school. Public schools were responding then to the wave of children blind due to retrolental fibroplasia, and many were already implementing itinerant and resource room programs for children with visual impairments. In fact, many of the older students who lived at that residential school for the blind attended the local public high school. We didn't call it mainstreaming, integration, or inclusion, but just attending school.

Immediately after Jerry's mother withdrew him in favor of public school, I was on the carpet and nearly under it for causing the school to lose the per capita state funding it received for every enrolled student. This aftermath was predictable and unpleasant, and it encompassed the major issues with which we still struggle—who we special educators are and how we practice our profession, who we are to serve, individualization of services, and placement concerns.

SPECIAL EDUCATION
AS A PROFESSION

Hallahan and Kauffman (1994; see also introduction to Part I in this book) are concerned that the seeds of destruction of the special education profession inadvertently sown by Dunn (1968) and Deno (1970) may be sprouting. No doubt, the profession has grown a few big weeds in recent years, but the field of special education will survive. Special education, by whatever name or organizational structure, is inherent in the bell-shaped distribution of many human learning characteristics. Regular education, even reformed or renamed, is a system that by its very essence is group oriented. Even if it were to adopt an individualized approach to the group enterprise, that individualized approach would be less than maximally effective and appropriate for the students at the extremes, the outliers. As long as resources are finite, regular education will have fallout. The fallout may be shifting and relative, as it always has been, and special educators will be there struggling with how to designate the children and how and where to serve them. The forces that gave rise to special education are basic and strong and are not going to go away. They may be temporarily glossed over or stifled, and that is a concern. If the foundations of the profession are eroded away under the current assault, or the next, the rebuilding process will be difficult, expensive, and time-consuming. But it will happen.

Special educators are the progeny of both science and compassion, and like all of our species we bring diverse values to our chosen profession. It is no wonder, therefore, that we are not all of one mind or cut from the same cloth. Some of the divisions between camps are deep and wide. These divisions have been variously described.

Deno spoke of two opposing armies of special educators divided over the very nature of special education as a discipline. One camp would have had us focus only on individuals; the other would have preserved categorical labels as a means of preserving identity and funding. Hallahan and Kauffman note the same split today and observe that labeling can focus unduly on negative aspects of disability, yet not labeling may result in no services being provided. More on this problem later.

Semmel, Gerber, and MacMillan (1994) focus on the dual aspects of progressivism and pragmatism. The pragmatists' interest they characterize as the "structural arrangements and placements—the inputs—that promise greater managerial control of limited resources." This reactive concern is in stark contrast, they say, to the progressive visionaries in special education who proactively and literally mean "full" participation by all students. When these progressive visionaries focus on outcome-based education, they envision powerful curricular and instructional interventions. Semmel et al. observe that prior to Dunn, special educators focused on long-term outcomes, and after Dunn, on the equity of procedures, at least until the mid-1980s, when the visionaries arose again. This outcome versus process distinction is a pervasive and fundamental one. Finn (1990) believes a fundamental paradigm shift is under way in all of education—away from education as process to education as outcome, that is, the result of process. Finn noted that during a paradigm shift, both "conflicting world views can exist side-by-side for many years, perhaps for generations" (p. 586). In special education, both views are alive and well.

That special education should be so divided is not surprising. Some people are drawn to special education just as to regular education by a set of values we could describe as holistic and child centered. They value children's engagement in the process of education, be it placement in a regular class, a cooperative learning group, or a developmentally appropriate practice engaged in with a chronologically age-appropriate peer. Inclusion is a process, not an outcome.

Others are drawn by the traditional scientific aspects of special education and place more emphasis on outcomes and their assessment. This division is not sharp, perfect, or unique to special education. But it is there. A closely related and fundamental distinction that seems to cut across many others can be drawn by the extent of a special educator's reliance on data. This is not to say that all data-based decision makers are always on the same side of every issue, but it is to say that they can and do communicate. The often unbridgeable communication chasm is between those educators—special or regular—who look primarily to hard evidence and those who do not.

MacMillan, Semmel, and Gerber (1994; see Chapter 3 in this text) make this exact distinction between program advocacy and child advocacy. Program advocacy, for example, on behalf of deinstitutionalization and full inclusion, has disregarded evidence about the effects of the program with children. MacMillan et al. plead for empirical validation and demonstrable generalization of intervention effects. These pleas go largely unheard by those whose primary focus is on the process of intervention or on the structure of a placement rather than on the accomplishment of specified outcomes.

Semmel et al. (1994) suggest that Dunn's legacy included this renewed tension between visionaries who want to reform without adequate data and managerial pragmatists, and they say it was after Dunn that special education's focus shifted away from outcomes to process and to the fairness of procedures. To the extent that this shift has occurred, it is an aspect of education's never-ending effort to achieve both equity and excellence, although they often seem at least partially mutually exclusive.

Closely related to the fact that not all special educators are empiricists is the fact that our discipline seems not to learn from our own history. In Deno's (1994) words, we fail to recognize that today's "bright idea" may have already been tried and abandoned for good reason. Cuban (1990) pointed out that education "reforms do return again, again, and again. Not exactly the same as before or under the same conditions, but they persist" (p. 11). Special educators fail to learn from the past because we fail to teach the past or perhaps we sometimes, being taught, choose to ignore the lessons. A discipline that has no sense of its own past not only repeats its mistakes, but also spins in place, failing to advance on the solid foundation of research. We now have a generation of graduate students in special education who have never heard of Precision Teaching or Project Follow-Through and who have no idea that the concept of learning styles was thoroughly studied over 30 years ago and found wanting, to give just three examples. Sadly, hundreds more could be cited.

Gottlieb, Alter, Gottlieb, and Wishner (1994) noted that many of the problems and unresolved issues the field faced 25 years ago are still with us today. Artiles and Trent (1994) observed that 25 years after Dunn and Deno we are still grappling with the issues of overrepresentation of and appropriate services for minority and/or poor children, and they said that one reason for our failure to move on is our failure to look at the problems in historical perspective. However, special education graduate students who are told to use only references and research less than 10 years old do not know that such problems and issues have already been raised. We must stop throwing away our history and begin teaching it and using it. Wheels truly do not need reinvention.

Relationships Between Special Educators and Regular Educators

An ongoing, troublesome aspect of working as a professional special educator has been an often difficult relationship with some regular educators. Dunn (1968) reflected, "We have been living at the mercy of general educators who have referred their problem children to us" (p. 5). We frequently, if not always, believed we could serve those children better than regular education did. As a result, communication between special and regular educators sometimes encountered difficulties around this perception that special educators were, or considered themselves, better trained and qualified. However, Dunn believed that we were in fact ill prepared and ineffective, at least with the socioculturally deprived slow learners about whom he was concerned. And he believed that by 1968 regular teachers were "increasingly better trained to deal with individual differences" (p. 10), but that there was yet a way to go. Perhaps regular education has now gone that distance, and that is why many now believe a proper model for delivery of special education is one where special educators work with regular educators, on their own turf, to deal with the entire class, including the children who have disabilities. It may be, too, that the stresses on regular education have increased to the point that teachers welcome help from any source, even one perceived as elitist.

Perhaps the real plea to special educators from their regular education counterparts is to either enable them to comfortably serve students with special needs or remove them. If we do neither, communication deteriorates and pressures mount.

WHO IS TO BE SERVED?

Special education is now both a service to children with disabilities and a safety net to some of the regular education fallout, by whatever changing name, and regardless of whether it is the best system to do the catching. Must there be fallout from regular education? As Hallahan and Kauffman (1994) point out, as regular education uses more effective methodologies, the variance in student outcomes will increase, not decrease. As I said before, regular education by its very essence deals with norms, averages, and groups, while special education focuses on outlier individuals, a difference that underlies much of the tension between special education and regular education. Better regular education results in more outliers, not fewer. Another reason for fallout is that regular education sometimes adopts unproven practices that result in increased fallout. For example, it is painfully ironic that as the evidence on the importance of phonological awareness and segmentation skills in learning to read becomes ever more conclusive, regular education rushes to adopt beginning reading approaches that minimize or omit altogether phonologically based instruction. Whenever instructional gaps or lapses appear or grow in regular education, the pressure of increased numbers needing better instruction is felt by special education.

Another factor in increased fallout is the inability of regular education to individualize. This hesitation is perfectly highlighted in the discipline of special education students. Only the rare regular education administrator understands either the educational or legal necessity for individualized disciplinary procedures and consequences for students whose disabilities cause their misconduct. Other issues related to individualization are treated later. Here the point is that there are and will always be students who require more individualization than regular education can provide.

In addition to failures in instruction and individualization, we are also seeing an actual increase in the proportion of children with categorical disabilities. Hallahan and Kauffman's (1994) discussion of this increase, especially in children with learning disabilities, is compelling and correct. Gottlieb et al. (1994) also discussed those increases and predicted that the children will be increasingly impaired. Let us just hope that 25 years further down the education road, no one has to write that we ignored these warnings or these children's needs.

Most districts seem now to serve and collect subsidies for both categorically defined IDEA students and many others who do not qualify but who are labeled learning disabled. We also frequently hear that some children who need services are not being served because they do not fit the eligibility criteria. When we place a child in special education who ought not be there, often Dunn's socioculturally deprived slow learner, it is the fault of none but special educators themselves. Every child to be served under IDEA must need special education in order to be eligible (34 CFR 300.7(a)(1)). Furthermore, professional judgment, not test score, must always be the final authority in eligibility decisions. If we choose to yield to pressure from regular educators, we are only delaying the day we all look unblinkingly at the needs of children now in the gap between regular and special education.

Given that we are legally and in every other way free to serve only and all the children who we professionally believe ought to be served, why are so many special educators upset about the population actually served? A few outright erroneous decisions are made, often because they are made by people who don't know the child well and/or because of improper reliance on tests. Better training can provide the correction for those cases. However, professional judgment, observation procedures, portfolios, or curriculum-based assessment, standardized tests, or any combination thereof will never be perfect 100% of the time. There will always be room for legitimate discussion about the effects of the diagnostic processes used on the numbers of children deemed in need of services.

Another not-so-legitimate source of variation in numbers served is the reliance upon those discrepancy formulas that allow identification of only a preset percentage of students as learning disabled. Few practices speak any more clearly to our loss of the vision of a child-centered discipline providing individualized services to children in need.

Another source of dispute is the extent to which a particular regular education program is able to serve children. Some districts, schools, and teachers can adequately serve a wider range of children than can others. Therefore, some children need special education in one district and not another and therefore are eligible in one and not the other. We could develop eligibility criteria that would ignore this match between the child and the educational system, but to do so would favor foolish consistency, which is hardly a virtue. Arguably, then, we have two somewhat different populations in those who have actual mental or physical disabilities and those who, for the reason discussed or others, such as cultural difference, fail to thrive in regular education. An issue that preceded Dunn and Deno, was addressed by them, and remains with us today is whether special education ought to serve all those children who are not successfully served in regular education—for whatever reason—or only those students who have actual disabilities and therefore need special services. One reason this is an issue is that somehow we have allowed the monetary subsidization of some special education students to become our sole focus.

The field has acted as if the IDEA subsidy for providing a free, appropriate public education to defined groups had somehow prevented states or local districts from appropriately serving additional children who do not meet the IDEA criteria. Nothing could be further from the truth. Those who wish to identify and serve additional children simply on the basis of need, failure, percentile, or achievement measures are totally free to do so. They may not, however, charge taxpayers in other states for that decision.

In short, a state or district may continue to provide special education to categorically defined IDEA students and receive a small federal subsidy for doing so. It may also provide special education, without the federal subsidy, to any other students it wishes. The choice of who to serve may and should be made on professional grounds, not on funding.

When we receive a subsidy for doing what's right, that may be helpful. However, it is not good to fail to serve children because we aren't paid a bonus to do it, nor is it good to claim falsely that a child fits the subsidy definition, even if the primary motivation is service.

Another aspect of who ought to be served by special education involves gender disproportion, a glaring but largely ignored phenomenon. Studies often report gender differences or nondifferences on some dependent variable, but much less is said about the fact that special education serves two boys for every one girl. The easy rejoinder is a combination of "boys have more disabilities" and "girls conform better to schools' behavioral expectations." Both are somewhat more easily said than established. For example, recent evidence suggests that reading disabilities may actually occur equally in males and females, contrary to most U.S. data on referrals and groups served. Amidst all the far worse sex discrimination in this country in 1993, underrepresentation of girls in special education may not be a large issue. It is, however, deserving of more attention than it receives. The underrepresentation of girls is obviously disproportional, but disproportion in itself is not desirable or undesirable. Legally, disproportion is discriminatory only when it is detrimental and lacking sufficient justification. Certainly, Dunn and his current followers believe that overrepresentation of some minority groups in special education is detrimental, unjustified, and therefore discriminatory. If this is so, is it not also the case that underrepresentation of girls would be beneficial for them? Both arguments are true only if special education services are deemed detrimental. A far more defensible position is that special education services may be either detrimental or beneficial, depending on the facts of a given case.

Disproportion may or may not be discriminatory, but ignoring it probably is. However, serious sex discrimination does still go on in special education. Referrals, evaluation processes, instructional programs, vocational opportunities, and more still reflect the sexism of the broader society. In addition, sexual victimization of students with disabilities, especially girls, is appalling and increasing. One might have predicted that special educators would be in the forefront of combating sex discrimination. Perhaps in the future we will be.

Another recurring question surrounds the shift from a melting pot model to a salad model of how society addresses diversity. Schools still largely reflect one major cultural and socioeconomic strand. We now see substantial mismatches between some schools and some cultural strands. It takes time for better matches to evolve, and the pace of change may never again be slow enough to eliminate all mismatches. Special education has tried to deal with some of these mismatches. It has not been perfect; it has been available. Gottlieb et al. (1994) argued that special education has not been an effective intervention for inner city children. One might ask whether educators are of one mind about what *has been* effective for low-achieving and/or low-ability students falsely or mistakenly labeled learning disabled. Inadequate regular education is not the answer, nor is inappropriate special education. As Gottlieb et al. said, neither cures poverty. Later I will look at one possible approach to the cultural–socioeconomic mismatch problem.

In sum, it seems that we have some students who do well in regular education and some who do not. The latter seem to be divisible into students with disabilities and some who fail for other reasons. It is this latter group that has caused so much concern.

INDIVIDUALIZATION

In the early 1960s and into the 1970s, the basic special education delivery model was categorical, not individualized. This was true for both placements and programs. Sarah was diagnosed as brain injured, so she was placed in a class of brain-injured children and taught by a method said to be for brain-injured and hyperactive children. In its extreme form, this could result in overlooking or downplaying much about Sarah's individual, unique needs.

This categorical service delivery model was so pervasive and ingrained that it was to us then as water is to fish. We didn't know it was there, it was just the omnipresent given. One aspect of the phenomenal appeal of the original *Illinois Test of Psycholinguistic Abilities* (ITPA; Kirk, McCarthy, & Kirk, 1968) was that it provided a way to individualize instruction and to organize educational programs around skills rather than labels. Popular as the ITPA was, it had not totally revolutionized practice by the time Deno (1994) urged individualization rather than categorization of program and services. She acknowledged her earlier fear of categorization and reemphasized her concern. She lamented the new categories of disability (presumably autism and traumatic brain injury) and preferred the safety net concept be used to define the population to be served by special education, rather than the categorical disability approach.

This debate might be resolved by recognizing that under IDEA, categorical information is required for eligibility only. All program and placement decisions are mandated to be totally individualized, and categorical decision making is prohibited. Special education has admittedly had a difficult time letting go of the categorical model, even though the law disallows it. The issue of labeling overlaps almost totally with that of categorization. One slight connotative difference, however, is that perhaps we fear a label has been affixed to the child without a connection to a subsequent action. Categorization seems to imply some more purposeful behavior with an intended action to follow. The term "label" also seems to connote a greater possibility or fear of stigma than does categorization.

Hallahan and Kauffman's (1994) analysis of the effects of labeling should and will become required reading for the next generation of special educators. One small postscript example might be added to the concern that current apprehension about labels may actually send an unintended message of shame. The parents, advocates, and courts who urge that a child who has a disability must be placed with those who do not have a disability too often send the message that children who have disabilities are not peers and are not fit to be with. Something is terribly and not very subtly insulting about saying a bright student with learning disabilities ought not attend a special school with other students who have learning disabilities because he or she needs to be with nondisabled students.

Another facet of individualization is how a student is treated within the educational system. Who among us has not heard an educator say, "If I make an exception for one, I'll have to make an exception for all, and I can't and I won't"? To make an exception is to individualize. Regular education by its present nature imposes limits on the individualization that can be accomplished. Special education has a mandate, on the other hand, to provide an individualized education program for every child served under IDEA.

This divergence between the two systems may be increased by the drive for excellence that is part of current reform. Semmel et al. (1994) report that schools that have good regular education programs are not the same schools that have effective special education. Semmel et al. suggest that diminishing resources, combined with reform pressures, may result in increasing regular education use of practices that are not effective for special education students.

While the goal, as Deno suggested, is individualization for all children, disabled and nondisabled alike, it may be nearly impossible to implement individualization for all within economic constraints. Even if one had unlimited resources, it is possible that the means of individualization that are effective for special education students might not be the same means as those for regular education students.

Deno's interest in individualization went beyond instructional program concerns into the arena of placement. In commenting on the cascade of services as it was implemented in Minnesota 2 decades ago, she observed that no one had assumed that mainstreaming would be appropriate for all children (Deno, 1994). This leads to our next ever-present issue—placement.

PLACEMENT

Placement issues loom as large as any raised in this retrospective view of the last quarter century of special education. Over a decade before Dunn's 1968 article, a course on gifted children was taught by James Gallagher. In the context of acceleration versus enrichment versus homogeneous grouping, he said something I recall as, "It isn't how you pile up the children that matters, it's what you do in the piles." I am now very sure he said it much more elegantly, but this profound and simple concept has been affirmed repeatedly as special education struggles ceaselessly with questions of how to best pile (place) children in the education setting.

The current placement battle rages over full inclusion versus the individualization placement decision-making process required by law. The substance of the war is placement of children, while its style reflects a deep and wide chasm dividing special educators. Individualized placement decisions can be made only if there is a continuum or variety of placements from which to select. The shape of Deno's cascade of services was tapered to reflect the numbers of children who need each level of service. In a strange twist, that numerical taper is now believed by some to reflect not only the amount of "restrictiveness" but also amount of "goodness" in the placements depicted.

Snell and Drake (1994) were extremely critical of Deno's cascade, claiming that it has "unfortunately" dominated the organization of special education. They characterized the cascade and its legal identity—the continuum of alternative placements—as "label, separate, and educate." They asserted that the cascade model requires that students must qualify for placement with nondisabled peers and that disability labels are rigidly associated with placement location. Further, they claimed that the legally mandated continuum is obsolete and prevents interaction with age peers. To whatever extent, if at all, any of these assertions is true, both the law and Deno's concepts are being violated. The position taken by Snell and Drake and other full inclusionists appears to be that only chronological age need to be considered in placement decisions. No legal or factual basis for this position is made explicit. Nor has it been evident to most courts. In a fairly typical case, the United States Fourth Circuit Court of Appeals dealt with the placement of 16-year-old Michael. His IQ was 72, his academic level about fourth grade, and he worked successfully at a fast food restaurant and related well to other teenagers in several small continuing groups, although he also had some difficulties with communication and social skills. The court approvingly noted the lower court's conclusion that at Annandale High School, which served 2,300 students, few of whom were disabled, Michael had "no appropriate peer group academically, socially, or vocationally." The court therefore upheld his placement at a vocational center 13 miles from his home, rather than at the public high school. The court also spoke to the fact he would have been simply monitoring classes at the high school and said that the disparity between his cognitive level and that of the other students would mean that he would glean little from the classes and his work would be at a much lower level than his classmates (*DeVries v. Fairfax County School Board*, 1989). The emphasis on access to typical, chronological-age peers seen in much of the advocacy for full inclusion is confusing, especially in light of the equally adamant support for "developmentally appropriate practices" now heard in many education reform circles.

Snell and Drake (1994) saw "no-referral intervention" as central to all successful reform. All students would be automatically placed in neighborhood schools, and yet at the same time the law's procedural safeguards would be continued. However, intervention without referral, evaluation, and identification would be a clear violation of several important procedural rights. Automatic placement with no individual decision making and with consideration only for chronological age also violates some very important procedural rights protected by IDEA. If in fact one advocates repeal of rights and protections central to IDEA, that advocacy might better be done openly. The placement battle illustrates perfectly the division in the field between process and outcome focus, between program advocacy and child advocacy, and between scholarly research and social philosophy.

A FEW FINAL THOUGHTS

Too many special educators are burning out after only a few years. Teachers' workloads are so heavy that teachers cannot be as effective as they want to be and know how to be. Much of the load is unproductive and unnecessary paperwork that results from administrators' lack of understanding of the law and fear that dire consequences will follow a failure of the forms. Most of these fears are groundless, although some state departments have put excessive and burdensome requirements on districts that go far beyond federal law. The field must find ways to reduce the paperwork and shift it away from teachers. Too often, the team concept, which is mandatory in the evaluation, program, and placement functions of IDEA, becomes translated in practice into the teacher assuming all the logistical and paperwork duties.

In addition to undue burdens of grossly misconstrued legal requirements and impossible caseloads, teachers must also build bridges with regular educators, sometimes in the face of value differences, half-hearted cooperation, and communication difficulties. Special education has never been a soft job, and it won't be one soon. Nevertheless, or perhaps because of that, the profession continues to attract outstandingly capable, dedicated, and hard-working people who care and who help children succeed against the odds. The details will change over the next 25 years, but the basic story line will be similar.

The Children We Serve

As a step toward better formulation and solution, we asked an observer from Venus to check out the U.S. education scene. Venus found that we have three groups of children—REKS, SPEKS, and OEKS. The regular education kiddos' (REKS) and special education kiddos' (SPEKS) education programs are reasonably under control, according to Venus. However, near chaos reigns for the others (OEKS). They are fallout—Dunn's socioculturally deprived slow learners and today's urban students with learning disabilities (Gottlieb et al., 1994). "Who is responsible for their education?" asked Venus. Until that fundamental question is answered, and answered fully in terms of funding and delivery systems, we cannot begin to resolve the issues. Perhaps instead of a perverse tug-of-war over the "others" by two camps that seem not to want the victory, a third camp will emerge. Already there are many individual program tents in it—remedial reading, "chapter," at-risk, "just say no," and more.

Deno (1994) believes that it is not ethical for regular education to be required to serve those children special education finds not eligible, given that regular education has already failed with them. We special educators often deplore what Deno characterized as bits and pieces, narrow legislation, separate bureaucracies, and fragmented services. However, the federal control we and Deno believe is excessive does not in any way limit who may be served. It only defines the students who must be served and prescribes procedures and protections for them. Let us immediately and clearly recognize that special education may serve all the children we wish to. Only we can decide which, if any, students we will serve beyond those who are IDEA-eligible. Special education has the expertise, but have we the necessary determination?

Individualization

One vital key to true individualization is constant monitoring of program efficacy. Gottlieb et al. (1994) proposed the innovative notion of trying special education intensively for a defined, limited period of time, and if it doesn't work, moving on to something else. While there are not a lot of something elses, the concept of preset time limits is well worth exploring. Evaluating interventions within a specific time frame is precisely what Individualized Education Program (IEP) objectives ought to be doing (Bateman, 1992). Too many IEP objectives are distinctly not serious, are barely measurable, and almost never measured. Once again, interestingly, we find that IDEA already provides the means, albeit neglected and abused, to the desired outcome.

Placement

Dunn advocated for socioculturally deprived, low socioeconomic students who were *labeled* mentally retarded, not who *were* mentally retarded. His thesis was that these children should not be labeled retarded and should not be placed as if they were retarded. In the best of the efficacy studies, Goldstein, Moss, and Jordan (1965) found that students in the 75 to 85 IQ range benefited more from regular classes, just as Dunn believed.

Under IDEA, every student whose education can be achieved satisfactorily in the regular classroom is entitled to be placed there. To insist that any one placement must be the only one for all children, regardless of unique needs or disabilities, is contrary to common sense and to law. Such decisions ought to be made on the basis of what is likely to be, and then shown to be, efficacious for each individual student.

One Last Thought

Special education today, just as 25 years ago, stands at a crossroads being challenged by divisions within. Differences within can keep us vibrant and growing as a discipline, or they can temporarily destroy us. These are chaotic and difficult times for all of education. Special education is vulnerable in the midst of reform. We must eschew slogans in favor of data, program advocacy in favor of child advocacy, and process focus in favor of outcome focus if we are to serve children effectively. Efficacy may be as much the issue as ethics in the tug-of-war between equity and excellence in the nation's schools.

REFERENCES

Artiles, A. J., & Trent, S. C. (1994). Overrepresentation of minority students in special education: A continuing debate. *The Journal of Special Education, 27,* 410–437.

Bateman, B. (1992). *Better IEPs.* Creswell, OR: Otter Ink.

Cuban, L. (1990). Reforming again, again, and again. *Educational Researcher, 19*(1), 3–13.

Deno, E. (1970). Special education as developmental capital. *Exceptional Children, 37,* 229–237.

Deno, E. (1994). Special education as developmental capital revisited: A quarter-century appraisal of means versus ends. *The Journal of Special Education, 27,* 375–392.

DeVries v. Fairfax County School Board, 882 F. 2d 876 (4 CA, 1989).

Dunn, L. M. (1968). Special education for the mildly retarded—Is much of it justifiable? *Exceptional Children, 35,* 5–22.

Finn, C. E. (1990). The biggest reform of all. *Phi Delta Kappan, 71,* 585–592.

Goldstein, H., Moss, J., & Jordan, L. J. (1965). *The efficacy of special training on the development of mentally retarded children.* Urbana: University of Illinois.

Gottlieb, J., Alter, M., Gottlieb, B. W., & Wishner, J. (1994). Special education in urban America: It's not justifiable for many. *The Journal of Special Education, 27,* 453–465.

Hallahan, D. P., & Kauffman, J. M. (1994). Toward a culture of disability in the aftermath of Deno and Dunn. *The Journal of Special Education, 27,* 496–508.

Kirk, S. A., McCarthy, J. J., & Kirk, W. D. (1968). *Illinois Test of Psycholinguistic Abilities* (Rev. ed.). Urbana: University of Illinois Press.

Semmel, M. I., Gerber, M. M., & MacMillan, D. L. (1994). Twenty-five years after Dunn's article: A legacy of policy analysis research in special education. *The Journal of Special Education, 27,* 481–495.

Snell, M. E., & Drake, G. P., Jr. (1994). Replacing cascades with supported education. *The Journal of Special Education, 27,* 393–409.

CHAPTER 3

The Social Context:
Then and Now

Donald L. MacMillan, Melvyn I. Semmel,
and Michael M. Gerber

loyd Dunn's (1968) article is among the most widely cited publications in the field of special education. Surveys of the most influential articles in special education (Patton, Polloway, & Epstein,
1989) and mental retardation (Heller, Spooner, Enright, Haney, & Schilit,
1991) reveal that respondents listed this article among the most influential
pieces to have been published. As such, there is no denying the extent to
which this publication is perceived to have influenced special education
policy and practices. We now have the luxury of reflecting back over the
past 25 years in an effort to examine the significance and impact of this article on special education. Moreover, we ask whether the subsequent policies and practices have benefited education for children with mild disabilities. Clearly, special education has changed markedly since publication of
Dunn's article. However, specifying those changes directly attributable to
this publication is virtually impossible. Instead, we can examine changes
and attempt to evaluate them in terms of the extent to which they are consistent with the case made by Dunn.

Consideration of the impact of Dunn's article on special education
requires that one distinguish between Dunn's literal position and what
some interpreted as "his message." That is, translators extrapolated liberally from Dunn's words to suggest that no children with mild mental retardation required special day class placement, that no minority group
children scoring in the 55 to 80 IQ range were "really retarded," and some
even extended the arguments to apply to children with severe and profound
disabilities—a population Dunn did not consider. Dunn certainly raised
some issues that most, if not all, would contend needed addressing, such
as the assumption that children with mild mental retardation constituted
a homogeneous population and that self-contained special classes and the
curriculum offered therein were appropriate for the students then served
as mildly mentally retarded or educably mentally retarded.

SOCIAL CONTEXT IN 1968

In 1975, Lee Cronbach published a paper analyzing 5 five decades of controversy surrounding mental testing, and a number of his observations bear
directly on the analysis of Dunn's article. Cronbach noted the importance
of the social context in considering the receptiveness of society to positions advanced by individuals. For example, when in 1923 Brigham char-

acterized certain immigrant groups as lacking intelligence, there was virtually no public outcry. Forty-five years later, however, when Jensen (1969) commented on Black–White differences in IQ, he was vilified. Sentiment in the late 1960s was antagonistic to Jensen's views, leading many scholars and the public to react negatively, aggressively, and in considerable numbers. Similarly, understanding the reaction to Dunn's article also requires consideration of the social context in the late 1960s—the field was *ready* for his message. Consider the probable reaction to the same points had they been raised at the height of the eugenics scare. In fact, only a few years before Dunn's article, G. Orville Johnson (1962) published an article entitled "Special Education for the Mentally Handicapped: A Paradox," which appeared in the same journal, *Exceptional Children,* and in which many points similar to those raised by Dunn were presented. The reason for the meager reaction to Johnson's article and the warm reception to Dunn's is best understood in terms of the different social contexts at these two points in time.

In order to understand the reaction to Dunn's article one must appreciate the differences that existed then in special education child categories and the delivery system as contrasted with the present. Moreover, one must understand the social context that prevailed in the late 1960s, because this context explains, in part, the receptiveness of the field to Dunn's message.

Special Education in the 1960s

Romaine Mackie (1969) reported that between 1948 and 1966 there was a 400% increase in the number of students served as mentally retarded in public schools. Moreover, when President Ford signed P.L. 94-142 into law in 1975, mild mental retardation constituted the highest incidence of the exceptional child diagnoses (Reschly, 1988a). Programs for students with educable mental retardation were the most numerous of all special education programs, and they served the largest number of children receiving special education services. In the middle and late 1960s, the categories of mild handicaps and educable mental retardation were almost synonymous. The field of learning disabilities, as we know it today, was essentially nonexistent. While efforts on behalf of children with "minimal brain dysfunction" had emerged and Title I of the Elementary and Secondary Education Act permitted services for children with "specific learning disabilities," categories of exceptional children at the state level and in the U.S. Bureau for the Education of the Handicapped were hazy on mild handicaps other than mental retardation. This left public educators in a somewhat awkward position. That is, a youngster encountering persistent academic and/or social failure was eligible for special education services only if he or she could be found eligible for, and served in, the educable mental retardation (EMR) program. At the time, the Heber (1961) definition served as the guide for most state codes defining mental retardation, and that definition permitted identifying children as mentally retarded with IQs as high as 85, including children who in the American Association on Mental Deficiency classification scheme were categorized as mildly mentally retarded (IQ 55 to 70) and borderline mentally retarded (IQ 70 to 85). As such, EMR programs in the 1960s served a majority of children who would not qualify as mentally retarded today, and who also were, in many ways, much more capable students academically and socially, considering that approximately 3% of the general population score IQ 70 or below, while 16% score IQ 85 or below (see MacMillan, 1989, for a discussion).

Overrepresentation

Because IQ was one of the defining features of mental retardation, the differing distribution for African American and White children (Kaufman & Doppelt, 1976) was to prove detrimental to EMR programs. One consequence of the use of IQ to establish eligibility, when coupled with the differing distributions for IQ by race and the disproportionate number of African American children reared in poverty, was the overrepresentation of minority children in EMR programs (see Reschly, 1988b). Although recognized for years, this issue would precipitate a series of court cases challenging the fairness of identification procedures for minority children (see Elliott, 1987; Reschly, 1988b, for discussion).

Social Context

The thinking about mental abilities and factors influencing them was also changing in the 1960s. Two publications in the early part of the decade would profoundly change our thinking on the relative impact of genetics and the environment. J. McV. Hunt (1961) published *Intelligence and Experience* and Benjamin Bloom (1964) authored *Stability and Change in Human Characteristics.* Both were highly regarded scholars, and their message was clear: We had been underestimating the influence of environmental factors on intellectual development. In describing this period, Zigler and Muenchow (1992) wrote: "It seemed that the whole country was captured by an environmental mystique: It was as if the biological law of human variability had been repealed, and all that was known about genetics was being denied" (p. 10). A wave of early intervention projects followed and were interpreted by some as efforts to intervene in the lives of children coming from impoverished homes in the belief that the quality of the environment, particularly in the early years, was a central determinant of subsequent intellectual development. The early 1960s was a watershed in terms of a change in thinking on the part of psychologists and educators from a belief in the dominant role of genetics to an optimism regarding the power of the environment to alter the developmental trajectory of intelligence. This "naive environmentalism" was not lost on some working in the area of mental retardation. A thorough treatment of the research and the interpretations of its results is provided by Spitz (1986). In describing this period, and in particular the role of Hunt's analyses, Spitz wrote: "Many influential workers considered that cultural deprivation was a major source of mild mental retardation, and consequently they prescribed early intervention as a preventive measure" (p. 86). In mental retardation circles, it was as if IQ were stable except in the range of 60 to 85 IQ, where the influence of the environment was operative in suppressing "true" scores in the normal range. Terms such as *pseudoretardation* and *the six-hour retardate* were invoked to suggest that there were some cases who appeared on superficial measures (i.e., IQ, school achievement, etc.) to be mentally retarded but who were "not really retarded." Such thinking is even apparent in some of the classification schemes on the American Association on Mental Deficiency (AAMD), where "retardation due to psychosocial disadvantage" suggested that we knew what the etiology of mild retardation was—the effect of cultural deprivation.

Coupled with this belief in the power of the environment was the influence of sociologists on the thinking of special educators. Although Mercer's book, *Labeling the Mentally Retarded,* was not published until 1973, the data reported in that book were collected during the early 1960s. Sociologists examined the influence of institutions on individuals, and Mercer's earlier presentations, which predated Dunn's article, emphasized the "Anglocentric" nature of the public schools, the influence of the medical model on the classification procedures used in the schools, and how these served to erroneously identify minority children as EMR. In addition, the famous *Brown v. Board of Education* (1954) case, although decided over a decade previously, precipitated study of, and debate over, the effect of resources in schools on achievement differences, particularly as these pertained to Black students. The post-Brown era included a serious examination of segregation/desegregation and the likely impact on school achievement. In essence, Dunn extended this examination to EMR classes, which were characterized at the time as suffering from de facto segregation. All of this made one of Dunn's major assertions very reasonable; namely, that if the public schools have denied equal educational opportunity to African American children in the form of racial segregation, then is it not reasonable to assume that the special educational component of the public schools is implicated by identifying many African American children as educably mentally retarded who are not, in fact, mentally retarded? Mercer's data seemed to support such an assertion, and those data were instrumental in the case presented by the plaintiffs in *Larry P. v. Riles* (1971, 1979, 1984).

UNIVERSAL PLACEMENTS, CURRICULUM, AND OUTCOMES

As noted in an earlier article (MacMillan, 1971), a major point made by Dunn was extremely helpful to the field. Namely, Dunn objected to the *universal* placement of students with educable mental retardation into self-contained special classes. At the time, special day class (SDC) placement was the service delivery model of choice, and it was universally applied to students with EMR. That is, if a student was certified as educably mentally retarded, he or she was placed and served in an SDC. Dunn appropriately noted the variability among students labeled EMR and questioned the appropriateness of the SDC and the nonacademic curriculum for *all* students so classified. Just as the predominant policy of assigning individuals with moderate, severe, and profound mental retardation in large residential institutions in the early decades of this century was found to be indefensible, so placement in special day classes for students labeled educably mentally retarded in the middle decades of this century was similarly misguided. Dunn challenged the utility of the special day class model for all students labeled educably mentally retarded, and outlined another service delivery model, the resource specialist teacher model, as potentially beneficial for a segment of the educably mentally retarded population. Some, unfortunately, interpreted Dunn's alternative model as a suggested replacement for the special day class model. Deno (1970) later explicated the need for a continuum of services, or cascade system, to accommodate the individual differences existing among students with disabilities.

In the years since Dunn's article appeared, we have witnessed the emergence of the resource specialist program (RSP) as the "almost universal" placement for students with mild handicaps. Mainstreaming, although difficult to define operationally (MacMillan & Semmel, 1977), entailed integration of students with mild handicaps with their nonhandicapped peers for some portion of the school day. In subsequent years we would experience pressure for the Regular Education Initiative (REI) (Will, 1984) and full inclusion—proposals that would shift responsibility for students with disabilities to regular education and would extend the range of children for whom integration was recommended. Throughout the period from 1970 to the present, the issue of *where* services are delivered remained the major topic of debate. Zigler, Hodapp, and Edison (1990), for example, invoked Bronfenbrenner's "social address" model of the environment, in which the only variable of importance is where the services are delivered. These authors noted that the field of mental retardation has been prone to conceptualize institutions "only as places, not as places *within which interactions occur*" (Zigler et al., 1990, p. 7). The preoccupation with settings and the apparent search for the universally best setting for delivering educational services to students with mild retardation deny the variability among children *and* the variability in social-psychological characteristics of settings within any given model (e.g., SDC, RSP). Project PRIME was the only comprehensive investigation of classroom observation variables among placement models that was conducted during the decade following Dunn's influential article (Kaufman, Agard, & Semmel, 1986). Results empirically demonstrated the wide variance within similarly classified classroom environments.

The civil rights movement, with its challenge to school arrangements on the basis of race, was not lost on special education. While special day classes had become the norm, the existence of a disproportionate number of minority children in these classes opened them to critical scrutiny as pockets of segregation within schools. This scrutiny, in turn, altered the fundamental way in which *schooling* was conceptualized and rekindled an awareness of individual differences. Special education was not a fixed set of clinical practices linked to a diagnosis or classification. Increased attention over the following decades was to be paid to individual differences within disability categories—an awareness that would lead logically to concepts of a "cascade" or continuum of services and the need for Individualized Education Programs (IEPs).

The shift from SDC to RSP as the preferred service delivery model had profound curricular implications as well. The curriculum orientation of the "EMR program" in place prior to Dunn's article, in fact, differed from the regular school curriculum in terms of goals, activities, and instructional units (see, e.g., DeProspo, 1955; Hungerford, DeProspo, & Rosenzweig, 1958; Kirk & Johnson, 1951). Although one might take issue with the appropriateness of this curriculum orientation for *all* students categorized as educably mentally retarded, the shift to RSP as the preferred service delivery model carried with it the adoption of the regular school curriculum, with its goals as appropriate for students with educable retardation, with the RSP services being designed to assist the student with the academic curriculum.

The primacy of the normal school curriculum had a longstanding tradition in the classification practices in mental retardation. The beliefs and practices dictated that there be a continuum of involvement in "normal" academic learning that should parallel students' relative severity of disability (e.g., educable mental retardation, trainable mental retardation, severe and profound mental retardation). Inability to learn in the normal curriculum was the original impetus for constructing an alternative curriculum for students with mental retardation, and it was the first step in the referral process for students being referred for psychological evaluation. The reasoning behind an alternative curriculum was that because the students could not learn in the curriculum designed to prepare them for normal occupations and life, they should be prepared for the inevitably limited social role that their level of ability dictated. Recommendation of the RSP model reiterated the belief that higher functioning students in the EMR category should learn the core curriculum to whatever extent possible. The validity of that position for the "higher functioning" students with educable retardation of the 1960s would prove difficult to test, because a change in the definition of mental retardation (Grossman, 1973) would eliminate children with IQs between 70 and 85 from eligibility.

CHANGES IN THE EDUCABLY MENTALLY RETARDED POPULATION

A central focus of Dunn's (1968) article was to question the utility of special education for many children then classified as mentally retarded who came from ethnic minority backgrounds. A disproportionate number of students with educable retardation were African American (Reschly, 1988b), a fact that would precipitate litigation for the next 20 years (*Larry P. v. Riles,* 1971, 1979, 1984; *Marshall et al. v. Georgia,* 1984; *PASE v. Hannon,* 1980; *S-1 v. Turlington,* 1979). It is important to realize that the educably mentally retarded population being addressed by Dunn resulted from the AAMD definition by Heber (1959, 1961). That definition permitted identification of individuals with IQs as high as 85 (actually 1 *SD* below the population mean). In 1973, AAMD published a new version of the definition (Grossman, 1973), which was responsive to the concerns raised regarding overrepresentation of minority group members, and shifted the upper cutoff from 1 *SD* to 2 *SD* below the mean (approximately IQ 70). The results of this change in definition include (a) a dramatic reduction in the number of children who are psychometrically eligible for classification as mentally retarded, and (b) a more patently disabled population with pervasive and serious learning problems (see MacMillan, 1989, for an extended discussion of these changes). Consider that Dunn's observations and recommendations for change were predicated on the previous definition of mental retardation and an educably retarded population that included youngsters who were far more capable than would be identified under the Grossman definition. Whether Dunn's concerns over achievement, stigmatization, negative effects of labels and segregation, self-fulfilling prophecies, and the like, extend to that segment of the mentally retarded population remaining after the change in definition, is open to conjecture. Nevertheless, his arguments concerning the negative aspects of the protective SDC for children with mild and borderline mental retardation can be found currently in much of the literature advancing full inclusion of children with severe handicaps—a literature with an even less substantive empirical basis than could be advanced by Dunn concerning children with mild mental retardation.

HOW BORDERLINE STUDENTS HAVE FARED: SOCIAL CONTEXT

Dunn hypothesized that the students in the EMR programs would fare at least as well in regular programs, although he was not specific in terms of which particular students (e.g., only those above IQ 70; minority students in the EMR category) were disserved by special education. In fact, Dunn listed a number of changes that had emerged in regular education that he believed would enable some/many students with EMR of the late 1960s to succeed in regular education. Debate centered on whether some children with EMR in the 1960s were "really retarded" or merely "6-hour retardates," but what was often overlooked was the fact that virtually all students placed in EMR programs at the time had been referred by their regular class teachers on the basis that these students were not keeping pace with their classmates. That is, referral was based on the teacher's perception that a child deviated markedly from classmates in achievement and social/personal adjustment and on the premise that the teacher had tried but failed to minimize the observed deficit. It was one thing to argue whether such children were truly mentally retarded; however, it was another to suggest that such children would be successful in regular education with no ancillary support, when they had not experienced success in earlier trials (Gerber & Semmel, 1984, 1985; MacMillan, Meyers, & Morrison, 1980).

Dunn also failed in his prognostications to anticipate changes that would occur in regular education that would reduce the likelihood for success by that segment of children targeted in his article. He apparently anticipated that the borderline students would be afforded more equal educational opportunity by being served in regular programs unlabeled. A number of features of special day classes, however, were sacrificed. For example, SDCs were characteristically associated with (a) low pupil–teacher ratios, (b) teachers with specialized training, (c) programs with vocational and social goals and sequences—and experiences for achieving these goals, (d) expenditures on the order of 1.75 to 2.5 times greater than costs per student in regular education ($2,000 to $4,000 more per student), and (e) greater individualization of instruction and periodic reviews of student progress (Reschly, 1988b). In exchange, these students were enrolled in regular programs with little or no ancillary services. Moreover, in the 1980s there was pressure to "return to basics" and to reinstitute "standards" viewed by many critics of public education as sorely lacking. These sentiments are captured in the report entitled *A Nation at Risk* (National Commission on Excellence in Education, 1983), in which consternation was expressed over the lack of standards indicated by diploma recipients who were barely literate. One response to this press for excellence came in the form of proficiency assessments, known as minimum competency examinations. Legislation was passed in some 40 states requiring minimum competency tests, frequently required in order for students to graduate from high school.

Dunn and his supporters who urged the return of children with EMR to regular grades did not anticipate these changes in regular education—changes that would dramatically compromise the chances of the borderline students to receive a high school diploma. In his provocative article, Dunn offered achievement data from efficacy studies to suggest that students in the IQ range of 70 to 85 achieved "significantly better" in regular grades. Overlooked was the fact that "significantly better" did not translate into achievement at grade level. In their review of the efficacy and mainstreaming literature, Semmel, Gottlieb, and Robinson (1979) reported that the highest mean reading achievement test score for students identified as educably retarded was 3.8, regardless of their age or the setting in which they were taught. It is instructive to note that the Balow, MacMillan, and Hendrick (1986) report on grade equivalence required to pass minimum competency tests indicated that not one district adopted a reading level anywhere near as low as 4.0 to pass the competency examination. As a result, those students who Dunn argued would be better accommodated in regular grades are very unlikely to achieve in reading at a level that would permit them to pass the minimum competency test (MCT) required for receipt of a high school diploma.

In a recently completed project (MacMillan, Balow, Widaman, & Hemsley, 1993), the educational circumstances of borderline students (i.e., IQ < 85 and achievement in the lowest quartile) were contrasted with those of learners with mild handicaps served by special education and regular class contrasts. The "back to basics" curriculum provides borderline students with a traditional academic curriculum, courses required for high school graduation, and proficiency tests. Failure of a proficiency test, or subtest, in ninth grade frequently results in the student being programmed into a remedial class until the student passes the proficiency test. For each remedial class taken, one less elective course can be taken by the student. MacMillan et al. (1993) found several interesting features of these remedial classes. First, they had disproportionately high ethnic minority enrollments, and the degree of the disproportion became greater as grade level increased. The "overrepresentation" noted by Dunn for EMR classes is currently present in remedial classes for students failing MCT subtests. The educational site of overrepresentation has shifted from EMR classes to remedial classes; however, the two types are comparable in that they *both* enroll a homogeneously grouped population with low academic achievement including a disproportionate number of ethnic minority students. A second finding was that the more remedial classes in which a student was enrolled, the less "relevant" they viewed the curriculum in terms of preparing them for their future.

Semmel, Gerber, and MacMillan (1994) collected longitudinal data demonstrating the effect of the academic orientation at the school level provoked by the recent "effective schools" and "school improvement" policy movements in general education on children with mild handicaps. Two-year academic gain on the California Assessment of Proficiency (CAP) Tests for schools as a whole was negatively correlated with 2-year academic gain of special education elementary school students with mild handicaps. This empirical finding supported the earlier contention of Zigmond and Semmel (1988), who contended that the economic need to compete with Pacific Rim nations has been the impetus for growing pressure on the schools for increasing the competency of pupils in mathematics and science. This general education policy initiative has provoked a significant increase in academic press for achievement in the schools. This trend is associated with greater frustrations, failures, and increased dropout rates among the most "nonacademic" children with mild handicaps in the schools.

The bright future for borderline students seen by Dunn in 1968 has proven to be an illusion. In 1968, students with generalized achievement deficits and IQs in the 70 to 85 range were portrayed by Dunn as candidates for success in regular education classrooms because of innovations and changes in practices in regular education. Although his argument that they were "not really retarded" was later reinforced by the AAMD (Grossman, 1973), even the most ardent critic of EMR programs would not have denied that these students presented persistent and serious academic difficulties. What awaited these students in regular education was a curriculum that was highly academic, a paucity of ancillary support services to meet their needs, large classes, and course requirements and MCTs that were serious barriers for them in light of their academic problems. Moreover, Gottlieb's (1981) analysis of the extent to which mainstreaming resulted in anticipated benefits to children with mild retardation provides further evidence that Dunn's anticipated consequences concerning achievement, social acceptance, and avoidance of de facto segregation have not been realized.

SHIFT FROM EMPIRICISM
TO ADVOCACY

In an earlier critical analysis of Dunn's position, MacMillan (1971) noted that the 1968 article lacked scholarly rigor. In many ways, Dunn utilized empirical data like the proverbial tippler who uses a lamppost—for support rather than illumination. Dunn argued for the relatively positive effects of regular classes based on the lack of empirical results of the "efficacy studies" of special classes (see Semmel et al., 1979; Semmel, Peck, & Lieber, 1985). Hence, the empirical support generated to buttress his views placed him in the weak scientific position of arguing in favor of a condition based on the lack of support for the efficacy of a contrasting condition (i.e., SDC). Furthermore, his review of empirical evidence on a given point (e.g., impact of labeling, existence of a self-fulfilling prophecy) was neither comprehensive nor penetrating. Instead, Dunn tended to selectively cite a study or two that supported a point he was making, and in the process, ignored other evidence that failed to support or even contradicted the evidence he cited. For example, Dunn argued that the label "mentally retarded" was not worn as a badge of distinction. He then extrapolated from Goffman's (1963) work on mortifications of self and stigma and Rosenthal and Jacobson's (1968) study on self-fulfilling prophecy in an attempt to empirically validate the assertion he was making, namely, that labeling children "mentally retarded" does irreparable harm to them. The Rosenthal and Jacobson study had been roundly criticized (see Elashoff & Snow, 1971; Thorndike, 1968). Goffman's research involved members of religious orders, the military, and incarcerated individuals who experienced removal of personal clothing and possessions, extreme regimentation of their daily lives, 24-hour close supervision, and the like. These are hardly analogous to the experiences of a child placed in a special day class. Moreover, Dunn ignored empirical evidence presented regarding the extension of Goffman's hypotheses to a mentally retarded population, albeit in a different environment, by Edgerton and Sabagh (1962). These investigators reported that higher functioning clients with mental retardation actually benefited from aggrandizements of the self by virtue of comparing themselves to less capable residents of the institution into which they were placed. On the broader topic of labeling children mentally retarded, MacMillan, Jones, and Aloia (1974) failed to confirm the negative effects hypothesized by Dunn. For a more detailed critique of the empirical evidence cited by Dunn (1968), see MacMillan (1971).

MARGINAL ROLE OF EMPIRICISM IN POLICY: AN UNFORTUNATE LEGACY

Special educational practices for children with EMR had been subjected to extensive, if not always sophisticated, empirical validation for years prior to publication of Dunn's article. Leaders in the field, such as Samuel Kirk (1964), Herbert Goldstein (1963, 1964, 1967), and Samuel Guskin and Howard Spicker (1968) had published extensive reviews of research summarizing critically the empirical evidence on various educational practices concerned with children with EMR. Most, if not all, of the research summarized in these reviews focused on the effects of educational practices (placement, methods of instruction, curriculum, etc.) on the child/adolescent/adult with EMR. Of importance to the present discussion is that researchers in special education sought *evidence* on which to try certain things, change practices, and recommend policy. It should also be noted that the focus of these efforts was on *outcomes*.

Coinciding with the publication of, and reactions to, Dunn's article is a shift away from focusing on outcomes and a new emphasis on *inputs—* that is, gaining *access* to regular classes for students with mild handicaps and to special education for those heretofore denied a public education because they were perceived as being too handicapped to benefit. The period of the early 1970s serves as a sort of watershed; since that time policies and treatments have been recommended, in many cases devoid of empirical support that they will in fact have a positive impact on children with mental retardation. Zigler et al. (1990) capture this shift:

> On the one hand, it is our duty to gather and evaluate information, to participate in our work as responsible scientists. Yet all too often, each side of the normalization debate has lapsed into an advocacy or apologist role vis-à-vis group homes or large institutions or mainstreamed versus special education classrooms.
>
> This sort of dogmatism intrudes as well into professional advice concerning the best placements for each specific retarded person. Nowadays, professionals often insist they know best, instructing families about what to do with their children or what to do with their retarded adult offspring. Again, a look at history provides us with instructive examples. Some years ago professionals advised institutionalizing most retarded individuals; today families who institutionalize their family members are made to feel inadequate or guilty, and these are problems that can be as

long-lasting and hurtful as the actual difficulties of dealing with a mentally retarded loved one. (p. 9)

While policy reform relative to special education was under way prior to 1968, the change in the basis on which academics urged change appeared to be informed by Dunn's strategy. Ride the tide of sentiment! Increasingly we see those in the academic community eschewing the need for evidence, and instead relying on ideology and slogans as the basis for the changes sought. "Label jars, not people" was the simplistic solution to some for the complex issue of classification. To the question of what evidence suggested a certain change in services being advocated, a frequent response was, "It didn't require Lincoln to have a research study to know that slavery was wrong." No longer were "best practices" determined by evaluation designs; rather, they were determined by those with the loudest voices, catchiest slogans, and most ability to simplify.

The current state of affairs in special education represents the most unfortunate legacy from Lloyd Dunn. He failed to review the evidence in a scholarly manner, he made broad, sweeping generalizations, and he recommended a blueprint for change that lacked any empirical support. Moreover, some of his disciples compounded these problems by misrepresenting what Dunn had stated or by blatantly extrapolating from his article to populations of children with disabilities not considered by Dunn. To his credit, he read the climate in the field and anticipated properly the reception his criticism and recommendations for change would receive. Within a short time, the professional publications in special education would abound with self-flagellation concerning all the ills of special education, usually ignoring the variation within categories of children, variations in specifics of any single administrative model or instructional strategy, and clearly taking on a sociological flavor in regard to the issue of how institutions harm people. Interestingly, special educators contributing such pieces typically saw no problems in general education and frequently none inherent in the individual child. School psychologists were portrayed as individuals ferreting out students with disabilities where no disabilities actually existed, and the tools they used were assailed in the courts and in the literature as causal factors in the academic problems encountered by children. In the 25 years since the Dunn article appeared, there has been a stream of topics in print and delivered at conferences suggesting that the "problem" would be solved if we abolished residential institutions, intelligence tests, special education settings, and disability categories and refrained from the use of categorical labels. Unfortunately, the simplistic casting of special education issues fails to capture the multivariate nature of the problems and thereby misleads those who would study the "problem" in the simplistic fashion suggested. A quote from H. L. Mencken summarizes this problem: "For every complex issue there is a simple answer, and it is wrong" (cited in Zigler & Hodapp, 1986, p. 223).

In the ensuing years, "advocacy" has become the umbrella term to subsume any number of activities designed to bring about change in the field of disability. Certainly, advocacy on behalf of children is desirable; however, the brand of advocacy we have seen has increasingly been "program advocacy" rather than "child advocacy." Advocacy on behalf of deinstitutionalization, mainstreaming, behaviorism, abolishment of aversives, facilitated communication, the Regular Education Initiative, and full inclusion, to mention only some, has been characterized by the uncritical advancement of a point of view in the absence of, or a disregard for, the evidence on the effects of that "program" on children. The noted psychologist Lee Cronbach (1975) distinguished between advocacy and scholarship:

> There is a fundamental difference between the style of the advocate, in law and in journalism, and the style of the scholar. An advocate tries to score every point, including those he knows he deserves to lose. The advocate who bridles his partisanship places his side at an "unfair" disadvantage. Our scholars chose to play advocate when they went before the public, and they abandoned scholarly consistency. (p. 12)

In this passage, Cronbach has captured the essence of what all too often has passed as scholarship in the special education literature. Ideology backed by testimonial has led to advocacy for certain practices as being the panacea, with a blatant disregard for the individual differences inherent in the population classified as disabled or within any one of the disability categories. Kauffman and Hallahan (1993) have vividly described the use of the term "all" in much of the reform literature describing entry level skills *all* children will bring to school, levels of achievement in math and science which *all* children will surpass; statements that fail to consider the severe disabilities present in *some* children. Advancing a treatment for *all* children in effect argues for the abandonment of *some* for the betterment of *others*. There is danger inherent in assuming that one treatment is appropriate for all children, or that a given treatment is never appropriate for any child.

Program advocacy, such as that mentioned above, gives the distinct impression to legislators and others concerned with special education that we know what works and how to best serve children with disabilities. However, after a decade of effort to implement some of Dunn's proposals, Gottlieb wrote that an "appropriate education for mentally retarded children has not yet been developed" (1981, p. 118). Similar conclusions have been reached by most empiricists taking a child perspective and examining the consequences of various educational placements and instructional procedures on child outcomes (e.g., achievement, social status, self-concept).

In closing, we reiterate our agreement with those who advocate for the rights of children with disabilities to free *access* to all of the real and potential advantages of education. However, we maintain a strong commitment to maximizing personal, social, and academic *outcomes* for these citizens throughout their lives. Advocacy demands compelling moral and ethical argument to achieve policy objectives. Effective educational interventions, however, demand empirical validation and demonstrable generalization. Advocacy defines opposing positions and perceptions as impediments to desired goals. Science, on the other hand, thrives on variation and controversy. Advances in new knowledge grow from testing competing views. Part of the tragedy of the contemporary atmosphere is that would-be reformers frequently denigrate the mores of science in the name of advocacy. They often promote and rationalize their subjective views as if these were buttressed by scientific rigor. There also appears to be a growing trend among some advocates to stifle debate about how children with disabilities are to be educated. Clearly, at a time when children with disabilities and special education are in danger of losing the protected resources and commitment won after long struggle, Dunn's views must not be uncritically embraced as an historical "affair complete." Rather, we advocate for continued professional debate and research on the salient issues that Lloyd Dunn so dramatically brought to public attention 25 years ago.

AUTHORS' NOTE

This chapter was supported, in part, by grants HC023C20002, H023C80072, and H023C30103 from the U.S. Department of Education to the first author, and grant H023C90038 to the Special Education Research Laboratory; University of California, Santa Barbara.

REFERENCES

Balow, I. H., MacMillan, D. L., & Hendrick, I. G. (1986). Local option competency testing: Psychometric issues with mildly handicapped and educationally marginal students. *Learning Disabilities Research, 2*(1), 32–37.

Bloom, B. S. (1964). *Stability and change in human characteristics.* New York: Wiley.

Brigham, C. C. (1923). *A study of American intelligence.* Princeton, NJ: Princeton University Press.

Brown v. Board of Education of Topeka, 347 U.S. 483, 493 (1954).

Cronbach, L. J. (1975). Five decades of public controversy of mental testing. *American Psychologist, 30,* 1–14.

Deno, E. (1970). Cascade system of special education services. *Exceptional Children, 37,* 229–237.

DeProspo, C. (1955). A suggested curriculum for the mentally retarded. In M. Frampton & E. Gall (Eds.), *Special education for the exceptional* (Vol. 3, pp. 472–478). Boston: Porter Sargent.

Dunn, L. M. (1968). Special education for the mildly retarded—Is much of it justifiable? *Exceptional Children, 35,* 5–22.

Edgerton, R. B., & Sabagh, G. (1962). From mortification to aggrandizement: Changing self-conceptions in the careers of the mentally retarded. *Psychiatry, 25,* 263–272.

Elashoff, J. D., & Snow, R. E. (1971). *Pygmalion reconsidered.* Worthington, OH: C. A. Jones.

Elliott, R. (1987). *Litigating intelligence.* Dover, MA: Auburn House.

Gerber, M., & Semmel, M. I. (1984). Teacher as imperfect test: Reconceptualizing the referral process. *Educational Psychologist, 19,* 137–148.

Gerber, M., & Semmel M. I. (1985). Microeconomics of referral and reintegration: A paradigm for evaluation of special education. *Studies in Educational Evaluation, 11,* 13–29.

Goffman, E. (1963). *Stigma.* Englewood Cliffs, NJ: Prentice-Hall.

Goldstein, H. (1963). Issues in the education of the educable mentally retarded. *Mental Retardation, 1,* 10–12.

Goldstein, H. (1964). Social and occupational adjustment. In H. A. Stevens & R. Heber (Eds.), *Mental retardation: A review of research* (pp. 214–258). Chicago: University of Chicago Press.

Goldstein, H. (1967). The efficacy of special classes and regular classes in the education of educable mentally retarded children. In J. Zubin & G. A. Jervis (Eds.), *Psychopathology of mental development* (pp. 580–602). New York: Grune & Stratton.

Gottlieb, J. (1981). Mainstreaming: Fulfilling the promise? *American Journal of Mental Deficiency, 86,* 115–126.

Grossman, H. J. (Ed.). (1973). *Manual on terminology and classification in mental retardation.* Washington, DC: American Association on Mental Deficiency.

Guskin, S. L., & Spicker, H. H. (1968). Educational research in mental retardation. In N. R.

Ellis (Ed.), *International review of research in mental retardation* (Vol. 3, pp. 217–278). New York: Academic Press.

Heber, R. (1959). A manual on terminology and classification in mental retardation. *American Journal of Mental Deficiency, 56,* Monograph Supplement (Rev.).

Heber, R. (1961). Modifications in the manual on terminology and classification in mental retardation. *American Journal of Mental Deficiency, 65,* 499–500.

Heller, H. W., Spooner, F., Enright, B. E., Haney, K., & Schilit, J. (1991). Classic articles: A reflection into the field of mental retardation. *Education and Training in Mental Retardation, 26,* 202–206.

Hungerford, R., DeProspo, C., & Rosenzweig, L. (1958). Education of the mentally handicapped in childhood and adolescence. In S. C. DiMichael (Ed.), *Vocational rehabilitation of the mentally retarded* (pp. 47–63). Washington, DC: U.S. Department of Health, Education, and Welfare, Office of Vocational Rehabilitation.

Hunt, J. M. (1961). *Intelligence and experience.* New York: Ronald Press.

Jensen, A. R. (1969). How much can we boost IQ and scholastic achievement? *Harvard Educational Review, 39,* 1–123.

Johnson, G. O. (1962). Special education for the mentally handicapped: A paradox. *Exceptional Children, 19,* 62–69.

Kauffman, J. M., & Hallahan, D. P. (1993). Toward a comprehensive delivery system for special education. In J. I. Gooddad & T. C. Lovitt (Eds.), *Integrating general and special education* (pp. 73–102). New York: Macmillan.

Kaufman, A. S., & Doppelt, J. E. (1976). Analysis of WISC–R standardization data in terms of the stratification variables. *Child Development, 47,* 165–171.

Kaufman, M. J., Agard, J., & Semmel, M. I. (1986). *Mainstreaming: Learners and their environments.* Cambridge, MA: Brookline Books.

Kirk, S. A. (1964). Research in education. In H. A. Stevens & R. Heber (Eds.), *Mental retardation: A review of research* (pp. 57–99). Chicago: University of Chicago Press.

Kirk, S. A., & Johnson, G. O. (1951). *Educating the retarded child.* Boston: Houghton Mifflin.

Larry P. v. Riles, No. 7 1-2270 (N.D. Cal. 1971), 495 F. Supp. 926 (N.D. Cal. 1979) (decision on merits), *aff'd,* 80-427 (9th Cir. 1984).

Mackie, R. (1969). *Special education in the United States: Statistics 1948–1966.* New York: Teachers College Press.

MacMillan, D. L. (1971). Special education for the mildly retarded: Servant or savant? *Focus on Exceptional Children, 2,* 1–11.

MacMillan, D. L. (1989). Equality, excellence, and the EMR populations: 1970–1989. *Psychology in Mental Retardation and Developmental Disabilities, 15*(2), 1, 3–10.

MacMillan, D. L., Balow, I. H., Widaman, K. F., & Hemsley, R. E. (1993). *Minimum competency tests and their consequences* (Final Report). Riverside: School of Education, University of California at Riverside.

MacMillan, D. L., Jones, R. L., & Aloia, G. F. (1974). The mentally retarded label: A theoretical analysis and review of research. *American Journal of Mental Deficiency, 79,* 241–261.

MacMillan, D. L., Meyers, C. E., & Morrison, G. M. (1980). System identification of mildly mentally retarded children: Implications for interpreting and conducting research. *American Journal of Mental Deficiency, 85*, 108–115.

MacMillan, D. L., & Semmel, M. I. (1977). Evaluation of mainstreaming programs. *Focus on Exceptional Children, 9*(4), 1–14.

Marshall et al. v. Georgia, U.S. District Court for the Southern District of Georgia, CV482-233, June 28, 1984; Affirmed (11th cir. no. 84-8771, Oct. 29, 1985); Order, February 13, 1987.

Mercer, J. R. (1973). *Labeling the mentally retarded.* Berkeley: University of California Press.

National Commission on Excellence in Education. (1983). *A nation at risk: The imperative for educational reform.* Washington, DC: Author.

PASE (Parents in Action on Special Education) v. Joseph P. Hannon, U.S. District Court, Northern District of Illinois, Eastern Division, No. 74 (3586)(1980).

Patton, J. R., Polloway, E. A., & Epstein, M. H. (1989). Are there seminal works in special education? *Remedial and Special Education, 10*(3), 54–59.

Reschly, D. J. (1988a). Introduction. In M. C. Wang, M. C. Reynolds, & H. J. Walberg (Eds.), *Handbook of special education: Research and practice* (Vol. 2, pp. 3–5). Oxford, England: Pergamon Press.

Reschly, D. J. (1988b). Minority mild mental retardation: Legal issues, research findings, and reform trends. In M. C. Wang, M. C. Reynolds, & H. J. Walberg (Eds.), *Handbook of special education: Research and practice* (Vol. 2, pp. 23–41). Oxford, England: Pergamon Press.

Rosenthal, R., & Jacobson, L. (1968). *Pygmalion in the classroom: Teacher expectation and pupils' intellectual development.* New York: Holt, Rinehart & Winston.

S-1 v. Turlington, Preliminary Injunction, U.S. District Court, Southern District of Florida, Case No. 79-8020-Civ-CA WPB (1979).

Semmel, M. I., Gerber, M. M., & MacMillan, D. L. (1994). Twenty-five years after Dunn's article: A legacy of policy analysis research in special education. *The Journal of Special Education, 27*, 481–495.

Semmel, M. I., Gottlieb, J., & Robinson, N. M. (1979). Mainstreaming: Perspectives on educating handicapped children in the public schools. In D. Berliner (Ed.), *Review of research in education VI.* Washington, DC: American Educational Research Association, Peacock.

Semmel, M. I., Peck, C., & Lieber, J. (1985). Effects of special education environments: Beyond mainstreaming. In J. Meisels (Ed.), *Mainstreaming the mildly handicapped child* (pp. 165–192). Hillsdale, NJ: Erlbaum.

Spitz, H. H. (1986). *The raising of intelligence: A selected history of attempts to raise retarded intelligence.* Hillsdale, NJ: Erlbaum.

Thorndike, R. L. (1968). Review of R. Rosenthal and L. Jacobson, *Pygmalion in the classroom. American Educational Research Journal, 5*, 708–711.

Will, M. (1984). Educating children with learning problems: A shared responsibility. *Exceptional Children, 52*, 411–415.

Zigler, E., & Hodapp, R. M. (1986). *Understanding mental retardation.* New York: Cambridge University Press.

Zigler, E., Hodapp, R. M., & Edison, M. R. (1990). From theory to practice in the care and education of mentally retarded individuals. *American Journal on Mental Retardation, 95*, 1–12.

Zigler, E., & Muenchow, S. (1992). *Head Start: The inside story of America's most successful educational experiment.* New York: Basic Books.

Zigmond, N., & Semmel, M. I. (1988). Educating the nation's handicapped children. In K. Lloyd (Ed.), *Risking American education competitiveness in a global economy: Federal education and training policies, 1980–90.* Arlington, VA: Center for Educational Competitiveness.

CHAPTER 4

The Pull of Societal Forces on Special Education

James J. Gallagher

I t is a pleasure to have the opportunity to comment on the current nature of the special education enterprise as seen by a series of highly capable leaders and to reflect upon the impact of the articles by Lloyd Dunn and Evelyn Deno from the perspective of 25 years later. As suggested in a number of the articles in this volume, the timing of the articles by Deno and Dunn had a great deal to do with their acceptance at the time. The 1960s and 1970s was an era when the importance of the cultural environment on the child's development was given substantial attention.

CORRELATION VERSUS CAUSATION

It is always difficult to distinguish causation from correlation in a series of events, even with the advantage of retrospective insight. To cite a personal example, one time when I was first taking tentative steps toward learning to cook, I was preparing a meal and turned on the oven. Immediately all the lights in the house went out. Not only did all the lights in the house go out, but all the lights in the neighborhood went out! The first agonizing thought to cross my mind was, "What have I done?" The answer of course was, "Nothing"; a failure in a power station had occurred as I turned the switch on the oven. But it is a typical human foible that we ascribe larger influences to our own actions than are justified.

There would seem to be a major parallel here about our arguments inside special education and the reality of its role in general education. To assume that the arguments that Deno and Dunn produced were the determining factor in the final decision to modify the patterns of American education is to be similarly ego involved. There is considerable evidence to suggest that such a conclusion is far from the truth. What was influencing policymakers, and what will influence the restructuring of education for the 21st century, will have more to do with larger societal issues and values than in-house arguments within our small subset of education.

The articles by Lloyd Dunn (1968) and Evelyn Deno (1970) *were* representative of these larger societal forces at work in the late 1960s, but it was these larger influences, in my opinion, that were the driving force to change special education. The drive toward desegregation and the heightened social consciousness of discrimination as a way of life surely had more to do with the reshaping of special education at that time than any of the arguments within the field (see Semmel, Gerber, & MacMillan, 1994, and Chapter 3 of this book).

Certainly no credence can be given to the notion that our programmatic structures were changed as the result of comprehensive research results that have yielded evidence moving us in one direction or another. Instead, it seems that the forces and people driving public policy often tend to extract, often from the research community and literature, those elements that seem supportive of the idea that they wish to promulgate and to ignore those that do not seem to support the current fashion (Gallagher, 1989). Such neglected research can hibernate in scholarly anonymity for a decade or more, only to be rediscovered when a different social and policy fashion comes into being.

In order for us to adequately understand our situation and for us to correctly identify what is needed to change it, we need to take a step back and look at these larger forces that seem to be affecting our organizations and institutions as well as our teaching methods. It is these hidden or more distant forces that I will focus on. The other articles in this issue [*The Journal of Special Education,* Vol. 27, No. 4] have touched upon these forces at one time or another (see, e.g., Gottlieb, Alter, Gottlieb, & Wishner, 1994).

EXPECTATIONS, OVER AND UNDER

What should we expect from our programs for exceptional children, given strong and positive educational intervention? The answer depends on our perception of the cause of the exceptionality in the first place. There has been substantial discussion about the likelihood that a poor cultural environment is responsible for a child being identified as mildly mentally retarded or learning disabled. We should ask questions about this assumption that rarely were asked in the 1970s. We have the luxury of posing issues long after the time when fundamental assumptions should have been challenged.

For example, consider a child of 6 now testing in the mentally retarded range of development. What do we have a right to expect of such a youngster who would benefit from an outstanding educational intervention program? Do we believe that such a youngster might become a neurosurgeon or a lawyer? Or if not that, then perhaps the head of a dressmaking company or a director of a construction crew? Not any of those things? Despite an outstanding intervention program? When we ask such questions, and answer them, we begin to see our own limited expectations for our educational intervention program. We are not downgrading our programs to adjust this limited impact on the child. These limitations are biological or constitutional in nature; they are present and largely determine the result in adulthood no matter what the nature of the educational program might be.

The tale of the Japanese admiral is illustrative of our problem:

> During World War II a Japanese admiral was faced with a very difficult decision as to what path his fleet should take in the war in the Pacific. Having been excellently educated at UCLA, he knew games theory and decision theory and put his skills and knowledge to work. He carefully calculated the weights that should be applied to his two reasonable options and carefully selected which option held out the best opportunity for him.

Sad to say for the Japanese admiral, his choice turned out most unhappily. His fleet was destroyed and he was disgraced. A natural question that could be posed is why, with his knowledge and skills, did he make such a mistake? Why did he choose the wrong path? The answer to this puzzle is even more interesting because, as it turns out, the admiral did not make a mistake. In fact, he *had* chosen the best of those paths available to him. The problem was that neither choice offered much hope for his fleet and his decision was only to maximize what turned out to be an unhappy set of choices under any circumstances.

When we apply this story to the situation faced by the 6-year-old youngster who has been identified as mentally retarded, we face a similar situation. We are faced with the same problem as the Japanese admiral: None of our potential options is extraordinarily favorable. We are faced with trying to maximize what is likely to be, in the end, a limited outcome no matter what choice we make.

We do not expect our 6-year-old youngster to become a neurosurgeon or a lawyer. We will be happy if he or she will become a skilled worker who is able to be self-sufficient and who is able to obtain consistent employment. When we try to assess the effectiveness of our educational intervention programs, we need to keep in mind the story of the Japanese admiral. We must understand that we have a limited set of options, and that, in all too many cases, few of the probabilities are in our favor.

If we are depressed by such facts, we shouldn't be. The fact that the youngster with cerebral palsy does not win the 100-yard dash does not make our habilitation program a failure, nor that our deaf child does not play Hamlet. We have to find a path between underestimating the potential of the child and being unrealistically optimistic about the outcome.

It is our expectations, our often unreasonable flights of fancy, that cause us to be depressed or to expect too much from ourselves and our colleagues, when we do, in fact, have the skills to help the child have a productive and happy life.

SPECIAL EDUCATION AS WE KNOW IT

There is little doubt that an era of special education ended in the late 1960s coincident with the publication of the two articles by Lloyd Dunn and Evelyn Deno. As many of the articles in this issue have pointed out, the reason for the impact of the two articles was only partially due to the arguments presented; it was also due to the times and the ecological circumstances. The articles were persuasive to many in the field of special education, who correctly perceived that they were telling the truth about our limitations (Edgar & Polloway, 1994).

Prior to the Dunn and Deno articles, there seemed to have been an unwritten treaty established between general education and special education. The essence of the treaty was that special education would agree to take from general education those students who were the most difficult to teach and most behaviorally difficult to manage in the classroom. In exchange, teachers and administrators in general education would support special education and its requirements for additional resources, with only the unspoken proviso that under no circumstances would special education bring these children back into the regular program. This treaty has now been broken by the new philosophy of *full inclusion,* and neither the special educators nor general educators are likely to be totally satisfied with the new situation.

The problem with the Dunn argument against special classes for children with mental retardation is that it assumed that if one type of environmental modification is a "failure," then "success" must lie in the opposite model. Instead, as Semmel et al. (1994) point out, success under any circumstances is a very difficult concept to identify or achieve, regardless of the type of environment or program that is provided to these students. In addition, there is very real evidence that the population of students now labeled as mentally retarded is quite different than it was merely a decade ago, when many youngsters of borderline mentality (based on IQ) were still being included in programs for students with mental retardation (Polloway, Patton, Smith, & Roderique, 1991).

As pointed out by Hallahan and Kauffman (1994), one of the limitations of special education has been to specify what "success" means in an educational program for children with mental retardation. Surely it does not mean that the students will perform at an average or superior level in academic coursework. It must mean, as Edgar and Polloway (1994) pointed out, that there should be an emphasis on outcomes of the program and the nature of the curriculum necessary to generate such outcomes. The outcomes that we are looking for are some kind of viable employment in adulthood and a reasonable life-style so that the student can enter the work force and have a productive and happy life. But to reach that goal, much work needs to be done at earlier stages of development.

SPECIAL EDUCATION AND DISCRIMINATION

We need to reassess at what developmental stage the decision should be made to separate those students who we expect will become skilled or semi-skilled workers from those students who are going on to more advanced and professional types of education. The reluctance to make this decision has stemmed in no small matter from educational administrators' fear of being called unfair. There is hardly a more devastating charge in the current social climate than to accuse someone of being unfair or discriminatory in their decision making toward various ethnic or social groups (Artiles & Trent, 1994).

The consequence of the fear of being accused of discrimination is that the decision to separate students for differential programming is delayed and delayed again by educational decision makers until relatively late in the secondary school program, by which time many students have been referred to special education or have been so discouraged and disheartened by their educational experience that they have dropped out, either physically or mentally, from the schools.

It is interesting to speculate the extent to which issues such as ability grouping would currently be before the public if the proportions of minority students in special education programs matched their proportions in the general population. In my opinion, it is the fear of courts and court action against special education for being discriminatory toward minorities that has been one of the prime driving forces toward restructuring of special education. Artiles and Trent (1994) spelled out the concern about overrepresentation. But what is overrepresentation? If children grow up in an environment unfavorable to education—or to the valuing of long-term goals, or of compliance to adult demands—then why should we be surprised that more youngsters from such families would be in educational difficulty than their proportions in the society?

In the end, it is the ability to master knowledge systems and to practice desirable skills that determines the success of students. Just as there is a disproportion of ethnic and racial membership in the National Basketball Association (few Asians, an "overrepresentation" of African American players), which rather truly represents the degree to which these physical skills have been honed over hours of practice, so it is also true that there is disproportionality of ethnic and racial groups in areas where reading and studying are concerned. This is not to deny that there is justification for the concern of minority advocates that *some* special education programs have become dumping grounds where students have been put aside as a bother to the general education program. Any overall structural solution to our problem must deal with the issue of discrimination.

SPECIAL EDUCATION AS AN ENTRY TO SERVICES

Deno's (1970) cascade of services, now being interpreted as a comprehensive set of services and programs to meet the needs of varying levels of child problems in the educational setting, appears to be a reaction to an earlier structural problem in education. In many school systems, the only way to provide extra services to young children in educational difficulty was to refer them to special education because that is where the school psychologists, the counselors, and the specially trained teachers were housed. It has been the inadequate special resources provided to the general education stream that has been the problem for educators interested in helping students.

Chalfant's (1987) teacher referral teams represented one constructive approach to this problem of too many referrals to special education, invoking the strategy of case staffing children in educational difficulties *before* they are referred to special education and recommending courses of action that can be taken by the classroom teacher. Under such programs, it is possible to defer or eliminate many referrals to special education by making meaningful changes in the general education program for these students having educational problems.

EDUCATIONAL REFORM, RESTRUCTURING, AND FULL INCLUSION

We seem to be in another critical transitional era similar in this respect to the general social climate in which the Dunn and Deno articles appeared a quarter century ago. The present seems to be a watershed in education, a time when major changes are expected and anticipated by political decision makers. Too little has been made of the significance of the National Governor's Conference of 1989, where 50 governors of all conceivable political persuasions signed off on the "National Goals for Education" (America 2000) and the president of the United States adopted these goals as his own. Such an event could only have been possible if there were widespread dissatisfaction with the educational status quo.

If we are correct in our earlier assumption that larger social forces are at work in the shaping of educational policy, then what are those forces this time? Clearly, there is concern for equity in education. Are children of poor families or families from culturally different backgrounds getting a fair chance at a quality education? Fairness and equity are the key concepts, and the educational reaction to such concerns has been to return to an educational setting where children of all levels of ability, achievement, motivation, and family backgrounds would be together, more or less, ensuring that no group has been siphoned off and placed in an inferior setting with less opportunity.

Somewhat paradoxically, there also is a societal concern about excellence, particularly with the various studies showing American students lagging behind badly in comparison with other national groups of students (Stevenson & Lee, 1990). How this is affecting education currently seems to be largely in the assessment area, where talk of world class standards and authentic assessments is widely heard.

Children with disabilities are brought along in this values scheme with the concept of *full inclusion,* meaning that children with disabilities will be educated with children without disabilities and that no separate educational channels should be supported except under the direst of circumstances (Biklin, Ferguson, & Ford, 1989; Brown & Snell, 1993; Stainback, Stainback, & Forest, 1990). In this way, fairness, rather than discrimination, can be demonstrated, and children with disabilities, who have much to learn from their social peers, can have a more defensible education.

The article by Gottlieb et al. (1994) stressed the community-based education idea. Their concern is that "educational inclusion" will merely replicate an earlier model that has proven to be a failure for those students identified and referred to special education. One of the major differences in our thinking patterns must be to stop thinking of education as a place (school) and think of education as a continuing community responsibility. This is particularly true for students with severe learning disabilities or mental retardation, who can often learn much more in a job than they can by sitting in a classroom.

If families in desperate economic and social conditions are sending their children to the schools, then the solution is only partly within the school and partly within the community itself to change the unfavorable environment in which these students exist. At the present time, there would seem to be a radical swing from the concept that the problem exists *entirely* within the child to the equally unjustified conclusion that the problem lies *entirely* within the environment. Many of the people in the educational restructuring movement (e.g., Oakes, 1985; Slavin, 1988) seem to want to create an educational environment in which there is not only equal opportunity, but also equal outcomes. The rather banal slogan, "All children can learn," deliberately ignores the significant proposition that all children will not learn at the same pace or from the same base of knowledge.

One essential difficulty of the full inclusion philosophy is that it presumes that the children with learning disabilities or with mental retardation would be studying the same curriculum as the average student—but perhaps at a slower pace (Will, 1984). In reality, at the middle school or junior high school level, many specialists in the field of mental retardation stress a *functional curriculum* with concrete tasks and usable skills, such as computing sales tax, reading job descriptions, or writing a menu for a balanced diet (see Kauffman, 1989). Many specialists recommend a curriculum for such students that focuses on learning useful skills and understandings that do not require a heavy burden of generalization or transfer (Deshler & Schumaker, 1986; Robinson, Patton, Polloway, & Sargent, 1989). Such a functional curriculum is not the preferred intellectual meal, however, for above-average students on their way to college. Nor is the abstract generalization required by the curriculum in college preparatory classes the proper educational diet for children with mental retardation.

THE INTEGRATION OF SPECIAL AND GENERAL EDUCATION

The problem of the melding of special education and regular education really is one of organization and structure. How does one administer the special services needed for exceptional children within a given school system? Should there be a parallel organization within the school system in which the director of curriculum for the regular program is paralleled to the director of special education, and there are various parallel levels of organization creating a special organizational unit of special education? Such an organizational structure has often been designed as a parallel system encouraging little communication between general education and special education. How does one integrate such programs at some point below the superintendent level (Goodlad & Field, 1993)?

We should be clear in our understanding that the issues here involve more than just educational efficiency (Cullen & Pratt, 1992). They are, instead, issues of power and influence. If special education becomes merely a minor part of the general education system, then special education loses its voice in the power circles of the educational system and loses much of its ability to influence policy in that system at the local, state, and federal levels. One major question is, who sits at the table, who is "in the room" when the major policy issues of the schools are being considered? If there is a director of special education visible in the hierarchy of the school program, then it is likely that that person will be sitting in the room where the policy decisions are made. If special educators are merely one of many assistants to the general education administration, they likely will not be participants in policy meetings. Apart from anything else, this absence removes an important voice for the child who is different from key decisions in the school system.

And what are we to make of the Peter Pan phenomenon that seems to be gripping both regular and special educators, that is, the temptation to consider that all children will remain forever within the 10- to 12-year range? Few children with disabilities will go to law school or medical school, or even to college, so somewhere in the developmental progression in education these children should be separated from their nondisabled peers. How and when should this be done?

Also, is there not a considerable literature in special education suggesting that a goal of vocational success for children with mental retardation has to be planned long before the student is 17 or 18, but rather must begin in a functional curriculum at middle school or before? So, how can we achieve both goals—a differentiated curriculum for exceptional children, but within the same social setting with other students?

SPECIAL EDUCATION RESPONSIBILITIES

Well, if we are being driven by these larger social forces, what are we to do? Are we merely a cue ball on the pool table of life to be pushed here and there as outside forces dictate? Not at all! We as special educators would seem to have two major sets of responsibilities; first within the special education community, and second outside that community.

Special educators have been blamed for so many things that are clearly not their fault or responsibility that it becomes an easy excuse for special educators to say they have been the victims of social policy. But there is one responsibility that special educators should not avoid, and that is the design of a developmental curriculum from age 4 or 5 to adulthood that delineates the necessary tasks and skills to be learned at each educational level for the exceptional child, and the progressive building on prior skills that will lead to the child's becoming an effective worker and citizen. We have too often focused on a narrow band of the developmental process. Full inclusion is something that would seem to be most applicable to 8- to 10-year-olds but certainly not 13- to 15-year-olds (Skrtic, 1991). Full inclusion may fit into a part of a total developmental process, but only a part, and the maintenance of such strategies across the entire age range of growing up is clearly inapplicable.

The responsibilities outside the special education profession require us to point out forcefully that there is something amiss in the full inclusion plan—that fairness does not consist of educating all children in the same place at the same time (and with the same curriculum?) but in ensuring that the student has basic needs met and is traveling a well-thought-out road to a career and a satisfying life-style. Whether that means being in the same educational setting from middle school onward is highly dubious in my opinion. It is not that we oppose "fairness"; rather, we wish to define it in a more appropriate way.

CONTRIBUTIONS
OF SPECIAL EDUCATION

In the past, special education has been a leader in fields such as educational technology and the use of psychological services. Special education, once again, has an opportunity to lead in multidisciplinary programming with an emphasis on the family in the early childhood field. Part H of IDEA has encouraged the states to provide a comprehensive, multidisciplinary, interagency program for infants and toddlers with disabilities and their families (Gallagher, Trohanis, & Clifford, 1989).

It is always easier to introduce substantial changes in the service delivery patterns when you are starting from scratch, as in the early childhood area, as opposed to trying to change well-established patterns, as would be necessary in the public schools. The long experience of special education in working with families and with working across agencies and disciplines can establish the pattern that will shape the early childhood field, as the general education early childhood effort is only now beginning to gather steam (Gallagher, 1989).

The future that we face may well require us to be sociologists and anthropologists as well as diagnosticians and planners of curriculum. We must be aware of those social forces that often are more important than the arguments within the academy in determining the shape of the future.

REFERENCES

Artiles, A. J., & Trent, S. C. (1994). Overrepresentation of minority students in special education: A continuing debate. *The Journal of Special Education, 27,* 410–437.

Biklin, D., Ferguson, D., & Ford, A. (1989). Schooling and disability. Part II. *Eighty-eighth yearbook of the National Society for the Study of Education.* Chicago: University of Chicago Press.

Brown, F., & Snell, M. E. (1993). Meaningful assessment. In M. Snell (Ed.), *Instruction of students with severe disabilities* (4th ed., pp. 61–98). New York: Merrill.

Chalfant, J. (1987). Providing services to all students with learning problems: Implications for policy and programs. In S. Vaughn & C. Bos (Eds.), *Research in learning disabilities: Issues and future directions.* Boston: Little, Brown.

Cullen, B., & Pratt, T. (1992). Measuring and reporting student progress. In S. Stainback & W. Stainback (Eds.), *Curriculum considerations in inclusive classrooms: Facilitating learning for all students* (pp. 175–196). Baltimore: Brookes.

Deno, E. (1970). Special education as developmental capital. *Exceptional Children, 37,* 229–237.

Deshler, D. D., & Schumaker, J. B. (1986). Learning strategies: An instructional alternative for low-achieving adolescents. *Behavioral Disorders, 7,* 207–212.

Dunn, L. (1968). Special education for the mildly retarded—Is much of it justifiable? *Exceptional Children, 35,* 5–22.

Edgar, E., & Polloway, E. A. (1994). Education for adolescents with disabilities: Curriculum and placement issues. *The Journal of Special Education, 27,* 438–452.

Gallagher, J. (1989). The impact of policies for handicapped children in future early education policy. *Phi Delta Kappan, 71,* 121–124.

Gallagher, J., Trohanis, P., & Clifford, R. (1989). *Policy implementation and P.L. 99-457.* Baltimore: Brookes.

Goodlad, J. I., & Field, S. (1993). Teachers for renewing schools. In J. Goodlad & T. Lovitt (Eds.), *Integrating general and special education* (pp. 229–252). New York: Merrill.

Gottlieb, J., Alter, M., Gottlieb, B. W., & Wishner, J. (1994). Special education in urban America: It's not justifiable for many. *The Journal of Special Education, 27,* 453–465.

Kauffman, J. M. (1989). The regular education initiative as Reagan–Bush education policy: A trickle-down theory of education of the hard-to-teach. *The Journal of Special Education, 23,* 256–278.

Oakes, J. (1985). *Keeping track: How schools structure inequality.* New Haven, CT: Yale University Press.

Polloway, E., Patton, J., Smith, J., & Roderique, T. (1991). Issues in program design for elementary students with mild retardation: Emphasis on curriculum development. *Education and Training in Mental Retardation, 26,* 142–150.

Robinson, G., Patton, J., Polloway, E., & Sargent, L. (1989). *Best practices in mild mental disabilities.* Reston, VA: Council for Exceptional Children.

Skrtic, T. (1991). *Behind special education.* Denver, CO: Love.

Slavin, R. (1988). Synthesis of research on grouping in elementary and secondary schools. *Education Leadership, 46,* 67–77.

Stainback, S., Stainback, W., & Forest, M. (Eds.). (1990). *Educating all students in the mainstream of regular education.* Baltimore: Brookes.

Stainback, S., Stainback, W., & Slavin, R. (1989). Classroom organization for diversity among students. In S. Stainback, W. Stainback, & M. Forest (Eds.), *Educating all students in the mainstream of regular education.* Baltimore: Brookes.

Stevenson, H. W., & Lee, S. (1990). Context of achievement. *Monographs of the Society for Research in Child Development, 55.*

Will, M. (1984). Educating children with learning problems: A shared responsibility. *Exceptional Children, 52,* 411–415.

CHAPTER 5

Comments from a Biased Viewpoint

William C. Morse

n their discussion of advocacy versus empiricism, MacMillan, Semmel, and Gerber (see Chapter 3) present a significant challenge to all who profess in special education. My essay [presented here] must be considered biased advocacy responding to but a few of the many significant concerns dealt with in this impressive series of articles [*The Journal of Special Education*, Vol. 27, No. 4]. My basis is personal experience with all of the biases that my experience introduces, and even then my comments [made in this chapter] are largely confined to programs for pupils with emotional and social disturbance. Thus, my observations come from a limited focus, and I make no claim as a generalist special educator. In addition, the segment of special education concerned with emotional and social disturbance is recognized as the most ineffective in terms of outcomes in general quality of life, academics, and employment—on the average, at least (Knitzer, Steinberg, & Fleisch, 1990). A close examination of the successes and failures does not encourage the view that this branch of special education is highly effective in general (Nelson & Pearson, 1991).

The Deno (1970) and Dunn (1968) contributions came at what was, for me, an interesting professional time. We were working in two school districts to transfer some of the techniques developed at a group therapy camp for disturbed boys to public school settings where programs for disturbed pupils lagged behind other specializations. The standard assistance was referral to child guidance clinics when referral was possible. School liaison was rare and limited. School psychologists and school social workers were growing in numbers but still inadequate. The education—mental health liaison had a fundamental dissonance then that persists today; it makes one wince to hear present predictions that final solutions for programs for disturbed pupils will be achieved through the shotgun marriage of the two agencies (Morse, 1992). Until both disciplines change substantively, there will be limited gains for their students/clients.

At any rate, we were working in two school systems to develop programs for disturbed pupils. One development eventually became the crisis of helping teachers using Life Space Interviewing: This style of aid flourished in the two systems until the legal requirements of the federal legislation co-opted resources. In this approach, children did not have to be labeled or admitted by formal special education rituals, were not removed from the mainstream as home base, and service was based on actual behavior. Simultaneously, the two school systems were initiating another service of the "cascade," special segregated classes employing both intensive special education and mental health intervention. And along came Dunn and Deno.

My reaction to Dunn was very superficial. As the excitement grew, I ignored his arguments as too broad, really conclusions from too little evidence. None of this was on the sophisticated grounds brought forth in the current papers. Dunn said nothing about the quality of the classes: A rotten class is a rotten class, special or regular. I knew of efforts to help disturbed kids that were really deleterious. Anyway, he was speaking of students with mental retardation, and I held then and now that there are differences in what particular special children need and where they can best be served. As an individual psychologist, I find it uncalled for to consider all children with the same designation as equal, as is done for a class action decision. Also, it would have been interesting to know if certain children in either of Dunn's settings made progress while others might have regressed. My suspicions about unanalyzed average differences have grown with the years.

Then and now, I wondered at the big impact of Dunn's article. Several of the current authors bring out that Dunn found a cordial climate where many professionals were suspicious about the promises of special education classes as they existed. As to the disproportion of African American students, failure to compare similar White socioeconomic groups prevents clarification of what part of overrepresentation is prejudice, as poverty is a devastating condition for all children, as Gottlieb, Alter, Gottlieb, and Wishner (1994) demonstrated so vividly. But added to poverty is the overt and covert racial prejudice, which most of us have seen firsthand, the causes and possible cures for which were analyzed in detail by Artiles and Trent (1994). This prejudice is reflected throughout education in discipline, exclusions, and career counseling, as well as special education.

As several of the authors state, Dunn should be neither damned nor praised for all that is attributed to his article. The total inclusion push became powerful not on the basis of Dunn, but as a product of a particular interpretation of a civil rights extension to those with disabilities, combined with severe budget problems in education. Such a combination of holiness and financial stress is difficult to resist, as is all too evident. Some professionals who helped to bring about the current rash of criticisms by overpromising results for special education classes are now overpromising again for inclusion. Who was in charge when we separated beyond functional need, ignored parents, neglected racial prejudice, and created a massive self-perpetuating infrastructure of rules and regulations? All of us were involved. If special education does collapse, there are many of us who participated. For those who are socioemotionally disturbed, it is professionals who are giving the sage advice to imitate mental health and deinstitutionalize.

Will we put them on streets or in the school halls, or remove them to solitary home-bound teaching?

Inclusion for students who are socially and emotionally disturbed has usually been accompanied by diminished services: In one district where they closed their day school but did maintain the same level of inservice, it was necessary to hire many additional staff to serve the dispersed population. Often, total inclusion is in reality for all but the disturbed pupils. Regardless of Dunn, these two school systems went ahead with plans for segregated classes, with integration where possible. In retrospect, we erred in not maximizing integration through creative planning. Since there was a waiting list of pupils with severe disturbance, there was no worry about those with mild disturbance being included. We did not see Dunn's propositions as being prescriptive for all extruded special education students. It is interesting that, as the plans for the two systems evolved, one school allowed only 1 year of separate class while the other had no limit. And it soon became clear that some children needed more than the special class. Because there were no day schools then, this meant hospital treatment—even more exclusion. We were fortunate to have a high-quality service available. Parents, for the most part, had high hopes for the special class placement: For once, they were not bombarded with calls from school to come and get their unmanageable offspring. Parents were not required to accept counseling, only to come to the regular parent–teacher conference. At the time Dunn wrote, none of us saw that he boded ill for special education. We were deaf to the possibility and blind to our own shortcomings.

One of the biggest changes in special education has taken place in ideology. Now there are those special educators who see their field as corrupt and damaging to children, even though they continue to produce new crops of teachers every year through their classes. Yet, at least in the area of disturbance, there are those special teachers working on the front line who still feel they are doing the right thing to help youngsters through special classes. Given a modicum of support, they continue to work and even in some cases to turn pupils' lives around in spite of confounding pupil ecologies. Turning around one life makes the class cost-effective to the community, to say nothing of the child's life gains. But the work is very taxing, and the field continues to have the highest turnover rate. Lack of adequate support, stultifying rules, and outlandish expectations induce fatigue.

In contrast to my reaction to Dunn's article, my reaction to Deno's article was positive. I saw it as relevant and encouraging to what the school districts were planning. The cascade concept supported our plans. Decisions were made informally at the start, justice being subject to professional ethic. We were not aware then that we were party to a buildup of a legal bureaucracy, especially one that was part and parcel of the increasingly flawed general educational system (Skrtic, 1991). We did worry about how one could decide where on the continuum of service to best help a student. Trial and error was patently unfair. Unfortunately or not, depending upon one's viewpoint, the promise of a continuum was never fully realized in most programs countrywide. Even when complete, every level felt helpless, with some children too damaged to respond to the resources available to them. The point is that, if Deno's cascade is to function as intended, there must be an assurance of services and utilization of services for that small percentage of the most serious cases.

Studying these sophisticated papers reflecting on 25 years of Deno and Dunn, one is impressed by the erudition and insight displayed. The experience is like attending an advanced special education seminar. In fact, this issue could be a text for such an enterprise. Even those who try to keep abreast of the literature on these matters stand to be impressed by the scrutiny of the literature and the astute search for meaning as well as the additional original research reported. Of course, there is the advantage of hindsight. What would these authors have written at the time of the original publications? Some of Dunn's references were suspect even then, and the violation of the scientific paradigm of randomness should have been evident. Ecological considerations have reduced blame of the victim to a considerable degree. The basic orientation has also changed from process to final outcome evaluation. In this respect, the outcomes for students who are disturbed are the poorest: The quality of their lives, school level, and employment all are discouraging. Follow-up studies suggest that, if you want the most favorable results, you should assess outcomes within a short time after intervening: The longer the delay, the more these pupils slip back *on the average,* even though some do successfully join the mainstream. This again illustrates that special education is not about categories, although such arguments are an academic pastime. It is about individual children, not labels. Disturbed children represent a polyglot group with even more polyglot environments. In what cases is special education the significant cause of success or failure in outcomes when the youngster usually goes back to the same school, family, and community ecology that was influential in creating the initial plight that made for eligibility? It is painful to acknowledge that special education was never meant to meet mental health needs of children and youth in the first place, but only to give some sort of emotional bandages, and then only for certain ones (not to exceed 2% of the population) whose school learning was fouled up by their emotional state. Surveys show that, at a minimum, twice that number are seriously disturbed and some 12% more are known to need some assistance. The valiant effort to reach parents (who have rights but not obligations and are often overwhelmed themselves) pays off when it can be managed. But the ecology is frequently impervious to change (Morse, 1993). Chaos theory certainly applies to the field of special education, as Guess and Sailor (1993) suggested. We are in an enterprise far too complex for simplistic answers.

UNDERLYING ISSUES

As one studies the two original articles and this current set, certain underlying issues emerge. Although these issues are not always explicit, each of us holds a position on these variables, and these positions bear on subsequent argument. Overt or covert, such positions become predispositions for advocacy decisions.

Does extruded special education have the potential for helping youngsters or is it inherently a flawed and negative intervention?
Another seldom-discussed matter in all the arguments about where the child sits is the real issue of the appropriateness and quality of what the child gets. Several of the authors point this out. There are individual differences in classes as well as differences in individuals, and by what criterion do we randomize classes? Dunn must have had some high-quality classes and some low, as well as pupils in each who flourished and others who regressed. The question for research should be this: For what pupils are what class elements appropriate? There are obviously indications and contraindications, as results in general are variable. It already looks as if, for children who are disturbed, ecological factors rather than class factors may be dominant in the long run. Generalizations in special education are as spurious and primitive as comparing those who had therapy with those who didn't, with no control of the essential variable: therapy. The match of templates between individual need and what is provided is at issue (Bem, 1979). Special education is supposed to be an individualized matter, and as yet we depend upon average differences (sometimes of minimal practical significance) for policy decisions, rather than examining subprofiles or templates.

Do the negative aspects of special education inevitably overbalance the positive? If special education means a lower teacher–pupil ratio, individualization, and highly trained teachers, how can it be a negative influence unless miserably executed? Once, when we were meeting to place a special pupil back in good old regular education, the receiving teacher could not see the value of haste: "You have the ideal education now, which I wished I had—small group, individualized curriculum. Every pupil should have it so good, especially some of my 28." There are still those who see special education as health producing rather than as a fatal disease. MacMillan, Semmel, and Gerber (see Chapter 3) raise this issue. Perhaps negative attitudes can be managed by special education subcultures, as Hallahan and Kauffman (1994) propose, or by direct counseling, as I have found. Of course, there will need to be overall antidiscrimination efforts as well, because we live in a scapegoating culture. Some of our pupils who are disturbed fought over being called "retards." They announced they were not "retards" but "disturbed." We cannot ignore the meaning of a label to the child who is given it, even though most have previously undergone self- and peer-labeling.

Rejecting the value of special education, as many pupils do, is a generic problem in education today, when many high school students hold negative attitudes about their education. They are joined by some high-powered critics. The services of education and the mode of delivery must be seen as relevant by the consumer. One self-referred adolescent refused the peer efforts at negative contagion because, as he told them, he saw the special class as a solution to his dilemma. The impact of being special turns out to be an individual person-ecology matter. Yet there are a number of special educators who "know" that special education is evil for all pupils. In the subtle process of any human helping, can we operate on pretense?

What should be the obligation of education in general to society, and in turn, what should be the relationship of special education to general education?
What purpose is assigned these two agencies? There is obvious disparity in the answers to this question. An economist once wrote that the function of the schools as a societal grant agency is to provide a massive child-sitting service and to keep adolescents off the streets and out of the employment market. The chain of relationships between society, education, and special education embodies profound philosophical arguments; we all have our opinions. Neither regular nor special education is a free-floating operation. We resist special education as handmaiden to regular education, thus "letting regular education continue in errant ways." Special

educators seem to be embarrassed by being forced to play second violin. Because the community seldom speaks with one voice, there are many power plays and compromises concerning obligations. General education finds itself forced to add to the basics in response to societal problems, from driver education to AIDS education. Special education adds new categories.

So much depends upon societal attitudes toward special children, which have waxed and appear now to have plateaued if not waned in the financial crisis. Outcome data replace guilt as a driving force. The papers collected in this issue are attentive to the social changes in the last 25 years and the implications for special services. Social change, as Deno (1994) emphasized, is a euphemism for the disintegration of the child-raising function. Neither regular education, with its push for excellence and higher graduation requirements, nor special education, with its spawning categories, has taken change seriously. At best, as Guess and Sailor (1993) have stated, the educational agencies look piecemeal at the situation, which calls for massive and coordinated alterations in society itself. Who really believes the changes proposed for Education 2000 will be accomplished? If the predictions turn out to be accurate, what will happen to special education?

Rather than dreams [of President George H. W. Bush], we can best expect spots of progressive change in the configurations of education, not universal metamorphosis. When change happens, it will be the consequence of a coming together of a series of conditions welded in shape by astute and ethical local leadership. It is fascinating how, when there is a scarcity of resources to help students in dire need, such as Gottlieb et al. (1994) described, special educators distort their system to get help for children by making them special pupils. It is easier to do this than to get the proper changes in the system. We are reminded again of the late Eli Bower's comment that institutions that start out to serve children gradually convert to the cause of self-perpetuation.

Perhaps some of the differences of opinion about the original two articles go back to assumptions about the respective roles of regular and special education in society. Fred Weintraub (personal communication, 1992) once explained that there are three different basic assumptions about education. One is that equity means providing each student with the same opportunity and that those who can learn do, with an expected range in achievement. A second theory is that we give to each on the basis of individual need, thus eliminating individual differences in accomplishment. A third is that we give to each according to need but still expect significant individual differences. The variant paradigms are latent in the minds of administrators, teachers, and parents in every Individualized Education Program conference.

At a gross level of abstraction, we all agree that every child deserves a free appropriate, public education. The pinch comes in allotment of scarce resources. It is similar to the public debate on health care: Who is to get how much? When it comes to tax support, districts that are eliminating distinctly visible special education programs (saving money in a reduction of the hands-on time by assuming that consultation will suffice) are finding it more difficult to pass taxes—no visible program, no money. I have heard one national leader of inclusion mention (but only in passing) that our special funds are something we will have to protect as we move to full inclusion. Next fantasy? It would be helpful if writers during the great debates would post their position on the role of regular education vis-à-vis special education.

A related source of different opinions rests in beliefs concerning the mutability of individual differences.
Our youngsters represent the extensions of the distribution in various dimensions. We hold different ideas about how and what children can learn. In truth, there may be no general answer to mutability, even though we hold our positions on the debate. The body politic led by the always changing scientific zeitgeist expects greater or less potential from environmental interventions. We are now seeing the ascendance of the neural-chemical explanation for variant behavior, even to the point of differential biological etiology for various modes of aggression! Chemical treatment is rising in importance. Even though the resolution of the malleability debate can be achieved only in a specific individual situation, some apply a fixed view to a variety of conditions in planning meetings. If a practice helps one child, it should also work for any child, and the school should implement the practice. In some instances, the sponsors of cures refuse to allow any evaluative research. Special education becomes a matter of faith.

Perhaps the most important contribution of the federal legislation was the recognition of individual differences as the cornerstone for the new special education. While we are all equal before the law in certain regards, we are not all equal before the blackboard. There was even the faint hope that regular education might embrace the concept and do away with their 12 categories known as grades. Some schools have achieved the semblance of individual planning. The preschool legislation requires a family plan— every child should have a continually evolving, developmentally appropriate life plan. The legislation made explicit the most important premise: Each child goes to her or his own school. Teachers are often hard put to motivate attendance at the school where they teach. However, we all know teachers who do pass this miracle every day, at least until the pupils are adolescents. Incidentally, the article on adolescence by Edgar and Polloway (1994) addressed a neglected aspect of individual differences—developmental age differences. The world of the child changes with age, and so must special education. Specifically, the implication of inclusion—separation will differ with age as well as specific individual factors.

Unfortunately, the individual differences that dominate the narrow-gauge, regular educational assembly line have to do with cognitive intelligence. As Gardner's (1991) conceptualization indicates, this is but one of the seven multiple intelligences. Special education has yet to capitalize on his formulation. There are individual differences not only in child capacity, but also in how various pupils learn. Part of the time, the arguments we have reside in our concepts of each child's uniqueness and the individuality of learning.

The power and central place of caring in special education are often ignored.

Special education is billed as a caring enterprise. Such an illusive quality as caring finds no home in our research, yet it may be a crucial variable. Perhaps because of my focus on pupils who are disturbed, I look for more attention to affective components in children's lives. Edgar and Polloway (1994) did indicate the need for caring. Several authors speak of self-concept and self-esteem, which are not always clearly distinguished. Hallahan and Kauffman (1994) discuss the ambiguity of the research on self-esteem in special pupils. Because of the centrality of self-esteem and self-efficacy, perhaps each concept deserves more attention. As Markus and Nurius (1986) have demonstrated, children have more than a single self-concept tied to their hopes for the future: Some future selves are fearful and others encouraging as they relate to sense of self-efficacy in controlling their lives. In talking with special children, it is seldom that the special education experience has been deeply related to the present and future self-potentials. Special education is just another adult manipulation in the pupil's oft-manipulated life. Adolescents often say, in retrospect, "If it hadn't been for that class and teacher, I would have never made it." The point of beginning in special education is to seek relevance to the self in this non-choice "opportunity." It is psychological abuse to ignore the meaning to the individual. The most difficult challenge is education for the delinquents who have lost hope. Many of them also believe the future self is in the bands of fate; as one said, "fifty-fifty"—it's college or prison for the future self. Deno (1994) talked in general about the social malaise, and she might even have gone sharper. There are special pupils who live in constant fear for themselves and their protectors. There are classes and even schools where our pupils don't feel protected.

Special education is declared a caring profession, yet little is said about the rehabilitative function of teacher caring as an essential special education ingredient, even in the discussion of the increasing number of children stultified by not being cared for. How many of Dunn's classes were caring places? It is difficult to be a partial surrogate parent to 30 youngsters and no simple matter even with 10. Caring by consultation requires even more imaginative extension. Yet caring is what many special children most need. Caring requires hands-on relationships. We would like to remake families as the central source of essential caring. Sometimes we can; too often such changes elude us. The school and other agencies will have to become caring if we expect to socialize our children and make them secure in this neglectful society. Noddings (1992) has delineated the challenge. Sarason (1985) for the first time added education to the mental health holy trinity in his book on caring and compassion. Of course, a special class does nothing more than increase the opportunity for caring; it does not give a guarantee.

While somewhat fleeting attention is given to the emotional life of pupils and teachers, there are glib expectations of great positive changes in public and teacher attitudes toward special children. This seems especially dubious in the present "skinhead" climate. But there is no argument that it is a task we must undertake. My caution: Go easy on the wishful thinking, and do not make our special children pay the price of exaggerated anticipations of acceptance.

There are a number of cogent observations about how society has changed in the years since the original articles, starting with Deno (1994). We have moved from a nation at risk to a nation of children at risk. In spite of well-intended Great Society programs, we now have an underclass in which poverty dooms the lives of many children, as Gottlieb et al. (1994) so well demonstrated. When these social changes are added up, it makes for a different world of childhood and thus a presumed different school life. The battle has been joined in the school change literature between excellence goals for world competition and the goals of compensatory support to meet the needs of those who are deprived. The matrix of forces from populist to professional is played out in local and state school boards, currently only superseded by budget dilemmas. While all levels of society are at risk for reactions to the vast social changes depicted, there is a concentration of multiple risk factors in large population centers. Studies in one state indicate that half the students are at risk for unproductive lives. While special education gets the fallout of the regular school, the regular school gets the fallout of society. It has been pointed out that the majority of the children in some schools are candidates for special services: Gottlieb et al. (1994) made this only too clear. The conditions are more than poverty, though they find poverty the major culprit. There is also the massive social disorganization in basic cultural institutions, particularly the family and the economy. Will the family structure restabilize or further diffuse? Will there ever be enough jobs above subsistence level to go around in the future? And are not special students the most in jeopardy?

The enormity of the task confronting us encourages retreats to the latest announced rapid cure-all for special children. Eli Bower characterized what happened to community psychology as a retreat to private office practice when confronted with the dismaying task of changing the community life. While pondering these papers, one can wonder if we are belaboring the most important issues. Certainly, the papers shed new light on special education with careful presentation of research. But is this where it's at?

Finally, are we paying enough attention to the impact of research findings and policy decisions on the role of the primary help given, the regular and special teacher?

Several of the papers, particularly those of Semmel, Gerber, and MacMillan (1994) and Hallahan and Kauffman (1994), took the refreshing stance of including the service deliverer in their analyses. Mandates come down from on high, but the nature of the child's experience is largely formulated by the regular or special teacher and the integrity of the support. If there are advantages to a special class, large credit goes to the teacher. If there are advantages to the mainstream class, again we must credit the teacher and the elements of the work setting. Special teachers often report their greatest frustration is not the problem children but the problem system, which stymies what they could be doing. In fact, many effective teachers are habitual rule breakers.

With the increased numbers of high-need, developmentally unfinished children in regular classes today, many teachers find themselves fatigued to the point of zombie-like responses. Daily survival becomes the main goal (Tompkins & Tompkins-McGill, 1993). If one asks an audience of teachers how many would quit and take another equal-pay position, it is not uncommon that half the professionals would leave. The turnover of teachers of students who are socially and emotionally disturbed is at the crisis level.

Whatever the argument concerning inclusion, what happens to the teacher role has to be a primary concern, second only to what happens to the child. There are examples of included children who are there but who are "out of it." They are sitting in a regular education seat but lost in the process because there is not enough square inch of teacher to individualize—which is the birthright of special education. This is not to say that there are no teachers who have the Midas touch, but there are many who do not. If inservice education (or preservice for that matter) were as successful as some seem to expect, we would not have many of the problems we now face. Many of the difficulties teachers face every day result from contagion and require group rather than individual solutions. Teachers are group workers, but most have little or no training in group dynamics.

ARE THERE HOPEFUL SIGNS EMERGING FROM OUR CHAOS?

Most of our authors give attention to what can be done about the problems their research raises, sometimes presenting solutions in explicit detail. Twenty-five years hence we will know how realistic the ideas were. Twenty-five years ago, and again today, much hope for a more justified special education rests on pending changes in regular education. Current crises and dissatisfaction with schools have produced federal, state, and local mandates for change, usually with little said about special education. Advocates of equity and excellence spar. Often the courts become the decisive arbiter. School reorganization ranges from waiting it out until the craze dies down, to cosmetic alterations and occasionally a significant revolution. Because reorganization emphasizes local empowerment and community participation, the tendency is to spend considerable effort on process and committees. Building principals, in whom local empowerment takes place, are confronted with power loss and role changes. Leadership by committee is a new turn for the educational bureaucracy. Local empowerment counters the imposition of any model or even effort to examine critically the available wisdom on problems. Each effort is an individual case study. We are a diverse society, so we expect diverse outcomes. But it would expedite matters to have some promising images as guidelines.

One of the few writers concerned with both how children learn and what they need to learn is Gardner (1991) and, to a lesser extent, Noddings (1992). It is interesting that both go back to Dewey, although with some critical additions. Gardner emphasizes relevancy, apprenticeship, and what he calls natural museum-type learning based on work being done in schools where he develops his ideas. Often special education is virtually ignored in school reorganization. For disturbed pupils, William Rhodes is about to publish a new curriculum/method aimed at empowering the students to control their own lives. This constitutes a specific example of restructuring in one area of special education. As important as cooperative learning and collaboration are, do we not have to go beyond this level for needed changes?

There is not much discussion about the role of prereferral to foster inclusion, though this is required in some special education programs. As an intervention, prereferral intends to reduce certifications by maximizing assistance in the mainstream setting. While the goal is to save money and prevent the negative effects of certification, if adequate service can be generated to alleviate the impasse of both the child and the teacher, what could be better as a first step in rational inclusion?

One of the resources not emphasized by Deno is crisis intervention support to the pupil, teacher, and classroom at the point of the pupil's failure to cope. If we are to include pupils who are disturbed, we need to have some immediate rescue service, such as the helping or crisis teacher mentioned above. This is direct hands-on service, not consultation. Intimate collaboration with the classroom teacher is essential. Such assistance need not require certification or separation beyond processing the precipitating episode, be it acting out or depressive withdrawal. But it also becomes the natural way to move in on persistent problems in a sustained way. Diagnosis is continual and driven by the particular problem rather than by the certification label. Because the curriculum aspects as well as behavior may be involved, the crisis person is trained both in teaching and mental health skills. It would seem that inclusion for pupils who are disturbed implies an available crisis resource.

But to some there is one movement pending that supersedes these changes. Thinking in broader terms of social restructuring to meet the needs of all children, there is the concept of the full service school (FSS). Perhaps I am enthusiastic about this new approach because it is the logical way to improve not only special education for children who are disturbed, but also the multiple service needs of many other children and their families. There are two major thrusts to agency collaboration. One is the generation of a community-based comprehensive spectrum of services (Epstein, Quinn, Nelson, Polsgrove, & Cumblad, 1993) called the Child and Adolescent Service System Program (CASSP; Stroul, 1985). The obstacles to getting broad agency collaboration are formidable, as anyone who has tried to get even two agencies to cooperate will attest (Schlenger et al., 1992).

A more manageable effort is the FSS, an alternative being developed in Florida and being monitored by Lynn Lavely and Neal Berger at the College of Education in the University of South Florida. In the FSS, community agencies serving children and their families have representatives on the school campus. The goal is one-stop service aimed at family preservation by connecting parents and children with relevant services through a case coordinator. The interagency working group proposes that a FSS serve as a central point of delivery for whatever education, health, social/human, or employment services are locally needed. A possible advantage is that, rather than expending huge amounts of energy to get agency collaboration, the thrust is providing actual services to those in need. The essential point is that restructuring schools or special education, no matter how well done, will not necessarily serve the needs of children, especially special children. The school cannot and should not be expected alone to meet all needs of children. The idea of "ancillary" as applied to special education services is misleading. No needed service is ancillary. The FSS is service oriented to individualized planning. There is also evidence of the various disciplines participating with teachers in relevant curriculum as well.

Finally, it will not suffice just to articulate services if the services continue doing their business as usual. All services, not just the school, face the need to reinvent their practice and become more caring. If education needs to restructure practice to be responsive to the social realities of the day, should not the same hold for health, mental health, legal, and welfare services as well?

REFERENCES

Artiles, A. J., & Trent, S. C. (1994). Overrepresentation of minority students in special education: A continuing debate. *The Journal of Special Education, 27,* 410–437.

Bem, D. J. (1979). Assessing persons and situations with the template matching technique. In L. R. Kahle (Ed.), *Methods for studying person–situation interactions* (pp. 1–17). San Francisco: Jossey-Bass.

Deno, E. (1970). Special education as developmental capital. *Exceptional Children, 37,* 229–237.

Deno, E. (1994). Special education as developmental capital revisited: A quarter-century appraisal of means versus ends. *The Journal of Special Education, 27,* 375–392.

Dunn, L. (1968). Special education for the mildly retarded—Is much of it justifiable? *Exceptional Children, 35,* 5–22.

Edgar, E., & Polloway, E. A. (1994). Education for adolescents with disabilities: Curriculum and placement issues. *The Journal of Special Education, 27,* 438–452.

Epstein, M. H., Quinn, K., Nelson, C. M., Polsgrove, L. & Cumblad, C. (1993). Serving students with emotional and behavioral disorders through a comprehensive community-based approach. *OSERS, 5*(1), 19–23.

Gardner, H. (1991). *The unschooled mind: How children think and schools should teach.* New York: Basic Books.

Gottlieb, J., Alter, M., Gottlieb, B. W., & Wishner, J. (1994). Special education in urban America: It's not justifiable for many. *The Journal of Special Education, 27,* 453–465.

Guess, D., & Sailor, W. (1993). Chaos theory and the study of human behavior: Implications for special education and developmental disabilities. *Journal of Learning Disabilities, 27*(1), 16–34.

Hallahan, D. P., & Kauffman, J. M. (1994). Toward a culture of disability in the aftermath of Deno and Dunn. *The Journal of Special Education, 27,* 496–508.

Knitzer, J., Steinberg, Z., & Fleisch, B. (1990). *At the school house door.* New York: Bank Street School.

Markus, H., & Nurius, P. (1986). Possible selves. *American Psychologist, 41,* 954–969.

Morse, W. C. (1992). Mental health professionals and teachers: How do the twain meet? *Beyond Behavior, 3*(2), 12–20.

Morse, W. C. (1993). Ecological approaches. In T. R. Kratochwill & R. J. Morris (Eds.), *Handbook of psychotherapy with children and adolescents* (pp. 320–356). Boston: Allyn & Bacon.

Nelson, C. M., & Pearson, C. A. (1991). *Integrating services for children and youth with emotional and behavioral disorders.* Reston, VA: Council for Exceptional Children.

Noddings, N. (1992). *The challenge to care in the schools: An alternative approach to education.* New York: Teachers College Press.

Sarason, S. B. (1985). *Caring and compassion in clinical practice.* San Francisco: Jossey-Bass.

Schlenger, W. E., Etheridge, R. M., Hansen, D. J., Fairbank, D. W., & Onken, J. (1992). The evaluation of state efforts to improve systems of care for children and adolescents with severe emotional disturbances: The CASSP initial cohort study. *The Journal of Mental Health Administration, 19,* 131–142.

Semmel, M. I., Gerber, M. M., & MacMillan, D. L. (1994). Twenty-five years after Dunn's article: A legacy of policy analysis research in special education. *The Journal of Special Education, 27,* 481–495.

Skrtic, T. M. (1991). The special education paradox: Equity as the way to excellence. *Harvard Educational Review, 61,* 85–99.

Stroul, B. (1985). *The child and adolescent service system program (CASSP) system change strategies.* Washington, DC: CASSP Technical Center at Georgetown University.

Tompkins, J. R., & Tompkins-McGill, P. L. (1993). *Surviving in schools in the 1990s.* Lanham, MD: University Press of America.

CHAPTER 6

The Concept of the Least Restrictive Environment and Learning Disabilities: Least Restrictive of What?

Reflections on Cruickshank's 1977 Guest Editorial for the Journal of Learning Disabilities

Jean B. Crockett and James M. Kauffman

A child placed in a so-called least-restrictive situation who is unable to achieve, who lacks an understanding teacher, who does not have appropriate learning materials, who is faced with tasks he cannot manage, whose failure results in negative comments by his classmates, and whose parents reflect frustration to him when he is at home, is indeed being restricted on all sides.

(Cruickshank, 1977, p. 193)

In a 1977 editorial for the *Journal of Learning Disabilities,* Bill Cruickshank suggested that policies defining the regular classroom as the least restrictive placement for all students reflect administrative wishful thinking. With his ironic portrayal of the hapless child whose opportunities for learning and acceptance are "restricted on all sides," Cruickshank made his educational position clear: Nothing restricts a child more than lost opportunities to learn.

Challenging state and local policies across the United States for ranking various instructional settings from "most restrictive" to "least restrictive," Cruickshank (1977) raised the question, "Least restrictive of what?" Inquiring how regular class placement came to be considered less restrictive than any other placement, he asked, "Was this an administrative decision based on thought? Based on theory? Based on research? Based on opportunism? Based on fears of parental pressures of legal threats?" (p. 193). Noting that no administrative remedy can compensate for inadequate instruction, he remarked, "The fact of the matter is that there is no research to demonstrate that one type of educational placement is less restrictive than others. All types are needed, but all must be high quality" (p. 193).

Concerned with educational consequences, Cruickshank asked, Who will be held accountable when the least restrictive placement fails to provide the magic cure? Will the focus of blame rightfully fall back on educational leaders who sought redemption through untested structural changes instead of appropriate pedagogy? Or will blame fall to the alleged inadequacies of the child, or his parents, or the supposed incompetencies of the educators who tried to teach him? Said Cruickshank, "The child with learning disabilities deserves more than this. If the concept of least-restrictive placement is to prevail and not result in a new generation of tragedy for learning disabled children, then school leadership must attack its deficiencies with unrelenting vigor" (p. 194).

CONTINUING CONTROVERSIES IN SERVICE DELIVERY

Twenty-five years after the publication of Cruickshank's (1977) editorial, controversy still surrounds service delivery to students with learning disabilities (LD) regarding which students should be served, which curricula and instructional methodology should be used, and where instruction should take place. Teachers and administrators, frequently coping with their own inadequate preparation for educating exceptional learners, continue to face professional challenges in accommodating increasing numbers of students with disabilities into general education classrooms (Crockett & Kauffman, 1998; Scruggs & Mastropieri, 1996). However, these challenges to professional knowledge and skills have not been exclusively an American experience. As Pijl and Meijer (1994) point out, "The integration of students with special needs into regular education and—and a wider context—the integration into society of all kinds of segregated groups have been debated in the last decades throughout practically the whole western world" (p. xi).

The field of special education has a long tradition of advocating for the educational rights and the social acceptance of children and youth with disabilities in both schools and the larger society. This advocacy has been important and significant in advancing the universal acceptance of persons with disabilities and increasing society's accountability for the well-being of each of its members. Now that access to an equitable education for all students has been established by legislation in many countries and total exclusion from schooling is less of a threat for students with disabilities, a more subtle but no less threatening challenge remains. For some students with learning disabilities, the *functional* exclusion Cruickshank (1977) described is still a reality in contemporary classrooms"Many students do not have the ability to keep pace with the curriculum the way it is structured within the general education classroom and thus may experience a different kind of segregation—the exclusion from the basic right to learn" (Schumm et al., 1995, p. 335).)

Cruickshank's Guiding Perspective

Cruickshank's (1977) editorial perspective is that of a special educator informed from scholarship and practice about educating students with learning difficulties—an educator armed not merely with hope and good intentions but also with knowledge of both students and schools. With his references to student failure and concern for those "unable to achieve," Cruickshank situates productive learning through specific instruction as the educational sine qua non for students with extreme individual differences. In characterizing the plight of the ill-served child "restricted on all sides," he realistically implies that schools and classrooms have ecological features that facilitate achievement for students with learning disabilities such as interactions with understanding teachers and peers, instructional interventions, and appropriate curricular organization and management.

Cruickshank troubles over the purpose of educational access for students with learning disabilities, the availability of opportunities to enhance their performance, and valid accountability to prevent their academic and social failure. He proceeds from the presumption that harm can befall individual students when appealing but theoretical, untested social policies are given priority over proven instructional approaches. Cruickshank's concerns are similar to our own.

The Framework for Our Discussion

In discussing the concept of least restrictive environment (LRE) for students with learning disabilities, we are mindful of contemporary special education's dual roots in the contexts of effective pedagogy and public policy. We organize our thoughts about the conceptual issues and practical realities affecting students with learning disabilities by addressing the following questions: (a) What is involved in providing students with *access to the general curriculum,* and ensuring that *the general education curriculum is accessible to* students with learning disabilities who might require extraordinary approaches to derive its benefits? (b) How can inclusive policies be balanced with imperatives for individually appropriate learning? (c) How can practitioners best respond to presumptive positivism when instruction in the general education class or curriculum is determined to be a flawed preference for individual students with learning disabilities?

Our intention is to examine the purpose of the LRE requirement in American public policy and to probe its character as a rebuttable presumption of inclusive placement. Legal reasoning frequently proceeds from presumptions of truth or benefit understood from a positivist perspective. Justice relies on the presentation of convincing evidence of ensuing harm to rebut presumptions about placement in individual cases. The most classic example in American law is the presumption of innocence until guilt is proven. In special education, "rebuttable presumptions are universal prescriptions for programming that are assumed innocent until proven guilty of not addressing the educational benefit of vulnerable students" (Crockett, 1999, p. 4). We believe it is critical for special educators to be knowledgeable about the characteristics of students with learning disabilities and to develop prowess in specialized instruction to address their needs. Teachers who know what to look for, what to do, and what data to collect to best guide and portray their students' progress have the best chance of blending the intents of pedagogy and public policy. They will have the skills of argument and the stores of evidence that allow them, when necessary, to rebut placement presumptions on behalf of students who often require different resources to achieve different results. In probing the legal presumptions surrounding the concept of LRE, we rely on data we gathered in the positivist tradition from the multiple perspectives of parents, legislative developers, and educational professionals in our comprehensive study of the origins and interpretations of LRE (Crockett & Kauffman, 1999).

Our intent in this discussion is to focus on the educational needs of students with learning disabilities and to consider how parents and professionals in the United States and elsewhere attempt to balance social policies with learning imperatives. We begin each major section of our discussion with Cruickshank's words.

PROCEEDING FROM THE PRINCIPLES
OF SPECIAL EDUCATION

There are few, if any, who would argue with the spirit of the concept of least restrictive placement. The fact of the matter is that in terms of current educational practices, the "least" *may more often be the most restrictive place for learning disabled children to receive their education.*

(Cruickshank, 1977, p. 5, emphasis in original)

The concept of LRE weaves together the educational elements of place and practice and raises questions of what schools are for and how they are to be judged. Cruickshank's (1977) characterization of the child most restricted by placement in what is supposed to be a least restrictive learning environment draws attention to a basic question of educational access: What is the purpose of providing access to the regular class for students with learning disabilities if appropriate learning is not made individually accessible to them there?

According to Cruickshank (1977), the context of American schools prevents the individual consideration required to provide appropriate instruction to students with learning disabilities. Among the factors that conspired to make the "least" the most restrictive placement, in his view, were thoughtlessness and haste in developing appropriate mainstreaming programs, lack of instructional preparation for regular teachers, an abundance of administrators unprepared to support mainstreamed instruction, and an overreliance on evaluation rather than instruction as the means to prevent school failure. Contemporary reviews of inclusive practice continue to identify the same factors, despite sincere efforts to restructure schools (Burdette & Crockett, 1999; Cook, Semmel, & Gerber, 1999).

In what he describes as the underresearched and rampant spread of public school programs that misconstrued mainstreaming to mean placements that are "unselectively appropriate" (p. 194), Cruickshank's concerns were prescient. Although early interpretations of LRE did not begin with the presumption of regular class placement in every case, recent changes in federal law have endorsed such placement as a rebuttable preference, despite the continuing absence of a defensible research base. If there were ready access to systematic knowledge from intervention research about the outcomes of inclusive schooling, Swanson (2000) suggests that the unfortunate controversy surrounding LRE might be avoided. Although he acknowledges that policy in special education is rarely inspired by research, Swanson takes the position that the full continuum of placements should be available unless it can be shown that all children with learning disabilities do not benefit from pullout programs. To do otherwise would jeopardize their educational opportunity.

Cruickshank (1977) and Swanson (2000) both grapple with the dual discourses endemic to the field of special education. Speaking from his years of experience at the intersection of pedagogy and public policy, Gallagher (1984) refers to a critical aspect of social policy: "It is necessary to have a clear sense of your goals and a determined persistence in pursuing them if you want a chance to succeed" (p. 214). The primary goal and centerpiece of the Individuals with Disabilities Education Act (IDEA) is its requirement that students with disabilities are to be assured the right to a free appropriate education. Also under IDEA, students with disabilities, to the maximum extent appropriate to their learning, are to be educated with children who are not disabled (20 U.S.C. Sec. 1412 (a) (5) (A)).

Setting Clear Goals

Because the IDEA guides individualized decisions about educational programming and placement, LRE problems occur when there is confusion about what a learning environment is supposedly restricting for a particular child—educational opportunity or social integration. Our concern is that the social goals of inclusion have been articulated but not clearly aligned with goals for enhanced student outcomes. For example, although the recent amendments to the 1997 IDEA target educational results, they advocate the inclusion of all students in the general education curriculum and in widescale accountability systems, which are often of questionable relevance to meaningful individualized instruction. Although this policy strategy might be described as presumptive positivism (Sunstein, 1996), it can sometimes obfuscate and distort the individualized intentions of the federal law.

In calling for agreement on common goals for educating students with learning disabilities, Swanson (2000) advocates for a guiding policy less obsessed with placement and more concerned with *minimizing errors* (weak gains in achievement) in instruction. Although admitting that nothing is foolproof and that some of his suggestions are tongue-in-cheek, Swanson offers ways of handling errors with multiple options to prevent a poor fit between environment and child needs. His suggestions address early identification and evaluation of students with learning disabilities, selective hiring of teachers and school psychologists, and teacher preparation and practice. If the instructional environment is still at risk, says Swanson, "Change the environment in which policy is developed" (p. 48). Swanson remarks, "The specific aim of meeting the needs of learning disabilities children is to prepare them for citizenship in general society. Providing an effective array of options does this. Sometimes, in the debate on full inclusion we find that our aim is not well focused" (p. 48).

Brooding Creatively About Purpose

Norman Cousins (1974), long-time editor of the *Saturday Review World*, remarked on the need for leaders "to brood creatively about purpose" (p. 4) without becoming overwhelmed by discontinuity and unremitting arbitration—two pitfalls familiar to decision-makers coping with issues of student placement. Worrying over the purpose of education in general, Sarason and Doris (1979) advocated for both academic and social development, proposing that education addresses coequal goals for American students: "Productive learning and mutuality of living" (p. 407). Expanding on this definition, Sarason (1996) characterized productive learning as the product of "the social contexts that are necessary to arouse and sustain a combination of intellectual curiosity and striving, a sense of personal worth and growth, and a commitment to the educational enterprise" (p. 261).

With regard to educating exceptional learners, Cruickshank (1967) noted that "democracy ... accepts the responsibility for the education of all children" (p. 21) but provides individual consideration when its responsibilities cannot be ordinarily met. "Thus, special methods and provisions must be developed for children who ... are termed exceptional and who often cannot be educated with the typical frame of reference deemed appropriate for the so-called normal child" (p. 21). Gallagher (1994) points out that educational equity "does not consist of educating all children in the same place at the same time (and with the same curriculum?) but in ensuring that the student has basic needs met and is traveling a well thought-out road to a career and a satisfying life style" (p. 528). Schooling is not a place, says Gallagher; it is a continuing educational responsibility.

Principled Leadership in Special Education

Noting the administrative tendency to lead from rules of policy rather than principles of instruction, Sarason and Doris (1979) remarked that when the purposes of the LRE concept are considered, discussions quickly become "mired in the controversies centering around law, procedures, administration, and funding" (p. 392). Consequently, decisions seem to spring more from compliance concerns than conceptual understanding. We suggest that this occurs because the goals of special education for students with learning disabilities are assumed to be understood by teachers and administrators rather than explained as part of a foundational set of principles that ensure the following: (a) universal educational access and accountability; (b) individual consideration; (c) educational benefit; (d) effective programming; and (e) productive partnerships among students, parents, professionals, and communities that foster high expectations, support research-based strategies, and target positive results for exceptional learners (Crockett, 1999).

LEGAL REASONING AND THE PRESUMPTION OF POSITIVISM IN REBUTTAL

Special education involves meeting the needs of children. This is not a hollow cliché, but a mandatory concept.

(Cruickshank, 1967, p. 47)

From the legal perspective of the IDEA, the purpose of schooling exceptional learners is very clear: "to ensure that all children with disabilities have available to them a free appropriate public education that emphasizes special education and related services designed to meet their unique needs, and prepare them for employment and independent living"

(20 U.S.C. Sec. 1400 (1) (A)). The requirement to provide students with farsighted, appropriate programming raises a basic question: How can inclusive policies be balanced with imperatives for individually appropriate learning? What kind of evidence will be taken as rebuttal of general education placement?

The Continuum of Alternative Placements

As an American scholar of education and human exceptionality, Bill Cruickshank's pedagogical views became an integral part of the foundation upon which the IDEA was based. Cruickshank's (1967) advice to teachers about educating exceptional children and youth reads like a primer to the IDEA; so much of what he describes as intensive and individualized practice for students with disabilities was incorporated into the statute. The main difference between the texts is that Cruickshank's prescriptions are couched in the educational context of pedagogy, and those of the IDEA are set in the legal context of students' rights. For example, this difference is particularly evident in the language Cruickshank chose to describe student placement; *selective placement* is his term. The process he describes, however, is the close, careful scrutiny from multiple perspectives that is required by what would become, in the legal discourse, "factor-guided placement in the LRE"—a more complex analysis than mere placement in classrooms ranked more or less restrictive regardless of students' needs.

From 1975 to the present, in approximately 15,000 school districts, the provision of an appropriate education has relied on the cascade of services model (see Deno, 1970) to operationalize the requirement of providing the LRE under American law. The cascade model offers students with disabilities instruction across a continuum of alternative placements extending from regular classrooms, separate classes, day schools, residential settings, to hospital and homebound services. The educational intent of the continuum of alternative placements is to provide a variety of settings in which appropriate individual programming might be offered to a student with disabilities. The legal intent of the continuum is to ensure that a free appropriate public education (FAPE) can still be provided to students who are not making satisfactory progress in the regular class, despite the assistance of supplementary aids and services.

Presumptive Positivism

Within the legal discourse, the least restrictive appropriate placement for any student is presumed to be the regular class. Pedagogy can rebut this presumption, however, if decision-making teams find a mismatched relationship between a student's unique learning characteristics and the ecological elements in the regular setting necessary to provide the student with appropriate educational access or benefit. Distinguishing legal presumptions from hard and fast rules is as critical to educational decision-makers as it is to legal advocates for the defense. Rebutting presumptions in special education placements requires an understanding of FAPE. It also requires that those who seek an alternative to the placement presumption possess both the drive to rebut it and the data (i.e., evidence in the positivist tradition) to succeed.

In allowing for presumptions about placements and their rebuttal, the law gives privilege to evidence and prevents discrimination. Presumptions about access to general education classrooms and curricula are considered to be preferences unless evidence suggests that such preferences would cause harm in particular cases. The term *presumptive positivism* (cf. Sunstein, 1996) describes a data-based alternative to the application of rules when rules might produce "weird or palpably unjust outcomes in particular cases" (p. 127). Sunstein suggests that this strategy, which allows for escape from rules in extraordinary circumstances, may be the best that we can do: "If exceptions will be made in cases of absurdity, then it is possible to ask, in every case, whether the particular application is absurd" (p. 127).

The Concept of LRE as a Rebuttable Presumption

In U.S. policy, the LRE concept has been variously interpreted as a legal principle enhancing integration and an educational strategy linking integration to appropriate programming. LRE was never intended to be an unyielding rule for the integrated placement of students with disabilities in the regular classroom. Rather, it is best described as a rebuttable presumption that favors the inclusion of disabled and nondisabled students in regular classes, but allows separation in certain instances (Turnbull, 1990; Yell, 1998).

In researching its legal roots, we found that the term *LRE* is derived from the concept of the least restrictive alternative (LRA), which has its legal basis in the U.S. Constitution and serves to accommodate both individual and state interests. "As long ago as 1819, Chief Justice Marshall of the United States Supreme Court ... indicated that regulation affecting citizens of a state should be both 'appropriate' and 'plainly adapted' to the end sought to be achieved" (Burgdorf, 1980, p. 278). This principle has been applied widely from cases of inter-state commerce to education, and it has been couched in various judicial forms, including the phrase "less drastic means for achieving the same basic purpose."

Edwin Martin, who served as Chief of the U.S. Bureau of Education for the Handicapped when the concept became part of the federal regulations, told us that the term LRE was not in the original statute, but that the reference to a continuum of placements was built into the law from the start:

> LRE was an important element of the law, but it was down the list of elements. The most important element was a "free appropriate public education." The assumption was not that all children would be educated in the regular classroom with non-handicapped children,... just where "appropriate." Appropriate placement is based not on the philosophy of the school but on the individual IEP under the law. (in Crockett & Kauffman, 1999, p. 75)

The LRE concept has been described as a means by which to balance the values surrounding the provision of an "appropriate education (the student's right to and need for an appropriate education) with the values of individual rights of association" (Turnbull, 1990, p. 148). "Presumptively ... [a] segregating placement is more harmful than regular school placement. Only when it is shown that such a placement is necessary for appropriate education purposes in order to satisfy the individual's interests or valid state purposes is the presumption overcome" (p. 163).

Turnbull views rebuttable presumptions as positive policy tools that offer affected parties greater *"freedom of choice"* (p. 163, italics in original), and protection from having no alternative to what they perceive as harmful. In the case of LRE, determining what constitutes a suitable rebuttal can be complex and relies on a fact-specific (positivist) inquiry. The concept of LRE "is inextricably tied to the notion of appropriateness, which makes it all the more complex because appropriate education itself is difficult to define" (Turnbull, 1990, p. 161). While the constitutional basis of LRE requires the government, when it has a legitimate interest, to take actions that least drastically restrict a citizen's liberty, "it is another thing altogether to answer the question: What is an unwarranted or unnecessary restriction of a handicapped child when the state is required to educate him or her appropriately?" (p. 162).

As Cruickshank (1977) suggested, *the concept of LRE was never intended to mean that the student could or should be situated solely in the regular classroom.* Congress, in developing the original Education for All Handicapped Children Act in 1975, viewed the regular class as the optimal setting but acknowledged the views of special educators like Bill Cruickshank that instruction should be offered in multiple environments if individual needs are to be appropriately met. However, when amending the statute in 1997, Congress shifted its presumptive stance. Acknowledging that decisions for students with disabilities are to be based on individual need, Congress, nevertheless, called for justification in the student's Individual Education Program (IEP) when decisions require an alternative placement to regular classes. Huefner (2000) remarked that "although the content of the statutory provisions governing the least restrictive environment and requiring a continuum of placement options did not change, Congress, in effect, introduced a shift via the side door" (p. 198).

Problems with Presumptions of FAPE

Although only minor changes have been made to the LRE provisions in the federal regulations, extensive alterations addressing each student's participation and progress in the general education curriculum are now prescribed under the heading of FAPE. The general school reform agenda has been grafted to each IEP in an effort to ensure that each special education student receives at least a comparable education to his or her classmates. However, the intent of the IDEA has long been to offer a more personalized standard of educational opportunity to students with learning disabilities through individualized, not comparable, educational programming. The pervasive emphasis on participation and progress in the general curriculum for each student with a disability, if not understood as a presumed preference of the law, could subtly shift the focus of accountability from the child's appropriate progress to the adequacy of the school district's service provision.

These policies endorsing curricular inclusion and accountability rely on a presumption that more children will be successful than we think if they are included in and tested on their competence in the general education curriculum. However, further presumptions are also implied: (a) the presumption that the general education curriculum is challenging, (b) the presumption that low expectations for their success will continue without a mandate to report on the progress of exceptional learners in that curriculum, and (c) the presumption that curricular and instructional alternatives are de facto less challenging without considering for whom they are less challenging and under what circumstances they are less challenging.

American parents and professionals welcome efforts to measure the educational progress of students with disabilities, but they do so with concerns about confusing the principles of ensuring universal access and accountability with providing effective programming that is reasonably calculated to provide individual students with educational benefit. In other words they are suspicious that presumptions of FAPE serve the political agenda of equalizing access for *all* students to the *same* high standards and the *same* curricular offerings without stopping to consider that access to these standards and this presumably rich curriculum might not help some students to achieve meaningful outcomes at all (Crockett, 1999).

Employing a System of Factors

It is one thing to apply presumptive positivism to the concept of LRE; placement concerns are only one factor in providing FAPE. But irony surrounds the application of presumptive generalities to the inherently individualized nature of FAPE. Presumptions are blunt instruments, ill-fitting and heedless of individual specifications. They neither respect what is individually considered to be true nor clarify what is not understood. They make a point that begs a counterpoint when the fortunes of the few are threatened by generalities. Presumptive rules are by nature confrontational; they are indigenous to the argument culture (cf. Tannen, 1998). Unlike the more refined legal tool of factors, presumptions provoke a challenge rather than provide procedures for thoughtful deliberation. Factors guide decision-making by setting out the elements to be considered in responding to rules or presumptions; for example, the presumptions of LRE are rebutted with (positivist) evidence guided by a set of mandatory and qualified factors set out in the federal regulations to the IDEA (cf. Bateman & Chard, 1995). Factors provide the counterpoint by looking at a range of particulars and allowing decisions to emerge from multiple criteria. A system based on factors requires appreciation for diversity, ambiguity, multiple perspectives, attention to much of the broad situation, attention to particulars, attention to how others in similar circumstances have been treated, allowance for different values placed on assumed benefits, and agreements based not on theory but on the particular circumstances and positivist data under review: "Tests of this sort imply a wide and close look at individual circumstances. On this view, justice is far from blind. It tries to see a great deal" (Sunstein, 1996, p. 144).

REALITIES OF PROFESSIONAL PRACTICE

If the concept of least-restrictive placement is to prevail and not result in a new generation of tragedy for learning disabled children, then school leadership must attack its deficiencies with unrelenting vigor. Time is not on the side of leadership any longer.

(Cruickshank, 1977, p. 194)

Students with learning disabilities will need double indemnity if administrators fail to balance social policies with learning imperatives and fail to ensure systematic and explicit instruction by teachers highly skilled in delivering it. *If* LRE, as a legal concept, is to be considered as a rebuttable presumption of inclusive placement, *and if* requirements for FAPE are linked with general school reform, *then* practitioners need to know when and how to make legitimate exceptions. These concerns raise the following question: How can practitioners best respond to *presumptive positivism* when instruction in the general education class or curriculum is determined to be a flawed preference for individual students with learning disabilities? As Cruickshank suggests, the task requires more than hope and good intentions. Reliable data are critical.

Cruickshank's Remedies: Addressing Conceptual and Practical Deficiencies

Among the remedies Cruickshank (1977) suggests is the establishment of universal in-service training through which all teachers can be brought to a basic understanding about the complex problems of students with learning disabilities. For master teachers, however, he recommends "in-depth preparation under competent professors" (p. 6). He offers two final prescriptions: the subordination of diagnosis to instruction, and the provision of a variety of educational programs to serve a variety of student needs. In addressing the realities of professional practice, we consider his prescriptions in reverse order, addressing first his conceptual concerns with variety, and tackling second his practical concerns with what teachers and administrators need to know and be able to do.

Offering a Variety of Educational Programs

Cruickshank's (1977) vision of corresponding varieties of students and programs is similar to the positions taken by several groups advocating for the educational benefits of students with disabilities. Although many students with learning disabilities benefit from inclusion in regular classes, The Learning Disabilities Association of America (LDA) posits that "the regular education classroom is not the appropriate placement for a number of students with learning disabilities who may need alternative instructional environments, teaching strategies, or materials that cannot or will not be provided within the context of a regular classroom placement" (LDA, 1993).

Cruickshank's calls for variety are also reminiscent of Hornby's (1999) appeals for responding to inclusion with diversity in England. Hornby targets inclusion in the community after students have left school "as the actual end that educators are seeking. Inclusion in mainstream school may be a means to that end but is not the end itself" (p. 125). Hornby suggests that accessing high-quality instruction that leads to a successful postschool life relies less on an obsession with curricular or classroom inclusion for special education students and more on providing a diversity of settings, strategies, and curricular options responsive to their diverse needs and strengths.

Special educator Karen Silver's observations reflect an appreciation for the variety and diversity of programs that are hard-won through parental advocacy and professional support. Speaking from her perspective as the parent of a special education student, she cautions that not all parents of children with disabilities view the regular classrooms in their neighborhoods as having the capacity to provide meaningful opportunities to learn.

> Not all children who require special education are the same. The diversity of programs which exist today came about because parents and educa-

tors fought for them, recognizing that there was no single setting which could possibly meet the wide-ranging needs of the disabled school-age population. (Silver in Crockett & Kauffman, 1999, p. 184)

As Cruickshank (1977) suggests, a variety of program options requires teacher development and instructional expertise. Time is definitely not on the side of unprepared practitioners any longer.

Specific Requests for Specific Instruction

Some parents of students with learning disabilities have given up on unresponsive schools and are removing their children from public programming at increasing rates, attributing learning gains to instructional methods used in private schools (e.g., Kingsley, 2000). In recent instances, challenges to placement have been associated with parental requests for alternative curricula and specialized methodology in reading instruction. After reviewing 27 legal decisions involving students with learning disabilities and parental requests for specific reading methods, Bhat, Rapport, and Griffin (2000) observed that when making their decisions, hearing officers and justices relied most frequently on the twin criteria of appropriateness of district programming and the academic progress of the student with learning disabilities.

Student performance was at the center of each case, with hearing officers and judges sympathetic to parental complaints when student achievement in reading and spelling fell below 3 or more years of grade level. In the 16 decisions that found district programming appropriate to the needs of the particular students with learning disabilities, the school districts each offered a variety of language-based programs targeting decoding and spelling skills. Of particular interest is the fact that a majority of these cases involved students with learning disabilities in the secondary grades whose parents were alarmed at their lack of academic achievement. Parental optimism with standard reading instruction in the early grades faded from exposure to the obvious disparities between classmates and their child as academic demands increased. "As parents became acutely aware of the skill deficits their children experienced, they also realized how essential it was for them to have highly effective instructional interventions that would provide immediate benefits" (Bhat et al., 2000). Perhaps these cases best illustrate courts' presumptive positivism—their tendency to presume that data, not theory alone, will be the basis for judgment.

What Do Practitioners Need To Know About Students with Learning Disabilities?

Judicial demands for data rather than assumptions about the performance of students with learning disabilities continue to rely on pedagogical decision-making by teachers highly skilled in assessment and specialized instruction. In asserting that there is something special, indeed, about special education, Cruickshank (1967) remarked, "special education exists because some children present problems which cannot be readily solved by general education" (p. 21). Cruickshank (1977) expressed concern that educators had little understanding about the complex problems faced by students with learning disabilities and called for both universal teacher in-service and in-depth special education preparation for master teachers to understand both the characteristics of students with learning disabilities and programming demonstrably effective in helping such students to learn.

Special Education Means Specialized Instruction

After researching issues of mainstreaming and inclusion for 30 years, Naomi Zigmond (2000) notes from her observations that what the IDEA describes as special education is not being provided to students with learning disabilities. Her conclusion is that special education needs to be reinvented according to its initial design.

> As others have said before me, special education is, first and foremost, instruction focused on individual need. It is carefully planned. It is intensive, urgent, relentless, and goal directed. It is empirically supported practice, drawn from research. To provide special education means to set priorities and select carefully what needs to be taught. It means teaching something special and teaching it in a special way.... To provide special education means monitoring each student's progress ... and taking responsibility for changing instruction when the monitoring data indicate that sufficient progress is not being made. (Zigmond, 1997, pp. 384–385)

According to Zigmond, none of these elements was visible in the multiple classrooms she studied in a comprehensive report of what inclusion looks like in American elementary schools (cf. Baker & Zigmond, 1995). She advocates reinventing special education as an effective medium of instruction for students with learning disabilities by redefining the responsibilities of general educators to address the individual differences of students who require less than the specialized, intensive attention demanded by the IDEA. For students with learning disabilities who require more than an education comparable to that received by the majority, Zigmond calls for a return to "special education that is temporary, intensive, and delivered in a pull-out setting … because the general education classroom learning environment is not conducive to intensive instruction" (pp. 386–387). She also advocates for preserving a unique and specialized preparation for special educators so that "special education can be provided by a highly trained professional capable of assessing the child, of planning a teaching program based on this assessment, and implementing the teaching plan" (p. 386). Zigmond's essential message for practitioners, policy makers, advocates, and researchers in special education is to focus "on defining the nature of special education and the competencies of the teachers who will deliver it" (p. 389).

In reflecting on the links between research and service delivery, Keogh (1999) remarks that parents and professionals continue to rely on availability and advocacy, not appropriateness or effectiveness in making programming decisions. Bryan (1999) also notes that effective programming in both general and special education is often undermined by circular and recurrent changes rather than progressive reforms based on scientific data. "How can 40 years of research, some of it quite elegant, be swept aside by fads?" she asks. "Does the adoption of fads or nonscientifically supported methods of instruction mean the field of education is fundamentally anti-science? The field of education should be the bastion of scientific endeavor" (p. 445).

What Do Practitioners Need To Do
To Demonstrate Instructional Results?

Considering that legal reasoning relies on fact-specific, positivist evidence to rebut placement presumptions, we would expect teachers and administrators to be cognizant of the characteristics of students with learning disabilities and knowledgeable about research-validated practices for their instruction. We would also expect special educators to be skillful in prescribing and applying these practices appropriately for a particular student in a particular set of circumstances. In addition, we suggest that practitioners come to recognize when elements of educational law constitute presumptions so that rebuttals can be made when appropriate, and, in the case of placement presumptions, evidence can demonstrate when a learning environment might restrict rather than facilitate a child's learning.

CONCLUDING THOUGHTS

Three decades after the publication of Cruickshank's (1977) editorial, Swanson (2000) restated Cruickshank's theme: "The major premise guiding policy for children with learning disabilities should be concerned with minimizing errors in terms of instruction" (p. 47). This statement encapsulates the view of positivist science, which has as its foundation stone "the admission that one can simply reach a wrong conclusion due to various forms of error" (Kauffman & Brigham, 2000, p. 168). As we have noted, the courts rely upon concepts of science and positivism to judge whether the presumption of appropriate placement of students with learning disabilities (and other disabilities) in general education is tenable. Yet antiscientific, antipositivist, "dubiously coherent relativistic views about the concepts of truth and evidence really have gained wide acceptance in the contemporary academy ...," and "this onset of relativism has had precisely the sorts of pernicious consequences for standards of scholarship and intellectual responsibility that one would expect it to have" (Boghossian, 1998, p. 23). Special education and general education reformers today seem particularly likely to abandon the positivist view for the notion that the key to improvement is structural change. However, others contend that structure is not the heart of the problem of improving special education (e.g., Kauffman & Hallahan, 1993).

Experts in the field of educational administration would seem to agree that structure is not the central problem, suggesting that issues of instruction are ill-served by structural solutions. Murphy (1995) takes the position that inclusion is primarily an organizational, not an educational intervention. Agreeing that results of inclusive programming should not be assumed and assessment of student outcomes should be pursued, Murphy acknowledges a theoretical dilemma: "Organizational changes—whether of the macro-level variety, such as the centralization or decentralization of governance and management, or of the more micro-level variety, such as student grouping—have not, do not now, and never will, predict organizational effectiveness" (p. 210). Elmore, Peterson, and McCarthey (1996) point out that reforms, such as inclusion, are based on the shaky premise that changing structure changes practice: "Stripped to its essentials, school restructuring rests on a fundamental belief in the power of organizational structure over human behavior. In this belief, traditional school structures are the enemy of good teaching practice, and fundamental structural changes are the stimulus for new practices" (p. 4). A more realistic approach to the issue of instructional placement—an approach less reliant on "administrative wishful thinking"—might suggest that norms and behaviors of schools and teachers need to change before structures are eliminated and redesigned. Such an approach "would require reformers to treat structural change as a more contingent and uncertain result of change in practice, rather than as a means of reaching new practice" (Elmore, 1995, p. 26). As Conquest (2000) puts it, "certainty on matters in which our knowledge is inevitably imperfect is the enemy of good understanding and good policy" (p. 14).

In his closing remarks, Cruickshank (1977) suggested that "there is nothing magical about an administrator's decision to foster less-restrictive placement of children" unless, at a minimum, the elements he identified as needing remedy were addressed. Several generations later, yet still without thoroughly trained teachers, informed administrators, intensive instruction, and a variety of educational programs, students with learning disabilities risk "failure to thrive" in supposedly least restrictive placements. We wonder if their low achievement, despite their inclusive participation in general education settings, might turn the optimism of some advocates into cultural critique and despair if they perceive, erroneously, that there is little else that educators can do to improve the performance of students with learning disabilities. We suspect that Bill Cruickshank would say in response: "The child with learning disabilities deserves more than this."

REFERENCES

Baker, J. M., & Zigmond, N. (1995). The meaning and practice of inclusion for students with learning disabilities: Themes and implications from the five cases. *The Journal of Special Education, 29,* 163–180.

Bateman, B., & Chard, D. J. (1995). Legal demands and constraints on placement decisions. In J. M. Kauffman, J. W. Lloyd, B. P. Hallahan, & T. A. Astuto (Eds.), *Issues in educational placement: Students with emotional and behavioral disorders* (pp. 285–316). Hillsdale, NJ: Erlbaum.

Bhat, P., Rapport, M. J., & Griffin, C. (2000). A legal perspective on the use of specific reading methods for students with learning disabilities. *Learning Disabilities Quarterly, 23,* 283–297.

Boghossian, P. A. (1998). What the Sokal hoax ought to teach us. In N. Koertge (Ed.), *A house built on sand: Exposing postmodernist myths about science* (pp. 23–31). New York: Oxford University Press.

Bryan, T. (1999). Reflections on a research career: It ain't over till it's over. *Exceptional Children, 65,* 438–447.

Burdette, P. J., & Crockett, J. B. (1999). An exploration of consultation approaches and their implementation in heterogeneous classrooms. *Journal of Education and Training in Mental Retardation and Developmental Disabilities, 34*(4), 2–22.

Burgdorf, R. L., Jr. (1980). *The legal rights of handicapped persons: Cases, materials, and text.* Baltimore: Brookes.

Conquest, R. (2000). *Reflections on a ravaged century.* New York: Norton.

Cook, B. G., Semmel, M. I., & Gerber, M. M. (1999). Attitudes of principals and special education teachers toward the inclusion of students with mild disabilities. *Remedial and Special Education, 20,* 199–207, 243.

Cousins, N. (1974, November 16). Thinking through leadership. *Saturday Review World, 4.*

Crockett, J. B. (1999). *Preventing disabilities from handicapping the futures of our children.* Keynote address presented at the annual conference of the Association of Special Education Administrators in Queensland, Australia, September 20, 1999.

Crockett, J. B., & Kauffman, J. M. (1998). Classrooms for students with learning disabilities: Realities, dilemmas, and recommendations for service delivery. In B. Y. L. Wong (Ed.), *Learning about learning disabilities* (2nd ed., pp. 489–525). San Diego, CA: Academic Press.

Crockett, J. B. & Kauffman, J. M. (1999). *The least restrictive environment: Its origins and interpretations in special education.* Mahwah, NJ: Erlbaum.

Cruickshank, W. M. (1967). *Education of exceptional children and youth.* Englewood Cliffs, NJ: Prentice-Hall.

Cruickshank, W. M. (1977). Least-restrictive placement: Administrative wishful thinking. *Journal of Learning Disabilities, 10,* 193–194.

Deno, E. (1970). Special education as developmental capital. *Exceptional Children, 37,* 229–237.

Elmore, R. F. (1995). Structural reform and educational practice. *Educational Researcher, 24*(9), 57–64.

Elmore, R. F., Peterson, P. L., & McCarthey, S. J. (1996). *Restructuring in the classroom: Teaching learning, and school organization.* San Francisco: Jossey-Bass.

Gallagher, J. J. (1984). The evolution of special education concepts. In B. Blatt & R. J. Morris (Eds.), *Perspectives in special education: Personal orientations* (pp. 101–124). Glenview, IL: Scott, Foresman.

Gallagher, J. J. (1994). The pull of societal forces on special education. *The Journal of Special Education, 27,* 521–530.

Hornby, G. (1999). Inclusion, exclusion, and confusion. *Liberty, 46,* 121–125.

Huefner, D. S. (2000). The risks and opportunities of the IEP requirements under IDEA '97. *The Journal of Special Education, 33,* 195–204.

Individuals with Disabilities Education Act of 1997. 20 U.S.C. §1400 *et seq.*

Kauffman, J. M., & Brigham, F. J. (2000). Editorial. *Behavioral Disorders, 25,* 168–169.

Kauffman, J. M., & Hallahan, D. P. (1993). Toward a comprehensive service delivery system. In J. I. Goodlad & T. C. Lovitt (Eds.). *Integrating general and special education* (pp. 73–102). Columbus, OH: Merrill/Macmillan.

Keogh, B. (1999). Reflections on a research career: One thing leads to another. *Exceptional Children, 65,* 295–300.

Kingsley, E. (2000, March 14). Rescued from the mainstream: One mom learns that special treatment is best for her son with ADHD. *The Washington Post/Health,* 9.

Learning Disabilities Association of America. (1993). Position paper on full inclusion of all students with learning disabilities in the regular education classroom. *LDA Newsbrief, 28*(2).

Murphy, J. (1995). Insights on "the context of full inclusion" from a non–special educator. *The Journal of Special Education, 29,* 209–211.

Pijl, S. J., & Meijer, C. J. W. (1994). Introduction. In C. J. W. Meijer, S. J. Pijl, & S. Hegarty (Eds.), *New perspectives in special education: A six-country study of integration* (pp. xi–xiv). London: Routledge.

Sarason, S. B. (1996). *Barometers of change: Individual, educational, and social transformation.* San Francisco: Jossey-Bass.

Sarason, S. B., & Doris, J. (1979). *Educational handicap, public policy, and social history.* New York: Free Press.

Schumm, J. S., Vaughn, S., Haeger, D., McDowell, J., Rothlein, L. & Saumell, L. (1995). General education teacher planning: What can students with learning disabilities expect. *Exceptional Children, 61,* 335–352.

Scruggs, T. E., & Mastropieri, M. A. (1996). Teacher perceptions of mainstreaming/inclusion, 1958–1995: A research synthesis. *Exceptional Children, 63,* 59–74.

Sunstein, C. R. (1996). *Legal reasoning and political conflict.* New York: Oxford University Press.

Swanson, H. L. (2000). Issues facing the field of learning disabilities. *Learning Disabilities Quarterly, 23,* 37–50.

Tannen, D. (1998). *The argument culture.* New York: Random House.

Turnbull, H. R. (1990). *Free appropriate public education: The law and children with disabilities.* Denver, CO: Love.

Yell, M. L. (1998). *The law and special education.* Upper Saddle River, NJ: Prentice-Hall.

Zigmond, N. (1997). Educating students with disabilities: The future of special education. In J. W. Lloyd, E. J. Kameenui, & D. Chard (Eds.), *Issues in educating students with disabilities* (pp. 377–390). Mahwah, NJ: Erlbaum.

Zigmond, N. (2000). Reflections on a research career: Research as detective work. *Exceptional Children, 66,* 295–304.

CHAPTER 7

Enabling or Disabling? Observations on Changes in the Purposes and Outcomes of Special Education

James M. Kauffman, Kathleen McGee, and Michele Brigham

This chapter is from "Enabling or Disabling? Observations on Changes in the Purposes and Outcomes of Special Education," by J. M. Kauffman, K. McGee, and M. Brigham, 2004, *Phi Delta Kappan, 85,* pp. 613–620. Reprinted with permission.

The emphasis of special education has changed from habilitation and re-mediation to inclusion and accommodation regardless of ability or per-formance. The consequence of this change is more disabling than en-abling for students with disabilities. Description of changes in attitudes toward disability and special education is followed by discussion of prac-tices in placement and accommodation that may further disable rather than enable students with disabilities.

Schools need demanding and distinctive special education that is clearly focused on instruction and habilitation (Kauffman & Hal-lahan, 2005). Abandonment of special education is a prescription for disaster. But special education has lost its way in the single-minded pursuit of full inclusion. Once, special education's purpose was to bring the performance of students with disabilities closer to that of nondis-abled peers in regular classrooms, to move as many students as possible into the mainstream with appropriate support (Fuchs, Fuchs, Fernstrom, & Hohn, 1991). For students not in regular education, the goal was to move them toward a more typical setting in a cascade of placement op-tions (Deno, 1970; Huefner, 1994). Any good thing can be ruined by extremes. We see special education suffering from extremes of inclusion and accommodation.

Aiming for as much normalization as possible gave special education a clear purpose. Some disabilities were seen as easier than others to reme-diate. Most speech and language disorders, for example, were considered eminently remediable. Other disabilities, such as mental retardation and many physical disabilities, were assumed to be permanent or long-term and less remediable, but movement *toward* the mainstream and increasing independence from special educators were clear goals.

The emphasis in special education has shifted away from normaliza-tion, independence, and competence. The result has been students' de-

pendence on whatever special programs, modifications, and accommodations are possible, particularly in general education settings. The goal
seems to have become the *appearance* of normalization without the *expectation* of competence. Many parents and students seem to want more
services as they learn what is available. Some have lost sight of limiting
accommodations and challenging students to achieve more independence.
At the same time, many special education advocates want all services to be
available in mainstream settings, with little or no acknowledgement that
the services are atypical. Although teachers, administrators, and guidance
counselors often are able and willing to make accommodations, these are
not always in students' best long-term interests. They give students with
disabilities what anthropologist Robert Edgerton called a cloak—pretense,
a cover, which actually fools no one—rather than actual competence
(Edgerton, 1967, 1993; Kauffman, 2003a). We discuss how changes in attitudes toward disability and special education, placement, and modifications can perpetuate disability. We also explore the problems of ignoring or
perpetuating disability rather than helping students lead fuller, more independent lives. Two case examples illustrate how we believe good intentions
can go awry—how attempts to accommodate students with disabilities can
undermine achievement.

 ### *"But he needs resource ..."*

Thomas, a high school sophomore identified as emotionally disturbed
was assigned to a resource class designed to help students who have organization problems or need extra help with academic skills. One of the
requirements in the class is that students keep a daily planner in which
they enter all assignments, share their planner with the resource teacher
at the beginning of class, and discuss what academic subjects will be
worked on during that period. When Thomas consistently refused to
keep a planner or do any work in resource (he slept!), a meeting was set
up with the assistant principal, the guidance counselor, Thomas, and the
resource teacher. As the meeting was about to begin, the principal announced that he would not stay because Thomas felt intimidated by so
many adults. After listening to Thomas's complaints, the guidance counselor decided that he would not have to keep or show a planner, that the
resource teacher should not talk to him unless Thomas addressed her
first, and that Thomas would not be required to do any work in the class!
When the resource teacher suggested that, under those circumstances,
Thomas should be put in a study hall, because telling the parents that he

was in a resource class would be a misrepresentation, the counselor said, "But, he *needs* the resource class."

 "He's too bright ..."

Bob, a high school freshman with Asperger's syndrome, was scheduled into three honors classes and two advanced placement (AP) classes. His IEP included a two-page list of accommodations. In spite of his having achieved As and Bs, with a single C in math, his mother did not feel that his teachers were accommodating him appropriately. She e-mailed his teachers and case manager in the evening almost daily to request more information or more help for him, and she angrily called his guidance counselor if she didn't receive a reply by the end of the first hour of the school day. A meeting was scheduled with the IEP team, including five of his seven teachers, the county special education supervisor, the guidance counselor, the case manager, the principal, and the county autism specialist. When the accommodations were reviewed, Bob's mother agreed that all of them were being made. However, she explained that Bob had been removed from all outside social activities because he spent all night, every night, working on homework. The *accommodation* she demanded was that Bob have *no* homework assignments. The autism specialist agreed that this was a reasonable accommodation for a child with Asperger's syndrome. The teachers of the honors classes explained that the difference between homework in their classes, which was elaboration and extension of concepts, was even more essential to the honors class than to the advanced placement classes. In AP classes, homework consisted primarily of practice of concepts learned in class. The honors teachers explained that they had carefully broken their long assignments into segments, each having a separate due date before the final project. They gave illustrations of their expectations. The director of special education explained the legal definition of accommodations (the mother said she'd never before heard that accommodations could not change the nature of the curriculum). The director also suggested that perhaps instead of sacrificing his social life, it would be more appropriate for Bob to take standard classes. What Bob's mother was asking, he concluded, was not legal. She became very angry. She agreed to give the team a "little more time" to serve Bob appropriately, but she would "be back with her claws and broomstick" if anyone ever suggested he be moved from honors classes without being given the no-homework accommodation. "He's too bright to take anything less than honors classes, and if you people would provide this simple accommodation, he would do just fine," she concluded. She got her way.

ATTITUDES TOWARD DISABILITY AND SPECIAL EDUCATION

Not many decades ago, disability was considered a misfortune, not something to be ashamed of but a generally undesirable, unwelcome condition to be overcome to the greatest extent possible. Ability was considered more desirable than disability, and things that helped people with disabilities (devices or services) do what those without disabilities can do were considered generally valuable, helpful, desirable, and worth the effort, cost, and possible stigma associated with needing them.

The disability rights movement did have certain desirable outcomes. It helped overcome some of the discrimination against people with disabilities. Overcoming such biases and unfairness in everyday life is a great accomplishment, but the movement also has had some unintended negative consequences. One of these is the outright denial of disability in some cases, illustrated by the contention that disability exists only in attitudes or as a function of social power to coerce (see, e.g., Danforth & Rhodes, 1997; Smith, 1999).

The argument that disability is only a "social construction" is particularly vicious in its effects on social justice. Even if we assume that disabilities are socially constructed, what should that mean? Should we assume that socially constructed phenomena are not "real," not important, or should be discredited? If so, then consider that dignity, civil rights, childhood, poverty, social justice, and nearly every other phenomenon that we hold dear and want to work for are social constructions. Many social constructions are not merely near and dear to us but real and useful in benevolent societies. The question is whether the idea of disability is useful in helping people attain dignity or whether it is more useful to assume that disabilities are not real (i.e., that, like social justice, civil rights, and other social constructions, they are fabrications that can be ignored when convenient). The denial of disability is sometimes expressed as an aversion to labels, so that we are cautioned not to communicate openly and clearly about disabilities but to rely on euphemisms. But this is counterproductive. When we are able only to whisper or mime the undesirable difference called disability, then we inadvertently increase its stigma and thwart prevention (Kauffman, 2002).

The specious argument that "normal" does not exist because abilities of every kind are varied and the point at which normal becomes abnormal is arbitrary leads to the conclusion that no one actually has a disability or, alternatively, that everyone has a disability. Then, some argue, either no one or everyone is due an accommodation so that either everyone or no one is identified as disabled. This unwillingness to draw a line defining something (e.g., disability, poverty, childhood) is based either on ignorance regarding the nature of continuous distributions or on rejection of the unavoidably arbitrary decisions necessary to provide special services to those who need them and, thereby, to foster social justice (Kauffman, 2002).

Another unintended negative consequence of the disability rights movement is that disability has for some people become either something that does not matter one way or the other or, even, something to love, take pride in, flaunt, claim as a privilege, adopt as a positive aspect of one's identity, or cherish as something wanted or a badge of honor. When disability makes no difference to us one way or the other, then we are not going to try to attenuate it, much less prevent it. At best, we will try to accommodate it. When we view disability as a desirable difference, then we are very likely to try to make it more pronounced, not ameliorate it.

Several decades ago, special education was seen as a good thing, a helpful way of responding to disability, not something everyone needed or should have but a useful and necessary response to the atypical needs of students with disabilities. This is why the Education for All Handicapped Children Act (now the Individuals with Disabilities Education Act) was written. Special education has been transformed in perception from something helpful to something awful (Kauffman, 2003b). The image of special education has become very negative in the minds of many.

The full inclusion movement did have some desirable outcomes. It helped overcome some of the unnecessary removal of students with disabilities from general education. However, the movement also has had some unintended negative consequences. One of these is that special education has come to be viewed in very negative terms, to be seen as a second-class and discriminatory system that does more harm than good. Rather than being seen as helping, a way of creating opportunity, it is now often portrayed as a means of shunting students into dead-end programs and killing opportunity (see, e.g., Bolick, 2001; Cottle, 2001).

Another unintended negative consequence of full inclusion is that general education is now seen by many as the place—the *only* place—where fair and equitable treatment is possible and opportunity to learn is extended to all equally (see, e.g., Lipsky & Gartner, 1996; Stainback & Stainback, 1991). The argument has been that special education is good only as long as it is invisible (or almost so), an indistinguishable part of a general education system that accommodates everyone, regardless of their hyper-abilities or disabilities. Usually, this is described as a "unified" (as opposed to "separate") system of education (see, e.g., Gartner & Lipsky, 1989; for an alternative view, see Kauffman & Hallahan, 1993). Special education is thus something to be avoided altogether or attenuated to the greatest extent possible, regardless of inability to perform. When special education is seen as discriminatory, unfair, an opportunity-killing system or, as one writer put it "the gold-plated garbage can of American schooling" (Fisher, 2001), then it is understandable that people will loathe it. But this way of looking at special education as undesirable is like seeing the recognition and treatment of cancer as the cause of difficulty.

The reversal in attitudes toward disability and special education—disability from undesirable to inconsequential, special education from desirable to awful—has clouded the picture of what special education is and should do for students with disabilities. Little wonder that special education stands accused of failure, calls for its demise are vociferous, and contemporary practices are often more disabling than enabling. An unfortunate outcome of changing attitudes toward disability and special education is that the benefit of special education is now sometimes seen as freedom from expectations of performance, the feeling that if a student has to endure the stigma of special education then the compensation should include escape from work.

PLACEMENT

Placing all students, regardless of their abilities, in regular classes has exacerbated the tendency to see disability as something existing only in people's minds. It fosters the view that students are fitting in when they are not able to perform anywhere near the normal level. It perpetuates disabilities; it does not compensate for them.

Administrators and guidance counselors sometimes place students in programs for which they do not qualify, even as graduation requirements are increasing and tests are mandated. Often, these students' *testing* is modified although their *curriculum* is not. These students may then feel they have beaten or gamed the system. They are taught that the system is unfair and that beating it is the only way to win. Hard work and individual responsibility for one's education are often overlooked, or at least discounted.

Students who consistently fail in a curriculum must be given the opportunity to deal with the natural consequences as a means of learning individual responsibility. For example, social promotion in elementary and middle school until students reach high school teaches them that they really don't have to be able to do the work to pass. Suddenly, usually in high school, no one passes them on and no one gives them undeserved credit. Many of these students do not graduate in four years. Some never recover, while others find themselves forced to deal with a very distasteful situation. But students who have been conditioned to rely on social promotion do not believe the cycle will end until it does so—usually very abruptly.

No one wants to see a student fail, but to alter any standard without good reason is to set that same student up for failure later in life. Passing a student with disabilities along in regular classes, pretending that he or she is performing at the level of most age peers or that it does not really matter (arguing that the student has a legal "right" to be in the class) is another certain prescription for later disappointment and failure. Often this failure comes in college or on the job.

Some people with disabilities need assistance. Others do not. Consider Deborah Groeber, who struggled through degenerative deafness and blindness. The Office of Affirmative Action at the University of Pennsylvania offered to intercede at Wharton, but she knew that she had more influence if she spoke for herself. Today she is a lawyer with three Ivy League degrees (Tener, 1995). Not every student with disabilities can do or should be expected to do what Ms. Groeber did. Our concern is that too many students with disabilities are encouraged only by pretense when they could do much more with appropriate special education.

TYPES OF ACCOMMODATIONS

Two popular IEP modifications are the use of calculators and extended time on tests and assignments. Calculators can be a great asset, but they should be used when calculating complex problems or application/word problems. Indiscriminate use of a calculator renders many math tests invalid, as they become a contest to see if buttons can be pushed successfully and in the correct order rather than an evaluation of ability to do arithmetic or test mathematical knowledge.

Extended time on assignments and tests can also be a useful modification, but it can easily be misused or abused. Extended time on tests should mean *continuous* time so that a test is not studied first, taken later. Sometimes a test must be broken into smaller parts that can be completed independently. However, this could put students with disabilities at a disadvantage, as one part of a test might help with remembering another part. Extensions of assignments need to be evaluated, not just given because they are written in the IEP. If a student is clearly working hard, then extensions may be appropriate. If a student has not even been attempting assignments, then more time might be an avoidance tactic. Sometimes extended time means that assignments pile up and the student gets further and further behind. The result is overwhelming stress and inability to comprehend discussions because the concepts must be acquired in sequence (e.g., in math, science, history, and foreign language).

Reading tests and quizzes aloud to students can be beneficial for many, but great caution is demanded. Some students and teachers want to do more than simply read a test. Reading a test aloud means simply reading the printed words on the page *without* inflections that reveal correct answers and without explaining vocabulary. Changing a test to open notes or open book without the knowledge and consent of the classroom teacher breaches good-faith test proctoring. It also teaches dependence rather than independence and accomplishment. Similarly, scribing for a student can be beneficial for those who truly need it, but the teacher must be careful not to add details and to write only what the student dictates, including run-on sentences and fragments. After scribing, if the assignment is not a test, the teacher should edit and correct the paper with the student the same as any other written work. This must be done *after* the scribing.

HOW MISGUIDED ACCOMMODATIONS CAN BE DISABLING

"Saving" a child from his or her own negative behavior reinforces that behavior and makes it a self-fulfilling prophecy. Well-intentioned guidance counselors often feel more responsibility for their students' success or failure than the students feel themselves. Sometimes students are not held accountable for their effort or work. They seem not to understand that true independence comes from *what* you know, not *whom* you know. Students who are consistently enabled and never challenged are never given the opportunity to become independent. Polar explorer and dyslexic, Ann Bancroft, claims that although school was a torment, it was disability that forged her iron will (Cheakalos et al., 2001). Stephen Cannell's fear for other dyslexics is that they will quit trying rather than struggling and learning to compensate for their disability (Cheakalos et al., 2001).

Most parents want to help their children. However, some parents confuse making life *easier* with making life *better* for their children. Too often parents feel that protecting their child from the rigors of academic demands is in his or her best interest. They may protect their child by insisting on curriculum modifications and accommodations in assignments, time, and testing. Children learn by doing, and not allowing them to do something because they might fail is to deny them the opportunity to succeed. These students eventually believe they are not capable of what typical students can do, even if they are. Sometimes it is difficult for teachers to discern what the student actually can do and what the parent has done until an in-class assignment is given or a test is taken. At that point it is too late for the teacher to do much remediation. The teacher may erroneously conclude that the student is simply a poor test taker. In realty, the student may have been "protected" from learning, which will eventually catch up with him or her. Unfortunately, students may not face reality until they take a college entrance exam, go away to college, or apply for a job. Students who "get through" high school in programs of this type often go on to flunk out of college. Unfortunately, the parents of these students are often upset at the college for the student's failure and blame the postsecondary institution for not doing enough to help their child. They should be upset at the secondary institution for not preparing their child adequately for the task to come and at their own demands for overprotection.

THE BENEFITS OF DEMANDS

Many successful adults with disabilities respond with common themes when asked about their ability to succeed in the face of a disability. Tom Gray, a Rhodes Scholar at Oxford who has a severe learning disability, claims that having to deal with the hardest experiences have given him the greatest strength (Cheakalos, 2001). Stephen J. Cannell believes that if he had known there was a reason beyond his control to explain his low achievement, he might not have worked so hard. Today, he knows he has a learning disability, but he is also an Emmy Award winning television writer and producer (Cannell, 2000). Paul Orlalea, the dyslexic founder of Kinkos, believes God gave him an advantage in his disability, and that others should work with their strengths. Charles Schwab, the learning disabled founder of Charles Schwab, Inc., cites his ability to think differently and make creative leaps that more sequential thinkers don't make as a chief reason for his success. Fannie Flagg, the learning disabled best selling author, concurs by insisting learning disabilities become a blessing *only if you can overcome them* (Cheakalos et al., 2001). Not every student with a disability can be a star performer, but all should be expected to achieve all they can.

Two decades ago, special educators thought it was their job to assess a student's achievement, understand what the student wants to do and what an average peer can do, and then develop plans to bridge the gap, if possible. Most special educators wanted to see that each student had the tools and knowledge to succeed as independently as possible. Helping students enter the typical world was the mark of success for special educators. The full inclusion movement now insists that *every* student will benefit from placement in the mainstream. However, some of the modifications and accommodations now being demanded are so radical that we are doing an injustice to the entire education system (Dupre, 1998). Special education must not be associated in any way with "dumbing down" the curriculum for students presumed to be at a given grade level, disabled or not.

Counselors or administrators who want to enable students must focus the discussion on realistic goals and plans for that student. An objective, in-depth discussion and evaluation must be completed to determine how far along the continuum of successfully completing these goals the student has progressed. If the student is making adequate progress independently, or with minimal help, special education services might not be necessary. If assistance is required to make adequate progress on realistic goals, then special education may be needed. Every modification and accommodation should be held to the same standard—"Will this help the student attain these goals?" *not* "Will this make life easier for the student?" Knowing where the student is aiming can help a team guide a student toward success.

The student must be part of this planning. A student who claims to want to be a brain surgeon, but who refuses to take science courses, needs a reality check. If a student is unwilling to attempt to reach intermediate goals or does not meet them, then special education cannot "save" him. At that point the team must help the student revisit his or her goals. Goals should be explained in terms of the amount of work required to complete them, not whether or not the teacher or parent feels they are attainable. Presented this way, the student can often make an informed decision regarding the attainability versus the desirability of the goal. Troy Brown, a university dean and politician who has both a doctorate and a learning disability, studied at home with his mother. He estimates that it took him over twice as long as the average person to complete assignments. Every night he would go to bed with stacks of books and read until he fell asleep, because he had a dream of attending college (Cheakalos et al., 2001).

General educators and special educators need to encourage all students to be responsible and independent, to set realistic expectations for themselves. Then teachers must assist students in meeting these expectations in a more and more independent manner. Special educators do not serve students well when they enable students with disabilities to become increasingly dependent on their parents, counselors, administrators, or teachers, or even when they fail to increase students' independence and competence.

CONCLUSION: WHERE WE STAND

We want to make it clear that we think disabilities are real and that they make doing certain things either impossible or very difficult for the people who have them. We cannot expect people with disabilities to be "just like everyone else" in what they can do. Other writers have said:

> The human service practices that cause providers to believe that clients (students) have inadequacies, shortcomings, failures, or faults that must be corrected or controlled by specially trained professionals must be replaced by conceptions that people with disabilities are capable of setting their own goals and achieving or not. Watered-down curricula, alterna-

tive grading practices, special competency standards, and other "treat them differently" practices used with "special" students must be replaced with school experiences exactly like those used with "regular" students. (Ysseldyke, Algozzine, & Thurlow, 2000, p. 67)

We disagree. In our view, students with disabilities *do* have specific shortcomings and *do* need the services of specially trained professionals to achieve their potential. They *do* sometimes need altered curricula or adaptations to make their learning possible. If students with disabilities were just like "regular" students, then there would be no need whatever for special education. The school experiences of students with disabilities obviously will not be—obviously *cannot* be—just like those of students without disabilities. We sell students with disabilities short when we pretend that they are not different from typical students, and therefore pretend also that they must *not* be expected to put forth *extra* effort to learn to do something or learn to do something in a different way. We sell them short when we pretend that they have competencies they do not have or pretend that the competencies we expect of most students are unimportant for them.

No legitimate purpose is served by (a) pretending that students with disabilities are not different from the norm, (b) expecting or demanding that students with disabilities do what they simply cannot, (c) allowing students with disabilities to escape the demands of learning all that they can, or (d) pushing students into predictable failure. Like general education, special education must push students to become all they can be. Special education must not countenance the pretense of learning or the avoidance of reasonable demands.

REFERENCES

Bolick, C. (2001, September 5). A bad IDEA is disabling public schools. *Education Week,* pp. 56, 63.

Cannell, S. (2000, August). How to spell success. *Reader's Digest,* pp. 63–66.

Cheakalos, C., Frankel, B., Plummer, W., Schindette, S., Baughn, A. J., Grisly, L., et al. (2001, October 30). Heavy mettle: They may have trouble reading and spelling, but those with the grit to overcome learning disabilities like dyslexia emerge fortified for life. *People,* pp. 18, 58.

Cottle, M. (2001, June 18). Jeffords kills special ed. reform school. *The New Republic,* pp. 14–15.

Danforth, S., & Rhodes, W. C. (1997). Deconstructing disability: A philosophy for education. *Remedial and Special Education, 18*(6), 357–366.

Deno, E. (1970). Special education as developmental capital. *Exceptional Children, 37,* 229–237.

Dupre, A. P. (1998, Winter). Disability, deference, and the integrity of the academic enterprise. *Georgia Law Review,* pp. 393–473.

Edgerton, R. B. (1967). *The cloak of competence: Stigma in the lives of the mentally retarded.* Berkeley: University of California Press.

Edgerton, R. B. (1993). *The cloak of competence: Stigma in the lives of the mentally retarded* (rev. ed.). Berkeley: University of California Press.

Education for All Handicapped Children Act of 1975, 20 U.S.C. § 1400 *et seq.*

Fisher, M. (2001, December 13). Students still taking the fall for D.C. schools. *The Washington Post,* p. B1.

Fuchs, D., Fuchs, L. S., Fernstrom, P., & Hohn, M. (1991). Toward a responsible reintegration of behaviorally disordered students. *Behavioral Disorders, 16,* 133–147.

Gartner, A., & Lipsky, D. K. (1989). *The yoke of special education: How to break it.* Rochester, NY: National Center on Education and the Economy.

Huefner, D. S. (1994). The mainstreaming cases: Tensions and trends for school administrators. *Educational Administration Quarterly, 30*(1), 27–55.

Individuals with Disabilities Education Act of 1990, 20 U.S.C. § 1400 *et seq.*

Kauffman, J. M. (2002). *Education deform: Bright people sometimes say stupid things about education.* Lanham, MD: Scarecrow Education.

Kauffman, J. M. (2003a). Appearances, stigma, and prevention. *Remedial and Special Education, 24,* 195–198.

Kauffman, J. M. (2003b). Reflections on the field. *Education and Treatment of Children, 26*(4), 325–329.

Kauffman, J. M., & Hallahan, D. P. (1993). Toward a comprehensive delivery system for special education. In J. I. Goodlad & T. C. Lovitt (Eds.), *Integrating general and special education* (pp. 73–102). Columbus, OH: Merrill.

Kauffman, J. M., & Hallahan, D. P. (2005). *Special education: What it is and why we need it.* Boston: Allyn & Bacon.

Lipsky, D. K., & Gartner, A. (1996). Equity requires inclusion: The future for all students with disabilities. In C. Christensen & F. Rizvi (Eds.), *Disability and the dilemmas of education and justice* (pp. 144–155). Philadelphia: Open University Press.

Smith, P. (1999). Drawing new maps: A radical cartography of developmental disabilities. *Review of Educational Research, 69*(2), 117–144.

Stainback, W., & Stainback, S. (1991). A rationale for integration and restructuring: A synopsis. In J. W. Lloyd, N. N. Singh, & A. C. Repp (Eds.), *The regular education initiative: Alternative perspectives on concepts, issues, and models* (pp. 225–239). Sycamore, IL: Sycamore.

Tener, E. (1995, December). Blind, deaf and very successful. *McCall's,* pp. 42–46.

Ysseldyke, J. E., Algozzine, B., & Thurlow, M. L. (2000). *Critical issues in special education* (3rd ed.). Boston: Houghton Mifflin.

CHAPTER 8

Dedicated, Not Segregated: Suggested Changes in Thinking About Instructional Environments and in the Language of Special Education

Michael F. Gliona, Alexandra K. Gonzales, and Eric S. Jacobson

---

Two common practices in special education are both inappropriate and damaging to children and the field: (a) misusing the concept of the least restrictive environment by referring to alternative placements as representing different levels of restriction and (b) denigrating alternative placements by calling them "segregated." A new model of alternative placements is introduced, the Direct Access Model. The term *dedicated* should replace *segregated.*

Two of the most damaging practices in special education today are the misuse of the phrase least restrictive environment (LRE) and the persistent references to alternative placements as segregated. Under the Individuals with Disabilities Education Act (IDEA), all disabled students are entitled to a free, appropriate public education (FAPE) in the LRE. To ensure FAPE for students with a wide range of disabilities and varying levels of severity, IDEA requires that several types of educational settings or environments be made available and chosen by the team writing the individualized education program (IEP). This range of choices or continuum of alternative placements (CAP) includes at least the following:

- Full-time placement in regular classes with consultation from special educators or other specialists
- Special classes with part-time placement in regular classes
- Resource rooms or classes
- Special classes in regular schools
- Special day schools
- Homebound schooling
- Hospital or residential schools

From the year of enactment of IDEA (in 1975, then known as the Education for All Handicapped Children Act, EAHCA, or Public Law 94-142), and perhaps even earlier in the writings of Reynolds (1962) and Deno (1970), the CAP has been misunderstood by many to be a system of place-ment levels (see Bateman & Linden, 1998, and Huefner, 2000, for discussion of the law by special educators who are lawyers). The widely known Cascade Model or cascade of placement options depicted by Reynolds (1962) and Deno (1970) graphically represents the notion that the various placement options have inherent levels of restrictiveness, as shown in Figure 8.1. This model has led to much controversy and to an emphasis on place itself rather

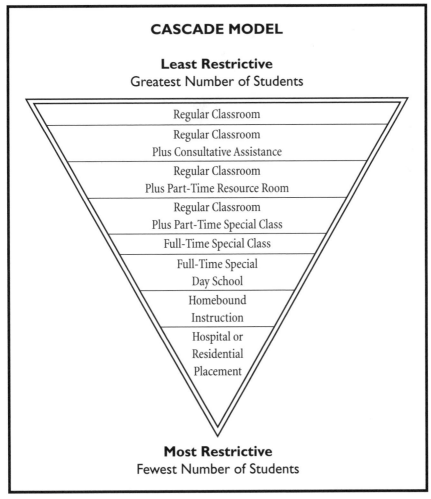

CASCADE MODEL

Least Restrictive
Greatest Number of Students

Regular Classroom

Regular Classroom
Plus Consultative Assistance

Regular Classroom
Plus Part-Time Resource Room

Regular Classroom
Plus Part-Time Special Class

Full-Time Special Class

Full-Time Special
Day School

Homebound
Instruction

Hospital or
Residential
Placement

Most Restrictive
Fewest Number of Students

FIGURE 8.1. Cascade Model, or cascade of placement options.

than instruction (see Crockett & Kauffman, 1999; Hallahan & Kauffman, 2003; Kauffman, 2002).

In the Cascade Model, the more dedicated or specialized the setting the more restrictive it is assumed to be, with placements in our list above (or in the model depicted by Deno and Reynolds) starting with the least restrictive at the top and becoming more restrictive as one proceeds down to the bottom of the list. Thus, special classes or special schools are at much lower levels compared to placement in the regular classroom, and such dedicated settings are seen as very restrictive.

It is not clear how students would benefit from the Cascade Model. How and where does the individual student fit in? How does the student move from one level to the next? And how does the student attain the ideal LRE way up at the top? The Cascade Model makes it appear that students placed at the "lower" levels are hopelessly separated from the LRE. This conception of the CAP is so pervasive in special education and now in the public mind that it is frequently assumed to be part of the IDEA. It is not. Even though the IDEA requires that disabled students be educated with nondisabled students to the maximum extent *appropriate*, it does not suggest that the regular classroom is the one and only LRE or that a residential school is the most restrictive placement for any student. Nowhere in the law does IDEA say that placement choices have inherent levels of restrictiveness. The LRE is not exclusively the general education classroom, nor is it necessarily inclusion in general education. The CAP does not represent settings that range from the least restrictive to the most restrictive. It does, in fact, represent settings that range from general to more specialized or dedicated, but the restrictiveness of each is determined by the needs of the student, not by the existence of the placement option. The LRE to which every child is entitled by IDEA is the setting that best supports implementation of the IEP and ensures the greatest amount of success. This is why placement is determined after the child's goals are set. The placement environment must, above all, be appropriate for the individual student. That is why there is a CAP in the first place. *Every option on the continuum of alternative placements is some child's least restrictive environment* (Gonzales, 2003, and previous unpublished statements).

If a disabled student must be personally escorted everywhere on a general education campus but can get around with relative independence on a more protective special education campus, then probably the special campus is the LRE for that student. If a student's IEP contains toilet training and self-feeding goals, then a classroom with kitchen and bathroom facilities will probably be the LRE for that student. If a student can perform at grade level with certain accommodations, then a general education classroom with consultation for the regular classroom teacher is probably the LRE for that student.

A student's LRE can change over time. A blind child might ordinarily be expected to move from a more dedicated environment early in his or her school career to a more general educational setting or campus as he or she learns Braille. However, an autistic child might (though not necessarily) increasingly need a more dedicated setting or campus as he or she gets older. A developmentally disabled child might do well on a general education campus in the elementary grades but need a more dedicated setting later in life as his or her educational needs diverge from those of the general education students. This does not mean that the student is regressing or that mainstreaming has been a failure. It means merely that the student's needs have changed vis-à-vis those of typical children. In each of these cases, however, there are other factors besides the disability itself to consider as well, so there can be no pre-established rules about which placement is best or the LRE. The IEP team must decide each student's LRE individually.

Some students will need access to several different placements during the course of their schooling. For example, one mother told us about the educational struggles of her son, who has a life-threatening combination of problems, including weak immune system, heart defects, severe epilepsy, and ADHD. Due to multiple surgeries, broken bones, and memory-shattering seizures, this student needed, at different times, virtually every option in placement from regular classes to hospital care. Frequently, for the mother, obtaining the right placement for her son required fighting school district officials over the meaning of LRE and educating them about her child's rights. This student was able to graduate from high school and went on to complete a course in hotel management. This salutary outcome would never have been possible without a wide range of services and placement options.

Portraying the general education classroom as the single best setting has contributed to some very negative thinking about special education and threatens the ability of parents, such as the mother we mentioned, to make necessary choices for their children's education. Calling the regular classroom the LRE for every child leads one to believe that any other placement is, by definition, undesirable and should always be avoided, or at least be provided only with regret and after great and sustained resistance to the placement. The full inclusion movement (FIM) depicts regular classroom placement as desirable for all children and portrays alternative placements, and frequently, special education itself, in the worst possible light. Advocates of the FIM want to do away with placement choices because they view them as inherently restrictive and as a form of segregation. In the name of "integration," they want to place all students with disabilities in general education classrooms, regardless of their individual needs, regardless of the harm it could cause, regardless of parents' wishes, and regardless of the data about student outcomes other than placement (Kauffman, Lloyd, Baker, & Riedel, 1995; Mock & Kauffman, 2005).

The FIM is not only a movement in school districts but has been harbored, fostered, or even mandated in some university teacher education programs. According to first-hand reports given to us by students in special education teaching programs, at certain universities those who choose to teach in special schools may find their views suppressed or censored. Students may not be allowed to do their student teaching at special schools. This happened to one of the authors, Michael Gliona, at a state university in southern California. If students in certain classes dare to submit papers critical of the FIM, they may receive failing or lower grades or have their work marked "incorrect" simply because they do not tout the benefits of the FIM. Some students find their views openly denigrated by instructors in front of their classroom peers and bypass certain professors to avoid such unpleasantness.

If college students never are exposed to the small, but significant population of severely disabled children who attend special schools, indeed, if students are actively discouraged from teaching at these schools, that means an entire group of children, who need highly trained specialist teachers, is being abandoned by these universities. These university programs are where our future teachers and administrators get their foundation of knowledge. The CAP is surely doomed when teachers and administrators operate on the basis of faulty assumptions about the LRE. Too many university professors teach fallacies about the law and the nature of LRE. Too many use demeaning language for dedicated special classes and schools and express demeaning attitudes toward anything other than the FIM.

Using the word *segregated* in reference to alternative placements has gone largely unchallenged in special education and has become a pervasive practice. This damning term is used most perniciously in reference to special schools, which are being threatened with extinction, even though they are mandated by the IDEA regulations as part of the CAP. Just how destructive this term can be is illustrated by what happened in the *Chanda Smith et al. v. Los Angeles Unified School District* (LAUSD) class action law suit. What began as a suit to correct the LAUSD's deficiencies in serving its disabled students quickly took on a full inclusion agenda to "integrate" every disabled student in the district.

Part of the FIM agenda was a plan to eliminate the "segregated" special education schools by gradually converting them to general education campuses. This plan, called "LRE Plan 12," was one of the proposed remedies in the suit. It was put forward in spite of the desperate pleas of the parents of students in these special schools not to take their schools away. When the LAUSD lost a motion to overturn the Chanda Smith Consent Decree, Plan 12 became a federal court order by default. In order to save their schools, the parents had to band together on their own, to oppose the very attorneys who were supposed to be representing their children in the class action suit. Together with some courageous educators within the LAUSD, they formed a coalition, which became Save Our Special Schools (SOSS), Inc. Throughout this battle between parents of children at the special schools and those opposed to the special schools, the local press depicted the case as a *segregation* issue. The Chanda Smith attorneys finally relented on this issue, but even after all parties agreed that the special schools would remain intact the headline in the *Los Angeles Times* read, "L.A. Unified to Keep 16 Schools Segregated for Special Education" (Hayasaki & Moore, 2002).

Many students with disabilities can succeed in general education classrooms with the right support, and by law they are fully entitled to do so. However, students who need alternative placements also have rights, and the fact remains that for many of the most vulnerable children and their families the availability of alternative settings, such as special schools, in particular, is a blessing and a necessity. There are good reasons why the parents in Los Angeles fought so hard to keep their special schools open. Special schools, in particular, provide students with severe disabilities a safe environment tailored to their individual needs; an environment in which they can learn from teachers who understand their disabilities and who teach specifically because they *want* to serve the disabled. Special schools provide classrooms with low teacher/student ratios. They provide services by highly trained specialists, such as speech–language therapists, hearing specialists, physical therapists, and occupational therapists in addition to special education teachers. Yes, these services are provided on general education campuses with varying degrees of effectiveness, acceptance and support, but at the special schools they are integral to the mission to which everyone is dedicated.

Special schools are not segregated, and they are not needlessly restrictive for the students they serve. It is wise to remember that every environment is restrictive of some things, that a totally nonrestrictive environment does not exist, and that therapeutic environments are designed for particular purposes (Kauffman, 1995; Kauffman & Hallahan, 1997). Enrollment in special schools is not based on race, creed, nationality, sex, or any other factor than the student's needs. On the contrary, these schools serve students of many cultures. They provide students with real opportunities to form friendships, to participate in school activities, and to participate in community life. Students at special schools do not need "Circle of Friends" committees or "person-centered" assessment procedures to oversee their social life (see Miller, Cooke, Test, & White, 2003; Vandercook, York, & Forest, 1989; Westling & Fox, 2000). They interact freely with one another and choose their own friends. They do not just attend assemblies; many are on the stage performing. In school sports, many are on the teams, working together and competing fiercely with other special schools. Others are cheer leaders, performing their routines and loving it. They live full and satisfying lives. They are out in the neighborhood, learning how to use public transportation, learning how to shop, learning how to earn money at a job. For the students who need them, *special education schools go way beyond mere inclusion in general education as prescribed by proponents of the FIM.* Special schools provide real opportunities for first-hand participation in life.

SOSS proposes a new way of looking at educational choices for students with disabilities, showing clearly what the CAP means and dispensing with the derogatory term *segregated.* To correct the Cascade Model, with its levels of restrictiveness, SOSS offers a replacement called the Direct Access Model (DAM) shown in Figure 8.2. As the DAM correctly shows, the student does not have to work his or her way up through layers of "lower" settings to achieve the LRE, nor is any setting relegated to a lower status. There is direct access to any placement, or combination of placements, that is judged by the IEP team to be the most appropriate and least restrictive. An additional advantage of this model is that it can be used to illustrate an individual student's LRE, as shown in Figure 8.3. Perhaps most important of all, the DAM makes intuitive sense to parents and educators alike, as they immediately can see the CAP as an array of available options. This model is based on SOSS President Alexandra Gonzales's description of the CAP, when speaking to parent groups and at school staff development meetings, as an arc. It was first printed in an SOSS brochure (Gonzales, 2003), and it has been received very enthusiastically. The DAM shows clearly what is intended by the IDEA—a constantly available, full range of choices, meaning that students have the right to *continuous direct access* to their individually determined LRE.

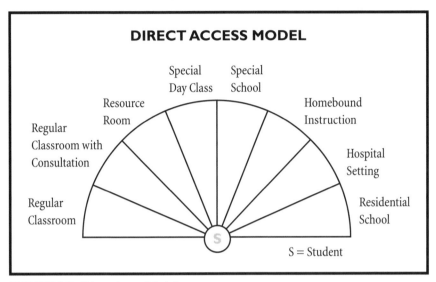

FIGURE 8.2. Direct Access Model.

As we stated earlier, use of the term segregated in describing alternative placements is entirely inappropriate and causes real harm to students and families. This terminology serves no purpose but to denigrate special education. It is a terrible and unwarranted insult to brand those who serve disabled students in alternative settings as segregationists. The history of segregation in this country is that of a comprehensive system of exploitation, repression, and mistreatment created to insure the complete dominance of one color of person over another. The practices associated with segregation have nothing whatsoever to do with the alternative placements that are designed to benefit students who need specific kinds of help (Kauffman & Lloyd, 1995). The IDEA ensures that students with disabilities are not forced into particular settings as was true with racial segregation. In special education that is lawful, there are no automatic placements of students by type of disability, much less by color, ethnic origin, or gender. Placement is decided at an IEP team meeting, which includes parents as co-equal participants. Under the IDEA, nothing can be decided upon without parental input and permission. SOSS proposes replacing the term segregated with the term dedicated. Dedicated means (a) wholeheartedly devoted to or committed to a goal, cause, or job and (b) designed and designated to carry out only one task; set aside for a single purpose. Here is a word (*dedicated*)

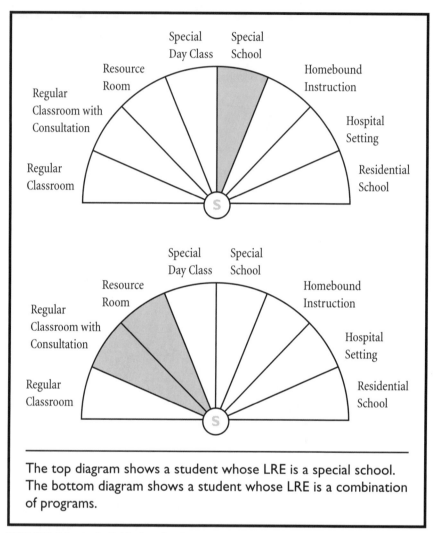

The top diagram shows a student whose LRE is a special school. The bottom diagram shows a student whose LRE is a combination of programs.

FIGURE 8.3. An individual student's Least Restrictive Environment (LRE) as shown using the Direct Access Model.

that is entirely consistent with the mission of special education. At its best, special education is a beneficial system practiced in a variety of alternative settings, a system built, maintained, and staffed by idealistic, caring professionals. Let us stop putting special education down. Of course, it can be greatly improved, like any other institution. However, special education is an eminently humanitarian enterprise, filled with dedicated professionals, paraprofessionals and specialists, each serving students in dedicated classrooms and dedicated schools.

REFERENCES

Bateman, B. D., & Linden, M. A. (1998). *Better IEPs: How to develop legally correct and educationally useful programs* (3rd ed.). Longmont, CO: Sopris West.

Chanda Smith v. L.A.U.S.D. et al., District Court case no. CV93-7044 RSWL.

Crockett, J. B., & Kauffman, J. M. (1999). *The least restrictive environment: Its origins and interpretations in special education.* Mahwah, NJ: Erlbaum.

Deno, E. (1970). Special education as developmental capital. *Exceptional Children, 37,* 229–237.

Education for All Handicapped Children Act of 1975, 20 U.S.C. § 1400 *et seq.*

Gonzales, A. (2003, Summer). *Bringing you the truth about the LRE (least restrictive environment) and CAP (continuum of alternative placements).* [Save Our Special Schools Brochure]. Los Angeles: SOSS.

Hallahan, D. P., & Kauffman, J. M. (2003). *Exceptional learners: Introduction to special education* (9th ed.). Boston: Allyn & Bacon.

Hayasaki, E., & Moore, S. (2002, October 4). L.A. Unified to keep 16 schools segregated for special education. *Los Angeles Times,* pp. B1, B10.

Huefner, D. S. (2000). *Getting comfortable with special education law: A framework for working with children with disabilities.* Norwood, MA: Christopher-Gordon. (Additional information and updates on federal special education law can be found at http://www.ed.utah.edu/~huefner/sped-law/spdlawbk.htm)

Individuals with Disabilities Education Act of 1990, 20 U.S.C. § 1400 *et seq.*

Kauffman, J. M. (1995). Why we must celebrate a diversity of restrictive environments. *Learning Disabilities Research and Practice, 10,* 225–232.

Kauffman, J. M. (2002). *Education deform: Bright people sometimes say stupid things about education.* Lanham, MD: Scarecrow Education.

Kauffman, J. M., & Hallahan, D. P. (1997). A diversity of restrictive environments: Placement as a problem of social ecology. In J. W. Lloyd, E. J. Kameenui, & D. Chard (Eds.), *Issues in educating students with disabilities* (pp. 325–342). Hillsdale, NJ: Erlbaum.

Kauffman, J. M., & Lloyd, J. W. (1995). A sense of place: The importance of placement issues in contemporary special education. In J. M. Kauffman, J. W., Lloyd, D. P. Hallahan, & T. A. Astuto (Eds.), *Issues in educational placement: Students with emotional and behavioral disorders* (pp. 3–19). Hillsdale, NJ: Erlbaum.

Kauffman, J. M., Lloyd, J. W., Baker, J., & Riedel, T. M. (1995). Inclusion of all students with emotional or behavioral disorders? Let's think again. *Phi Delta Kappan, 76,* 542–546.

Miller, M. C., Cooke, N. L., Test, D. W., & White, R. (2003). Effects of friendship circles on the social interactions of elementary age students with mild disabilities. *Journal of Behavioral Education, 12,* 167–184.

Mock, D. R., & Kauffman, J. M. (2005). The delusion of full inclusion. In J. W. Jacobson, J. A. Mulick, & R. M. Foxx (Eds.), *Fads: Dubious and improbable treatments for developmental disabilities* (pp. 113–128). Mahwah, NJ: Erlbaum.

Reynolds, M. C. (1962). A framework for considering some issues in special education. *Exceptional Children, 28,* 367–370.

Vandercook, T., York. J., & Forest, M. (1989). The McGill Action Planning system (MAPS): A strategy for building the future. *The Journal of the Association of Persons with Severe Handicaps, 14,* 205–215.

Westling, D., & Fox, L. (2000). *Teaching students with severe disabilities* (2nd ed.). Upper Saddle River, NJ: Prentice-Hall.

PART II

Policy Analyses, Commentaries, and Research

The essays in Part II address the conceptual bases and policy implications of the full inclusion movement. The first chapter in this section (9) explains why the movement to merge general and special education is misguided and offers an alternative set of assumptions regarding the relationship between general and special education. The second chapter (10) goes further in explaining why we need a diversity of environments to provide appropriate education for all of a very diverse population of students. The next two chapters (11 and 12) analyze full inclusion as a policy issue from empirical and historical perspectives. Chapter 13 raises questions about the preparation of teachers for full inclusion, and Chapter 14 discusses the delusions necessary to support full inclusion or see it as successful. Chapter 15 is an essay imagining what might happen to special education if full inclusion becomes federal policy and challenging readers to think through the story they might write about special education and its future. Part II ends with a review of why the place of instruction is not the important issue (Chapter 16).

Together, these commentaries and analyses raise questions about how and why the full inclusion movement has become the focal point of controversy in special education. They also raise questions about the conceptual and research bases of full inclusion and offer alternative views on what a prudent course for the field would be. They suggest that special education is something to be preserved and that special education can indeed have the desired effect of ensuring an appropriate education for every child, regardless of disability. However, such preservation and appropriate education will continue to be available to all students only if the full continuum of placement options is preserved (Fuchs & Fuchs, 1991, 1995; Kauffman & Hallahan, 2005).

The full inclusion movement suggests that diversity is good, except diversity in placement or type of environment. But, as Hallahan and Kauffman (1994) ask, why should we not celebrate the diversity of environments in which students can find acceptance, support, and success? In Part II, writers suggest that specialized placements can be very good indeed for some students and that special environments should not be called "segregated" or described by other demeaning words, as Gliona, Gonzales, and Jacobson suggest in Chapter 8.

REFERENCES

Fuchs, D., & Fuchs, L. S. (1991). Framing the REI debate: Abolitionists versus conservationists. In J. W. Lloyd, A. C. Repp, & N. N. Singh (Eds.), *The regular education initiative: Alternative perspectives on concepts, issues, and methods* (pp. 241–255). Dekalb, IL: Sycamore.

Fuchs, D., & Fuchs, L. S. (1995). Special education can work. In J. M. Kauffman, J. W. Lloyd, D. P. Hallahan, & T. A. Astuto (Eds.), *Issues in educational placement: Students with emotional and behavioral disorders* (pp. 363–377). Hillsdale, NJ: Erlbaum.

Hallahan, D. P., & Kauffman, J. M. (1994). Toward a culture of disability in the aftermath of Deno and Dunn. *The Journal of Special Education, 27,* 496–508.

Kauffman, J. M. & Hallahan, D. P. (2005). *What special education is and why we need it.* Boston: Allyn & Bacon.

CHAPTER 9

Toward a Comprehensive Delivery System for Special Education

James M. Kauffman and Daniel P. Hallahan

Your design must be directed primarily at helping all students meet world class standards in five core subjects" (Blount & Kean, 1991, p. 3). This constraint on designs for a "new generation of American schools" was proposed by the chief executive officer and the chairman of the board of the New American Schools Development Corporation (NASDC). The NASDC was created in response to President Bush's unveiling in April 1991 of his new strategy for American education. Its emphasis on the achievement of world-class standards by all students follows a spate of "system-wide 'crisis rhetoric'" (Carson, Huelskamp, & Woodall, 1991, p. 172) and a rush of calls for "radical reform," "restructuring," and "transformation" of American public education, including appeals for integrating general and special education (see also Lloyd, Singh, & Repp, 1991).

Much of the current language of education reform consists of disparaging commentaries on the failure of American education and calls for inclusiveness (all students) and unity of service delivery structures (integrated, merged). Some researchers have observed that American education does not appear by objective standards to be the miserable failure portrayed by its contemporary critics (Bracey, 1991; Carson et al., 1991). In appeals for integration of general and special education the two are frequently described as separate systems, yet one might note the ways in which special education already exists as an integral component of public general education. In this context, we must consider carefully the implications of key concepts in reform rhetoric and the ways in which general and special education have been, are, and should be integrated in a comprehensive delivery system.

Special education evolved as an integral part of public general education in the early 20th century, as MacMillan and Hendrick explain (see Hendrick & MacMillan, 1989). In conception, special education was—and we argue that it remains—a necessary and integral part of a comprehensive general education delivery system. A comprehensive education delivery system addresses the educational needs, but not all the needs, of all children, not merely most. Special education originated because the education designed for most children was not having the desired effect on some. Educators saw that the appropriate education of all children required different instruction (i.e., special education) for a minority.

A central issue in designing a comprehensive education delivery system is the definition of *all,* a word with desultory meanings. More than the rhetorical meaning of *all* is at stake in designing a comprehensive delivery system. What is at stake is (1) whether general education will have a special-purpose branch to serve the exceptional needs of some children and (2) how that branch will be articulated with the trunk program of education. Thus, the varied meanings of *all* in controversies regarding special and general education, and the implications of these meanings for a comprehensive delivery system, are central issues in our discussion.

THE VARIED MEANINGS OF ALL

The implicit and explicit meanings of *all* are critical for understanding political and educational dialogue because one typically assumes that the freedoms, rights, and responsibilities addressed in these exchanges are limited, not absolute. The user of the word *all* does not usually intend that it be interpreted literally because either tradition or rational discourse (or both) suggests exceptions, meaning that *all* usually represents only an approximation (and sometimes not a very close approximation) of every individual. *All*, then, is frequently understood to exclude certain individuals, sometimes for reasons that are justifiable and sometimes for reasons that are not. The varied meanings of *all* are therefore of considerable consequence to those who may be tacitly excluded.

Impoverished and Exclusionary Meanings of *All*

The meaning of *all* can be impoverished, either by unintelligible exclusions or by extreme literalness. In today's political rhetoric regarding education, and too often in the speaking and writing of educators, we encounter the cliché "all children can learn" proffered without clarifications that might make it more than a hint of an allusion. One must ask for answers to follow-up questions to this slogan: What can all children learn? At what rate? With what allocation of instructional resources? To what degree of proficiency or mastery? For what purpose? These are particularly important questions when we are considering students who are exceptional—markedly different from their typical age-mates in ways that are directly related to learning and instruction (thinking, communicating, or moving).

One might interpret the hackneyed "all children can learn" to mean that most children can learn what most teachers are supposed to teach at about an average rate and to a generally acceptable degree of mastery. Perhaps it is intended as a reminder that students differ in some ways that are very seldom inherent constraints on teaching and learning (e.g., color, gender, or socioeconomic status) and that teachers have sometimes been guilty of lowered expectations based on these differences that have relatively trivial implications for instruction. But "all children can learn" is a hollow slogan when we consider the full range of child characteristics. It is devoid of meaning because it merely reifies two facts: (1) many students, but not literally all, can learn what we expect of the typical student, and (2) most children, but not literally all, can learn something worthwhile. Historically, users of this slogan have not meant it to include all children with disabilities because some of them cannot learn that which, presumably, "all children" can.

Until the 1970s, many children with disabilities were routinely excluded from public schools. Educating "all children" once meant, in the common parlance of many state legislators and local school officials, something considerably less than teaching every youngster who can learn useful skills. Since enactment in 1975 of the federal legislation known commonly as P.L. 94-142 (Education for All Handicapped Children Act of 1975, now the Individuals with Disabilities Education Act, or IDEA), the courts have interpreted the education of "all handicapped children" to mean the inclusion of literally all, regardless of the nature or severity of their handicaps. The blunt literalness of high court interpretations of federal special education law apparently allows no living child to be found ineducable, meaning that schools must provide a free appropriate public "education" to children with scant cortical function and even to those with no cerebral cortex and no possibility of consciousness (*Timothy W. v. Rochester, New Hampshire School District*, 1989; see also McCarthy, 1991). Whether attempting to educate children who are permanently unconscious is a moral imperative or a mockery is an open question for philosophical debate, but legislation and litigation have left no room for educators' clinical judgment on the matter.

We are unable to describe educational needs of permanently unconscious and semicomatose children, although these children have obvious needs for humane treatment. We realize, nonetheless, that what constitutes a sufficient state of consciousness or cortical function to create an educational need is a matter of informed judgment in the individual case. Our point is that *all* can be impoverished of meaning in discussions of education in either of two ways: when it is used glibly and insidiously to exclude children who are not typical in what they can learn or, on the other hand, as a cudgel of literalness that equates inability to learn only with total brain death.

The most extreme cases of cognitive disability and their deliberate inclusion in "all handicapped children" in federal mandates are not merely distracting aberrations for two reasons: (1) they demand that any serious discussion of the inclusion of all children in general education confront the full range of disability without implicit exclusions, and (2) they force us to consider the careless use of *all* and the implications for designing a service delivery system that includes children whose special educational needs are tacitly ignored. The excluded and ignored children often are not only those with such profound intellectual impairments that they arguably have no educational needs but many who have impairments of a far milder form and who can clearly be educated, including children with mild or moderate mental retardation, emotional or behavioral disorders, and learning disabilities.

As efforts to reform, restructure, or "reinvent" American schools have gained momentum, many educators have suggested that schools must become more inclusive of children with diverse educational needs—that schools must serve the needs of all children. Thus we must consider carefully the meanings of *all* in discussions of education reform.

Meanings of *All* in Education Reform

In the language of current education reform, *all* often does not mean literally every student. In fact, it clearly must be interpreted to exclude many students who do not have profound cognitive impairments. The educational goals for the year 2000 set by President Bush and the states' governors are a case in point. We recognize that many students with disabilities are fully capable of meeting or exceeding the expectations set by the nation's leaders if they are provided appropriate education. Yet the goal that by 2000 "all children will start school ready to learn," for example, is vague in its implications for gifted and handicapped children. To say that "all" students will be ready to learn and be literate is appealing rhetoric, but it renders actual achievement of these goals impossible. We believe that President Bush and the governors are serious in their hope that public education will be improved, but we do not believe that they have considered the ramifications of their goal statements for students with disabilities.

We interpret such goal statements as indicating a lack of awareness of the full range of children's abilities, with the implicit assumption that *all* means, in actuality, "most" or "a somewhat greater percentage." What will children be ready to learn when they start school? What is the meaning of "ready"? At what age will children start school? Clearly, we might expect very dissimilar answers for children with severely limited cognitive abilities, those of near average intelligence, and those with extremely high intellectual abilities. Without answers to these questions, we see *all* in most of the goal statements of education reform as implicitly excluding many exceptional children.

Special education and the problem of constructing a service delivery system that includes exceptional children have been ignored or mentioned only in passing in discussions of general education reform. "The silence about the needs of, or outcomes for, handicapped children in the current reform movement is deafening" (Hocutt, Martin, & McKinney, 1991). The omission may be interpreted in at least two ways. One interpretation is that the needs of exceptional children are considered by most educators not to merit special attention. Accordingly, *all* in the language of reform means those children who are not so different from the norm that the goals established for "all students" are reasonable. Thus, for example, when the president and governors established the goal "By the year 2000 every adult American will be literate and possess the knowledge and skills necessary to compete in a global economy and exercise the rights and responsibilities of citizenship," they were apparently unconcerned about students whose cognitive disabilities preclude their learning to read or to understand concepts such as rights and citizenship and those who can only acquire rudimentary knowledge and skills that will neither make them competitive in a global economy nor enable them to exercise responsibilities of citizenship in meaningful ways. The implication is that special education will be necessary to address the needs of those forgotten in the press to restructure general education.

An alternative interpretation is that the reforms proposed for general education will be (or can be) so sweeping and revolutionary that the need for special education as such will be obviated. In essence, the trunk program of general education should assimilate its special education branch; general education must become special for all students, such that all students are treated with the same care for meeting individual differences, hence without marking any person or service as extraordinary. Special education will, in effect, become "normal" or standard educational practice. Special and general education will be merged into a single entity described in the language of reform as "supple," "flexible" (Lipsky & Gartner, 1987), and even as intended to provide *"an elite education for everyone"* (National Center on Education and the Economy [NCEE], 1989, p. 9). The implication is that restructured general education will provide sufficient safeguards for meeting the needs of exceptional children, an assumption that, we shall show, is untenable.

Even when special education is specifically at issue in discussions of reform, however, *all* is sometimes apparently used with the tacit assumption that no one will ask whether *all* is meant to be taken literally. One widely cited education reform program, known as Success for All (Slavin, 1990a; Slavin et al., 1991) and commonly offered by its author as an alternative to special education, clearly does not address the needs of all students (see Semmel & Gerber, 1990; Slavin, 1990b). It might more candidly be called "Higher Achievement for Most." Another program widely lauded in the special education reform literature is the Adaptive Learning Environments Model (ALEM) of Wang and her colleagues (see, e.g., Wang, Reynolds, & Walberg, 1986, 1988; Wang & Zollers, 1990). Some have stated, "All types of students can be accommodated in ALEM classrooms" (Biklen & Zollers, 1986), yet it is clear that ALEM has not been demonstrated to meet the needs of all students, particularly not all students with mild or moderate disabilities (Bryan & Bryan, 1988; Fuchs & Fuchs, 1988).

Claims of success for all students in any given program said to be an alternative to special education as it is currently structured are sometimes qualified by explicit exclusions, for example, "Those who are retarded or severely emotionally disturbed, as well as those with physical, speech, or language deficits and those with severe learning disabilities" (Slavin et al., 1991). Excluded students are sometimes described as those who are not "judgmentally" handicapped (Reynolds, Wang, & Walberg, 1987). These exclusions are logical contradictions, namely, that success must be defined as impossible for some students in programs claiming success for all or, on the other hand, that the success of some students must be judged by a different standard from that presumably applicable to all students. We shall return to the problem of these lacunae in the logic of reform.

Candor and prudence in stating goals and making claims for the inclusiveness of educational programs might make innovations and reform proposals less beguiling and create less confusion about what is possible and desirable in public education. Unfortunately, the relentless hyperbole regarding programs said to be alternatives to special education, combined with current political and economic pressures for the reform of both special and general education, have led to much confusion regarding the nature of special programs and their roles in a comprehensive service delivery system designed to meet the educational needs of all students.

THE PRESS FOR SPECIAL EDUCATION REFORM

Extreme unhappiness with American public education is today de rigueur, although many of the bases for its condemnation are questionable (Carson et al., 1991). Perhaps dissatisfaction with special education is an indication of the degree to which it is now seen as an integral part of the public education system. Before discussing how we might work toward a comprehensive service delivery system, we examine problems created by current reform rhetoric. Although we recognize that education—special education included—needs substantial improvement, we believe that much of the current press for radical restructuring is based on misrepresentations, tortured ideologies, and conceptual confusion.

Misrepresentations

Part of the press for special education reform and the integration of special with general education has been created by scathing commentaries on educational outcomes for children with disabilities who have received special education and by ardent claims that alternatives to special education are known to produce superior outcomes for all children. Critics of the current system of special and general education charge bluntly that it does not work, provides no benefit, and therefore cannot be justified, whereas restructured programs are highly successful and serve all children well (Biklen & Zollers, 1986; Gartner & Lipsky, 1989; Lipsky & Gartner, 1991; Reynolds, 1989).

Space does not allow us to review the findings here. Suffice to say that research has yielded mixed findings for both prevalent service delivery models and restructured programs. We believe that the conclusions that special education has failed and that restructured programs have not are overgeneralizations. They can be reached only by ignoring substantial findings to the contrary, and they can be maintained only by assiduously avoiding critical analysis of both rhetoric and research (Fuchs & Fuchs, 1991; Hallahan, Kauffman, Lloyd, & McKinney, 1988; Kauffman, 1989, 1991; Kauffman & Hallahan, 1990; Kauffman & Pullen, 1989). In our view, they are dangerous exaggerations that distort perceptions and create a climate in which research data are devalued in favor of ideologies that, although otherwise defensible, have been twisted into parodies.

Tortured Ideologies

Special education is accurately portrayed as justified in part by two ideologies: civil rights and normalization. Both ideologies have been of considerable value to special education, but both have been invoked inappropriately in attempts to justify proposals that undermine its conceptual foundations.

Civil Rights

Equal protection of law and equal educational opportunity are concepts supporting special education for exceptional students. These same concepts support the integration of diverse ethnic groups in public schools. The educational rights of exceptional children and those of ethnic minorities rest on the same foundation, namely, that children's characteristics must not be used as a justification for unfair treatment (i.e., treatment that denies them equal opportunity to learn). Nevertheless, unfairness in education has historically had very different meanings for ethnic minorities and exceptional children. In the case of ethnic minorities, providing different education for children with the same needs has been seen as creating unfairness; in the case of exceptional children, however, providing the same education for children whose needs are significantly different from others' has been viewed as unfair. When one disregards these differences in the nature of unfairness and applies the same criteria for judging discrimination to exceptionality and ethnicity, civil rights arguments become non sequiturs.

Some calls for radically restructured special and general education assume an isomorphism of ethnicity and disability, which yields the conclusion that separating exceptional children for instruction is as unfairly discriminatory as maintaining schools segregated by ethnicity (Lipsky & Gartner, 1987; Stainback & Stainback, 1991; Will, 1984). Some have used the argument that separate education is inherently and unfairly unequal when children are segregated by skin color or ancestry to justify the conclusion that grouping children for instruction based on their performance is inherently and unfairly unequal, particularly when children differing in performance are instructed in different classrooms. This line of reasoning ignores the fact that racial segregation was the total separation of children for instruction according to the dichotomous and, presumably, instructionally irrelevant variable of skin color, whereas schools separate children into groups for special education for varying amounts of time (a relatively small amount of the school day for most) based on assessment of their academic performance and instructional needs (Kauffman, 1991; Kauffman & Hallahan, 1990).

Those who have recently proposed to establish special academies for Black male students have reversed the argument that separate education is inherently and unfairly unequal when the basis for separation is ethnic identity or gender. In our view, these proposals have merit precisely to the extent that one can make the case that ethnic identity and gender are characteristics determining what or how students can best be taught. Our interpretation of equal educational opportunity is that students must not be grouped for instruction by caprice or by criteria that are irrelevant to their learning and social development but that they must be grouped by criteria directly related to what they are to learn and how they can be taught most effectively.

Normalization

Normalization, the concept on which landmark legislation and litigation in special education has been built, has lost much of its meaning. Rather than a guiding principle for developing services for persons with disabilities, it has become codified as a rule requiring that all students with disabilities be educated in general education classrooms. It has been reduced to a slogan standing for the politically correct position of total integration or inclusion, but it is a much more complex notion than many realize.

Some proponents of educational reform have misconstrued the normalization principle as a rationale for abolishing pullout programs (e.g., Gartner & Lipsky, 1987). Wolfensberger has addressed this misconception, stating that normalization and mainstreaming should not be considered synonymous (Wolfensberger, 1980). Today's advocates of total integration have fashioned the meaning of "normalization" for their own purposes. They would certainly have a difficult time reconciling their push for total integration with Wolfensberger's position on the subject. Regarding the misconception that normalization means that people with retardation should *always* work in culturally normative settings, for instance, Wolfensberger has stated, "In fact, I do not recall meeting a single normalization advocate or even zealot who has not recognized the need for at least some type of sheltered work conditions and circumstances for at least some retarded persons" (Wolfensberger, 1980, p. 98).

Furthermore, although favoring small residential arrangements, Wolfensberger (1980) is a strong proponent of a variety of different options. For those requiring psychiatric services, for example, he has proposed no less than 15 different types of models varying in separateness as a function of the characteristics of the clients. Currently, public school programming for students with disabilities appears to be headed in the opposite direction. Instead of multiple service delivery options, the rush toward total integration is reducing the number of alternatives for educational placement.

Although Wolfensberger was not clear on the subject in his earliest formulation of the normalization principle, he later clarified that he did not mean to equate normalization with the statistical norm (Wolfensberger, 1980). His later conceptualization places more importance on the *perceived* value of the means to achieving normalization. Even so, however, one can argue that the most effective treatment methods may not always be those that are most culturally normal or valued. Mulick and Kedesdy, for example, contend that in the case of self-injurious behavior in persons with autism, culturally normative responses worsen the behavior, and some of the most efficacious treatment techniques for self-injurious behavior in persons with autism run counter to normalization principles (Mulick & Kedesdy, 1988). The culturally normative response to someone who injures him- or herself is consolation or a response that draws attention to the injured person. Social attention to self-injurious behavior, however, actually leads to increases in self-injury. Techniques that would not be high on a list of cultural normality, such as restraint and punishment, are the ones that researchers have found most effective in reducing self-injury.

A less dramatic, but more common, example of how the best educational techniques are not always culturally normative pertains to the learning problems of children. Placing students in small groups and using a highly teacher-directed, drill-and-practice approach is not the way most children are taught to read, nor is it consistent with current trends in educational reform. Research has documented, however, that just such an approach is the most successful for students with learning disabilities (White, 1988). Such an approach, however, would meet Wolfensberger's later conceptualization of perceived value.

To us, it seems that the almost obsessive concern for normalization promulgated by some advocates of mainstreaming and deinstitutionalization promotes a demeaning attitude toward those with disabilities. There needs to be a balance between focusing on changing the person with a disability to be more "normal," by attending regular schools and classes and being included in the standard curriculum, versus changing society to accept people who have disabilities. As Hauerwas notes,

> We usually associate movements toward justice in our society with the
> language of equality. We assume to be treated equally is to be treated

justly, but on reflection we may discover that is not the case. Often the language of equality only works by reducing us to a common denominator that can be repressive or disrespectful. (Hauerwas, 1986, p. 213)

Because the originators of the principle of normalization—Bank-Mikkelsen, Nirje, and Wolfensberger—have often written passionately about the validity of the concept, they have probably given present-day normalization proponents justification for imbuing it with status equivalent to one of the Ten Commandments (see Bank-Mikkelsen, 1969; Nirje, 1969; Wolfensberger, 1980). We note that Wolfensberger describes normalization on the societal level, meaning that society should be more tolerant of the differences of people with disabilities, and that he has stated, "Normalization does not mean that only normative human management tools and methods are used—merely that these be as normal *as feasible*" [italics added] (Wolfensberger, 1972, p. 238).

Advocates of total integration have unfortunately twisted the original intent of the principle of normalization. As a guiding principle, it provides an appropriate rationale for much of what we should be trying to do in educating children with disabilities; as a pretext for total integration or a rationale for wholesale mainstreaming and deinstitutionalization, its meaning is distorted to such an extent that it is in danger of becoming an empty slogan.

Conceptual Confusion

Proposals for integrating special and general education have reflected considerable confusion about basic concepts, including as they do the juxtaposition of incongruous meanings, the use of self-contradictory lines of argument, and antipathy toward critical analysis of purposes and means to achieve them. Such confusion leads inevitably to a circularity of reasoning that thwarts the good intentions of reformers.

Incongruities of Meaning

Much of the language of radical restructuring is peculiarly oxymoronic, containing appeals for common specialness, excellence without exception, and the normalization of exceptionality. Lipsky and Gartner conclude that "it is time to move on to the struggle of changing the educational system to make it both one and special for all students," (Lipsky & Gartner, 1987, p. 73), ignoring the inherent contradiction of the concepts *same* and *spe-*

cial. Another example of puzzling disregard of meanings in the reform literature is the statement of the National Center on Education and the Economy that "the challenge is to provide *an elite education for everyone*" (NCEE, 1989, p. 9). These nonsensical "struggles" and "challenges" are similar to others one might construct from combinations of opposite meanings, such as "The challenge is to foster democracy without involving ordinary citizens" or "It is time to move on to the struggle for standards of excellence not derived from comparisons." Perhaps such language has become the norm in the sound bites associated with advertising and political campaigns in which success is based on the assumption that the public will not think critically and analytically, but we hope for a higher level of discourse about educational reform—at least among educators. Language of this type belies any intent to bring intellectual integrity to the tasks of educating children and their teachers (see Goodlad, 1990), and it carries a peculiar irony when the avowed intent of reform is to promote critical thinking, prepare students to "render critical judgment," and produce students "whose understanding runs deep" (Carnegie Forum on Education and the Economy, 1986, p. 20).

Self-Contradictory Arguments

Lines of arguments offered in support of radical restructuring are often incoherent. One commonly finds self-contradictions in stated assumptions about why special and general education have failed and how their failures can be reversed.

In a paper circulated by the National Center on Education and the Economy, Gartner and Lipsky state that we must abandon the notion that learning problems are inherent in children: "The current practice of special education operates on a deficit model; that is, it identifies something as wrong or missing in the student" (Gartner & Lipsky, 1989, p. 20). Yet one of their recommendations for improving student productivity is "Do not waste time on 'teaching,'" and they go on to say that "the outcome of an education is student learning, [and] it is only the student who can do that learning" (Gartner & Lipsky, 1989, p. 28). On the one hand, they fault special education for identifying something wrong with the student; on the other hand, they argue that students, including those who have failed, hold the keys to their own failure and success.

Criticism of special education is occurring in the larger context of criticism of public education. General education, critics claim, is failing to reach its goals with many students, including those identified as handicapped and many who are not. We agree with Keogh that "it is a strange logic that calls for the regular system to take over responsibility for pupils it has already demonstrated it has failed" (Keogh, 1988, p. 20). MacMillan and Hendrick (1993; see also Hendrick & MacMillan, 1989) buttress Singer's observation that "special education was the solution to the regular educator's thorny problem of how to provide supplemental resources to children in need while not shortchanging other students in the class. Nothing else has happened within regular education to solve this problem" (Singer, 1988, p. 416). We note also that many of the instructional reforms so far implemented in general education and widely favored among general educators (e.g., less explicit, more child-directed, more "developmental" instruction) are those that researchers have found most likely to lead to failure for handicapped and at-risk students (Carnine, 1991; Carnine & Kameenui, 1990).

Critics have characterized special education as a failure (Lipsky & Gartner, 1991), as segregationist (Stainback & Stainback, 1991), as a way of diminishing children (Lipsky & Gartner, 1987), and as a second-rate system (Wang et al., 1986, 1988). Yet the same writers have suggested that special education provides a model of what general education should become and that, were special education merged with general education, all students would benefit, none would be diminished, and general education could become first-rate. We do not understand how the alleged failures—general and special education—will be transformed by this fusion, particularly how losing its separate identity will turn special education from evil to good. We understand that reformers propose that purportedly nefarious aspects of special education (e.g., special identities called labels, students taught in places other than their home school or regular classroom) will not be parts of restructured education. But special programs present dilemmas, not the least of which is that when special identities of students are lost, so is the capacity to provide special services (see Minow, 1987), and that stigma and separation can be greater problems in home schools and regular classes than in alternative schools and classes.

Antipathy Toward Analyzing Purposes and Means
As Fuchs and Fuchs have noted, some have presented the goals of restructured general and special education in impressionistic, nonempirical terms (Fuchs & Fuchs, 1991). Reformers say that special and general education as they currently exist have failed, and often we read and hear that neither "works" (e.g., Lipsky & Gartner, 1991). Yet we are not told, except in impressionistic and even surrealistic language, how we should judge that either is "working" (Kauffman, 1990). The aversion to logical analysis of pur-

poses and means is particularly evident in discussions of performance outcomes and policy (i.e., structure and regulation of access to programs).

What would characterize the distribution of outcomes if general or special education, or both, worked? If all students received an appropriate education, if not the best education possible, would we have fewer or more children who compare unfavorably to the majority on important outcomes? Would the disparities between the achievement of high and low performers become smaller or greater? That is, would we expect education that works to increase or decrease population variance? To us, it is apparent that these and other questions that must be addressed in careful analyses of performance goals have been sidestepped in appeals for reform. If they are not addressed, however, reform proposals are merely bravado, which leaves all of us confused about just what is intended.

Reformers also skirt questions regarding the relationship between special and general education. If special and general education are to become a unitary system, as some suggest (e.g., Lipsky & Gartner, 1991; Stainback & Stainback, 1991), what are the criteria for judging that they are unitary, not separate? What makes a program special or separate? Designated personnel? Special personnel training? Budget lines? Separate professional organizations? What percentage of time must a student be taught in a different curriculum to make a program separate or segregated from that received by others? What physical distance from another group of students constitutes segregation? If a unitary system is to be "supple" and "flexible," what are the criteria for judging that these characteristics have been achieved? Should it contain no option for special classes or schools, no different curricula or goals for different types of students, no "standard" expectations for any group of students? What would a supple, flexible system allow, and what would it disallow? Who will be the arbiters of what is acceptable and what is prohibited in a flexible system?

Given that certain components of a service delivery system are deemed essential, how does one create and maintain the policy structures necessary for their inclusion? Some reform advocates propose a unitary system of service delivery in which current federal regulations are reduced or eliminated (e.g., Gartner & Lipsky, 1987; NCEE, 1989). We can think of no case in which important rights and protections are safeguarded without legislation and regulation, human nature being what it is. As Fuchs and Fuchs conclude, the appeal for a unitary, deregulated system is more than an ahistorical, nonempirical perspective; its naiveté invites the neglect of students with disabilities whenever there are competing interests, and there are always competing interests (Fuchs & Fuchs, 1991; see also Hocutt et al.,

1991). That a particular school or community appears, at least temporarily, to have gone beyond current regulations in the care of its students must not be interpreted to mean that public policy can be based on the assumption of public goodwill toward children with disabilities or that what is possible in one school is possible in any.

SPECIAL EDUCATION AS PART OF A COMPREHENSIVE SERVICE DELIVERY SYSTEM

To this point we have discussed only problems with the revisionist critique of special education. We acknowledge that special education is beset by substantial problems that must be addressed in any serious effort to improve it. We believe that these problems are primarily a result of inept professional practice and misunderstanding of what special education is. Contrary to the assertion that special education is flawed in its basic conception (Lipsky & Gartner, 1991), we maintain that the basic idea of special education is as sound as the very notion of public education. What is needed is not the reconceptualization or reinvention of special education but a sober look at the postulates on which a comprehensive service delivery system might be based and a careful examination of the extent to which the practice of special education so conceptualized falls short of the ideal. To this end we propose eight postulates and corollaries that might provide the framework for making special education an effective branch of a comprehensive service delivery system.

Postulate 1: Public schooling must serve equitably the educational needs of all children by helping them achieve a level of academic, social, and vocational competence commensurate with their potential.

This postulate reaffirms our belief that public schools must serve more than academic needs and that it must address the full range of students' educational needs, from those of the most talented or educationally gifted to those of students with such severe intellectual impairments that they will be able to learn only simple self-care skills. It recognizes that students have needs that are not educational and acknowledges that some children, though a very few in number, may have no educational needs.

Corollary 1a: Because public education must serve all children who have educational needs, the largest part of general education must be designed for the modal characteristics of students and teachers.

Public education by definition must serve the masses. Like any product or service designed for the public, most of public education must be designed to fit the most common (modal, "standard") characteristics of consumers. Economies of scale require that products and services designed for the general public be structured by the size, shape, and abilities of citizens falling within a limited band of variability around a mean. This does not mean that individuals with characteristics very different from the average cannot be accommodated by services or product lines designed and produced by public agencies; it does mean, however, that the needs of exceptional individuals will not be met by the standard products and services that are appropriate for most persons.

Likewise, education must be structured so that the modal teacher is capable of accomplishing the tasks of education with most students. This does not mean that the performance capability of the average teacher cannot be raised through better training; it does mean, however, that expectations for the performance of most teachers must not outstrip what the average teacher can do with appropriate training.

Corollary 1b: Because public education must address all children's educational needs, it must include explicit structures ensuring the accommodation of exceptional students.

Explicit structures creating differentiation of public services are required to meet extraordinary needs. Exceptional children by definition require extraordinary education—that which is different from the standard education that serves most students well. The structure of education includes goals, lines of authority, roles and responsibilities of personnel, budgets and purchases, allocation of time and space, curriculum, selection and assignment of students to classes, and evaluation. Failure to create and maintain explicit structures accommodating exceptional individuals inevitably results in the neglect of those for whom the core services are inadequate. The necessary explicit structures may become a predictable or required part (a "normal" part) of public services, but without these structures we can predict that exceptional individuals will be ill served.

Dramatic changes in certain school structures—lowering the typical class size to 12 or fewer students or placing 2 competent teachers in every class of 25 students, for example—would allow teachers to accommodate greater variability in student characteristics. Even assuming these desirable (but highly improbable) changes in standard school structures, however, teachers will not be able to accommodate every student within the new, standard structure. No single teaching arrangement is infinitely flexible.

Postulate 2: Exceptional students differ significantly from the modal or typical student in instructionally relevant ways that result in their inevitable failure, given standard educational goals and programs.

Abilities to access and process specific information are directly relevant to instruction. The extreme differences in such abilities of some students preclude their attainment of certain educational goals that are appropriate for most students. Moreover, standard instructional programs that are successful with most students cannot accommodate extreme differences in students' abilities to perceive, organize, store, retrieve, and apply information to the solution of specific problems. Thus, some exceptional students will fail to meet standard educational goals regardless of the instructional program that is provided; others will be able to meet standard educational goals but not with standard instructional programs.

Teachers must not be led down a path of fantasy or intellectual duplicity regarding what is possible and what their moral responsibility is when confronted by students whose needs they have not the resources to meet. Goodlad (1990) suggests, "For teacher education programs not to be models of educating is indefensible" (p. 59). He notes, further, that teacher education programs have a moral responsibility to confront their limitations:

> Even supposing it could be argued that all traits are amenable to education, teacher education programs possess neither the resources nor the time to redress severe personality disorders; and they appear ill-equipped to perform much lesser tasks. Consequently, the moral and ethical imperatives of selection require that applicants be counseled out if they fall seriously short in characteristics that are deemed important but for which there are no programmatic provisions. Failure to so counsel is morally wrong, and the consequences are costly. (Goodlad, 1990, p. 284)

We believe that the same moral responsibility applies to teachers in our public schools who are aware that they are ill equipped to redress the limitations of their students' ability to learn.

Corollary 2a: The requirements of alternative educational goals and programs must be made explicit for exceptional students.

When standard goals or instructional methods are inappropriate for a student, appropriate alternatives must be available. These alternatives will not be available in all school systems unless they are explicitly required by law and regulation, as public attention and economies of scale are inevitably centered on meeting modal needs. The implicit or explicit assumption that standard educational goals and programs will accommodate the educational needs of all students is not only logically untenable but places the onus of proof on the student when questions regarding an individual student arise. The explicit requirement of alternatives to meet the needs of exceptional students places the burden of proof on the school's service delivery system.

Corollary 2b: Alternative goals and programs must be expressed as alternative curricula and methods for exceptional students.

Educational goals and programs entail instructional materials, teaching procedures, and an array of activities designed to result in the acquisition of specific skills, attitudes, and values. Thus, goals and programs for exceptional students involve alternative curricula or methods, beyond the range of the standard materials, procedures, and activities that produce acceptable outcomes for most students.

Corollary 2c: Alternative curricula and methods sometimes require alternative grouping of students.

It is axiomatic that a teacher cannot teach all things to all students at the same time. Students are necessarily grouped for instruction in specific content according to the teachers' instructional capabilities and the germane pupil characteristics. Moreover, the greater the variability in a group of the students in their characteristics germane to instruction (beyond a base level of manageable variability), the smaller the number of students a teacher is able to instruct successfully. Efficient and effective instruction of non-exceptional students can best be accomplished by forming standard patterns of grouping (i.e., groups designed for instruction of students falling within a band of teachability in specific skills). Effective and efficient instruction of exceptional students sometimes requires nonstandard groupings to facilitate the use of alternative curricula and methods.

Both general and special educators teach heterogeneous groups of students. Teachers observe variability between students on specific characteristics and within individual students in various domains such as academic, social, and vocational skills. Instructional grouping must be designed to limit the heterogeneity of students to facilitate effective and efficient instruction.

We recognize that some categorical groupings do not achieve their intent of substantially reducing the variability among students to be instructed. Moreover, we recognize that it is neither possible nor desirable to reduce the variance of instructionally relevant characteristics in groups of students to near zero. Effective teaching demands the ability to accommodate a tolerable level of student variance. Nevertheless, we assert that, as Goodlad argues for teacher education, a moral commitment to educating children and youth carries with it the clear implication that teachers must recognize the limitations of their ability to accommodate student variance and seek alternative instruction for those whom they are not equipped to serve competently (Goodlad, 1990). A further implication is that in a comprehensive service delivery system, the student whose characteristics are judged to be incompatible with those of an instructional group must be included in an alternative group of students for whom alternative instruction is offered. A final implication is that individual instruction in one or more areas of the curriculum may be required for some students.

We note that alternative grouping of students for special education may sometimes be necessary to avoid significant deleterious effects for nonhandicapped students. At times, students with disabilities may be so disruptive or otherwise require so great a proportion of the teacher's resources that the educational needs of other members of the class suffer to a significant degree. We recognize that the degree of interference with the education of other students is a matter of professional judgment, but we think it better that the issue be addressed rather than ignored. We believe that it is the moral responsibility of the teacher to see that all students are receiving a fair chance to succeed. The consequences of failure to make such judgments in education are, as Goodlad (1990) points out, costly.

Postulate 3: Exceptional students must have open to them the full range of options for instructional grouping and environments for delivery of educational services. No single curriculum, instructional approach, grouping plan, or learning environment is appropriate for all students.

Given the extreme differences in the instructionally relevant characteristics of children and youth, a very wide range of options for instructional grouping and learning environments is required. It is self-evident that not all kinds of instruction and environmental conditions can be present in one classroom or school at the same time. Recognition of variance in instructional needs, beyond lip service to designing individualized programs, demands recognition of the need for variance in service delivery options. Restriction to one or a few service delivery options increases the rate of poor fits between students and the curricula and methods employed in their instruction (for comments regarding learning disabilities, see Kauffman & Trent, 1991).

Corollary 3a: The full range of grouping options ranges from full-time placement in standard educational curricula and groups with special assistance to special residential schools.

We may assume that for educational purposes students are not exceptional if their needs are adequately met in standard educational groups and by standard curricula and methods without supplementary services. Some exceptional students' appropriate education is possible without alternative grouping, so long as they are provided supplementary services (e.g., alternative instructional strategies) not required by modal students. Thus, not all exceptional students need alternative grouping for instruction. Other students, however, are exceedingly unlikely to receive appropriate education without placement in alternative instructional groups or alternative learning environments. The relevant characteristics of some students are so different from those of most students that they require substantially different environments for learning in one or more areas of their curriculum. These different environments may be best constructed in part-time or full-time special classes, alternative day schools, or residential schools.

Corollary 3b: Selection of instructional and grouping options should be guided by the policies and procedures established in IDEA (P.L. 94-142); parents and teachers must together select the least restrictive appropriate option from a full range of alternatives.

In 1975, P.L. 94-142 (now IDEA) established the expectation that appropriate education of children with disabilities will be a part of all schools' service delivery system. The policy represented in this law is that decisions regarding appropriate education and the least restrictive environment will be made jointly by educators and parents of students with disabilities on an individual basis. Procedural protections in the law are designed to ensure that a full range of instructional and grouping options is available and that the environment (placement) option judged least restrictive is chosen from those that are first judged appropriate.

Postulate 4: Alternative goals and instruction needed by exceptional students will not be ensured without explicit, permanent structures that include them in a comprehensive system of public education.

Public education itself was established by explicit, permanent structures, *first* those creating public schools, then those involving mandatory school attendance, later those granting equal access to schooling by students of color, and more recently those ensuring accommodations of students with disabilities. In each case, explicit and permanent structures were required to produce the intended benefits to students and the larger society. In the case of special education, the basic structures were provided by IDEA.

Corollary 4a: These structures must include special education as an integral but clearly differentiated part of a comprehensive service delivery system; the structures must include special teachers, administrators, funding mechanisms, and procedures.

IDEA established, within the larger structure of general education, mechanisms designed to require attention to the needs of students with disabilities. These mechanisms include fiscal, administrative, procedural, and instructional requirements that are necessary to ensure the inclusion of special education in school systems' service delivery. Without identifiable special personnel, specific funding channels, and procedural requirements, school systems are unlikely to be held accountable for their accommodation of students with disabilities; without these structures, the burden of proof of failure to accommodate is on the student and parents.

Corollary 4b: Special education structures must be ongoing; they must not be viewed as temporary measures that can be eliminated once their objectives have been achieved and special education is ensconced in public education.

The structures that created public schools, required student attendance, demanded equal access by students regardless of color, and required accommodation of students with disabilities cannot be abandoned under the assumption that once they have accomplished their purpose they are superfluous. Without constant attention to their preservation and maintenance, these structures and the practices they support will inevitably deteriorate and collapse. Special education has become an integral part of public education service delivery, but it will be maintained as such only if its supportive structures are maintained.

Postulate 5: The structures needed to ensure appropriate education of exceptional students require carefully regulated decisions regarding which students shall receive specific educational options.

Special provisions for at least some students with special needs have been "normal" components of the public education service delivery system of most state and local education agencies for two decades or more. Only since 1975, however, has federal education policy set the expectation that special education for all students with disabilities will be a part of the total symmetry of schools. Prior to the enactment of IDEA, the designation of students as having special needs, and therefore as needing special education programs, was not carefully regulated in most states. Consequently, decisions regarding the selection of individual students for specific instructional options were often capricious, and parents were often excluded from participation in the processes of identification and placement of their children.

Students cannot be provided educational options that are substantially different from the standard program without someone's making the decisions regarding which students should receive such options and which students should not. If one argues that no student should receive a "standard" program—that all students' programs should be individualized, and therefore "special"—we can predict that the vast majority of students' programs will be highly similar and hence "special" only in name. That is, it is predictable that a limited range of variability will define what is typical, expected, or unremarkable for students of a given age. Some students, however, will need programs that are remarkable outliers (i.e., very different from most).

The question remains, should the decision that a student needs a substantially different program from that appropriate for most students be regulated, such that special consideration and parental participation are required? One might argue that the same level of care and parental participation should be required in decisions regarding all students' programs. We question whether this argument can be grounded in the realities of public schooling and understanding of the responsibilities of teachers. Moreover, we see this argument as reducing all students' needs to unity, not merely to a common denominator. It is based on the denial of difference, not its recognition. The consequences of educators treating decisions regarding all students' programs with the same level of scrutiny would be predictably disastrous for students with special needs, much as the failure of professionals in other fields (law and medicine come immediately to mind) to discriminate cases requiring a special level of scrutiny would predictably result in grotesque malpractice.

Corollary 5a: Selection of education options is unavoidably judgmental, requiring informed professional and parental judgment of the individual student's abilities and needs.

There are two ways for educators to avoid making difficult judgments about which students should be granted special options. One is to treat all cases the same, which, as we have discussed, is tantamount to malpractice. The other is to set forth criteria based on psychometric data and to make these criteria the sole basis for decisions, which may seem to remove subjectivity from the decision-making process but also leads inevitably to abrogation of professional responsibility.

Education, like every other profession, is inherently judgmental. To speak of the "judgmentally handicapped" is as trite as to speak of the "judgmentally guilty," the "judgmentally ill," or an automobile that is "judgmentally unsafe." When disability or guilt or danger is said to be "obvious," we must ask, "Obvious to whom?" When the consequences are significant for the individual about whom a decision is made, society imposes regulatory mechanisms for making judgments, including procedural and authority structures.

True, there are cases in which most or all casual observers might judge an individual to have a disability—the "obvious" cases. Nevertheless, the great majority of cases of disability are not "obvious" to the casual observer. Moreover, the suggestion that special education should serve only the "obvious" cases or those whose disabilities are "severe" does not make special education nonjudgmental. "Obvious" and "severe" are themselves judgments about which well-informed persons may disagree. A structure is needed, therefore, for decision making in the case of students who may need nonstandard educational options. IDEA and attendant regulations set forth such a structure, which requires that the informed and combined judgment of educators and parents be the basis for the identification of handicapped students and for designing their programs.

Corollary 5b: The procedures for making judgments regarding educational options must be explicit, not covert.

As we have seen, judgments regarding the educational options students are eligible to receive cannot be avoided. All options should be available to all students who need them, but it is obvious that not all students will need all options. How, then, are decisions regarding options to be made? Asserting that general education should be sufficiently "flexible" or "supple" to accommodate all students begs the question; it is a ruse for driving the decision-making process underground, unless the regulatory mechanisms for decision making are explicated. IDEA was enacted in large measure because identification and placement decisions regarding handicapped children were not aboveboard. Moreover, the law was designed precisely to require that public education be flexible, supple, and accommodating of special needs.

When explicit structures for making decisions are not present, decisions regarding selection of curriculum and programming options cannot be monitored effectively (Feniak, 1988). Appeals to deregulate special education eligibility decisions are a direct appeal to abandon the structures— the procedural protections—that are necessary to maintain open and accountable decision making.

Corollary 5c: Judgments regarding educational options must not be made solely on the basis of psychometric data; teachers and parents must be the primary decision makers.

Psychometric assessments may yield useful information for decision making, but they are not sufficient in themselves for determining students' educational needs. Parents and those who are responsible for teaching the student must be the primary decision makers. Their decisions may be imperfect, but they are nevertheless the best equipped to make decisions regarding individual pupils when their judgment is informed by the best available data (Gerber & Semmel, 1984). This principle is embodied in IDEA.

Corollary 5d: Selection of specific educational options unavoidably results in labeling.

Individuals who receive educational programs (or any other treatment or recognition that others do not) are labeled by whatever language we use to describe them. The labels may not be the traditional ones associated with special education, but they are labels nonetheless (see Feniak, 1988; Minow, 1987). Care must be taken to avoid letting labels turn into abusive epithets, but our choice is clear: Either we label students with disabilities by speaking of their special needs, or we label them only as students, thereby denying the possibility of providing special programs for them.

Furthermore, the suggestion that programs but not students should be labeled (Reynolds, 1991; see also Stainback & Stainback, 1991) is gratuitous, as IDEA requires special education labels only for reporting purposes. The law does not require that students themselves be given labels, nor does it require that students be grouped by traditional special education categories. With regard to labels, the law requires only that programs for students with specific handicapping conditions be available and that students with disabilities be placed in programs designed to meet their special individual needs. The appeal for restructuring that eliminates labeling, then, must be seen for what it is—an appeal based on misrepresentation of the law and one not cognizant of the consequences of ignoring differences.

Postulate 6: Appropriate education of exceptional students depends on adequate preparation of professional personnel.

Teaching exceptional students well requires specialized training as surely as specialized training is required for other professionals who deal with unusual cases. We recognize that basic professional training must prepare the teacher to respond appropriately to a wide range of students. All professions see the need for a core of common training as well as the need for specialized training for those who will serve clients with particular needs.

Corollary 6a: All professional educators must be prepared to accommodate diversity among students and to recognize the need of some students for alternative instruction.

All teachers must be prepared to deal with diversity among the students they teach. It is also axiomatic that all teachers have limitations in the diversity they are able to accommodate. A critical aspect of ethical practice in any profession is recognition of one's limitations of training and expertise. Teachers who are unprepared or unwilling to request consultation from others and to refer a student for possible alternative placement when they are not able to meet the student's needs are in violation of federal special education policy as stated in IDEA. Moreover, they are violating standards of professional conduct.

Corollary 6b: Special educators must be prepared first as general educators and, following a period of successful practice as general educators, receive additional extensive training in specialized instruction.

One of the most substantial problems faced by special education is improving the competence of its classroom practitioners. Our belief is that special education has erred in its preparation of preservice teachers. Special education teachers must have prior training and experience as general educators if their training is to be truly specialized and if they are to collaborate effectively with teachers in general education classrooms. More than a cursory textbook understanding of the conditions and rigors of teaching in general education is required of special teachers who are to be collaborators with general educators.

Corollary 6c: Optimum accommodation of exceptional students depends on preparation of general and special educators to collaborate with other professionals and parents.

Teachers will become effective collaborators only if they are taught the procedures and skills involved in working with professional colleagues. Both general and special educators must receive training in how to work with each other for the benefit of exceptional students, how to work with noneducation professionals whose related services are required for their students, and how to work with parents as partners. The neglect of these procedures and skills in teacher training programs is a serious problem limiting the effectiveness of special education as part of a comprehensive service delivery system.

Postulate 7: The outcomes used to judge the effectiveness of general education are not always appropriate as criteria for judging the effectiveness of special education.

Special education is sometimes assessed by noting discrepancies between the performance of students with disabilities and that of the general population of students. Predictably, special education so weighed is found wanting, as the measure of success is inappropriate. Many students with disabilities can, if they are provided appropriate education, be expected to achieve outcomes similar to those of their nondisabled peers. It is predictable, however, that the rate of failure by those standards (e.g., graduation rate, number of passing grades, transition to higher education, successful employment) will be higher for students with disabilities than among students without disabilities, given equally appropriate education for the two groups. Special education must be conceptualized as a continuing support system for students who cannot be enabled to participate in programs appropriate for modal students as well as a means of addressing academic and social deficits that are remediable.

> **Corollary 7a:** Appropriate education for exceptional students will not necessarily result in their performance within the range deemed adequate, expected, or "normal" for nonexceptional students.

The expectation of a "cure" for educational disabilities—enabling all disabled students to function as if their disabilities no longer existed—is not realistic. If appropriate education is assumed to be only that which allows the student to achieve "normal" educational progress, then many exceptional students, their teachers, their parents, and the public face uninterrupted failure and censure.

> **Corollary 7b:** The informed, ethical behavior of practitioners is an important criterion for evaluating the appropriateness of special education and evaluating its practices.

The extent to which special education improves students' performance over what they would otherwise achieve is an important criterion for evaluating its practice, but it must not be the sole criterion. As is the case in other professions, the outcome of individual cases must be evaluated in the light of the best professional practices under the circumstances. The extent to which procedures designed to protect the interests of the involved parties were followed and the extent to which the behavior of professional practitioners was informed and ethical must be weighed in the balance.

Postulate 8: Special education may not be the only special compensatory program serving students who have difficulty in school, but it must be maintained as a branch of general education having special identity and articulation with other programs.

It is a truism that many students have difficulty in school. Nevertheless, we can safely assume that the effective education of all students will not eliminate variance in the desired performance outcomes of the student population. In fact, we venture that a uniform degree of improvement in the education offered every student would increase the population variance in such outcomes, which would make the educationally "disadvantaged" even more so. This is one of the reasons we believe compensatory education programs are necessary for students who perform poorly; such programs are a means of "leveling the playing field" somewhat in the interests of fairness and human compassion as well as the eventual economic benefits of the habilitation of those who are given special assistance.

All compensatory programs are by definition failure-driven; they are intended to compensate for conditions producing actual or predicted failure of individuals. Access to compensatory programs is knowingly granted only to individuals judged to be in jeopardy, and for good reason: Access by all squanders the resources intended for those "at risk" and, predictably, quickly bankrupts the program. When the risk factors that predict failure are complex, poorly understood, and pandemic, as they are in many schools, extraordinary care must be taken to protect the interests of specific groups through special allocations of compensatory resources. Attention to either prevention or remediation alone is insufficient; special resources must be allocated both to programs designed to avoid failure and to those designed to cope with the reality of failure.

Corollary 8a: An array of special programs with specific eligibility criteria for participation is an appropriate means of creating a comprehensive service delivery of general education.

Given the range of educational needs in most school systems, it is not reasonable to believe that one compensatory program will be sufficient to provide the comprehensive services necessary. Even those who argue passionately for restructuring to eliminate special program authority recognize the need for an array of special programs for selected students. One can imagine a school situation that has programs such as the following (Reynolds's list includes five more):

- The Braille Reading Program
- The Reading Recovery Program
- The Intensive Basic Skills Program
- The Social Skills Program
- The White Cane and Mobility Program (Reynolds, 1991, p. 35)

As we have seen, the issue of eligibility for special programs cannot be avoided. The criteria and procedures for determining individual students' eligibility for specific programs must be regulated explicitly. Otherwise, eligibility will be covertly determined, the reasons and processes for program selection being matters one cannot monitor effectively.

Corollary 8b: Efforts to marginalize or disable special education by obscuring its identity through its assimilation into general education must be resisted.

To flourish, a program of education must enjoy visibility, status, budget, and personnel—those things that give it borders and identity. Without these, the program inevitably becomes increasingly derelict in both intent and accomplishment. Goodlad describes the unhappy situation of teacher education:

> First, the farther down in a university's organizational structure teacher education finds itself, the less chance it has to obtain the conditions necessary to a healthy, dynamic existence. Second, the farther down in the hierarchy teacher education finds itself, the less likely it is that it will enjoy the tender loving care of those tenure-line faculty members universities strive so hard to recruit. Who, then, speaks for teacher education? Who speaks for those who would become teachers? (Goodlad, 1990, p. 277)

We might substitute *special education* for *teacher education* in this statement. Goodlad goes on to suggest the minimum essentials for making teacher education "[fit] comfortably into the context of a college or university":

1. A school or center of pedagogy with a sole commitment to teaching
2. "Its own budget, determined in negotiation at the highest level of budget approvals, and this budget must be immune to erosion by competing interests"

3. Authority and responsibility for student selection and personnel
4. A full complement of faculty
5. Control over specification of prerequisites for admission (Goodlad, 1990, p. 278)

We suggest that the same minimum essentials are necessary for special education to fit comfortably into the context of the public school. Those who encourage general education to assimilate special education fully or urge special education to merge with general education cannot be both aware of the realities of educational organizations and concerned for special education's viability.

CONCLUSION

The capacity of American public education to respond humanely and effectively to variance among students should be expanded, but this can be accomplished only by maintaining and strengthening the essential structures on which a comprehensive delivery system is based. Although general and special education are now distinctive parts of an integrated system, their interface needs more attention.

Many of the suggestions for restructuring or integrating special and general education, however, are based on notions that have a highly charming surface appeal but are the antitheses of a reflective, analytical approach to the problems of designing a comprehensive service delivery system of education to serve an extremely diverse student body. They suppose a world in which one never need take a hard look at realities, one in which inspirational rhetoric and the callousness of policymakers in the Reagan–Bush era to the plight of the socially, economically, and educationally disinherited will carry the day. We return to Goodlad's observations on the conditions of renewal in teacher education. He calls for substantially increased resources to conduct the enterprise.

And these resources must be made secure for the purposes intended. That is, they must be earmarked for and assigned to a unit with clear borders, a specified number of students with a common purpose, and a roster of largely full-time faculty requisite to the formal and informal socialization of these students into teaching. Put negatively, these resources must not go to the larger, multipurpose unit of which teacher education is a part; there they run the danger of being impounded by entrepreneurial program heads and faculty members. (Goodlad, 1990, p. 152)

The people responsible for teacher education, suggests Goodlad, must have clear focus, identity, and authority. His prediction of the alternative: "Otherwise, teacher education will remain an orphan, dependent on charity and goodwill" (Goodlad, 1990, p. 153). We believe that the same is true for special education if its mission is to be taken seriously. Special education once was what Goodlad describes as the inevitable consequence of lack of focus, identity, and authority—an orphan, dependent on charity and goodwill in a larger, multipurpose unit, its resources constantly in danger of impoundment by competing interests. The interests now competing most overtly for special education's resources are (1) concern for underachieving students who are at risk for greater failure and (2) pursuit of the higher performance of "all" students out of concern for America's economic competitiveness. These interests will, of course, seek to attach special education's resources by arguing that these assets must not be protected from infringement because their reallocation or redistribution can serve not only children with disabilities but the common good as well.

After a long period of struggle, special education has finally achieved the status of a normal part of public general education and been integrated into the fabric of our thinking about students' special needs. It has done so only by recognizing the realities of which Goodlad speaks, and it will remain such only if it is successful in fending off the entrepreneurial interests and irresponsible attacks that threaten its hard-won position.

AUTHORS' NOTE

Preparation of this manuscript was supported in part by the Commonwealth Center for the Education of Teachers, Curry School of Education, 405 Emmet Street, University of Virginia, Charlottesville, VA 22903. We are grateful to Doug Fuchs for his helpful comments on an earlier version of this chapter.

REFERENCES

Bank-Mikkelsen, N. E. (1969). A metropolitan area in Denmark: Copenhagen. In R. B. Kugel & W. Wolfensberger (Eds.), *Changing patterns of residential services for the mentally retarded* (pp. 227–254). Washington, DC: President's Committee on Mental Retardation.

Biklen, D., & Zollers, N. (1986). The focus of advocacy in the LD field. *Journal of Learning Disabilities, 19,* 583.

Blount, W. F., & Kean, T. H. (1991). *Designs for a new generation of American schools: A request for proposals.* Arlington, VA: New American Schools Development.

Bracey, G. W. (1991). Why can't they be like we were? *Phi Delta Kappan, 73,* 104–117.

Bryan, J. H., & Bryan, T. H. (1988). Where's the beef? A review of published research on the adaptive learning environment model. *Learning Disabilities Focus, 4*(1), 9–14.

Carnegie Forum on Education and the Economy. (1986). *A nation prepared: Teachers for the 21st century.* New York: Carnegie Foundation.

Carnine, D. (1991). Increasing the amount and quality of learning through direct instruction: Implications for mathematics. In J. W. Lloyd, N. N. Singh, & A. C. Repp (Eds.), *The regular education initiative: Alternative perspectives on concepts, issues, and models* (pp. 163–175). Sycamore, IL: Sycamore.

Carnine, D., & Kameenui, E. (1990). The regular education initiative and children with special needs: A false dilemma in the face of true problems. *Journal of Learning Disabilities, 23,* 141–144.

Carson, C. C., Huelskamp, R. M., & Woodall, T. D. (1991). *Perspectives on eduation in America: Annotated briefing–Third draft.* Albuquerque, NM: Systems Analysis Department, Sandia National Laboratories.

Education for All Handicapped Children Act of 1975, 20 U.S.C. § 1400 *et seq.*

Feniak, C. A. (1988). Labelling in special education: A problematic issue in England and Wales. *International Journal of Special Education, 3,* 117–124.

Fuchs, D., & Fuchs, L. S. (1988). An evaluation of the adaptive learning environments model. *Exceptional Children, 55,* 115–127.

Fuchs, D., & Fuchs, L. S. (1991). Framing the REI debate: Abolitionists versus conservationists. In J. W. Lloyd, N. N. Singh, & A. C. Repp (Eds.), *The regular education initiative: Alternative perspectives on concepts, issues, and models* (pp. 241–255). Sycamore, IL: Sycamore.

Gartner, A., & Lipsky, D. K. (1987). Beyond special education: Toward a quality system for all students. *Harvard Educational Review, 57,* 367–395.

Gartner, A., & Lipsky, D. K. (1989). *The yoke of special education: How to break it.* Rochester, NY: National Center on Education and the Economy.

Gerber, M. M., & Semmel, M. I. (1984). Teacher as imperfect test: Reconceptualizing the referral process. *Educational Psychologist, 19,* 137–148.

Goodlad, J. I. (1990). *Teachers for our nation's schools.* San Francisco: Jossey-Bass.

Hallahan, D. P., Kauffman, J. M., Lloyd, J. W., & McKinney, J. D. (Eds.). (1988). Questions about the regular education initiative [Special issue]. *Journal of Learning Disabilities, 21*(1).

Hauerwas, S. (1986). *Suffering presence: Theological reflections on medicine, the mentally handicapped, and the church.* Notre Dame, IN: University of Notre Dame Press.

Hendrick, I. G., & MacMillan, D. L. (1989). Selecting children for special education in New York City: William Maxwell, Elizabeth Farrell, and development of upgraded classes, 1900–1920. *Journal of Special Education, 22*, 395–417.

Hocutt, A. M., Martin, E. W., & McKinney, J. D. (1991). Historical and legal context of mainstreaming. In J. W. Lloyd, N. N. Singh, & A. C. Repp (Eds.), *The regular education initiative* (p. 24). Sycamore, IL: Sycamore.

Individuals with Disabilities Education Act of 1990, 20 U.S.C. § 1400 *et seq.*

Kauffman, J. M. (1989). The regular education initiative as Reagan–Bush education policy: A trickle-down theory of education of the hard-to-teach. *Journal of Special Education, 23*, 256–278.

Kauffman, J. M. (1990, April). *What happens when special education works? The sociopolitical context of special education research in the 1990s.* Invited address to the Special Interest Group: Special Education Research at the Annual Meeting of the American Educational Research Association, Boston.

Kauffman, J. M. (1991). Restructuring in sociopolitical context: Reservations about the effects of current reform proposals on students with disabilities. In J. W. Lloyd, N. N. Singh, & A. C. Repp (Eds.), *The regular education initiative: Alternative perspectives on concepts, issues, and models* (pp. 57–66). Sycamore, IL: Sycamore.

Kauffman, J. M., & Hallahan, D. P. (1990). What we want for children: A rejoinder to RET proponents. *Journal of Special Education, 24*, 340–345.

Kauffman, J. M., & Pullen, P. L. (1989). An historical perspective: A personal perspective on our history of service to mildly handicapped and at-risk students. *Remedial and Special Education, 10*(6), 12–14.

Kauffman, J. M., & Trent, S. C. (1991). Issues in service delivery for students with learning disabilities. In B. Y. L. Wong (Ed.), *Learning about learning disabilities* (pp. 465–481). New York: Academic Press.

Keogh, B. K. (1988). Improving services for problem learners: Rethinking and restructuring. *Journal of Learning Disabilities, 21*, 20.

Lipsky, D. K., & Gartner, A. (1987). Capable of achievement and worthy of respect: Education for handicapped students as if they were full-fledged human beings. *Exceptional Children, 54*, 69–74.

Lipsky, D. K., & Gartner, A. (1991). Restructuring for quality. In J. W. Lloyd, N. N. Singh, & A. C. Repp (Eds.), *The regular education initiative: Alternative perspectives on concepts, issues, and models* (pp. 43–57). Sycamore, IL: Sycamore.

Lloyd, J. W., Singh, N. N., & Repp, A. C. (Eds.). (1991). *The regular education initiative: Alternate perspectives on concepts, issues, and models.* Sycamore, IL: Sycamore.

MacMillan, D. L., & Hendrick, I. G. (1993). Evolution and legacies. In J. I. Goodlad & T. C. Lovitt (Eds.), *Integrating general and special education* (pp. 23–48). Columbus, OH: Merrill/Macmillan.

McCarthy, M. M. (1991). Severely disabled children: Who pays? *Phi Delta Kappan, 73*(1), 66–71.

Minow, M. (1987). Learning to live with the dilemma of difference: Bilingual and special eduation. In K. T. Bartlett & J. W. Wenger (Eds.), *Children with special needs* (pp. 375–429). New Brunswick, NJ: Transaction Books.

Mulick, J. A., & Kedesdy, J. H. (1988). Self-injurious behavior, its treatment, and normalization. *Mental Retardation, 26*(4), 223–229.

National Center on Education and the Economy (NCEE). (1989). *To secure our future.* Rochester, NY: National Center on Education and the Economy.

Nirje, B. (1969). The normalization principle and its human management implications. In R. Krugel & W. Wolfensberger (Eds.), *Changing patterns in residential services for the mentally retarded* (pp. 179–195). Washington, DC: President's Committee on Mental Retardation.

Reynolds, M. C. (1989). An historical perspective: The delivery of special education to mildly disabled and at-risk students. *Remedial and Special Education, 10*(6), 7–11.

Reynolds, M. C. (1991). Classification and labeling. In J. W. Lloyd, N. N. Singh, & A. C. Repp (Eds.), *The regular education initiative: Alternative perspectives on concepts, issues, and models* (pp. 29–41). Sycamore, IL: Sycamore.

Reynolds, M. C., Wang, M. C., & Walberg, H. J. (1987). The necessary restructuring of special and regular education. *Exceptional Children, 53*, 391–398.

Semmel, M. I., & Gerber, M. M. (1990). If at first you don't succeed, bye, bye again: A response to general educators' views on the RET. *Remedial and Special Education, 11*(4), 53–59.

Singer, J. D. (1988). Should special education merge with regular education? *Educational Policy, 2*, 416.

Slavin, R. E. (1990a). General education under the regular education initiative: How must it change? *Remedial and Special Education, 11*(3), 40–50.

Slavin, R. E. (1990b). On success for all: Defining "success," defining "all." *Remedial and Special Education, 11*(4), 60–61.

Slavin, R. E., Madden, N. A., Karweit, N. L., Dolan, L., Wasik, B. A., Shaw, A., et al. (1991). Neverstreaming: Prevention and early intervention as an alternative to special education. *Journal of Learning Disabilities, 24*, 373–378.

Stainback, W., & Stainback, S. (1991). A rationale for integration and restructuring: A synopsis. In J. W. Lloyd, N. N. Singh, & A. C. Repp (Eds.), *The regular education initiative: Alternative perspectives on concepts, issues, and models* (pp. 225–239). Sycamore, IL: Sycamore.

Timothy W. v. Rochester, New Hampshire School District, 875 F.2d 954 (1st Cir. 1989), cert. denied, 110 5. Ct. 519 (1989).

Wang, M. C., Reynolds, M. C., & Walberg, H. J. (1986). Rethinking special education. *Educational Leadership, 44*(1), 26–31.

Wang, M. C., Reynolds, M. C., & Walberg, H. J. (1988). Integrating the children of the second system. *Phi Delta Kappan, 70*, 248–251.

Wang, M. C., & Zollers, N. J. (1990). Adaptive instruction: An alternative service delivery approach. *Remedial and Special Education, 11*(1), 7–21.

White, W. A. T. (1988). A meta-analysis of the effects of direct instruction in special education. *Education and Treatment of Children, 11*(4), 364–374.

Will, M. C. (1984). Let us pause and reflect—But not too long. *Exceptional Children, 51,* 11–16.

Wolfensberger, W. (1972). *Normalization.* Toronto, Canada: National Institute on Mental Retardation.

Wolfensberger, W. (1980). The definition of normalization: Update, problems, disagreements, and misunderstandings. In R. J. Flynn & K. E. Nitsch (Eds.), *Normalization, social integration, and community services* (pp. 71–115). Baltimore: University Park Press.

CHAPTER 10

A Diversity of Restrictive Environments: Placement as a Problem of Social Ecology

James M. Kauffman and Daniel P. Hallahan

This chapter is from "A Diversity of Restrictive Environments: Placement as a Problem of Social Ecology," by J. M. Kauffman and D. P. Hallahan, 1997, in *Issues in Educating Students with Disabilities* (pp. 325–342), by J. W. Lloyd, E. J. Kameenui, and D. Chard (Eds.), Mahwah, NJ: Erlbaum. Copyright 1997 by Erlbaum. Reprinted with permission. Portions of this chapter were published in "Why We Must Celebrate a Diversity of Restrictive Environments, by J. M. Kauffman, 1995, *Learning Disabilities Research and Practice, 10,* pp. 225–232.

The overriding policy issue in special education in the 1990s has been the assignment of students to a place of schooling. Many special education reformers have centered attention on the least restrictive environment (LRE) provisions of the Individuals with Disabilities Education Act (IDEA), suggesting that the inclusion of all students with disabilities in general education classes in their neighborhood schools—and only such inclusion—will fulfill the letter and spirit of the law (e.g., Gartner & Lipsky, 1989; Laski, 1991; Lipsky & Gartner, 1991; Stainback & Stainback, 1991). Policymakers' enthusiasm for inclusion rhetoric and the assumption that the general education classroom in the neighborhood school is, in fact, least restrictive for all students has resulted in rapid erosion of placement options for students with disabilities, especially those identified in the categories of learning disabilities, emotional and behavioral disorders, and mild mental retardation. Many communities have seen the not-so-gradual disappearance of special self-contained classes, and in some schools pull-out programs of any kind have virtually disappeared.

The rapid policy shift from commitment to a full continuum of placement options, which in fact is mandated by IDEA, toward a severe limitation of options has occurred in the absence of adequate consideration of the logical or empirical bases for grouping students for schooling. Our purpose is to extend the discussion we have begun elsewhere (e.g., Hallahan & Kauffman, 1994; Kauffman, 1988, 1989, 1991, 1993, 1994; Kauffman & Hallahan, 1993; Kauffman & Lloyd, 1995) by considering the meaning of LRE in ecological perspective.

As we have pointed out elsewhere, *place*—that is, physical location, not to mention rank or status—is a highly emotionally charged issue (Kauffman & Lloyd, 1995). In fact, place is so highly emotionally charged that it tends to breed fanatics—zealots willing to sacrifice everything else for the sake of a place. Fanatics of nearly every stripe elevate some aspect of place to the supreme value, which they then use to justify illogical and morally indefensible behavior. The tribal, ethnic, religious, and national warfare of the 20th century demonstrates how reverence for holy places can produce rage and violence. Temples and other holy places, motherlands, fatherlands, and promised lands have been the excuses for the coercive tactics of terror, torture, degradation, slaughter, and vandalism used by religious, nationalistic, and political zealots. These observations led Kauffman (1992) to articulate the hope that in the 21st century "we will understand that special education has no holy place and no promised land" (p. 344).

Our concern is that the inclusion movement is leading to designation of the general education classroom in the neighborhood school as the "promised land" or a "holy place" for students with disabilities. The implication is that special education is in danger of being radicalized into a group who will justify whatever tactics are necessary to claim that promised land for students with disabilities. The claim that all students should be promised placement in general education classes is based on the assumption that the general education classroom is least restrictive for all, which is a serious misunderstanding of LRE.

MISUNDERSTANDING OF LRE AND THE MEANING OF ENVIRONMENT

A basic assumption of proponents of full inclusion is, apparently, that any placement other than the general education classroom is inherently more restrictive and, therefore, less desirable. This assumption reflects a common misunderstanding about environments in general and the general education classroom environment in particular—that an environment can be either least restrictive for all or totally nonrestrictive.

Every environment is inherently restrictive. "Nonrestrictive environment" is an oxymoron, like "universal excellence" or "an elite education for everyone." The concept of environment implies surroundings—both physical and social—that impinge on our behavior. Surroundings by definition constrain what we can and may do. That is, physical and social contexts alter the probability that we can and may do certain things. The significance of an environment is not that it is restrictive in a general sense but that it is restrictive of specific things. As Cruickshank (1977) suggested, a given environment can be less restrictive of social interaction but more restrictive of learning than another; talk of environmental restrictiveness is therefore essentially meaningless unless we ask, "Restrictive of what?"

To make an environment least restrictive of some things—academic learning or socialization, for example—other things may need to be made more restrictive, such as the tasks presented, the responses demanded, the consequences provided, and so on. In fact, the restrictions placed on antecedents, behaviors, and consequences are the very stuff of education. What IDEA envisions is the least restriction of the educational environment *that will produce the desired educational outcomes for individual students.* Restrictions are necessary to produce outcomes, and the same restrictions will not produce the same outcomes for all students. Furthermore, *a single environment cannot contain all manner of restriction, for no environment is infinitely flexible.*

A common assumption of the proponents of full inclusion is that the LRE concept embodied in Public Law 94-142 (now called IDEA) requires that students be placed in the schools and classes they would attend if they were not identified as having disabilities. This assumption probably is the basis for the argument by some that the LRE for all students is, in fact, the general education classroom in the neighborhood school. However, the assumption that there exists a universally least restrictive place is at odds with both the law and the best available scientific evidence (see Bateman, 1994; Bateman & Chard, 1995; Huefner, 1994, for commentary on legal issues).

The framers of IDEA made no assumption that the general education classroom in the neighborhood school would be least restrictive for all students. Clearly, they thought that a cascade of placement options ranging from general education classrooms and resource rooms through special self-contained classes to residential or hospital care would be necessary to achieve the appropriate education of all children and that each of these placements would be least restrictive for some but not for others (Hocutt, Martin, & McKinney, 1991). The law is consistent with the principles of ecological psychology that had emerged a decade before Public Law 94-142 was enacted in 1975.

IMPLICATIONS OF ECOLOGICAL CONCEPTS FOR SPECIAL EDUCATION PLACEMENT

The restrictiveness of environments requires consideration of human ecologies. Ecological principles have important implications for human services, including special education. They are especially critical in constructing the social ecologies in which particular academic and social goals for individual students can be reached. Human and nonhuman social ecologies are in many ways governed by the same principles, but it is important to note some differences between them.

In natural biological ecologies, things are in balance. Various species, varieties, groups, and individuals may support each other's survival, often by one species, group, or individual preying on another to sustain itself and keep another in check. We accept the natural order as good, although it may involve the violent aggression of one species, variety, group, or individual against another. We do not try to turn raptors into eaters of cereal or even carrion. Only a real kook, like the demented Dr. John Harvey Kellogg of Boyle's (1993) novel *The Road to Wellville,* would claim to have trained—or even try to train—a wolf to be vegetarian.

In subhuman social ecologies, the concept of a "natural" order also applies. Dominance, pecking order, flocking, schooling, and congregation into a closed group or segregation of individuals from the group are typically merely observed by scientists, not manipulated. Scientists often worry that the manipulation of subhuman social ecologies might upset the ecological balance. Another important aspect of subhuman ecologies is that the individual is not typically essential to ecological balance or to what is considered acceptable. There are sacrificial lambs. We do not want to prevent the fox from eating the mouse or those species that do so from eating their young, nor do we intervene to prevent the harsh domination of one primate by another in its natural environment. The individual's life is expendable, and the individual's social standing in the group is accepted, whether the individual is a despot or an outcast. The group, the species, is the center of concern.

In contrast, in human social ecologies the concept of "natural" is ambiguous. We do not admire the feral child. We describe uncontrolled human social ecologies as having devolved to the law of the jungle, to predatory behavior. We see the manipulation of individuals and groups as not only acceptable but desirable or essential. Acceptable human social ecologies are constructed deliberately, and we are constantly seeking to refine them, to make them more caring, more supportive of prosocial behavior. In human social ecologies, especially in Western cultures, the focus of concern is at least as much on the individual as on the group; the individual is seldom deemed to be expendable.

Perhaps Mark Twain was right in his assessment that we humans are morally inferior to the so-called "lower" animals. He observed that, "To create man was a quaint and original idea, but to add the sheep was tautology" (Library of America, 1976, p. 946). Mark Twain's unsettling wit notwithstanding, we must proceed as if we are superior to subhumans in intelligence and in our ability to construct deliberately a social habitat that supports the kind of behavior we want to flourish and to suppress the kind of behavior we consider destructive. However, we ignore the basic principles that govern all species only at our own risk. We are part of a social ecosystem as surely as the sheep or the baboon. The behavior of individual human beings is interconnected, and the basic principles of ecological systems apply in large measure to human social intercourse and the structure of human social groups.

Since the early work of ecological psychologists (e.g., Barker, 1968; Hobbs, 1966), we have understood that the behavior of individuals shapes and is shaped by the environment—by those physical and social restrictions that are the stuff of an environment. More recently, Gallagher (1993) has said:

> The same environmental unit provides different inputs to different persons, and different inputs to the same person if his behavior changes....
> The whole program of the environment's inputs changes if its own ecological properties change; if it becomes more or less populous, for example. (p. 205)

Taking an ecological perspective, whether in biology or psychology or special education, requires consideration of the totality or pattern of relationships between individuals and their environments. Educators and social scientists with an ecological bent are interested in the development and structure of human communities and the ways in which the presence of individuals with certain behavioral characteristics alters the pattern, rhythm, or course of social interactions or relationships.

Interest in applying ecological concepts to the study of special education dates back at least to the 1960s (e.g., Hobbs, 1966; Rhodes, 1967). Contemporary psychological and behavioral research includes relatively sophisticated ecobehavioral analyses of the problems of maintaining and teaching individuals with disabilities in specific social environments (e.g., Kamps, Leonard, Dugan, Boland, & Greenwood, 1991; McWilliam & Bailey, 1995). The work of Farmer and his colleagues applies developmental and ecological concepts to the study of social networks in general education and special classes (e.g., Farmer, 1994; Farmer & Farmer, 1996; Farmer & Hollowell, 1994; Farmer, Pearl, & Van Acker, 1995; Farmer, Stuart, Lorch, & Fields, 1993).

Two terms important for understanding sociobehavioral ecologies are *niche* and *ecodeme.* Niche refers to a site or habitat supplying the support necessary for an individual or group to survive. It also refers to the role of an individual or group in an interdependent community, especially its way of life in a community and the effects of its behavior on the environment. Thus, an ecological niche involves both location and interaction. An ecodeme is a population occupying a particular ecological niche. In sociobehavioral ecology, the ecodeme is comprised of the group occupying the location and forming the community and structure into which an individual might be introduced or from which an individual might be ejected.

The concept of ecological niche has very important implications for special education placements. It is important to remember, for example, that certain ecological niches are notoriously hospitable to some species, varieties, and individuals and equally notoriously inhospitable to others. An ecosystem may be thrown out of balance or destroyed by the introduction of certain individuals or groups, and individuals or groups that find a particularly hospitable niche may, if uncontrolled by others, destroy the very ecosystem that initially sustained them. Our own uncontrolled behavior as a species, for example, threatens to destroy our entire ecosphere. All experienced teachers understand how a given individual can undermine and quickly destroy the social structure of a class.

Natural scientists who are concerned with ecologies study the limits of the adaptability of various species, varieties, and individuals to various habitats and the effects of niches on survival. However, social and behavioral scientists, including educators, are interested in more than survival; they study also how the quality of human life of an individual or group is altered by someone's occupying a given niche and how humans create and maintain ecodemes and niches for themselves and others.

CREATION OF EDUCATIONAL ECOLOGIES

Social ecologies are constructed and maintained in large measure through two processes: by the congregation and segregation of individuals. Congregation and segregation are not peculiar to humans; they are pervasive biological processes. Subhuman species congregate into groups, separate individuals from groups, and segregate themselves from other groups in the interests of survival. These processes of congregation and segregation are part of the natural order. However, human beings have the capacity and the moral duty to construct a social order that does more than protect the species. We must construct a social order that also serves humanely the interests of the individual. Nevertheless, we cannot avoid congregation and segregation, because these are basic processes in any social ecology. The conceptual bases and strategies for clustering individuals in certain locations—the rationales for and the construction of ecodemes and niches through congregation and segregation—are the turning points for controversies about placement.

For example, it is important to recognize that on the one hand the legal racial segregation of American society has been rightly condemned as a great evil and that de facto segregation resulting in lowered opportunities is often and rightly decried. On the other hand, the segregation of dangerous criminals from the general society for most or all of their lives and the segregation of people with specific medical needs in hospitals are practices that most would agree are not only just but necessary to the preservation of a humane social fabric.

Likewise, congregation, depending on the purposes and circumstances, may be judged either an evil or a good. On the one hand, we condemn the congregation of people for evil purposes, such as lynching or performing violent acts in a gang. On the other hand, we condone or extol the virtues of congregating people in many other ways for mutual support, comfort, and special purpose. We approve of families, family reunions, and social, civic, recreational, and political clubs of great variety—some even though they are congregations determined primarily by race or ethnicity or gender. The congregation of African Americans in churches, colleges, and other social or political organizations is often defended as not only legal but ethical, advantageous, and worthy of preservation. Our point is that we must understand the words *congregation* and *segregation* in their broader meanings as we examine placement issues and not make the assumption that segregation and congregation for educational purposes are equivalent (Hallahan & Kauffman, 1994; Kauffman & Hallahan, 1993; Kauffman & Lloyd, 1995; Semmel, Gerber, & MacMillan, 1994).

The ideals of a democratic society include the freedoms of movement and association. Consequently, we view the assignment of someone to a special ecodeme or niche with great caution, if not suspicion, fearing that the assignment may be coerced or result in restricted opportunities. The contemporary ideals of American society also include tolerance if not deliberate maintenance of a rich social and behavioral diversity. Consequently, we view the removal of an individual from an established ecodeme or niche with great wariness, if not misgiving, fearing that removal may limit awareness and tolerance of those who are different. The primary focus of intervention in some human social ecologies, such as schools and classrooms, is therefore on altering the behavior of individuals within a given location—that is, the focus is on refurbishing the existing social habitat in some way to modify the individual's niche. We are hesitant to move a child to a new location, place him or her with a different ecodeme, and require the child to find a new niche in that group.

A common suggestion, for example, is that special services be brought to students in the habitat of their general education classroom and school; that is, that students should not be brought to services offered at another place. Another is that we should try to develop friendships in an existing group rather than move a child to a new group where other friendships might be developed. The inclusionary bias is to foster academic learning and desirable social networks for children with disabilities among an ecodeme comprised of nondisabled peers in a general education class of the neighborhood school rather than to offer academic instruction and introduce children with disabilities to social networks in special classes or special schools in which their peers have similar disabilities.

An inclusionary bias may be proper and ethical, as long as it does not lead to ignoring important realities. Unfortunately, the ideology of full inclusion ignores or distorts the literature on social ecologies, and in so doing ignores or distorts the realities our students and teachers must face daily. It ignores or distorts the responsibilities we have to construct the most habilitatively restrictive environments we can for our students. The study of human social ecologies, including the social ecologies of schools and classrooms, may lead to the recognition of several realities that will temper but not lead to the abandonment of a bias toward refurbishing the ecodemes and niches of students with disabilities and highlight the value of moving *some* students to different ones. An ecological approach to placement issues requires the recognition of the complexity, variety, and purposes of social systems.

Complexity

Full inclusion ideology seems to imply that the congregation of students in neighborhood schools for general education purposes is sacrosanct, that this congregation has superior moral status for all students, and that this ecodeme is the one to which all students should belong regardless of their characteristics or preferences. The assumption is that being educated alongside their general education classroom peers is the only acceptable solution to the challenge of meeting the special needs of students for academic instruction and socialization, that constant proximity to normal peers in regular classrooms is necessary to foster learning and appropriate social relationships. However, this simplistic view is inconsistent with the science of social systems. It denies the complexity of social relationships. Consider, for example, Dunbar's (1988) comments on the social systems of primates. Dunbar pointed out that a problem with the traditional conception of societies is that sociality or social interaction has been seen as synonymous with living in a group:

> But this is a very simplistic conception of what is involved in social existence, at least in mammals as advanced as primates. In these species, groups exist through time not because animals are arbitrarily forced to associate, as, for example, dungflies do on a cow dropping, but because of the relationships that they have with each other. Those relationships exist independently of whether or not the animals actually live in physical proximity in the same group. Just because animals live semi-solitary lives, it does not follow that their relationships with each other are not as complex as those in species that live in formal groups. (p. 11)

Full inclusionists make much of the notion of the neighborhood school. They insist, for example, that students with disabilities be educated in the same schools as those of their peers, and in making this argument they frequently refer to these schools as "neighborhood schools." We have to wonder if they are not holding to a rather outdated notion of neighborhood schools. Forty or 50 years ago, schools tended to be either rural or urban, and the latter often were, indeed, neighborhood schools in the sense that virtually everyone knew everyone else and every child lived within walking distance of the school. The suburbanization of the United States, however, has resulted in a large percentage of the school-age population living relatively great distances from each other and from the schools they attend. The idea of a neighborhood school, in the traditional sense, has disappeared for many students. With this disappearance, the supposed advantages of having students with disabilities attend the same schools as students from their neighborhoods has greatly diminished.

The point here is not that grouping students is unimportant, but that physical proximity is neither necessary nor sufficient to ensure social relationships, either in subhumans or in human beings. Socialization is far more complex a phenomenon than much of the rhetoric about full inclusion suggests (see Schroeder, 1990). For example, recent work with young children with and without disabilities in various social groupings (McWilliam & Bailey, 1995) "challenges us to understand the complexity of various environmental influences—particularly, the social dimensions of environments" (Wolery, 1995, pp. vii–viii). Research by Schroeder et al.

(1982) showed that the presence or absence of a single newcomer or disruptive individual dramatically changed the rates of many behaviors, both adaptive and maladaptive, of other individuals in group settings. Commenting on these findings, Mulick and Meinhold (1994) noted:

> It was as if the entire habitual set of social and individual interactions in the setting had been thrown out of balance by such intrusions. This is what we mean by a social ecology. Literally, changes in one part of such complex social environments produce dramatic changes in other parts of the social environments. The reality of these potential effects is the context in which teaching and treatment procedures. as well as new social relationships, are imposed on people with handicaps by planners and programmers. (p. 119)

The suggestion that environments judged "normal" will facilitate the emergence of "normal" behavior of all individuals is contradicted by the fact that aberrant behavior often develops and is sustained in normal environments. Furthermore, we know that nonnormal environments are sometimes required to produce normal behavior. Contrary to ideological reasoning about normalization, normal environments are not equally habilitative for everyone, and a single environment cannot be engineered to include all of the features necessary to produce desirable outcomes for every individual. Every environment imposes limitations on what is possible and what is feasible. Mulick and Meinhold (1994) concluded that:

> Normal-appearing environments by themselves, even environments characterized by social advantage, do not assure normal behavioral outcomes. Handicaps sometimes require extraordinary environmental modifications, including modifications of quite normal rules for social conduct. We do not suggest that segregation and devaluation of people with handicaps is indicated by a scientific analysis, just that rules derived from an abstract and idealized sociopolitical analysis may not be useful in developing effective individualized treatment approaches.... Normal environments make some things easier and some things remarkably harder. (p. 121)

The way children learn through observation and social interaction is often grossly oversimplified. A very common part of the rationale for full inclusion is that placement of students with disabilities in the general education classroom in their neighborhood schools is important because that is where they will see appropriate peer models. This rationale is suspect to those who work in the area of emotional and behavioral disorders, not only because it is simplistic but, in the words of John Irving's (1989) character Owen Meany, "Made for television" in its obfuscation of reality. As Rhode, Jenson, and Reavis (1992) have stated about the students they call "Tough Kids":

> By definition, Tough Kids exhibit significant social skills deficiencies when they are compared with their successful peers. There are those who propose that students with severe behavior problems need only spend time with their normal peers to learn the desired skills. However, Tough Kids are poorly accepted by their "normal" peers, resulting in minimal interaction between them even when they do spend time together. When interaction does occur, it is often negative. It becomes clear that if all that was needed was to expose Tough Kids to their normal peers in order for them to acquire appropriate social skills, they would have acquired acceptable social skills already. (p. 95)

The simplistic notion that appropriate peer models is the key to behavioral improvement is suspect for several reasons. First, if children tend always to imitate appropriate peer models, then one might expect the behavior of children in general education classes—where, presumably, the appropriate peer models exist—to become progressively more tractable. If appropriate peer models are indeed a more powerful influence than are the contingencies arranged by teachers, then a much higher proportion of students in general education classes than now do should be expected to imitate the appropriate behavior of their peers and thus avoid ever being identified as having emotional or behavioral disorders. Furthermore, those students who exhibit disruptive behavior might be just as likely, or perhaps even more so, to imitate other disruptive students in regular classrooms (Patterson, Reid, & Dishion, 1992). Finally, it may be possible for students to find appropriate and effective peer models in special classes (Farmer et al., 1993).

The truth is that socialization through modeling and imitation is far more complex than the proponents of full inclusion have let on (Gresham, 1982). As Hallenbeck and Kauffman (1995) pointed out in a review of research on observational learning, if regular classroom teachers are to make effective use of appropriate peer models, then they have a very substantial job cut out for them. They must find ways to (a) provide explicit models, including explicit instructions to imitate certain behaviors, plus guided practice in exhibiting those behaviors; (b) monitor the extent to which desirable imitation occurs; (c) provide direct and frequent reinforcement for imitation of desired behaviors; (d) make the models salient to the observers by increasing the observers' perceptions of similarity to the models; (e) decrease the likelihood that students with emotional or behavioral disorders will respond to seeing others obtain reinforcement as if they (observers) were being punished; and (f) create regular class conditions in which students with emotional or behavioral disorders do not experience frequent academic or social frustration.

Variety

Animal societies, including human societies, include many different groupings constructed for different purposes at different times. Dunbar (1988) described how a population of primates might group itself into coalitions, units, teams, bands, and communities. All levels of grouping serve specific functions in the community, and individuals may sort themselves or be sorted by the social system into different groups at different times (see also Chance & Jolly, 1970). In primate societies, for example, groups may be formed to protect against predators, to defend resources, to increase efficiency in foraging, or to improve caregiving. Humans form groups for the purposes of teaching and learning new skills, transporting or marketing goods and services, observing religious rites, engaging in athletics, celebrating kinship, providing the national defense, providing health care, creating the legal rules for the society, advocating legal rights, and so on. In fact, our daily lives can be characterized by movement from one social group to another for varying periods of time and for various purposes. We are constantly being pulled out of, being pushed into, and selecting ourselves in or out of groups—and most of these groups are not formed on the basis of prior physical proximity.

One line of argument is that students should not be pulled out of general education classrooms because it does not prepare them for life after school. As we have heard suggested more than once, "We don't live in a pull-out world." Nevertheless, the everyday social world of most adults includes a lot of pull-out groups, most of which are considered functional, ethical, and self-enhancing or self-protective. People are pulled out of a group and put in another or they move themselves out of one group and into another for training, work, moral support, recreation, and self-protection, and most individuals do not define themselves or their existence simply by reference to a single group with which they affiliate. One could make the case that preparing students to live in the adult world requires that they be taught to adopt a variety of group affiliations and be prepared to move and be moved from one to another.

Purpose

Analysis of placement decisions demands that we ask why we form groups for purposes of education: Just what are we trying to accomplish? How do we define place for educational purposes? What constraints or restrictions does the place of instruction put on how we accomplish our goals? Ultimately, we must ask what kind of social ecology is best for accomplishing each of our purposes.

Special education should be designed to accomplish two things, both of which are necessary and neither of which is alone sufficient to claim success: first, to offer effective instruction in the academic and social skills students should acquire; second, to foster social networks that induce and sustain desirable social behavior and that lead to satisfying relationships. Educational placement is defined by more than the physical space students occupy. It also involves the methods, materials, and equipment used in instruction, the particular students being taught, the teacher or teachers who provide instruction, and the tasks students are asked to perform. Clearly, the number and characteristics of the students present, the training and expertise of the teacher, and the instructional methods are constraints on the effects any placement might have. These dimensions of an educational environment are restrictive. The difficult task is designing an environment that is restrictive in the most helpful way for individual students.

Students with disabilities present an extremely varied set of instructional problems. The question for advocates of full inclusion is: Are these needs met most effectively for all students in the context of a general education classroom? We think it strains credulity to believe so. More important, the best available evidence to date suggests that a substantial proportion of students with disabilities are very poorly served in general education classrooms, even when strenuous and sustained efforts are made to accommodate their special needs (e.g., Zigmond et al., 1995). Moreover, the best available research belies the claim that the most effective instruction is provided in heterogeneous groups (Grossen, 1993). Students sometimes make greater academic progress in pull-out settings than in regular classes (e.g., Marston, 1987–1988). The fact that they *sometimes* make greater gains in separate settings is an important qualifier. As we have argued elsewhere (Hallahan & Kauffman, 1994), in comparing students' progress under fully inclusive versus separate settings, if researchers were to find significant differences favoring the former, this should not be used to justify the elimination of separate settings unless *all* students progressed better under the inclusive setting. When comparing two groups of students, those in inclusive settings and those in separate settings:

> There is almost always some overlap of the distributions…. Because of the mandate to provide the most appropriate education to *each* student with a disability, it would be unethical to eliminate special classes unless research consistently demonstrated that general education classes were superior to special classes and there was virtually no overlap between the distributions on the dependent variables. (Hallahan & Kauffman, 1994, p. 502)

Some might object that using such a stringent criterion in deciding what placement options to make available loads the deck in favor of having a wide assortment of placements available. To this, we readily admit and point out that this is precisely why the framers of IDEA were so wise in insisting on a variety of placement alternatives. Furthermore, special classes and special schools are places in which students with serious behavior problems can be taught self-evaluation, self-control, and other important social skills (e.g., Cosden, Gannon, & Haring, 1995; Kern et al., 1995). In short, the best evidence we have indicates that differently restrictive instructional environments are necessary to provide the best learning outcomes for all students.

The constraints of placement on socialization need to be examined more closely. We want students to learn important social skills and to develop social networks that enhance and sustain their social behavior. The outcomes we want depend on instruction in social skills, opportunities to practice under controlled conditions and obtain feedback on their performance, and the presence of a peer group containing members with whom they are likely to develop a desirable social network. For many students, placement in the general education classroom does or can provide the ecology we want, at least with careful management by the teacher. For some students, however, it is highly questionable whether the general education classroom can meet the requirements of desirable ecodeme and niche. As Farmer and his colleagues have found, students tend to form social networks based on homophily—on the basis of similarity of salient characteristics (Farmer & Farmer, 1996). For example, students gravitate socially to others who share their shyness, their prosocial behavior, or their antisocial behavior.

The niche a student fills in a classroom depends in large measure on the peer group available and the social networks already formed in the class. More important, habilitative social networks may be found in special classes or residential schools, and undesirable social networks can be developed in general education classes. We need much more knowledge of how students who exhibit problem behavior negotiate social ecologies of various types, and we need to know more about how to help students construct social networks that are most supportive of prosocial behavior. In all likelihood, increasing support will be found for well-implemented special classes and schools as ecologies that are most beneficial for some students during some phases of their development.

The preponderance of the evidence supports the conclusion that human responses to any given environment are extremely varied. People are diverse in their perceptions of how hospitable an environment is, in their ability to learn specific skills under specific environmental conditions, and in the friendship networks that support prosocial behavior in a given environment. True, we may be able to write a general prescription for the environment in which many or even most individuals will find a niche that we consider desirable. However, if we wish to construct a general social system that is hospitable to all, it must include a variety of places—a variety of environments with restrictions calculated to address the varied characteristics of individuals in the population.

Finally, we note the potential value of recognizing the culture of disability. Some groups of persons who receive special education services view themselves as cultural groups. Those who are blind and especially those who are deaf make it a point to emphasize the cultural aspects of their conditions. Many people who are deaf, for example, have their own set of cultural norms and behaviors (Padden & Humphries, 1988). Rather than seeing separate settings as evil, those who are blind or deaf often advocate for separate settings. They see congregating with other deaf or blind people as important for maintaining their culture. They emphasize their differences from the larger, nondisabled society and seek to maintain their identities as blind or deaf. A large part of their reasoning is that, by congregating, younger deaf or blind children can learn the ways of the culture from their elders and each other.

Elsewhere, we have speculated that there might be value in other populations of people with disabilities, such as those with learning disabilities, considering themselves as part of a culture (Hallahan & Kauffman, 1994). For example, adults with learning disabilities who are not hesitant to refer to themselves as learning disabled, who see their learning disability as a part of their identity, are more likely to be successful than those who tend to deny their disability (Gerber, Ginsberg, & Rieff, 1992; Spekman, Goldberg, & Herman, 1992).

Full inclusionists have argued that separate settings are detrimental to students with disabilities because they learn inappropriate behaviors from others who have the same disabilities. Ironically, it may be that students with disabilities may actually have the potential to be positive role models for other students with the same or similar disabilities:

> Perhaps association with others who have similar problems could be used to transmit the culture of what it is like to be learning disabled, mentally retarded, and so forth. This would require a shift, however, in how disability and disability labeling is viewed In our view, we should weigh the possibility and probability of reducing stigma and increasing learning by banning labeling and grouping by disability against the feasibility and likelihood of reducing stigma and increasing learning by developing esprit de corps among congregations of people with disabilities. (Hallahan & Kauffman, 1994, p. 505)

For decades, we special educators have found coherence, unity, and mutual support in the notion that we should celebrate the diversity of the characteristics of children and youth. We have been, to be sure, congregated and united by our dedication to the task of changing for the better the characteristics of our students who have disabilities. However, we are in no way disparaging of the students whose characteristics we hope to change. We value these young people in all their diversity for who they are and hope that our profession will soon stop disparaging special placements and see renewed value in retaining a diversity of alternatives.

For a variety of reasons, our profession has been seriously divided, and therefore weakened, by the ideology of full inclusion. The doctrine of full inclusion defines diversity of placement as morally suspect, if not the Great Satan of special education. It seeks the elimination of placement options under the assumption that only one environment can be least restrictive, that the general education classroom is the promised land of all children. Special educators should reject the notion of a special education promised land and become united around another celebration—the celebration of the diversity of restrictive environments that are necessary to meet the needs of students with a wide variety of exceptionalities.

At present, we special educators are having trouble knowing just where we fit in the scheme of public education. Perhaps we will be more willing to celebrate a diversity of restrictive environments when we feel that our own niche in public education is secure.

REFERENCES

Barker, R. G. (1968). *Ecological psychology.* Stanford, CA: Stanford University Press.

Bateman, B. D. (1994). Who, how, and where: Special education's issues in perpetuity. *The Journal of Special Education, 27,* 509–520.

Bateman, B. D., & Chard, D. J. (1995). Legal demands and constraints on placement decisions. In J. M. Kauffman, J. W. Lloyd, D. P. Hallahan, & T. A. Astuto (Eds.), *Issues in educational placement: Students with emotional and behavioral disorders* (pp. 285–316). Hillsdale, NJ: Erlbaum.

Boyle, T. C. (1993). *The road to Wellville.* New York: Penguin.

Chance, M. R. A., & Jolly, C. (1970). *Social groups of monkeys, apes and men.* London: Jonathan Cape.

Cosden, M., Gannon, C., & Haring, T. G. (1995). Teacher-control versus student-control over choice of task and reinforcement for students with severe behavior problems. *Behavioral Education, 5,* 11–27.

Cruickshank, W. M. (1977). Guest editorial. *Journal of Learning Disabilities, 10,* 193–194.

Dunbar, R. I. M. (1988). *Primate social systems.* Ithaca, NY: Cornell University Press.

Farmer, T. W. (1994). Social networks and the social behavior of youth with emotional and behavioral disorders: Implications for intervention. *B.C. Journal of Special Education, 18,* 223–234.

Farmer, T. W., & Farmer, E. M. Z. (1996). The social relationships of students with exceptionalities in mainstream classrooms: Social networks and homophily. *Exceptional Children, 62,* 431–450.

Farmer, T. W., & Hollowell, J. H. (1994). Social networks in mainstream classrooms: Social affiliations and behavioral characteristics of students with emotional and behavioral disorders. *Journal of Emotional and Behavioral Disorders, 2,* 143–155, 163.

Farmer, T. W., Pearl, R., & Van Acker, R. (1995). *Expanding the social skills deficit framework: A developmental perspective, classroom social networks, and implications for the social growth of students with disabilities.* Unpublished manuscript, University of North Carolina, Chapel Hill.

Farmer, T. W., Stuart, C. B., Lorch, N. H., & Fields, E. (1993) The social behavior and peer relations of children with emotional and behavioral disorders in residential treatment: A pilot study. *Journal of Emotional and Behavioral Disorders, 1,* 223–234.

Gallagher, W. (1993). *The power of place: How our surroundings shape our thoughts, emotions, and actions.* New York: Poseidon.

Gartner, A., & Lipsky, D. K. (1989). *The yoke of special education: How to break it.* Rochester, NY: National Center on Education and the Economy.

Gerber, P. J., Ginsberg, R., & Rieff, H. B. (1992). Identifying alterable patterns in employment success for highly successful adults with learning disabilities. *Journal of Learning Disabilities, 25,* 475–487.

Gresham, F. R. (1982). Misguided mainstreaming: The case for social skills training with handicapped children. *Exceptional Children, 48,* 422–433.

Grossen, B. (1993). Focus: Heterogeneous grouping and curriculum design. *Effective School Practices, 12*(1), 5–8.

Hallahan, D. P., & Kauffman, J. M. (1994). Toward a culture of disability in the aftermath of Deno and Dunn. *Journal of Special Education, 27,* 496–508.

Hallenbeck, B. A., & Kauffman, J. M. (1995). How does observational learning affect the behavior of students with emotional or behavioral disorders? A review of research. *Journal of Special Education, 29,* 45–71.

Hobbs, N. (1966). Helping the disturbed child: Psychological and ecological strategies. *American Psychologist, 21,* 1105–1115.

Hocutt, A. M., Martin, E. W., & McKinney, J. D. (1991). Historical and legal context of mainstreaming. In J. W. Lloyd, N. N. Singh, & A. C. Repp (Eds.), *The regular education initiative: Alternative perspectives on concepts, issues, and models* (pp. 17–28). Sycamore, IL: Sycamore.

Huefner, D. S. (1994). The mainstreaming cases: Tensions and trends for school administrators. *Educational Administration Quarterly, 30,* 27–55.

Irving, J. (1989). *A prayer for Owen Meany.* New York: Ballantine.

Kamps, D. M., Leonard, B. R., Dugan, E. P., Boland, B., & Greenwood, C. R. (1991). The use of ecobehavioral assessment to identify naturally occurring effective procedures in classrooms serving students with autism and other developmental disabilities. *Journal of Behavioral Education, 1,* 367–397.

Kauffman, J. M. (1988). A revolution can also mean returning to the starting point: Will school psychology help special education complete the circuit? *School Psychology Review, 17,* 490–494.

Kauffman, J. M. (1989). The regular education initiative as Reagan–Bush education policy: A trickle-down theory of education of the hard-to-teach. *Journal of Special Education, 23,* 256–278.

Kauffman, J. M. (1991). Restructuring in sociopolitical context: Reservations about the effects of current reform proposals on students with disabilities. In J. W. Lloyd, A. C. Repp, & N. N. Singh (Eds.), *The regular education initiative: Alternative perspectives on concepts, issues, and methods* (pp. 57–66) Sycamore, IL: Sycamore.

Kauffman, J. M. (1992). Special education into the 21st century: An educational perspective. In *Challenge for change: Reform in the 1990s. Conference proceedings, 16th national conference of the Australian Association of Special Education* (pp. 343–344). Perth, Western Australia: Australian Association of Special Education.

Kauffman, J. M. (1993). How we might achieve the radical reform of special education. *Exceptional Children, 60,* 6–16.

Kauffman, J. M. (1994). Places of change: Special education's power and identity in an era of educational reform. *Journal of Learning Disabilities, 27,* 610–618.

Kauffman, J. M., & Hallahan, D. P. (1993). Toward a comprehensive delivery system for special education. In J. I. Goodlad & T. C. Lovitt (Eds.), *Integrating general and special education* (pp. 73–102). Columbus, OH: Merrill.

Kauffman, J. M., & Lloyd, J. W. (1995). A sense of place: The importance of placement issues in contemporary special education. In J. M. Kauffman, J. W. Lloyd, D. P. Hallahan, & T. A. Astuto (Eds.), *Issues in educational placement: Students with emotional and behavioral disorders* (pp. 3–19). Hillsdale, NJ: Erlbaum.

Kern, L., Wacker, D. P., Mace, F. C., Falk, G. D., Dunlap, C., & Kromrey, J. D. (1995). Improving the peer interactions of students with emotional and behavioral disorders through self-evaluation procedures: A component analysis and group application. *Journal of Applied Behavior Analysis, 28,* 47–59.

Laski, F. J. (1991). Achieving integration during the second revolution. In L. H. Meyer, C. A. Peck, & L. Brown (Eds.), *Critical issues in the lives of people with severe disabilities* (pp. 409–421). Baltimore: Brookes.

Library of America. (1976). *Mark Twain collected tales, sketches, speeches, & essays 1891–1910* New York: Author.

Lipsky, D. K., & Gartner, A. (1991). Restructuring for quality. In J. W. Lloyd, N. N. Singh, & A. C. Repp (Eds.), *The regular education initiative: Alternative perspectives on concepts, issues, and models* (pp. 43–57). Sycamore, IL: Sycamore.

Marston, D. (1987–1988). The effectiveness of special education: A time series analysis of reading performance in regular and special education settings. *Journal of Special Education, 21*(4), 13–26.

McWilliam, R. A., & Bailey, D. B. (1995). Effects of classroom social structure and disability on engagement. *Topics in Early Childhood Special Education, 15,* 123–147.

Mulick, J. A., & Meinhold, P. M. (1994). Developmental disorders and broad effects of the environment on learning and treatment effectiveness. In E. Schopler & G. B. Mesibov (Eds.), *Behavioral issues in autism* (pp. 99–128). New York: Plenum.

Padden, C., & Humphries, T. (1988). *Deaf in America: Voices from a culture.* Cambridge, MA: Harvard University Press.

Patterson, G. R., Reid, J. B., & Dishion, T. J. (1992). *Antisocial boys.* Eugene, OR: Castalia.

Rhode, G., Jenson, W. R., & Reavis, H. K. (1992). *The tough kid book: Practical classroom management strategies.* Longmont, CO: Sopris West.

Rhodes, W. C. (1967). The disturbing child: A problem of ecological management. *Exceptional Children, 33,* 449–455.

Schroeder, S. R. (Ed.). (1990). *Ecobehavioral analysis and developmental disabilities: The twenty-first century.* New York: Springer.

Schroeder, S. R., Kanoy, J. R., Mulick, J. A., Rojahn, J., Thios, S. J., Stephens, M., & Hawk, B. (1982). Environmental antecedents which affect management and maintenance of programs for self-injurious behavior. In J. C. Hollis & C. E. Myers (Eds.), *Life-threatening behavior* (Monograph No. 5). Washington, DC: American Association on Mental Deficiency.

Semmel, M. I., Gerber, M. M., & MacMillan, D. L. (1994). Twenty-five years after Dunn's article: A legacy of policy analysis research in special education. *The Journal of Special Education, 27*, 481–495.

Spekman, N. J., Goldberg, R. J., & Herman, K. L. (1992). Learning disabled children grow up: A search for factors related to success in the young adult years. *Learning Disabilities Research and Practice, 7*, 161–170.

Stainback, W., & Stainback, S. (1991). A rationale for integration and restructuring: A synopsis. In J. W. Lloyd, N. N. Singh, & A. C. Repp (Eds.), *The regular education initiative: Alternative perspectives on concepts, issues, and models* (pp. 226–239). Sycamore, IL: Sycamore.

Wolery, M. (1995). Foreword. *Topics in Early Childhood Special Education, 15*, vii–viii.

Zigmond, N., Jenkins, J., Fuchs, L. S., Deno, S., Fuchs, D., Baker, J. N., et al. (1995). Special education in restructured schools: Findings from three multi-year studies. *Phi Delta Kappan, 76*, 531–540.

CHAPTER 11

Full Inclusion: An Empirical Perspective

Donald L. MacMillan, Frank M. Gresham,
and Steven R. Forness

It is argued that educational treatments of children with disabilities should be empirically validated. From this perspective the current press for full inclusion is examined against empirical evidence bearing on the major assertions of advocates for full inclusion. Students with emotional and behavioral disorders (EBD) are among the most difficult to include, and the unique problems presented by such children often are ignored by advocates for full inclusion. Arguments for full inclusion, particularly as they apply to children with emotional and behavioral disorders suffer from: (a) the failure to specify what constitutes full inclusion, (b) the weakness of relying on anecdotal reports and single case studies to validate the utility of full inclusion of all children with disabilities, and (c) the fact that the evidence that does exist fails to include children with emotional and behavioral disorders. Finally, evidence is summarized that contradicts the position that "more restrictive" placements are never beneficial and that regular class placement is always beneficial to all children with disabilities.

I t is instructive to recall the history of special education and to learn from it. George Santayana wrote, "Progress, far from consisting in change, depends on retentiveness.... Those who cannot remember the past are condemned to 1979" (p. 414). Proponents of full inclusion in its most radical form should heed this advice lest they succeed in achieving changes that ultimately prove harmful to the very children they claim to represent. As a field we have an history of embracing untried treatments, only to find out subsequently that they were ineffectual, or in some cases, actually fraudulent. At various times, we have seen significant numbers of our colleagues endorsing the "program" of Bernardine Schmidt (see Spitz, 1986), patterning as prescribed by Doman and Delacato (see Robbins & Glass, 1969; Zigler & Seitz, 1975), the Feingold diet (see Kavale & Forness,

1983), and most recently the utility of facilitated communication (see Wheeler, Jacobson, Paglieri, & Schwartz, 1993).

Full inclusion is among the recent banners behind which a number of special educators are rallying in spite of the lack of evidence on its efficacy. In discussing the writings of the Stainbacks' advocacy of full inclusion, Vergason and Anderegg (1989) wrote: "And we, as parents and professionals, should be equally frightened by this proposal. The Regular Education Initiative (REI) proponents at least had a flawed data base. These proposals appear to have no data base" (p. 8). A recent paper by Fuchs and Fuchs (1994) provides a careful and insightful analysis of the REI and Inclusive Schools movements noting the reliance on rhetoric and absence of evidence. Reactions by professional organizations were noted by Vaughn and Schumm (1995) to run the entire spectrum:

> (a) unqualified enthusiasm for full inclusion (The Association for Persons with Severe Handicaps, 1991), (b) concern that inclusion practices do not provide appropriate services for students with learning disabilities (Council for Learning Disabilities, April, 1993; Division for Learning Disabilities, 1993; Learning Disabilities Association, January, 1993; National Joint Committee on Learning Disabilities, 1993), (c) enthusiasm for the philosophy of inclusion, but concern for maintaining a continuum of services (Council for Exceptional Children, 1993; National Association of State Boards of Education, 1992), and (d) concerns about the responsibilities of general education teachers and the effects of inclusion on all students (American Federation of Teachers, 1993). (p. 264)

One lesson that we should have learned by now is that we have perseverated in posing questions about service delivery in terms of where children with disabilities are served. Zigler, Hodapp, and Edison (1990) reminded us of this when they recounted the history of deinstitutionalization and mainstreaming. Around 1900 there were those who advocated that institutions were the only appropriate placement for individuals with disabilities. There is a close analogy between the philosophy of full inclusion and policies of deinstitutionalization of individuals with mental illness (Lieberman, 1992). Fuchs and Fuchs (1994) point out that deinstitutionalization caused over 250,000 people with schizophrenia and manic-depressive illness to live in shelters, in jails, or on the streets: all in the name of "normalization." Proponents of deinstitutionalization in the 1960s and 1970s and the full inclusionists of the late 1980s and 1990s share the same logical flaw:

that physical placement in a "mainstream" setting equates to integration into that setting. In fact, evidence presented in this article suggests just the opposite. The position that institutions were the placement of choice for all individuals with disabilities was later deemed untenable. In 1965, Robinson and Robinson accurately captured the sentiment of the times when they wrote, "the consensus of special educators today definitely favors special class placement for the mildly retarded" (p. 436). Within two decades, special day class settings were in disfavor, being replaced by resource specialist pull-out programs which, in turn, were assailed by critics and advocates of the REI who sought to abolish the dual system. Today, full inclusion is being advanced by some who demand that all children with disabilities be educated in their neighborhood school in age-appropriate regular classes. The lessons of history have not been learned, as the exclusive emphasis on *setting* ignores the fact that settings are merely contextual variables in which the interactions of importance occur. The focus on *where* students with disabilities should be taught has led to very different recommendations at different times. In fact, Zigler et al. (1990) observed that "yesterday's orthodoxy has become today's heretical view" (p. 2).

Another lesson to be learned from our history is that approaches designed to meet the needs of children with disabilities should be adopted on the basis of empirical validation, and not based on ideology, persuasive slogans, or the volume and stridency of voices advocating a particular treatment or position. It has been noted elsewhere (MacMillan, Semmel, & Gerber, 1994) that one of the unfortunate legacies of Lloyd Dunn's 1968 influential article has been the tendency for policy in special education to be influenced more by ideology than by research.

In the following pages the press for full inclusion is examined from an empirical perspective. In so doing, an effort is made to critically analyze (a) what constitutes full inclusion, (b) evidence bearing on claims made by proponents of full inclusion, (c) the "types" of children with disabilities for whom evidence on inclusion has been offered (and the virtual absence of evidence on students who are the most difficult to include—seriously emotionally disturbed, severely/profoundly mentally retarded).

One reason for the polarization of the field over the issue of full inclusion derives, in part, from the fundamental difference concerning what should constitute the dependent variable in the discussion and the research. One way to conceptualize the empirical question concerning inclusion is to examine the effect or impact of full inclusion (i.e., the treatment or independent variable) on any number of child outcomes expected to be impacted (e.g., achievement, self-concept, social acceptance, social skills;

i.e., that would constitute the dependent variables). Advocates for full inclusion tend, however, to examine the effects of factors (e.g., teacher attitudes, parent beliefs, and so forth that are treated as independent variables) on the willingness to implement inclusive programs (i.e., the dependent variable). The latter approach presupposes that we *know* that full inclusion is beneficial, while the former approach assumes that the consequences of full inclusion are unknown and have to be examined. The consequence of these differences is a failure to communicate. Those examining full inclusion as the independent variable feel the assumption of beneficial effects of full inclusion, made by those treating full inclusion as the dependent variable, is premature. Moreover, proponents of full inclusion often reject the need to empirically test the effects of inclusion and take the position that it is a moral, not empirical, issue.

Before any effort to evaluate inclusive programs is undertaken, however, there must be agreement in terms of what constitutes full inclusion. Let us turn our attention to that question.

What Constitutes Full Inclusion?

At present one encounters considerable variability in the actual practices referred to as full inclusion. In some instances, full inclusion refers to the full-time placement of an individual student with disabilities in a regular education class. That is, Forrest Gump participates in full inclusion by virtue of his being enrolled in a regular class. In this case, *full* refers exclusively to the fact that one child is included for the entire school day and for all of his educational day. Testimonial evidence is then gathered to buttress the contention that if it works for Forrest Gump, then it works. The experiences of Shawntell, related by her parents (Strully & Strully, 1989), illustrates this perspective. Yet another meaning is inferred from those who argue that all students with disabilities, regardless of the nature or severity of their disability, should be enrolled in age-appropriate classes in their neighborhood school for the entire day. In this context, the *full* refers to both the entire population of students with disabilities *and* the entire school day. Stainback and Stainback (1992) articulate such a position when they write: "An inclusive school or classroom educates all students in the mainstream. No students, including those with disabilities are relegated to the fringes of the school by placement in segregated wings, trailers, or special classes" (p. 34). However, there is disagreement even among proponents of inclusion as to the wisdom of full-time placement in regular classes. For example, Lou Brown (Brown et al., 1991) wrote: "Regular education classrooms are heavily laden with abstractions. Thus, students with severe intellectual disabilities can be expected to learn relatively little. When abstract activities dominate, it is often more appropriate for these students to be elsewhere" (p. 41).

In fact, what extremely limited empirical (using the term broadly) evidence is available on full inclusion is based on yet another definition of full inclusion. Our reading of anecdotal accounts suggests that full inclusion, in the accounts available, refers to the full-time placement of students *whose parents prefer regular class placement* and who manifest, in most cases, moderate disabilities and are quite young (e.g., preschool or early elementary grades). The self selective factor of parents cannot be overlooked in terms of its importance, as *full* inclusion is being advanced as *the* program for all children with disabilities—and if adopted would deny parents who do not desire regular class placement for their child the option of placement in one of the other alternatives on the continuum of placements now available.

From an empirical perspective, however, it is essential that there be a clear specification of what constitutes full inclusion. If it only means that regular class placement should be available for *some* children with disabilities, then it has been available for years, and there is no need for a specific term "full inclusion." If it refers to the placement of all children with disabilities in age-appropriate regular classes all day in their neighborhood schools, then its adoption requires the abolition of the continuum of placements provided for in the Individuals with Disabilities Education Act (IDEA).

Ideological Impetus Lacking Logic and Empirical Backing

Fuchs and Fuchs (1994) clearly chronicle how The Association for Persons with Severe Handicaps (TASH) emerged as the ideological leader in the inclusive schools movement and how the rhetoric of its leading spokespersons (e.g., Gartner & Lipsky, 1987; Stainback & Stainback, 1984) became increasingly radical. For a perspective on the emergence of TASH as the primary advocate of full inclusion one should read the Fuchs and Fuchs (1994) article. Clearly, the impetus for advocates of full inclusion was never empirically driven, but rather ideologically driven and spokespersons frequently employed offensive statements, misrepresentations of extant evidence, and tortured logic to attract followers.

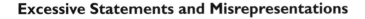

Excessive Statements and Misrepresentations

Extreme statements and inappropriate analogies appear in the literature that misrepresent the evidence and contribute to the polarization of professionals. For example, Forest and Pearpoint wrote: "In common is the label *disabled* pinned on them, like the yellow star pinned on people labeled Jewish, and the pink triangle pinned on people labeled homosexual during World War II" (1992, p. 81). Casting aspersions and representing the effects of labeling in this overly simplistic fashion both misrepresents the evidence on labeling (see MacMillan, Jones, & Aloia, 1974) and divides unnecessarily professionals sincerely concerned with serving children with disabilities.

Grenot-Scheyer and Lynch (1992) wrote: "While there is much controversy regarding what constitutes the least restrictive environment,... there are no published data which *do not support integration or inclusion* [italics added]" (p. 81). These authors might have considered Gottlieb's (1981) review or that of Semmel, Gottlieb, and Robinson (1979) which both report published data that fail to support the benefits of integration to students with disabilities. This statement is simply inaccurate, as evidence contra-indicating the beneficial effects of integration going back to the poor social position of mildly retarded children in regular grades reported by Johnson (1950; Johnson & Kirk, 1950), the literature on mainstreaming (e.g., Gottlieb, 1981), and meta-analytic reviews on self-concept (Chapman, 1988). Such statements are misleading and should be exposed as such.

Proponents also have extrapolated from racial segregation in schools and attempted to draw parallels between race and disability. For example, Gartner and Lipsky drew the following parallel "concerning the inherent inequality of separate education,... to recognize that advocacy efforts in the 1960s and 1970s on behalf of persons with disabilities were drawn from the context of the Civil Rights movement" (1987, p. 368). Similarly, terminology used by proponents attempts to further the link as placements in more protective and restrictive settings are referred to as "segregationistic." However, Kauffman and Hallahan (1993) have exposed the weakness in this parallel. Equal protection and equal educational opportunity provide that child characteristics *irrelevant to their learning* must not be used to justify unfair treatment; that is, denying them equal opportunity to learn. In the case of minority group children, these provisions assert that providing a different or separate education for children on the basis of race, which is irrelevant to how a child learns, is unfair. In the case of children with disabilities, however the characteristics defining the disability (e.g., blindness, low general intelligence) are extremely relevant to how a child learns. In fact, providing the same curriculum and instructional methods used with children free of disabilities for children with different learning needs is patently unfair.

Tortured Logic

A basic premise of those advancing inclusion of children with disabilities is that the regular classroom provides "better models" of behavior, and that children with disabilities will benefit socially from being able to observe the behavior of nonhandicapped students. Snell (1991) argued that full inclusion facilitates the development of social skills, improves the attitudes of peers toward students with disabilities, and promotes the development of friendships between students with disabilities and peers. The experimental data to date fail to support such a view. In fact, Gresham's 1982 review of the mainstreaming literature concluded the opposite, and a recent review of the more current literature (Gresham & MacMillan, 1997) drew the same conclusion. Gresham (1982) found that: (a) mainstreamed students with disabilities are less accepted and more often rejected by peers, (b) that social interactions between students with disabilities and their peers occurred at low frequencies or were more negative in nature, and (c) there was little evidence to suggest that integration promoted beneficial modeling effects. In addition, proponents argue that inclusion affords benefits to nonhandicapped students in that they will benefit from exposure to, and interactions with, students with disabilities. In many ways, this latter argument is reminiscent of the *contact hypothesis* advanced as a potential benefit of mainstreaming. Illustrative of the first point, Brown et al. (1991) wrote that "The best language, social, dress, and behavior models are in regular education classrooms" (p. 40). Visits to a variety of schools lead these authors to question this assertion. In many cases the language of adolescents is inappropriate (i.e., *mother* is half a word), gang and "skater" attire abounds in many of our schools, and behavior is cited by teachers as an area of concern. The belief that modeling of appropriate behaviors occurs appears to be unfounded, given the recent review by Hallenbeck and Kauffman (1995) concerning the notion that placement in regular classes somehow guarantees or even facilitates the modeling of appropriate behaviors of nondisabled children by those with disabilities. These authors asked: "If desirable models are both readily available and have a pervasive influence on behavior in neighborhood schools and regular classes, then one might ask why these models do not prevent students from acquiring maladaptive patterns of behavior?" (p. 47).

Research addressing the contact hypothesis was examined in depth by Jay Gottlieb in his writings. Contrary to the hypothesized benefits, Gottlieb's reviews demonstrated that the more nonhandicapped students came to know the students with disabilities *the less they liked them*. There are no assurances that contact, per se, will yield more favorable attitudes as they are influenced by the quality of the observations and interactions. When children exhibit behaviors that are objectionable, contact is likely to promote less favorable attitudes. Mere placement will not ensure that more favorable attitudes will be developed by nonhandicapped classmates (Gottlieb, 1975, 1981; Gresham & MacMillan, 1997; Kauffman, 1995).

In cases of mildly handicapped students who begin their educational careers in regular classes, encounter difficulty, and are subsequently identified for special education programs the logic behind this position is even more baffling. If the presence of "good" models is of such benefit to these children, why did they not "match to model" their behavior when they were enrolled in regular classes initially? One might argue that modeling only occurs after a certain age; that is, they did not effectively model the good behavior in first grade but they will in fifth. However, that would require a modification in the advocacy position—that is, children with disabilities will only benefit from the "good" models beyond some developmental stage and that contradicts the position that it is good for all disabled children, including those in the primary grades.

While the evidentiary base on sociometric status of children having serious emotional disturbance (SED) or behavior disorders is somewhat limited (Gresham & MacMillan, 1997), the evidence that does exist suggests that these children are much more likely to be rejected by their nondisabled peers (Sabornie & Kauffman, 1985; Sabornie, Kauffman, Ellis, Marshall, & Elksnin, 1987–1988; Walker & Bullis, 1991). Moreover, a large data base exists concerning the behavioral correlates of various sociometric groups (e.g., rejected, neglected, controversial) that shows a positive relationship between externalizing behaviors (aggressive, disruptive, noncompliant) that define children with emotional and behavioral disorders and being rejected (Newcomb, Bukowski, & Pattee, 1993).

Extant empirical evidence fails to support either the hypothesized beneficial effects of inclusion on peer acceptance or the hypothesized beneficial effects on self-concept. This being the case, how can proponents offer so much promise to parents of children with disabilities of anticipated social benefits of full inclusion to their children? In part, we believe they do so because: (a) they essentially distrust research and (b) rely on anecdotal cases and testimonial. Let us examine the role of such evidence in deciding educational policy.

Anecdotal Case Reports, Testimonials, and Educational Policy

Proponents of full inclusion have relied heavily (almost exclusively) on anecdotal reports and descriptions of individual cases where a child with disabilities is included in a regular class and has a good experience. Probably the most widely cited case by proponents of full inclusion has been that of Shawntell (Strully & Strully, 1989), a severely disabled girl who experienced successful integration. It is crucial, however, to realize that single anecdotal cases cannot confirm theories concerning universals. Nevertheless, they can challenge universals—that is, when a single case defies a universal. In the present context, we would argue that the case study of Shawntell serves to discredit a universal position that no children with disabilities can benefit from placement in regular classrooms or that all children with disabilities require protective placements. It does not, however, constitute confirmation for the position that all children with disabilities can benefit from inclusive placements. To paraphrase Lieberman (1992), the fact that Stevie Wonder is a talented musician cannot be taken as supporting a position that therefore all blind individuals are talented musicians.

Single case studies also can serve to challenge the universal position of proponents of full inclusion that it is beneficial to all children with disabilities. For example, Dorris (1989) related the experiences of his son, Adam, who also was integrated into a regular class. According to Dorris, the teacher wrote that Adam "demonstrated good ability and understanding with regard to our unit on geography" and provided other glowing progress reports. "Yet, at age 18 he cannot tell time or read a map; he has no notion of money and will cheerfully pay $10 for a doughnut" (p. 112). Yearly report cards proclaimed Adam's great progress in making friends. Yet according to Dorris, in all his school days Adam "never once received so much as a telephone call or an invitation from a 'friend'" (p. 112). Ohanian (1990) related the experiences of her third graders who were tolerant of Charles, an included child with disabilities. Their tolerance, according to Ohanian, was "because I was there, I have to admit that I never saw any evidence of friendship ... I would wager a sum that Charles has never received a phone call from a classmate, either" (p. 218). These case studies clearly challenge the universal position that inclusion is beneficial for all students with disabilities.

Testimonial can be elicited to support and refute the utility of inclusive placement for students with disabilities. On balance, such single case anecdotal evidence supports the position that *no* single placement is universally beneficial to *all* students with disabilities. For this reason, the radical full inclusionists' attempt to obliterate the continuum of placements provided for in IDEA cannot be sustained based on the evidence they present.

The Assault on the Continuum of Placements

The position of inclusionists is that "least restrictive environment" (LRE) is synonymous with regular school and regular class placement of all children with disabilities. There can be no mistaking that some proponents of inclusion are calling for the abolition of the continuum. Laski (1991) wrote:

> Three generations of children subject to LRE are enough. Just as some institution managers and their organizations—both overt and covert—seek refuge in the continuum and LRE, regional intermediate unit, and special school administrators and their organizations will continue to defend the traditional and professionally pliable notion of LRE ... In terms of placement, the home-school focus renders LRE irrelevant and the continuum moot. (pp. 413–414)

The earlier quoted passage from Stainback and Stainback (1992) which refers to "no student" being placed in "segregated wings, trailers, or special classes" (p. 34) precludes the possibility of placement in certain options. Similarly, Taylor (1988) argued against maintaining the continuum of placement options. However, evidence and experience with certain types of children with disabilities, particularly those with emotional and behavioral disorders and mental retardation, suggests that they present unique problems in regular classrooms that argue against inclusion. For example, students exhibiting severe behavioral problems (e.g., aggressive, violent behavior), particularly those weighing 150 pounds or more, are often placed *out of the district* when supports in special day classes are insufficient to manage the behavior problems. The expense to the district frequently exceeds $25,000 per year, yet this is judged a necessary expense in order to meet the needs of that child.

All, Never, and Every: One Size Never Fits All

Special education historically has been dedicated to individual differences and has recognized that not only do children differ but so do teachers, schools, parents, and peers. We defy proponents of inclusion to identify a single educational treatment that benefits *all* children. Combination classes, phonics approach to teaching reading, cooperative learning, special day classes for students with learning disabilities (LD), and, yes, even regular class placement for children with disabilities are beneficial to *some* students but not *all* students. The fundamental proposition that *all* children will benefit from regular class placement in neighborhood schools is contraindicated by reason and by extant empirical evidence reviewed later in this paper. Essentially, the rationality for regular class placement for all children with disabilities is reduced to the argument that "one size fits all."

In order to support this proposition it would be necessary to demonstrate (a) that a single placement is beneficial to *all,* and (b) that alternative placements are *never* beneficial for *any.* Moreover, the proposition that all students with disabilities will benefit more from placement in age-appropriate grades in their neighborhood schools than they would in any more protective settings defies reason and lacks empirical validation. Let us examine the empirical evidence as it informs assertions made by spokespersons for full inclusion.

One article frequently cited presumably to document that pull-out programs have failed is the report of a meta-analysis by Carlberg and Kavale (1980). This article has been cited by Gartner and Lipsky (1989), Laski (1991), Lilly (1988), and Wang and Walberg (1988) to support the position that removal of students with disabilities from regular classrooms has failed. Gartner and Lipsky (1989), characterizing special education programs that remove children with disabilities from regular classes, wrote: "… little or no benefit for students of all levels of severity placed in special education" (p. 13). However, a closer examination of Carlberg and Kavale's (1980) findings reveals that, although regular class placement produced slightly better results than special class placement *when all types of disabilities were considered together,* in fact, special class placement produced substantially better outcomes than did regular class placement for students classified as learning disabled, emotionally disturbed, and behavior disordered (see Singer, 1988). It also should be noted that meta-analysis can accommodate errors across studies the results of which are subjected to meta-analysis if those errors are randomized across studies. However, studies used in this meta-analysis shared a *common flaw* of sampling bias (i.e., errors were not random) where more capable and less behaviorally disordered students were systematically found in the regular class setting. As a result, it is virtually impossible to interpret the effect size statistic to reflect treatment/placement effects alone. Instead, interpretation of differences cannot disentangle the placement × severity of subject problem confound that characterizes the studies examined.

Ample evidence exists to demonstrate the efficacy of pull-out programs that is often ignored when advocates for full inclusion summarize evidence. While space precludes an extensive listing of such evidence, let us present illustrative investigations pendium of results attesting to the generalizable beneficial effects of pull-out programs for students with disabilities. O'Connor, Stuck, and Wyne (1979) combined highly structured instructional and behavior management programs implemented in a resource room for elementary children who were a year or more behind in basic skills and exhibited serious behavior problems. During the 8-week intervention, the on-task behavior and academic achievement of these children improved significantly compared to a control group of children with similar problems who remained in the regular classroom. These advantages were maintained when the children returned to regular classes (i.e., during a 4-month follow-up period). In another study, Marston (1987–1988) provided daily instruction in reading in a resource room for LD students and used curriculum-based measurement to track progress in the regular class and in the resource room. For 10 of the 11 students, progress in the resource room was markedly faster than in the regular classroom; on average, they gained about twice as much in reading during the 10 weeks of resource instruction than they had in 10 weeks in the regular classroom.

Specialized treatments in protective settings have been successful with students with disabilities. Walsh and McCallion (1987) reported on a program at Vineland Training School in New Jersey where staff developed a group home to serve clients with Prader-Willi syndrome. Food choice, food preparation, and intake were supervised by staff who used behavior modification techniques. This specialized treatment group home (i.e., nonnormalized, noninclusive) produced weight reduction in the Prader-Willi clients resulting in a reduction in behavior problems. While the program might be characterized by some as "restrictive" and "exclusive," it was successful in improving the quality of life enjoyed by these clients.

Contrary to the previously quoted assertion of Grenot-Scheyer and Lynch (1992)—that there is no evidence that fails to support integration or inclusion—the findings summarized above do in fact constitute just such evidence. These findings attest to the fact that a number of students with disabilities profit from specialized treatments provided in protective environments. To abolish access to more protective settings in the name of inclusion would deny those students with disabilities who benefit from such protectiveness the alternatives now provided for in the IDEA.

The notion that inclusive programs will provide beneficial outcomes for all students with disabilities is also impossible to support with existing research. As discussed earlier, the failure to adequately define what constitutes an inclusive program makes it impossible to ascertain what collection of features and practices can be taken as marker variables of an inclusive program. Nevertheless, there have been efforts to restructure schools and districts for the inclusion of students with disabilities. In fact, there have been several federally funded projects designed to explore the extent to which restructuring would permit more successful integration of students with disabilities. Findings from these projects were disappointing in the area of academics (Deno, Maruyama, Espin, & Cohen, 1990; Jenkins, Jewell, Leicester, Jenkins, & Troutner, 1991). In a recent article (Zigmond et al., 1995) findings are presented from three research projects (located at the University of Pittsburgh, the University of Washington, and Vanderbilt University and funded by the Division of Innovation and Development of the Office of Special Education Programs. U.S. Department of Education) representing innovative efforts at reform in regular education to serve students with LD in regular education settings. The projects focused on academic gains, and the findings failed to support the benefits alleged by proponents of full inclusion for "inclusive settings." To quote: "Taken together, the findings from these three studies suggest that general education settings produce achievement outcomes for students with learning disabilities that are neither desirable nor acceptable" (Zigmond et al., 1995, p. 539).

The successes of special educational efforts on behalf of children with disabilities are described and documented in a recent chapter by Fuchs and Fuchs (1995a). The empirical evidence reviewed attests to the success of academic and behavioral strategies employed by special education teachers in special education settings. Moreover, the evidence further documents the inability or unwillingness of regular educators to incorporate these strategies into general education classes. One description of regular educators' failure to employ these strategies was described by Gottlieb et al. (1994):

> It is not even clear what forms of support would be required to retain children in general education classes ... to prevent referrals. In our sur-

vey of 206 referring teachers in two separate urban school districts, other than indicating that children need one-to-one instruction, classroom teachers were not certain what support they needed to [help] the children. Almost two-thirds (63%) could not indicate what resources they would need. Only 16% indicated they could be trained with the necessary skills to retain the referred children in their classes Only 10% presented activities that could reasonably be described as curriculum adaptations. (p. 462)

Similarly, the Adaptive Learning Environments Model (ALEM) is cited frequently as a successful approach by advocates of full inclusion, despite the fact that this model was designed for, and evaluated on, students with mild disabilities, *many of whom did not meet criteria for special education eligibility.* Even when used exclusively with mildly handicapped students and ignoring the flaws in the methodology (see Bryan & Bryan, 1988; Fuchs & Fuchs, 1988a, 1988b; Hallahan, Keller, McKinney, Lloyd, & Bryan, 1988), the most generous interpretation of results is that ALEM may provide appropriate services for some students with disabilities: clearly, it does not do so for *all* students with mild disabilities.

The empirical evidence reported to date fails to support major assertions of spokespersons for full inclusion—in fact, the evidence contraindicates the recommendation of regular class placement for *all* children with disabilities. Furthermore, the research cited by inclusionists utilizes preschool and primary grade children, and the children with disabilities who are included are more likely to be representative of children with *moderate* disabilities. In fact, two proponents of full inclusion share this observation as shown in the following: "Most of the available research literature on best practices appears not to have addressed the most severely disabled population" (Halvorsen & Sailor, 1990, p. 112). The nature and degree of a child's disability are very germane to issues of placement, curriculum, and service needs (see Lieberman, 1992). The research to date on integration, mainstreaming, and inclusion has not included those children who present the most difficult challenge to those implementing such programs—children with serious emotional disturbances and children with severe and profound degrees of mental retardation. Children exhibiting physically dangerous behavior or those exhibiting behaviors offensive by any reasonable standard (e.g., pica, rectal digging) can reasonably be assumed to adversely impact other children into whose class they are integrated. The research base does not to date demonstrate the efficacy of including these types of children in regular classes, and while they represent extreme forms of behaviors they must be considered when advocates speak of *all* children with disabilities.

Figures from the *Sixteenth Annual Report to Congress* (U.S. Department of Education, 1994) reveal that slightly less than 16% of children nationally served as SED are in regular classes. At the same time, approximately 37% are educated in separate classrooms, 8% in public separate facilities, 6% in private separate facilities, and slightly over 5% in residential facilities/hospital/homebound settings. Unless one assumes wholesale noncompliance by the public schools, in over half of the cases of children served as SED the IEP committee has considered a separate class or even a more protective setting to be the least restrictive environment for these children. Radical advocates for full inclusion would deny such placements as options for these children.

Continuum Permits Inclusion and Other Options

There is nothing in IDEA that prevents children with mild, moderate, or severe disabilities from being placed in an age-appropriate regular classroom in their neighborhood school. Then why do some advocating full inclusion (e.g., Taylor, 1988) seek to abolish the continuum of placement alternatives currently provided for in IDEA? We submit that the explanation derives from the ideological position that the concept of least restriction is operationalized as regular class placement. Yet, as Lieberman (1992) argued so persuasively, we need to preserve special education and the range of options currently provided for those students who need them. He observed that children classified as SED are among those most frequently in need of more protective settings and more intense treatments. Even proponents of inclusion recognize the inappropriate nature of a regular class curriculum for *certain* children with disabilities (Halvorsen & Sailor, 1990).

There is ample evidence suggesting the need to be cautious about inclusion of children with serious emotional or behavioral disorders in regular classrooms (Braaten, Kauffman, Braaten, Polsgrove, & Nelson, 1988; Kauffman, 1993; Kauffman, Lloyd, Astuto, & Hallahan, 1995; Kauffman, Lloyd, Baker, & Riedel, 1995; Lewis, Chard, & Scott, 1994). Efficacy studies on full inclusion of such children suggest either that such placements are not as successful as special education classes or that the energy and resources needed for success in the regular class may not be commensurate with the questionable gains achieved (Clarke, Schaefer, Burchard, & Welkowitz, 1992; D. Fuchs, L. Fuchs, Fernstrom, & Hohn, 1991; Meadows,

Neel, Scott, & Parker, 1994; Walker, 1984; Walker & Bullis, 1991). In a careful review of such studies Schneider and Leroux (1994) note that on follow up "only the minority appear to have achieved total reintegration after a number of years" (p. 200). One of the assumptions of full inclusion is that children with emotional or behavioral disorders will benefit from social modeling of nondisabled peers in the regular classroom. Hallenbeck and Kauffman (1995) dispel this notion as well in their review of studies on observational learning which suggests, in particular, that there may be far too much disparity between children with emotional and behavioral disorders and their nondisabled peers for effective modeling to take place. In fact, a recent study on social networks of such children in regular classrooms demonstrates that they tend to gravitate toward other nonidentified peers with more equal levels of aggressive and disruptive behaviors (Farmer & Hollowell, 1994). Thus, as Long (1994) has suggested, there are some students with emotional or behavioral disorders whose needs far exceed the resources and talents of regular education and "any attempt to force them into a predetermined setting would be a violation of their civil rights" (p. 22).

There are some children who exhibit behaviors that are likely to impact adversely the learning of nondisabled children into whose classes they would be included. Kauffman, Lloyd, Baker, and Riedel (1995) alerted us to the unique problems presented by children with emotional and behavioral disorders. These children can exhibit behaviors that are "so severe that they require comprehensive and intensive intervention" (p. 543). The following case describes a child with emotional and behavioral problems. Consider the kinds of services required to regulate the behaviors exhibited and also the probable reactions of parents of the nondisabled students in Tom's class:

> Tom, a third-grade boy with serious academic deficits, has exhibited severe behavior problems with every teacher he has had. In first grade, he frequently urinated in the classroom and other inappropriate places and picked fights with other children. Now, not only is he highly aggressive, but also he frequently steals from the teacher and his classmates and is labeled a thief by his peers. His mother does not see his stealing as a serious problem; his father is in jail. Neither Tom nor his mother is receiving any counseling or mental health services. The school's pre-referral team has found no strategy to control his aggressive behavior. In the middle of his third-grade year, Tom was placed with an exceptionally strong male teacher, who finds it impossible to control Tom's behavior and to teach

the rest of his class at the same time. This teacher wants Tom to be evaluated for special education. (p. 543)

The possibility of violent and dangerous behaviors must be considered when deciding on the least restrictive environment for a given child in light of the nature and severity of his or her disability. What are the consequences for nondisabled children, and what is the feasibility of providing the number of trained personnel to ensure benefits to the child with disabilities being included? In addition to children with emotional and behavioral problems, there are students with profound mental disabilities who are often unable to benefit from enrollment in a regular classroom. The position that *all* children with disabilities belong in an age-appropriate regular classroom ignores that some such children currently reside in acute hospital wards in state hospitals in a comatose state. To reiterate, these extreme cases and others even less extreme have not been among those studied by those reporting positive effects from inclusive placements. Yet, they are included among all children with disabilities and before adoption of full inclusion it is essential that they be included in the evaluation of any such efforts if the policy is to be advanced for *all* children with disabilities.

The recommendation to obliterate the continuum of placements provided for in IDEA and taking the position that the regular class constitutes the least restrictive environment for *all* students with disabilities is illogical, unsupported by evidence, and, if implemented, would be a disservice to *some* children with and without disabilities. It is crucial that choice and options be preserved—for those who need them. Lieberman (1992) argued that it was important to preserve the *choice* of placement options included in the continuum of placements provided for in IDEA. However, he goes on to explain that to be against inclusion of all children with disabilities does not suggest that one is for *exclusion*. Parents want, and are entitled to, choices when it comes to the placement of their children with disabilities. This sentiment is expressed by a recognized scholar and parent of a child with disabilities, Bernard Rimland (1993), who wrote: "I have no quarrel with [full] inclusionists if they are content to insist upon inclusion for *their* children. But when they try to force me and other unwilling parents to dance to their tune, I find it highly objectionable and quite intolerable. Parents need [placement] options" (p. 3).

The feasibility of placing a student with disabilities successfully in a regular class depends not only on the nature and severity of the student's disability, but also on the features of the regular class into which the student is to be enrolled. Schools, like the students they serve, are highly varied in terms of the ability level of the students, the languages spoken, the resources available, and the qualifications of the teachers. Schools and classrooms within schools differ along salient dimensions that directly impact the feasibility of inclusion. Furthermore, the grade level of the class is proxy for a number of variables likely to make inclusion more or less feasible. For example, primary grade students are more tolerant than are, say, junior high age students who are likely to ostracize on the basis of a complexion problem. Teachers at the elementary level are more student-oriented than subject-matter oriented, and the opposite goes for most high school teachers. The point to be made here is that students are not included into a vacuum, but rather into real classrooms in which characteristics of students, teachers, and programs vary quite markedly.

The current zeitgeist in regular education places considerable emphasis on *outcome-based education* which is strongly aligned with academic priorities, particularly in math, reading, and science. Achievements in these academic domains are problematic for learners with mild disabilities and often inappropriate (at the level taught) for students with severe disabilities. It is paradoxical that the emphasis in regular education is on academic achievement, while the literature advocating full inclusion for students with severe disabilities stresses the anticipated benefits on social outcomes. To what extent is it realistic to expect a regular class teacher with a class of 35 students to achieve the academic goals emphasized in the outcome-based education model *and* the social goals stressed by advocates of full inclusion for the students with disabilities? The answer to this question is reflected in a research synthesis by Scruggs and Mastropieri (in press) in which they summarized 27 investigations in which regular education teachers were surveyed regarding their perceptions of including students with disabilities in their classes. There were 9,772 teachers across the 27 studies, and results were strikingly consistent across the 1958 to 1995 period in which these surveys were published. We have summarized the results of this synthesis in Table 11.1 according to the mean percent of agreement by teachers for six general statements relating to inclusion. Note that regular education teachers are generally, but not overwhelmingly, in favor of the idea of inclusion and express willingness to try full inclusion. However, when asked if inclusion will be the best placement for children with disabilities fewer than a third are in agreement, and about 30% definitely feel that including such children will be disruptive to the regular classroom. Little more than a fourth feel that they have sufficient time for inclusion efforts, that they are currently prepared, or that they will receive

TABLE 11.1

Scruggs and Mastropieri's Findings on Research Synthesis
of 27 Studies on Teacher Perceptions of Inclusion

Survey Item	No. of Studies	No. of Teachers	Mean % of Agreement*	Range of Percentage
General support for inclusion	8	4523	68.2	60.1–76.6
Willingness to include	8	1414	59.6	55.8–70.3
Best for child with disability	8	1223	31.0	12.8–50.0
Negative impact on classroom	4	363	30.3	10.0–41.7
Sufficient time	4	614	27.7	10.0–35.6
Sufficient expertise/training	9	2122	27.1	9.2–41.8

*Mean % of agreement = synthesis across studies of teachers in agreement with survey item.

sufficient training for inclusion. Even when afforded specialized training and ongoing support, substantial variability exists both in the extent to which regular education teachers are able to implement inclusive programs and in the progress their pupils with disabilities achieve as a result (L. Fuchs, D. Fuchs, Hamlett, Phillips, & Karns, 1995; Janney, Snell, Beers, & Raynes, 1995).

Some Final Observations About Empiricism and Inclusion

Special education has long been dedicated to the importance of individual differences. We attempt to provide for children who differ in visual acuity, hearing, intellectual ability, behavioral problems, and other dimensions when they differ on these dimensions to such a degree that they cannot maximally profit from regular instruction. Moreover, we are constantly alerted to the fact that "not all EBD kids are alike," and we provide for this with "individualized" education plans. Nevertheless, proponents of full inclusion suggest that all students with disabilities, regardless of the nature of their disability or individual differences among students with the same disability, will benefit from the same placement in age-appropriate regular classes. Such a recommendation derives from ideology, not from empirical evidence suggesting beneficial effects across children. In truth, we do not know the extent to which full inclusion, however defined and operationalized, benefits students with disabilities. Moreover, the possibility of negative effects of inclusion on children with disabilities and/or their non-handicapped peers has received little or no attention by inclusionists. Research addressing the nature and extent of negative effects of full inclusion is simply lacking at this time.

Visits by the authors to districts claiming to operate "inclusive" programs have uncovered several common situations that contradict the assertions, however well-intended, that they include all students with disabilities. For example, when personnel in these districts are asked whether they send any students out of the district they indicate that they, in fact, do. When visits are made to the special schools to which these "out-of-district" placements are made, we encounter students who can be described as follows: (a) they exhibit externalizing behavioral problems, (b) these behaviors are exhibited by students who have reached the age of 12 or 13 or weigh over 140 pounds, (c) the emotional and behavioral problems are frequently accompanied by comorbid problems of mild to moderate mental retardation, and (d) an alternative curriculum is appropriate for the students in question. When confronted with this operation, the personnel in the districts commonly explain that they "fully include" those students who can be included—not *all* students qualifying for special education services. These are not the kind of student for whom we have anecdotal accounts of successful inclusive efforts; instead, they represent a group of special education eligible students conveniently ignored in the "movement" for full inclusion.

In a recent article, MacMillan, Semmel, and Gerber (1994) proposed that one of the unfortunate legacies of Lloyd Dunn's (1968) paper was that it marked a watershed in special education. Prior to that time, empirical evidence was generated to address the issues of how well students with various disabilities were served by special education. Efficacy studies, while containing methodological problems, nevertheless reflected an effort on the part of the field to examine the extent to which practices impacted the achievement, sociometric status, and self-concept of students served. Since publication of Dunn's paper, however, decision making regarding policies and treatments has been conducted devoid of empirical support that the decisions will positively impact students with disabilities. In that paper we noted that there has been an increase in the academic community of those eschewing empirical evidence and instead relying on ideology and slogans in order to change practices. Complex issues of classification were simply addressed with slogans such as "Label jars not people." When others considered the complexities involved in mainstreaming and whether it benefited children, a frequently encountered response for those recommending it for all children was to *disregard* empirical evidence and rely on phrases: "Lincoln didn't require a research study to know that slavery was wrong." "No longer were (best practices) determined by evaluation designs; rather, they were determined by those with the loudest voices, catchiest slogans, and most ability to simplify" (MacMillan et al., 1994, p. 476). The issues confronting us are complex and the research examining these issues must capture the multi-variate nature of the issues if it is to inform as to the effectiveness of our treatments. We need more research on inclusion, not less, and that research must capture the variability between types of disabilities, among students with the same disability, regular class teachers and classrooms, the availability of resources and services, parent attitudes and preferences, and measures of child outcomes. Simplification will only mislead us into adopting untried treatments with the possibility of disserving children. H. L. Mencken captured this sentiment, when he stated: "For every complex issue there is a simple answer, and it is wrong" (quoted in Zigler & Hodapp, 1986, p. 223). Placing *all* students with disabilities in age-appropriate regular classes is a simple answer to a complex issue. And, it is wrong.

AUTHORS' NOTE

The present work was supported, in part, by grants No. H023C20002 and H023C30103 from the U.S. Department of Education. Opinions expressed herein are those of the authors alone and should not be intepreted to have agency endorsement. Requests for reprints should be sent to Donald MacMillan, School of Education - 82, University of California, Riverside, CA 92521-0128.

REFERENCES

American Federation of Teachers. (1993). *DraftAFT position on inclusion.* (Available from American Federation of Teachers, 555 New Jersey Ave., N.W., Washington, DC, 20001)

Braaten, S., Kauffman, J. M., Braaten, B., Polsgrove, L., & Nelson, C. M. (1988). The regular education initiative: Patent medicine for behavioral disorders. *Exceptional Children, 54*, 21–27.

Brown, L., Schwarz, P., Udvari-Solner, A., Kampschroer, E., Johnson, F., Jorgensen, J., et al. (1991). How much time should students with severe intellectual disabilities spend in regular education classrooms and elsewhere? *Journal of the Association for Persons with Severe Handicaps, 16*, 39–47.

Bryan, J. H., & Bryan, T. H. (1988). Where's the beef? A review of published research on the Adaptive Learning Environment Model. *Learning Disabilities Focus, 4*(1), 9–14.

Carlberg, C., & Kavale, K. (1980). The efficacy of special versus regular class placements for exceptional children: A meta-analysis. *The Journal of Special Education, 14*, 295–309.

Chapman, J. W. (1988). Learning disabled children's self-concepts. *Review of Educational Research, 58*, 347–371.

Clarke, R. T., Schaefer, M., Burchard, J. D., & Welkowitz, J. W. (1992). Wrapping community-based mental health services around children with severe behavioral disorder: An evaluation of project wraparound. *Journal of Child and Family Studies, 1*, 241–261.

Council for Exceptional Children. (1993). *CEC Policy on Inclusive Schools and Community Settings.* (Available from Council for Exceptional Children, 1920 Association Drive, Reston, VA 22091-9494)

Council for Learning Disabilities. (1993, April). Concerns about the "full inclusion" of students with learning disabilities in regular education classrooms. *Learning Disabilities Quarterly, 16*, 126.

Cronbach, L. J. (1975). Five decades of public controversy over mental testing. *American Psychologist, 30*, 1–14.

Deno, S., Maruyama, G., Espin, C., & Cohen, C. (1990). Educating students with mild disabilities in general education classrooms: Minnesota alternatives. *Exceptional Children, 57*, 150–161.

Division for Learning Disabilities. (1993). *Inclusion: What does it mean for students with learning disabilities?* (Available from Division for Learning Disabilities of the Council for Exceptional Children, 1920 Association Drive, Reston, VA, 22091-9494)

Dorris, M. (1989). *The broken cord.* New York: Harper & Row.

Dunn, L. M. (1968). Special education for the mentally retarded—Is much of it justifiable? *Exceptional Children, 35*, 5–22.

Farmer, T. W., & Hollowell, J. H. (1994). Social networks in mainstream classrooms: Social affiliations and behavioral characteristics of students with EBD. *Journal of Emotional and Behavioral Disorders, 7*(2), 143–155, 163.

Forest, M., & Pearpoint, J. C. (1992). Putting all kids on the MAP. *Educational Leadership. 50*(2), 81–86.

Fuchs, D., & Fuchs, L. S. (1988a). An evaluation of the adaptive learning environments model. *Exceptional Children, 55*, 440–446.

Fuchs, D., & Fuchs, L. S. (1988b). Response to Wang and Walberg. *Exceptional Children, 55*, 138–146.

Fuchs, D., & Fuchs, L. S. (1994). Inclusive schools movement and the radicalization of special education reform. *Exceptional Children, 60*, 294–309.

Fuchs, D., & Fuchs, L. S. (1995a). Special education can work. In J. M. Kauffman, J. W. Lloyd, D. P. Hallahan, & T. A. Astuto (Eds.), *Issues in educational placement* (pp. 363–377). Hillsdale, NJ: Erlbaum.

Fuchs, D., & Fuchs, L. S. (1995b). What's "special" about special education? *Phi Delta Kappan, 76,* 522–530.

Fuchs, D., Fuchs, L. S., & Fernstrom, P. (1993). A conservative approach to special education reform: Mainstreaming through transenvironmental programming and curriculum-based measurement. *American Educational Research Journal, 21,* 149–177.

Fuchs, D., Fuchs, L. S., Fernstrom, P., & Hohn, M. (1991). Toward a responsible reintegration of behaviorally disordered students. *Behavioral Disorders, 16,* 133–147.

Fuchs, L. S., Fuchs, D., Hamlett, C. L., Phillips, N. B., & Karns, K. (1995). General educators specialized adaptation for students with learning disabilities. *Exceptional Children, 61,* 440–459.

Gartner, A., & Lipsky, D. K. (1987). Beyond special education. *Harvard Educational Review, 57,* 367–395.

Gartner, A., & Lipsky, D. K. (1989). *The yoke of special education: How to break it.* Rochester, NY: National Center on Education and the Economy.

Gottlieb, J., Alter, M., Gottlieb, B. W., & Wishner, J. (1994). Special education in urban America: It's not justifiable for many. *The Journal of Special Education, 27,* 453–465.

Gottlieb, J. (1975). Public, peer, and professional attitudes toward mentally retarded persons. In M. J. Begab & S. A. Richardson (Eds.), *The mentally retarded and society: A social science perspective* (pp. 99–125). Baltimore: University Park Press.

Gottlieb, J. (1981). Mainstreaming: Fulfilling the promise? *American Journal of Mental Deficiency, 86,* 115–126.

Grenot-Scheyer, M., & Lynch, K. (1992). Full inclusion in Fullerton: Making schools work for all children. *California CEC: The Journal, 42*(1), 4, 7, 10, 13.

Gresham, F. M. (1982). Misguided mainstreaming: The case for social skills training with handicapped children. *Exceptional Children, 48,* 422–433.

Gresham, F. M., & MacMillan, D. L. (1997). Social competence and affective characteristics of students with mild disabilities. *Review of Educational Research, 67,* 377–415.

Hallahan, D. P., Keller, C. E., McKinney, J. D., Lloyd, J. W., & Bryan, T. (1988). Examining the research base of the regular education initiative: Efficacy studies and the adaptive learning environments model. *Journal of Learning Disabilities, 21,* 29–35.

Hallenbeck, B. A., & Kauffman, J. M. (1995). How does observational learning affect the behavior of students with emotional or behavioral disorders? A review of research. *The Journal of Special Education, 29,* 45–71.

Halvorsen, A. T., & Sailor, W. (1990). Integration of students with severe and profound disabilities. In R. Gaylord-Ross (Ed.), *Issues and research in special education* (pp. 110–172). New York: Teachers College Press.

Janney, R. E., Snell, M. E., Beers, M. K., & Raynes, M. (1995). Integrating students with moderate and severe disabilities into general education classes. *Exceptional Children, 61,* 425–439.

Jenkins, J., Jewell, M., Leicester, N., Jenkins, L., & Troutner, N. M. (1991). Development of a school budding model for educating students with handicaps and at-risk students in general education classrooms. *Journal of Learning Disabilities, 24,* 311–320.

Johnson, G. O. (1950). A study of the social position of mentally handicapped children in regular grades. *American Journal on Mental Deficiency, 55,* 60–89.

Johnson, G. O., & Kirk, S. A. (1950). Are mentally handicapped children segregated in regular grades? *Exceptional Children, 17,* 65–68.

Kauffman, J. M. (1993). Special problems in the inclusion of students with emotional or behavioral disorders in general education classrooms and schools. *Special Education Perspectives, 2*(1), 23–28.

Kauffman, J. M. (1995). How we might achieve the radical reform of special education. In J. M. Kauffman & D. P. Hallahan (Eds.), *The illusion of full inclusion* (pp. 193–211). Austin, TX: PRO-ED.

Kauffman, J. M., & Hallahan, D. P. (1993). Toward a comprehensive delivery system for special education. In J. I. Goodlad & T. C. Lovitt (Eds.), *Integrating general and special education* (pp. 73–102). New York: Macmillan.

Kauffman, J. M., Lloyd, J. W., Astuto, T. A., & Hallahan, D. P. (Eds.). (1995). *Issues in the educational placement of pupils with emotional or behavioral disorders.* Hillsdale, NJ: Erlbaum.

Kauffman, J. M., Lloyd, J. W., Baker, J., & Riedel, T. M. (1995). Inclusion of all students with emotional or behavioral disorders? Let's think again. *Phi Delta Kappan, 76,* 542–546.

Kavale, K., & Forness, S. (1983). Hyperactivity and diet treatment: A meta-analysis of the Feingold hypothesis. *Journal of Learning Disabilities, 16,* 324–330.

Laski, F. J. (1991). Achieving integration during the second revolution. In L. H. Meyer, C. A. Peck, & L. Brown (Eds.), *Critical issues in the lives of people with severe disabilities* (pp. 409–421). Baltimore: Brookes.

Lewis, T. J., Chard, D., & Scott, T. M. (1994). Full inclusion and the education of children and youth with emotional and behavioral disorders. *Behavioral Disorders, 19*(4), 277–293.

Lieberman, L. M. (1992). Preserving special education … for those who need it. In W. Stainback & S. Stainback (Eds.), *Controversial issues confronting special education: Divergent perspectives* (pp. 13–25). Boston: Allyn & Bacon.

Lilly, M. S. (1988). The regular education initiative: A force for change in general and special education. *Education and Training in Mental Retardation, 23,* 253–260.

Long, N. J. (1994). Inclusion: Formula for failure? *Journal of Emotional and Behavioral Problems, 3*(3), 19–23.

MacMillan, D. L., Jones, R. L., & Aloia, G. F. (1974). The mentally retarded label: A theoretical analysis and review of research. *American Journal of Mental Deficiency, 79,* 241–261.

MacMillan, D. L., Semmel, M. I., & Gerber, M. M. (1994). The social context of Dunn: Then and now. *The Journal of Special Education, 27,* 466–480.

Marston, D. (1987–1988). The effectiveness of special education: A time-series analysis of reading performance in regular and special education settings. *The Journal of Special Education, 21*(4), 13–26.

Meadows, N. B., Neel, R. S., Scott, C. M., & Parker, G. (1994). Academic performance, social competence, and mainstream accommodations: A look at mainstreamed and non-mainstreamed students with serious behavioral disorders. *Behavioral Disorders, 19*(3), 192–204.

National Association of State Boards of Education. (1992). *Winners all: From mainstreaming to inclusion.* (Available from National Association of State Boards of Education, 1012 Cameron St., Alexandria, VA 22314)

National Joint Committee on Learning Disabilities. (1993). Providing appropriate education for students with learning disabilities in regular education classrooms. *Journal of Learning Disabilities, 26,* 330–332.

Newcomb, A., Bukowski, W., & Pattee, L. (1993). Children's peer relations: A meta-analytic review of popular, rejected, neglected, controversial, and average sociometric status. *Psychological Bulletin, 113,* 99–128.

O'Connor, P. D., Stuck, G. B., & Wyne, M. D. (1979). Effects of a short-term intervention resource-room program on task orientation and achievement. *The Journal of Special Education, 13,* 375–385.

Ohanian, S. (1990). P.L. 94-142: Mainstream or quicksand? A heart-on-the-sleeve teacher confesses her fear that maybe a lot of youngsters are drowning in the mainstream. *Phi Delta Kappan, 72,* 217–222.

Oxford Dictionary of Quotations (3rd ed.). (1979). New York: Oxford University Press.

Rimland, B. (1993). Inclusive education: Right for some. *Autism Research Review International, 7,* 3.

Robbins, M. P., & Glass, G. V. (1969). The Doman-Delacato rationale: A critical analysis. In J. Hellmuth (Ed.), *Educational therapy* (Vol. 2) (pp. 323–377). Seattle, WA: Special Child Publications.

Robinson, H. B., & Robinson, N. M. (1965). *The mentally retarded child: A psychological approach.* New York: McGraw-Hill.

Sabornie, E., & Kauffman, J. (1985). Regular classroom sociometric status of behaviorally disordered adolescents. *Behavioral Disorders, 10,* 268–274.

Sabornie, E., Kauffman, J., Ellis, E., Marshall, K., & Elksnin, L. (1987–1988). Bi-directional and cross-categorical social status of learning disabled, behaviorally disordered, and nonhandicapped adolescents. *The Journal of Special Education, 21,* 39–56.

Schneider, B. H., & Leroux, J. (1994). Educational environments for the pupil with behavioral disorders: A "best evidence" synthesis. *Behavioral Disorders, 19*(3), 192–204.

Scruggs, T. E., & Mastropieri, M. A. (1996). Teacher perceptions of mainstreaming/inclusion, 1958–1995: A research synthesis. *Exceptional Children, 63,* 59–74.

Semmel, M. I., Gottlieb, J., & Robinson, N. (1979). Mainstreaming: Perspectives on educating handicapped children in the public schools. In D. Berliner (Ed.), *Review of research in education* (pp. 223–279). Washington, DC: American Educational Research Association.

Singer, J. D. (1988). Should special education merge with regular education? *Educational Policy, 2,* 409–424.

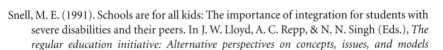

Snell, M. E. (1991). Schools are for all kids: The importance of integration for students with severe disabilities and their peers. In J. W. Lloyd, A. C. Repp, & N. N. Singh (Eds.), *The regular education initiative: Alternative perspectives on concepts, issues, and models* (pp. 133–148). Sycamore, IL: Sycamore.

Spitz, H. H. (1986). *The raising of intelligence: A selected history of attempts to raise retarded intelligence.* Hillsdale, NJ: Erlbaum.

Stainback, S., & Stainback, W. (1992). Schools as inclusive communities. In W. Stainback & S. Stainback (Eds.), *Controversial issues confronting special education* (pp. 29–43). Boston: Allyn & Bacon.

Stainback, W., & Stainback, S. (1984). A rationale for the merger of special and regular education. *Exceptional Children, 51,* 102–111.

Strully, J. L., & Strully, C. F. (1989). Friendships as an educational goal. In S. Stainback, W. Stainback, & M. Forest (Eds.), *Educating all students in the mainstream of regular education* (pp. 59–68). Baltimore: Brookes.

Taylor, S. J. (1988). Caught in the continuum: A critical analysis of the principle of the least restrictive environment. *Journal of the Association for Persons with Severe Handicaps, 13,* 41–53.

The Association for Persons with Severe Handicaps. (1991, July). *TASH resolutions and policy statement.* (Available from The Association for Persons with Severe Handicaps, 11201 Greenwood Avenue, N., Seattle, WA 98133)

U.S. Department of Education. (1994). *Sixteenth annual report to Congress on the implementation of the Individuals with Disabilities Education Act.* Washington, DC: Author.

Vaughn, S., & Schumm, J. (1995). Responsible inclusion for students with learning disabilities. *Journal of Learning Disabilities, 28*(5), 264–270, 290.

Vergason, G. A., & Anderegg, M. L. (1989). No more teachers! Bah humbug: An answer to Stainback and Stainback. *TASH Newsletter, 15*(11), 7–8, 10.

Walker, H. M. (1984). The Social Behavior Survival program (SBS): A systematic approach to the integration of handicapped children into less restrictive environments. *Education and Treatment of Children, 6,* 421–441.

Walker, H. M., & Bullis, M. (1991). Behavioral disorders and the social context of regular class integration: A conceptual dilemma? In J. W. Lloyd, N. N. Singh, & A. C. Repp (Eds.), *The regular education initiative: Alternative perspectives on concepts, issues, and models* (pp. 75–93). Sycamore, IL: Sycamore.

Walsh, K., & McCallion, P. (1987). The role of the small institution in the community services continuum. In R. Antonak & J. Mulick (Eds.), *Transitions in mental retardation: Vol. 3. The community imperative revisited* (pp. 216–236). Norwood, NJ: Ablex.

Wang, M. C., & Walberg, H. J. (1988). Four fallacies of segregationism. *Exceptional Children, 55,* 128–137.

Wheeler, D. L., Jacobson, J. W., Paglieri, R. A., & Schwartz, A. A. (1993). An experimental assessment of facilitated communication. *Mental Retardation, 31,* 49–60.

Zigler, E., & Hodapp, R. M. (1986). *Understanding mental retardation.* New York: Cambridge University Press.

Zigler, E., Hodapp, R. M., & Edison, M. R. (1990). From theory to practice in the care and education of mentally retarded individuals. *American Journal on Mental Retardation, 95,* 1–12.

Zigler. E., & Seitz, V. (1975). On "an experimental evaluation of sensorimotor patterning": A critique. *American Journal of Mental Deficiency, 79,* 483–492.

Zigmond, N., Jenkins, J., Fuchs, L. S., Deno, S., Fuchs, D., Baker, J. N., et al. (1995). Special education in restructured schools: Findings from three multi-year studies. *Phi Delta Kappan, 76,* 531–540.

CHAPTER 12

History, Rhetoric, and Reality: Analysis of the Inclusion Debate

Kenneth A. Kavale and Steven R. Forness

Issues surrounding the integration of students with disabilities into general education classrooms are explored in this article. The history of this debate is examined first by tracing the movement from mainstreaming and the least restrictive environment in 1975, to the call for a more integrated system during the 1980s under the Regular Education Initiative, and to full inclusion of all students in age-appropriate general education classrooms, with no separate special education. Next, the research investigating perceptions and attitudes about inclusion, the tenor of the general education classroom, and the preparation and ability of general education teachers to deal effectively with special education students is summarized. Finally, the dissonance between rhetoric and reality is explored. By ignoring research evidence, the inclusion debate has elevated discussion to the ideological level, where competing conflicts of vision are difficult to resolve. It is concluded that a rational solution requires the consideration of all forms of evidence if the best possible education for all students with disabilities is to be achieved.

I n the realm of special education, the word *inclusion* is likely to engender fervent debate. Inclusion is a movement seeking to create schools that meet the needs of all students by establishing learning communities for students with and without disabilities, educated together in age-appropriate general education classrooms in neighborhood schools (Ferguson, 1996). Although questions about the integration of students with disabilities should no longer be controversial, passionate discussion about inclusion continues to escalate because its philosophy not only focuses on students with disabilities of any type and severity level, but also seeks to alter the education for *all* students and hence general education. For some 25 years, integration has been the norm, according to the U.S. Department of Education (1997), which reported that about 95% of students with disabilities are served in general education settings. The movement toward greater integration has thus resulted in a significant change in the structure of special education, but questions remain about the success of special education. Empirical evidence about the efficacy of special education continues to be equivocal, and this has resulted in discussion being increasingly fueled by political and ideological concerns. These differences have often resulted in contentious discussion about how and for whom the inclusion of students with disabilities should be accomplished (see O'Neil, 1994–1995).

A CONFLICT OF VISIONS

Inclusion appears to have created an ideological divide in special education. In analyzing social policy, Sowell (1995) discussed such a divide as a conflict of visions by reference to the "vision of the anointed" versus the "vision of the benighted." The vision of the anointed involves the perceptions, beliefs, and assumptions of an elite intelligentsia whose revelations prevail over others in determining policy. On the other side there is the vision of the benighted, whose perceptions, beliefs, and assumptions "are depicted as being at best 'perceptions,' more often 'stereotypes,' and more bluntly 'false consciousness'" (p. 187). In special education, those who advocate most forcefully for full inclusion appear to hold the vision of the anointed. Such a vision, however, possesses a fundamental difficulty: "Empirical evidence is neither sought beforehand nor consulted after a policy has been instituted.... Momentous questions are dealt with essentially as conflicts of vision" (p. 2). Consequently, the anointed do not require clear definitions, logical arguments, or empirical verifications because their vision substitutes for all these things. Consequently, calls for more research to resolve fundamental problems are viewed solely as part of the vision of the benighted. Research evidence does not appear to be a major factor in the vision of the anointed.

What does appear to be a major factor in the vision of the anointed is assumptions about compassion and caring. Although these elements are seen as the special province of those with an anointed vision, in reality, they are also integral to the vision of the benighted. The reason for the emphasis on compassion and caring among the anointed is based on the assumption that their vision possesses a special state of grace for those who believe it. Those who accept this vision are deemed to be not merely factually correct but morally on a higher plane. Put differently, those who disagree with the prevailing vision are seen as being not merely in error, but in sin. For those who have this vision of the world, the anointed and the benighted do not argue on the same moral plane or play by the same cold rules of logic and evidence. The benighted are to be made "aware," to have their "consciousness raised," and the wistful hope is held out that they will "grow." Should the benighted prove recalcitrant, however, then their "mean-spiritedness" must be fought and the "real reasons" behind their arguments and actions exposed. (Sowell, 1995, pp. 2–3)

For the anointed, both a higher moral plane and significant ego preserve and insulate their vision. As Sowell (1995) said:

Despite Hamlet's warning against self-flattery, the vision of the anointed is not simply a vision of the world and its functioning in a causal sense, but is also a vision of themselves and of their moral role in the world. *It is a vision of differential rectitude.* It is not a vision of the tragedy of the human condition: Problems exist because others are not as wise or as virtuous as the anointed. (p. 5)

When applied to the case of inclusion, the anointed believe special education possesses problems, not as a result of limits on knowledge or resources, but because others lack their wisdom and virtue. Additionally, the anointed believe that special education is primarily a social construction and not a reflection of an underlying reality. Consequently, problems can be solved only by applying the articulated visions of the anointed. Any opposition to their vision is the result of an intellectual or a moral bankruptcy (or both), and not of a different reading of complex and often inconclusive research evidence. Because the vision of the anointed is independent of empirical evidence, Sowell (1995) said:

[This] is what makes it dangerous, not because a particular set of policies may be flawed or counterproductive, but because insulation from evidence virtually guarantees a never-ending supply of policies and practices fatally independent of reality. This self-contained and self-justifying vision has become a badge of honor and a proclamation of identity: To affirm it is to be one of *us* and to oppose it is to be one of *them.* (p. 241)

Special education appears to have drawn such a line between "us" and "them" over the question of inclusion. As Shanker (1994) pointed out, "Some full inclusionists talk as though they are in a battle pitting the forces of morality against the forces of immorality" (p. E7). In a later analysis. Sowell (1999) discussed the requirement to truly grasp basic ideas and concepts. In analyzing issues of justice, Sowell argued about the real need to untangle the confusions surrounding many problems by returning to square one. It is the purpose of this article to return to square one by analyzing the inclusion issue and to demonstrate that the truth is far simpler than the many elaborate attempts to evade the truth.

SPECIAL EDUCATION: HISTORY AND PERSPECTIVE

Mainstreaming

Historically, special education within the public school system developed as a specialized program separate from general education and was embodied in the categorical "special class" (e.g., MacMillan & Hendrick, 1993; Safford & Safford, 1998). The special class was seen as the best means for avoiding conflicts while providing universal education (Gerber, 1996). The special class was viewed as possessing the following advantages: low teacher–pupil ratios, specially trained teachers, greater individualization of instruction in a homogeneous classroom, and an increased curricular emphasis on social and vocational goals (Johnson, 1962). Although some discussion about alternative placement could be found prior to the 1960s (Shattuck, 1946), it was Dunn's (1968) famous article questioning whether separate special classes were justifiable that brought the legitimacy of special class placement to the forefront.

In analyzing the Dunn (1968) article, MacMillan (1971) noted that it lacked scholarly rigor. Dunn argued in favor of a position (i.e., less restrictive placement) based on the lack of support for the efficacy of a contrasting condition (i.e., separate special class). Nevertheless, the Dunn article was the impetus for a number of pieces calling for the abandonment of the special class (e.g., Christopolos & Renz, 1969; Lilly, 1970), even though summaries of empirical evidence offered no unequivocal conclusion about its efficacy (Goldstein, 1967; Guskin & Spicker, 1968; Kirk, 1964).

Within the social context of the time, the Dunn article initiated an attitude in special education that eschewed empirical evidence in favor of ideology to produce change (MacMillan, Semmell, & Gerber, 1994). This attitude was manifested in an emphasis on students in special education gaining access to general education. Advocacy thus shifted from the child to the program, but questions remained about what works in optimally serving students with disabilities in any setting (MacMillan & Semmel, 1977). The Dunn article must also be placed in the context of the strong antisegregation sentiments of the 1960s. The segregated (i.e., separate) nature of special education itself, rather than the particular practices used to teach students with disabilities, was targeted for change (Semmel, Gerber, & MacMillan, 1994).

The debate about integration culminated in the passage of the Education for All Handicapped Children Act (1975; now the Individuals with Disabilities Education Act [IDEA], 1990, 1992, 1997), which mandated that students with disabilities be provided an appropriate education designed to meet their unique needs in the least restrictive environment (LRE; K. Heller, Holtzman, & Messick, 1982; Weintraub, Abeson, Ballard, & LaVor, 1976). The act also required that students with disabilities be educated to the maximum extent appropriate with peers without disabilities (i.e., mainstreamed). Mainstreaming, however, was difficult to define operationally (Kaufman, Agard, & Semmel, 1986). The legal definition focused more on what mainstreaming was theoretically, rather than stipulating that students should be removed and placed in separate classes or schools only when the nature or severity of their disabilities were such that they could not receive an appropriate education in a general education classroom with supplementary aids and services (Bateman & Chard, 1995; Osborne & DiMattia, 1994). To ensure compliance with the act, school districts were required to make a complete continuum of alternative placement options available, as described by Reynolds (1962) and exemplified in Deno's (1970) "Cascade model." The continuum meant that the LRE was not a particular setting (i.e., general education classroom). Furthermore, although the LRE for some students with disabilities might be the general education classroom, it was neither required nor desirable in all cases (Abeson, Burgdorf, Casey, Kunz, & McNeil, 1975). This conclusion has been supported in a number of court cases in which the LRE concept was clarified by developing evidential tests for determining how compliance might be achieved (Thomas & Rapport, 1998; Yell, 1995). In no instance did the tests imply that the general education classroom was anything more than an option in the framework of the LRE (Zirkel, 1996).

The Regular Education Initiative

The LRE mandate brought structural change to special education by making the resource model the primary placement option. This option was defined by the resource room and special education teachers, who provided academic instruction for specified time periods to a special education student whose primary placement was the general education classroom (Hammill & Wiederholt, 1972). By spending at least half the school day in the general education setting, the student was considered to be in the mainstream. Nevertheless, answers to questions about the efficacy of special education remained equivocal (Madden & Slavin, 1983; Wang & Baker, 1985–1986; Wiederholt & Chamberlain, 1989).

Mainstreaming was primarily concerned with access, but questions about how students should be best taught still remained unanswered (Gottlieb, 1981; Kauffman, 1995). Despite increased calls for school reform during the 1980s, the needs of special education—especially how advocating for higher standards and enhanced excellence might affect students with high-incidence mild disabilities—were often not considered (Pugach & Sapon-Shevin, 1987; Shepard, 1987; Yell, 1992). In an effort to contribute to school reform, special education attempted to introduce more powerful instructional methodologies and professional practice (Biklen, 1985; Lipsky & Gartner, 1989; Wang, Reynolds, & Walberg, 1986). Along with a continued call for more inclusive placements, these efforts were termed the Regular Education Initiative (REI; Reynolds, Wang, & Walberg, 1987). Essentially, the goal was to merge general and special education to create a more unified system of education (Gartner & Lipsky, 1987; Will, 1986). The REI was based on the following assumptions: Students are more alike than different, so truly "special" instruction is not required; good teachers can teach all students; all students can be provided with a quality education without reference to traditional special education categories; general education classrooms can manage all students without any segregation; and physically separate education was inherently discriminatory and inequitable.

The REI did not receive uniformly positive responses (W. H. Heller & Schilit, 1987; Lieberman, 1985). For example, Kauffman, Gerber, and Semmel (1988) argued against the REI by indicating that students were not overidentified for special education, student failure should not be attributed solely to perceived shortcomings of teachers, more competent teachers did not necessarily possess more positive attitudes about students with disabilities, variability in student performance will increase rather than decrease when effective instruction is provided to all students, and teachers will be faced with the dilemma of maximizing mean performance versus minimizing group variance. Reynolds (1988) countered with the suggestion that perceived problems resulted primarily from traditional special education: "Present practices have themselves become problematic—causing disjointedness, proceduralism, and inefficiencies in school operations" (p. 355). The rhetoric continued and can be summarized in the question posed by Jenkins, Pious, and Jewell (1990): "How ready for the REI is this country's educational system?" (p. 489).

Research Evidence and the REI

In marshaling empirical evidence for the REI, supporters used the earlier "efficacy studies," the body of research that compared students with disabilities in special classes with those in general education placements. Dunn (1968) used this same research evidence, but the validity of these findings have long been open to serious question. For example, most efficacy studies did not use random selection and assignment of students, and thus they failed to meet standards associated with true experimental designs. In fact, the few studies that did use randomization provided some support for the efficacy of special classes (Goldstein, Moss, & Jordan, 1965). Thus, it was imprudent to cite the efficacy studies as having provided evidence that special classes were not effective (see Gartner & Lipsky, 1989; Lilly, 1988; Wang & Walberg, 1988).

Carlberg and Kavale (1980) conducted a meta-analysis that synthesized the findings from 50 of the best efficacy studies. The mean effect size was $-.12$, which indicated that the relative standing of the average special class student was reduced by about five percentile ranks after an average 2-year stay in a special class. Thus, a small negative effect was associated with special class placement. Larger effect sizes, however, were found for student classification. For students with mild mental retardation (MMR), a mean effect size of $-.14$ was found, but an effect size of $+.29$ was found for students with learning (LD) or emotional and behavioral (EBD) disabilities. Special class placement was thus found to be disadvantageous for students with below-average IQ, causing them to lose seven percentile ranks. In contrast, it was found to be advantageous for students with LD or EBD, who improved by an average of 11 percentile ranks and were better off than 61% of their counterparts placed in general education classrooms. These findings raise questions about whether *all* students with disabilities benefited from integration. Given the magnitude of associated effects, it was evident that placement per se had only a modest influence on outcomes. The place where students with disabilities resided was not a critical factor, suggesting that an examination of what goes on, instructionally and socially, in those placements was needed (Leinhardt & Pallay, 1982).

Empirical evaluations of models for educating students with disabilities in a general education setting have also been used to support the REI. A prime example is the Adaptive Learning Environments Model (ALEM), which was designed to deliver effective instruction to students with disabilities without removing them from the general education classroom (Wang, Gennari, & Waxman, 1985). Evaluations of ALEM (Wang & Birch, 1984a, 1984b; Wang, Peverly, & Randolph, 1984) have been analyzed critically, and ALEM was found to be deficient and inconsistent with respect to design, analysis, and interpretation, suggesting that ALEM cannot be endorsed as a prototypical model for integrating general and special education (Bryan & Bryan, 1988; D. Fuchs & L. S. Fuchs, 1988; Hallahan, Keller, McKinney, Lloyd, & Bryan, 1988).

Given its limited empirical support, the REI was buttressed primarily with ideological arguments. Rhetoric cast opponents of the REI as segregationists (Wang & Walberg, 1988) and the current system of special education as slavery (S. Stainback & W. Stainback, 1987) and apartheid (Lipsky & Gartner, 1987). Conversely, proponents of the REI were viewed as naive liberals (Kauffman, 1989). The essential issue was framed as a debate about the future of special education between "abolitionists and conservationists" (D. Fuchs & L. S. Fuchs, 1991). The REI proponents came to be divided over the question of who should be integrated, however. On one side, some proponents suggested that the REI was aimed primarily at students with high-incidence mild disabilities such as MMR, LD, and EBD. The option of alternative separate settings remained appropriate for students with severe and profound disabilities (Pugach & Lilly, 1984; Reynolds & Wang, 1983), with the possibility of a more progressive inclusion that was "describable in terms of a gradual shift, within a cascade model, from distal to proximal administrative arrangements and from segregated to integrated arrangements" (Reynolds, 1991, p. 14). On the other side, there was the suggestion that *all* students with disabilities be integrated, regardless of disability type or severity level (Gartner & Lipsky, 1987; S. Stainback & W. Stainback, 1984b). If all students were not integrated, then two separate systems of education would be maintained that represented merely "blending of the margins" (Gartner & Lipsky, 1989, p. 271) and did not "address the need to include in regular classrooms and regular education those students labeled severely and profoundly handicapped" (S. Stainback & W. Stainback, 1989, p. 43).

Inclusion: Part Time to Full Time

Special education was thus experiencing great tensions (Meredith & Underwood, 1995). Some called for radical change that would alter the fundamental nature of special education, and others called for a more cautious approach to change based on empirical analyses and historical considerations (Dorn, Fuchs, & Fuchs, 1996). Kauffman (1993) suggested that change in special education should be predicated on three assumptions:

1. The necessity of keeping *place* in perspective, because setting per se has limited impact on outcomes for students with disabilities.
2. Choosing ideas over image; for example, equating special education with segregation and apartheid was a gross oversimplification that distorted debate because image may become the measure of truth.
3. Avoiding fanaticism, a passion that has become dangerous because it can result in moral certainty with predetermined answers.

Finally, Kauffman called for the strengthening of special education's empirical base through experimentation with new programs, strategies, and policies.

D. Fuchs and L. S. Fuchs (1994) traced the origins of the inclusive schools movement and contrasted inclusion with the REI. A major distinction between movements was focused on the distinction between high- versus low-incidence special education populations. Many advocates for the low-incidence group (i.e., those students with severe intellectual deficits) continued to view the REI as policy directed primarily at students with high-incidence disabilities (i.e., MMR, LD, EBD) but nonetheless retained the goal of moving all students into the mainstream. Consequently, these disagreements resulted in special education not being successful in convincing general education about the merits of the REI (Pugach & Sapon-Shevin, 1987). In reality, the REI was primarily a special education initiative for high-incidence disabilities that had modest success in changing special, but not general, education.

The inclusive schools movement, however, possessed the larger goal of reducing special education, as defined in the continuum of placements (Gartner & Lipsky, 1989). Later, Lipsky and Gartner (1991) said, "The concept[s] of Least Restrictive Environment—a continuum of placements, and a cascade of services—were progressive when developed but do not today promote the *full* inclusion of *all* persons with disabilities in *all* aspects of societal life" (p. 52). The inclusive school was thus viewed as a setting essentially devoid of special education: "No students, including those with disabilities, are relegated to the fringes of the school by placement in segregated wings, trailers, or special classes" (S. Stainback & W. Stainback, 1992, p. 34). All models of inclusion were aimed at providing a restructured and unified system of special and general education (Skrtic, 1991). In the course of advocacy for inclusion, many proponents of the REI became disillusioned because of their limited influence on general education. But soon, a group associated with The Association of Persons with Severe Handicaps (TASH) "took the field by storm; they rushed into a vacuum created by others' inaction, no doubt intimidating by their vigor alone many who disagreed with their radical message" (D. Fuchs & L. S. Fuchs, 1994, p. 299). TASH had a significant effect on policy because of rhetoric calling for the elimination of special education in the form of a continuum of placements (W. Stainback & S. Stainback, 1991) and a curricular focus emphasizing socialization in order to foster social competence over academic achievement (Snell, 1991).

The proponents of full inclusion predicated their position on the assumption that special education was the basic cause of many of the problems experienced by general education (Skrtic, Sailor, & Gee, 1996). Consequently, there was no need for a continuum of placements because the LRE was, in fact, the general education classroom (Lipsky & Gartner, 1997; S. Taylor, 1988). This view of the LRE as a single place ignored important interactions between student needs and instructional processes (Korinek, McLaughlin, & Walther-Thomas, 1995; Morsink & Lenk, 1992). With all students in the same classroom (and no special education), TASH hoped that general education would be forced to deal with students previously avoided and thus transform itself into a more responsive and resourceful system. The essence of the message by TASH thus differed markedly from that of other advocacy and professional groups in special education (see Kauffman & Hallahan, 1995, pp. 307–348). For example, how could TASH speak for *all* students while supporting a diminished academic emphasis that represented the primary educational focus for almost all students with high-incidence mild disabilities? By rejecting alternative views, the TASH full inclusion position really reflected an exclusionary, not inclusionary, mind-set that radicalized reform in special education because the "full inclusionists' romanticism, insularity, and a willingness to speak for all is markedly different from REI supporters' pragmatism, big-tent philosophy and reluctance to speak for all" (D. Fuchs & L. S. Fuchs, 1994, p. 304). The radical proposal offered by full inclusion proponents was questioned by REI supporters who focused on repairing the disjointedness experienced by students and programs of the "second system" at the "school margins" (Reynolds, 1989, 1992; Wang, Reynolds, & Walberg, 1988). Additionally, special education renewed interest in demonstrating its real benefits (D. Fuchs & L. S. Fuchs, 1995a, 1995b; Kavale & Forness, 1999). Special education appeared, however, to reach a status quo, with limited consensus about the merits of the many approaches to integration (Putnam, Spiegel, & Bruininks, 1995). Martin (1995) indicated that "as a matter of public policy, a federal or state government, even a local school system, cannot responsibly adopt 'inclusion' without defining its proposed program" (p. 193).

SPECIAL EDUCATION PRACTICE AND EVIDENCE

The emphasis on special education as a place (i.e., a setting where students with disabilities are educated) deflected attention away from the fact that special education was a more comprehensive process whose actual dynamics were major contributors to its success or failure (Kavale & Glass, 1984). A significant part of the special education process was represented in the beliefs and actions of general education. In an integrated system, special education cannot act independently as a separate system, but must formulate policy in response to the attitudes, perceptions, and behaviors of general education (Gallagher, 1994).

Attitudes and Beliefs

It has long been recognized (Sarason, 1982) that a major factor in the success or failure of a policy such as mainstreaming is the attitudes of the
general education teacher (Hannah & Pliner, 1983; Horne, 1985). Early on,
general education teachers expressed some negative attitudes, especially
feelings of inadequacy in dealing with students with disabilities, although
they remained generally positive about the concept of integration
(Ringlaben & Price, 1981; Stephens & Braun, 1980). Although positive attitudes about students with disabilities could also be found (Alexander &
Strain, 1978; Yuker, 1988), these positive attitudes were often accompanied
by concern about the integration of students with severe disabilities, particularly those with significant intellectual deficits (Hirshoren & Burton,
1979; Shotel, Lano, & McGettigan, 1972). Teachers were also found to be
more willing to integrate students whose disabilities did not require additional responsibilities on their part (Gans, 1987; Houck & Rogers, 1994).
Otherwise, they revealed a resistance to greater integration (Margolis &
McGettigan, 1988). Although attempts to foster more positive attitudes
about integration have been made (Naor & Milgram, 1980), any positive
attitude changes achieved were found to be short-lived (Donaldson, 1980;
S. Stainback, W. Stainback, Strathe, & Dedrick, 1983).

The attitudes of peers toward students with disabilities have also been
investigated. Although they have not been uniformly positive, findings
generally revealed a tendency toward more tolerance with increased contact (Esposito & Reed, 1986; Towfighy-Hooshyar & Zingle, 1984; Voeltz,
1980). Generally, though, general education peers paid no particular
attention to students with disabilities (Lovitt, Plavins, & Cushing, 1999).
Any positive reactions about inclusion among students without disabilities also tended to be accompanied by feelings of discomfort, especially
about students with moderate and severe disabilities who may possess
significant communication difficulties and often lack positive social skills
(Helmstetter, Peck, & Giangreco, 1994; Hendrickson, Shokoohi-Yekta,
Hamre-Nietupski, & Gable, 1996). Although some found that students
with severe disabilities were accepted by nondisabled peers (Evans,
Salisbury, Palombaro, Berryman, & Hollowood, 1992; Hall, 1994; Janney,
Snell, Beers, & Raynes, 1995), Cook and Semmel (1999) found that this
was not the case, particularly when atypical behavior occurred. Cook and
Semmel also found that students with mild disabilities "do not typically
appear to engender peer acceptance" (p. 57).

For parents, generally positive attitudes about inclusion appeared to be the norm, although anxiety about the actual mechanics was also seen (Bennett, DeLuca, & Bruns, 1997; Gibb et al., 1997; Green & Shinn, 1994). The anxiety was most evident among parents who supported inclusion but had reservations about it for *their* children (Lovitt & Cushing, 1999). As a result, it was possible to find diverse opinion about inclusion among parents (Borthwick-Duffy, Palmer, & Lane, 1996). For example, Carr (1993) doubted whether inclusion would be appropriate for her child with LD because of the loss of special education services. The question and answer posed: "What has changed in education since the time my son was in elementary school that would ensure successful inclusion? The answer is, unfortunately, nothing really" (p. 591). B. R. Taylor (1994) disagreed and, in response, suggested that "regular education is not only where the responsibility lies, but also where those with learning disabilities *deserve* to be educated" (p. 579). In discussing her sons with special needs, Brucker (1994) stressed the need for change: "We have been generally unsuccessful in our current mode of service delivery, although we have had some individual successes. The operation may have been a success, but the patient died! Inclusion's time has come!" (p. 582). Grove and Fisher (1999) discussed these reactions as a tension between the culture of educational reform (opportunities offered by inclusive education) and the culture of the school site (day-to-day demands of schooling). The general public has also been found to possess positive attitudes about integration, but less positive if the students in question were likely to encounter difficulty in the general education classroom (Berryman, 1989; Gottlieb & Corman, 1975).

Administrators, because of their leadership positions, were viewed as playing a significant role in the success or failure of mainstreaming (Lazar, Stodden, & Sullivan, 1976; Payne & Murray, 1974). Principals, however, demonstrated a lack of their knowledge about students with disabilities (Cline, 1981), and often perceived little chance of success in general education, particularly students with the label "mentally retarded" (Bain & Dolbel, 1991; W. E. Davis, 1980). Additionally, principals indicated that pull-out programs were the most effective placements, that full-time general class placements offered more social than academic benefits, and that support services were not likely to be provided in general education classrooms (Barnett & Monda-Amaya, 1998; Center, Ward, Parmenter, & Nash, 1985). When the attitudes about mainstreaming of teachers and administrators were compared, the most positive attitudes were held by administrators, the individuals most removed from the reality of the classroom (J. C. Davis & Maheady, 1991; Glicking & Theobald, 1975).

Garvar-Pinhas and Schmelkin (1989) said that "principals appear to respond in a more socially appropriate manner than may actually be the case in reality" (p. 42). Additionally, Cook, Semmel, and Gerber (1999) found critical differences between principals' and teachers' opinions about inclusion, including differing perceptions concerning the possibilities for enhanced academic achievement, what really works best, and the level of resources being committed for inclusive arrangements. The optimistic views of principals were in sharp contrast to the more pessimistic views of teachers, and were assumed to be "at least in part, based on negative experiences regarding the outcomes of inclusion or the conviction that inclusion will not produce appropriate outcomes" (p. 205).

Summarizing Attitudes and Beliefs

Attitudes about integration have historically been multidimensional and reflective of a variety of underlying factors. Larrivee and Cook (1979) identified these factors, which included academic concerns—the possible negative effects of integration on general academic progress; socioemotional concerns—the negative aspects of segregating students with disabilities; administrative concerns; and teacher concerns—issues about support, experience, and training necessary to work with students with disabilities. These concerns appeared to be long-maintained, even after 20 years of inclusion experience (Cornoldi, Terreni, Scruggs, & Mastropieri, 1998).

The research evidence about attitudes surrounding integration tended to be inconclusive because of the widely disparate opinions held. Studies have shown general education teachers to hold negative views about integration (Coates, 1989; Gersten, Walker, & Darch, 1988; Semmel, Abernathy, Butera, & Lesar, 1991), and others have revealed more positive attitudes (Villa, Thousand, Meyers, & Nevin, 1996; York, Vandercook, MacDonald, Heise-Neff, & Caughey, 1992). These differences may be related to findings that suggest more experience with inclusion being associated with more positive attitudes (Minke, Bear, Deemer, & Griffin, 1996). The experiences with inclusion may also create sampling differences, however, that bias findings in one direction and make any generalizations suspect.

Soodak, Podell, and Lehman (1998) examined the relationships among teacher, student, and school factors in predicting teachers' response to inclusion. Two responses were found: a hostility/receptivity dimension reflecting teachers' willingness to include students with disabilities in their classrooms and their expectations about the success of such an arrangement;

and an anxiety/calmness dimension reflecting teachers' emotional tension when actually faced with serving students with disabilities. Both responses were found to be related to teacher attributes and school conditions. Teachers who possessed low efficacy (i.e., beliefs about the impact of their teaching), who had limited teaching experience, or who demonstrated limited use of differentiated teaching practices were generally less receptive to inclusion. Another major influence on both dimensions was type of disability: Teachers held more positive attitudes toward the inclusion of students with physical disabilities than toward inclusion of those with solely academic or behavior disorders (Mandell & Strain, 1978). The greatest hostility and anxiety were found for students with MMR, with these same perceptions found for students with LD as teachers gained more experience in special education (Wilczenski, 1993).

In an effort to harness the complexity surrounding attitudes about integration, Scruggs and Mastropieri (1996) conducted a quantitative research synthesis of 28 investigations that surveyed the perceptions of almost 10,000 general education teachers regarding the inclusion of students with disabilities. Although two thirds of general education teachers supported the concept of integration, only a small majority expressed a willingness to include students with disabilities in their own classrooms. Although there was support for the concept of integration, fewer than one third of general education teachers expressed the belief that the general education classroom either was the optimal placement or would produce greater benefits than other placements. The two factors that seem to influence these perceptions appeared to be the severity level of student disability and the amount of additional teacher responsibility required. Among about one third of the sample, these two factors appeared to be associated with the belief that including students with disabilities would have a negative impact on the general education classroom. Finally, only about one quarter of the teachers believed that they had sufficient classroom time for inclusion efforts, that they were currently prepared to teach students with disabilities, or that they would receive sufficient training for inclusion efforts. These findings were interpreted as support for the assumption that teachers viewed students with disabilities in the context of the reality of the general education classroom rather than as support for the prevailing attitudes about integration. General education teachers thus demonstrated a certain reluctance about inclusion that must be addressed if a policy change is to be successful (Welch, 1989).

THE REALITY
OF GENERAL EDUCATION

What Happens in the General Education Class?

Besides attitudes toward integration, there are also contextual realities associated with the general education classroom that might affect the success or failure of integration (Shanker, 1995). Baker and Zigmond (1990) asked, Are regular education classes equipped to accommodate students with learning disabilities? Their analysis indicated that the general education classroom was a place where undifferentiated, large-group instruction dominated and teachers were more concerned with maintaining routine than with meeting individual differences: "Teachers cared about children and were conscientious about their jobs—but their mind-set was conformity, not accommodation. In these regular education classes, any student who could not conform would likely be unsuccessful" (p. 519).

McIntosh, Vaughn, Schumm, Haager, and Lee (1993) found a similar scenario for students with disabilities in the general education classroom. Although they were treated much like other students, students with disabilities did not receive differentiated instruction or adaptations. Even effective teachers were found to make few adaptations because of the belief that many adaptations were not feasible (Schumm & Vaughn, 1991; Whinnery, Fuchs, & Fuchs, 1991; Ysseldyke, Thurlow, Wotruba, & Nania, 1990) or because students themselves did not view many adaptations favorably (Vaughn, Schumm, & Kouzekanani, 1993; Vaughn, Schumm, Niharos, & Daugherty, 1993). In fact, many students with disabilities preferred special education pull-out programs (i.e., resource rooms) over programs delivered exclusively in the general education setting (Guterman, 1995; Jenkins & Heinen, 1989; Klingner, Vaughn, Schumm, Cohen, & Forgan, 1998). Even though many students with disabilities experienced feelings of anger, embarrassment, and frustration in a special education setting and generally viewed it as undesirable (Albinger, 1995; Lovitt et al., 1999; Reid & Button, 1995), Padeliadu and Zigmond (1996) found that most students with disabilities also felt the special education setting to be a supportive and quiet environment where they could receive extra academic assistance. In a synthesis of eight studies examining students' perceptions about their educational placements, Vaughn and Klingner (1998) concluded that, "whether at the elementary or secondary level, many students with LD prefer to receive specialized instruction outside of the general education classroom for part of the school day" (p. 85).

In a later analysis of full-time mainstreaming with Project MELD (Mainstream Experiences for Learning Disabled), Zigmond and Baker (1994) investigated whether "the regular education class can provide an environment in which students with LDs have more opportunities to learn, to make greater educational progress in academic skills, and to avoid the stigma associated with being less capable in academic achievement" (p. 108). After examining outcomes, they concluded that special education students "did not get a *special* education" (p. 116). Lieberman (1996) attributed the situation to the increased demands on the general education teacher, and R. Roberts and Mather (1995) said that "regular educators are not trained to provide diversified instructional methods or to cope with the needs of diverse learners" (p. 50). In fact, general education teachers were most comfortable when using generic and nonspecific teaching strategies that were not likely to meet the individual needs of students with disabilities (Ellet, 1993; Johnson & Pugach, 1990).

In a more comprehensive evaluation of inclusive settings, Baker and Zigmond (1995) concluded,

> We saw very little "specially designed instruction" delivered uniquely to a student with learning disabilities. We saw almost no specific, directed, individualized, intensive, remedial instruction for students who were clearly deficient academically and struggling with the schoolwork they were being given. (p. 178)

Thus, a basic tenet of special education—individualization—was not being achieved (Deno, Foegen, Robinson, & Espin, 1996). Further confirmation of this was found in analyses of Individualized Education Programs (IEPs). Generally, findings suggested that the less restrictive the setting, the less individualized the IEP (Espin, Deno, & Albayrak-Kaymak, 1998; Smith, 1990): "The 'specialness' of special education, with its emphasis on individualized programming, seems to decrease in inclusive settings" (Espin et al., 1998, p. 173).

After analyzing three large-scale projects designed to restructure schools to better accommodate students with disabilities in general education classrooms, Zigmond et al. (1995) concluded that "general education settings produce achievement outcomes for students with LD that are neither desirable nor acceptable" (p. 538). In a review assessing the academic outcomes associated with eight different models for educating students with mild disabilities in general education classrooms, Manset and Semmel (1997) concluded, "The evidence clearly indicates that a model of wholesale inclusive programming that is superior to more traditional special education service delivery models does not exist at present" (p. 178). Although findings assessing academic outcomes associated with inclusion were mixed, they generally were not encouraging given the significant investment of resources necessary to provide these enhanced educational opportunities (Marston, 1996; Waldron & McLeskey, 1998). A similar scenario was found for the academic performance of students with disabilities who had been reintegrated into general education classrooms (Carlson & Parshall, 1996; D. Fuchs, L. S. Fuchs, & Fernstrom, 1993; Shinn, Powell-Smith, Good, & Baker, 1997).

The Social Situation in General Education

In addition to academic effects, social outcomes associated with general education placement have also been investigated. Although some positive social outcomes have been found, primarily in the form of increased tolerance and more social support from students without disabilities (Banerji & Dailey, 1995; Fryxell & Kennedy, 1995), there also appear to be continuing negative consequences, including limited self-confidence, poor self-perceptions, and inadequate social skills among students with disabilities (Tapasak & Walther-Thomas, 1999). Mixed findings also surrounded teacher–child interactions in inclusive settings. Although students with disabilities have been shown to engage in a greater number of positive interactions with teachers (Evans et al., 1992; Thompson, Vitale, & Jewett, 1984), studies have also shown far fewer such positive interactions (Alves & Gottlieb, 1986; Richey & McKinney, 1978). In a study of teacher–child interactions in inclusive classrooms over the course of a school year, Chow and Kasari (1999)—unlike Jordan, Lindsay, and Stanovich (1997), who found more interaction at the beginning of the school year—found that the number of teacher–student interactions did not differ over the course of the school year. Students with disabilities may, however, require continuing higher levels of interaction (Wigle & Wilcox, 1996), and "by receiving the same amount of interactions at the end of the year, the needs of children with disabilities and at-risk children may not have been sufficiently met" (Chow & Kasari, 1999, p. 231).

In a large-scale study, Vaughn, Elbaum, and Schumm (1996) assessed the effects of inclusive placements on social functioning and found that students with disabilities were less accepted by peers, and the degree to which they were accepted and liked declined over time. In sum, students with disabilities were less often accepted and more often rejected C. Roberts & Zubrick, 1992; Sale & Carey, 1995).

With respect to self-perceptions among students with disabilities in integrated settings, Bear, Clever, and Proctor (1991) found low levels of global self-worth, academic competence, and behavioral conduct. One problem noted by MacMillan, Gresham, and Forness (1996) was that for students without disabilities, simple contact with students with disabilities in itself does not result in more favorable attitudes and improved acceptance. Rather, the nature and quality of interactions were significant influences on the way attitudes developed, and any objectionable behavior on the part of students with disabilities quickly resulted in less favorable perceptions among their peers in general education. Additionally, if there was a strong academic focus in the classroom, then perceptions about students with disabilities not keeping up may result in less teacher tolerance and less peer acceptance (Cook, Gerber, & Semmel, 1997).

Teacher Skill and Ability

At a fundamental skill level, general education teachers were not well prepared for the inclusion of students with disabilities (Kearny & Durand, 1992; Myles & Simpson, 1989; Rojewski & Pollard, 1993), and consequently expressed a variety of concerns about the implementation of inclusion activities (Fox & Ysseldyke, 1997; Giangreco, Dennis, Cloninger, Edelman, & Schattman, 1993). For example, although Downing, Eichinger, and Williams (1997) found generally positive views about inclusion, they also found that teachers expressed concern about the time and effort required to meet the needs of students with disabilities that might limit their ability to provide an optimal education for students without disabilities. Special education teachers were most concerned about their perceived loss of control over the classroom, their modified job functions, and the possibility that needed resources and supports exceeded their availability (de Bettencourt, 1999; Werts, Wolery, Snyder, Caldwell, & Salisbury, 1996).

As a result of these perceived barriers and expressed concerns, the requisite individual planning for students with disabilities may not occur in general education contexts (Schumm & Vaughn, 1992; Schumm, Vaughn, Haager, McDowell, Rothlein, & Saumell, 1995; Vaughn & Schumm, 1994). Although instructional adaptations for students with disabilities were viewed as desirable (Bender, Vail, & Scott, 1995; Blanton, Blanton, & Cross, 1994; Schumm, Vaughn, Gordon, & Rothlein, 1994), they may not be used unless perceived as being easy to implement as well as requiring little extra time, little change in routine, or little additional assistance (Bacon & Schulz, 1991; L. S. Fuchs, D. Fuchs, Hamlett, Phillips, & Karns, 1995; Munson, 1986–1987). The experiences of general and special education teachers working collaboratively in inclusive settings revealed some success, but also revealed concerns stemming from differences in perceived roles, teaching styles, and philosophical orientation (Salend et al., 1997). Walther-Thomas (1997) noted pragmatic problems in collaborative arrangements related to scheduling planning time, coordinating teacher and student schedules, and obtaining administrative support. The failure of collaborative teaching teams was found to result primarily from an inability to communicate, a failure to resolve teaching-style differences, and an inability to adequately integrate special education students and teachers into the classroom (Phillips, Sapona, & Lubic, 1995).

Schumm and Vaughn (1995) summarized findings from a 5-year research project designed to determine whether general education was prepared for inclusive education and to gain insight into the success a student with a high-incidence mild disability might experience (see also Vaughn, Schumm, Jallad, Slusher, & Saumell, 1996). The findings affirmed many earlier conclusions suggesting that general education teachers believed they did not possess the necessary preparation to teach students with disabilities, lacked opportunities to collaborate with special education teachers, and made infrequent and unsystematic use of adaptations, even though students with disabilities preferred teachers who did make such instructional adaptations. In answering the question about whether the educational stage was set for inclusion, Schumm and Vaughn provided a generally negative response. The importance of having the stage properly set was demonstrated by Mamlin (1999) in an analysis of an inclusion effort that failed. The failure was attributed to a continuing culture of segregation in the school and a leadership style that demanded too much control. In conclusion, Mamlin said, "not all schools are ready to make decisions on restructuring for inclusion" (p. 47).

DISCUSSION

Special education is in a state of flux. Integration has been a prominent theme for some 25 years, but its final form remains unclear (Danielson & Bellamy, 1989; Katsiyannis, Conderman, & Franks, 1995). The lack of agreement is evidenced in the differing position statements offered by organizations promoting full inclusion (Association for Persons with Severe Handicaps, 1992; Council of Chief State School Officers, 1992; National Association of State Boards of Education, 1992) and those advocating inclusion being only one among a number of possible placement options (Council for Exceptional Children, 1993; Learning Disabilities Association, 1993; National Joint Committee on Learning Disabilities, 1993). Although the trend has been for greater integration for a greater number of students with disabilities, whether or not this means *all* students *all* the time has been subject to passionate debate (see Roberts & Mather, 1995, and response by McLesky & Pugach, 1995). A more cautious policy is thus warranted. Inclusion appears to be not something that simply happens, but rather something that requires careful thought and preparation. The focus must not simply be on access to general education, but rather the assurance that when inclusion is deemed appropriate, it is implemented with proper attitudes, accommodations, and adaptations in place (Deno, 1994; King-Sears, 1997; Scott, Vitale, & Masten, 1998).

The research evidence investigating inclusion clearly suggests caution (MacMillan et al., 1996; Salend & Gerrick Duhaney, 1999). Much is still not known, but what is known about the beliefs and operations of general education has not been uniformly supportive and suggests the need for careful and reasoned implementation (Downing et al., 1997; Idol, 1997). Analysis of the evidence also suggests that the effectiveness of practices associated with inclusion are mixed at best (Fisher, Schumaker, & Deshler, 1995; Hunt & Goetz, 1997). Generalizations about inclusion thus remain tentative, and it appears unwise to advocate for inclusion without ensuring that it is carried out effectively. Too much time has been spent talking about inclusion, and not enough time evaluating it in relation to alternative service delivery arrangements and practices (King-Sears & Cummings, 1996). Consequently, outcomes for special education have not been predictable, and students with disabilities may be at risk for adverse consequences with the indiscriminate implementation of a full inclusion policy.

Postmodernism and Inclusion

The realities of the general and special education nexus suggest that general education is neither ready nor willing to endorse a radical policy such as full inclusion. A segment of special education, however, appears to ignore this reality. The influence of postmodern thought among this segment is significant. Postmodernism rejects the modern view of science as a system that focuses on problem solving by constructing, evaluating, and testing different conjectures about optimal solutions (Gross & Levitt, 1994). The postmodern model questions the superiority of the modern over the premodern, eschews rigid disciplinary boundaries, and challenges the possibility of creating global, all-encompassing worldviews (Bauman, 1987; Griffin, 1988; Turner, 1990).

The postmodern perspective has been challenged, however (Koertge, 1998; Sokal & Bricmont, 1998). The differences between modern and postmodern were described by Rosenau (1992):

> Those of a modern conviction seek to isolate elements, specify relationships, and formulate a synthesis; post-modernists do the opposite. They offer indeterminacy rather than determinism, diversity rather than unity, difference rather than synthesis, complexity rather than simplification. They look to the unique rather than to the general, to intertextual relations rather than causality, and to the unrepeatable rather than the re-occurring, the habitual, or the routine. With a post-modern perspective, social science becomes a more subjective and humble enterprise as truth gives way to tentativeness. (p. 8)

Within the postmodern perspective, the most questionable assumption is the rejection of all science because it is believed to be untrustworthy. Consequently, alternative ways of knowing (e.g., special education), especially those based on an individual's own experience that is believed to be the only one really knowable, possess equal merit (Danforth, 1997; Sailor & Skrtic, 1996; Skrtic et al., 1996). Instead of discussion about the possibilities of inclusion in a real-world context buttressed by empirical evidence, some special educators have chosen to construct arguments within a postmodern framework This approach becomes even more unreal and extreme when also based on the view that special education is a fundamentally evil enterprise (Danforth & Rhodes, 1997; Lipsky & Gartner, 1996). For example, Brantlinger (1997) suggested that the current special education system is harming students because it is driven by a privileged ideology that has made it impossible to achieve equity. Consequently, the situation can be ameliorated only by placing all students in the general education setting. In reality, such a postmodern solution is neither practical nor reliable. Although postmodernism views radical transformation as the sole remedy, a more incremental approach to positive change, based on a substantive real-world empirical research foundation, offers the possibility for more rational and credible solutions (Carnine, 1997; Kauffman, 1993; Zigmond, 1997).

The role and validity of research, however, has become a contentious issue, particularly with respect to preferred research methodology, as evidenced in the quantitative–qualitative research debate (Simpson & Eaves, 1985; S. Stainback & W. Stainback, 1984a). Opposing sides in the inclusion debate tend to sort themselves into quantitative or qualitative camps, with much of the support for inclusion being based on qualitative research findings (Kozleski & Jackson, 1993; Salisbury, Palombaro, & Hollowood, 1993). Such findings are often presented in discourse form that emulates styles associated with literary criticism or cultural studies: "Post-modern delivery is more literary in character while modern discourse aims to be exact, precise, pragmatic, and rigorous in style" (Rosenau, 1992, p. 7). Although postmodernists may prefer "audacious and provocative forms of delivery" (p. 7), it must be emphasized that such characteristics offer no insight into the worth of the arguments presented. Contas (1998) also questioned the motivation behind the postmodern form of delivery: "Is this disciplinary shift part of a rhetorical strategy being used to give the impression of erudition?" (p. 29). Contas went on to say that definitive conclusions are often lacking because of "the spurious belief that ordered thinking and rational inquiry stifle the human spirit and oppress the political rights of the people we study" (p. 28). The consequences are seen in what has been termed the "cult of ambiguity and indeterminacy" (Eagleton, 1996).

The proper role of research may also be at issue. For example, in discussing the famous *Brown v. Board of Education* (1954) Supreme Court decision, Gerard (1983) argued that the supporting Social Science Statement was based on well-meaning rhetoric rather than solid research evidence:

> All that it said, in effect, was that because the minority child was now in a classroom with Whites, he or she would no longer have the status of an outcast or a panah. This knowledge would somehow impart to the child the self-image necessary to do well in school and later enter the mainstream of American society. (p. 869)

Substitute *child with disabilities* for *minority child*, and parallels to the present inclusion debate are apparent.

Ideology, Politics, and Beliefs

With an emphasis on ideology without reference to accompanying research evidence in making policy decisions, an objective rendering of the real-world situation may not be achieved (Kauffman, 1999). Ideology can cause arguments to be perceived in a selective manner (Cohen, 1993). A prime example is found in the contentious nature–nurture debate surrounding the role of heredity and environment in producing intelligence. In an early review, Pastore (1949) indicated that those taking the nature (heredity) side tended to be politically right of center, whereas those taking the nurture (environment) side tended to be left of center. Later, Harwood (1976, 1977) found a similar political dichotomy among those who either supported or objected to the position proposed by Jensen (1969), which suggested that the 15 IQ-point advantage for Whites over Blacks was about 80% due to heredity and only about 20% a result of environment. Consequently, theoretical positions may be partially formed by political beliefs.

The nature–nurture debate has not made significant progress in achieving closure. The primary reason is that not many new research data have been brought to bear on the question (Cartwright & Burtis, 1968). Consequently, the different sides tend to form conclusions using the same finite body of information, where differences are primarily the result of ideology, not scientific interpretation. With ideological differences paramount, the nature–nurture debate soon became testy. The nature side was accused of distortion, misrepresentation, and faulty logic (Deutsch, 1969; Hirsch, 1975; Lewontin, 1970), but the same charges were also leveled against those on the nurture side (Eysenck, 1971; Hernstein, 1973; Loehlin, Lindzey, & Spuhler, 1975). Thus, ideology was a significant factor in the positions taken.

Ideology, by itself, however, does not promote scientific advancement. In discussing Kuhn's (1970) ideas about paradigms and scientific development, Lakatos (1978) stressed the "research program" and its description as either progressive or degenerative. When there is a lack of evidence validating empirical research, theories experience experimental failure and must be modified to accommodate the earlier successes as well as the anomalies that brought the earlier theory into question. When this process is achieved successfully, the research program is termed progressive. If not progressive, the research program is termed degenerative. With no empirical successes, anomalies are met with ad hoc explanations that become increasingly inadequate and must be remedied through a new research program. The earlier-cited nature–nurture debate about IQ represents a case of competing research programs: Are the rival programs progressing or degenerating? Using Lakatos's (1978) critical methodology, Urbach (1974a, 1974b) concluded that the hereditarian (i.e., nature) position was stronger:

> Environmentalists have revised their theories in an ad hoc fashion. This patching-up process has left the environmentalist programme as little more than a collection of untestable theories which provide a *"passe partout"* which explains everything because it explains nothing. (Urbach, 1974b, p. 253)

Urbach also pointed out that such an analysis does not mean that the nurture (i.e., environmental) position was wrong: "The fact that the environmentalist programme has been degenerating does not mean that no progressive programme will ever be based on its hard core" (Urbach, 1974b, p. 253).

Empirical evidence is thus necessary to strengthen the research program so that it is progressive. Special education initially possessed a research program emphasizing the special class. The earlier-cited efficacy studies created an anomaly that was remedied by the continuum of placements embodied in the Cascade model. By 1980 the special education research program was manifested in the LRE concept, but anomalies were still present (e.g., students in special education not making the progress expected). Research dealing with resource models, collaborative models, adaptive education, peer tutoring, individualized education strategies, and innovative teaching strategies demonstrated the response of a progressive special education research program.

In contrast, advocates for full inclusion have failed to provide a progressive research program. In fact, a research program providing any empirical evidence is difficult to identify. In examining the same anomalies, the full inclusion research program simply upped the ante by calling for all students with disabilities to be fully integrated (Biklen, 1985; Lipsky & Gartner, 1997; S. Stainback, W. Stainback, & Forest, 1989; Villa, Thousand, Stainback, & Stainback, 1992). The supportive arguments were primarily based on ideology buttressed by anecdotal case studies and testimonials, but not on quantitative research evidence. Thus, a solution that simply calls for full inclusion without accompanying empirical support is neither logical nor rational and results in a degenerative research program with too many ad hoc explanations. More empirical research on inclusion is thus necessary, as suggested by MacMillan et al. (1996): "We need more research on inclusion, not less.... Simplification will only mislead us into adopting untried treatments with the possibility of disserving children" (p. 156).

Ideology may be useful in discussions attempting to establish goals and objectives, but actual practice is best derived from scientific inquiry. Special education had a previous example where ideology played a primary role in determining policy. The issue was deinstitutionalization, and Landesman and Butterfield (1987) pointed out that "as goals, normalization and deinstitutionalization are not terribly controversial; as *means* to achieving these goals many of the current practices related to deinstitutionalization and normalization are" (p. 809). They suggested that more data relevant to the care and treatment of individuals with mental retardation were required. In the absence of such information, there was no basis for judging the merits of deinstitutionalization policy. Shadish (1984), in discussing deinstitutionalization policy, pointed out the tendency to view negative consequences (e.g., increase in homelessness) as merely unfortunate happenstance not connected to the ideology that initiated the policy. More positive outcomes were then sought, not by using new research evidence to guide practice, but rather by using the same ideological foundation reshaped with more noble intentions and ending again with the same pragmatic difficulties. The parallels with the inclusion debate are again clear, and efforts should be directed at avoiding a similar scenario.

CONCLUSION

Questions about the integration of students with disabilities are not new. There has been, over the past 25 years, a steady press toward greater integration of students with disabilities. The law demands education in the LRE, but difficulties have resulted from this provision coming to be interpreted as solely the general education classroom, particularly for all students regardless of type and level of disability. Although there is ideological and political support for inclusion, the empirical evidence is less convincing. The reality of general education suggests that the requisite attitudes, accommodations, and adaptations for students with disabilities are not yet in place. Consequently, a more tempered approach that formulates and implements policy on the basis of research and evaluation findings as well as ideological and political considerations is necessary. In this way, real solutions may be forthcoming that do not reflect Sowell's (1995) visions of the anointed and benighted, but, rather, reflect a vision of the rational. It is possible to draw parallels to the inclusion debate from previous contentious issues in special education, and it would be prudent to learn from these past experiences. With a rational solution, special education may then be in a better position to pursue its real mission: providing the best possible education for all students with disabilities.

AUTHORS' NOTES

Kenneth A. Kavale, PhD, is a professor of special education at the University of Iowa. His research interests focus on the analysis of theory and policy for learning and behavioral disabilities. Address: Kenneth A. Kavale, Department of Special Education, N235 Lindquist Center, The University of Iowa, Iowa City, IA 52242.

Steven R. Forness, EdD, is a professor of biobehavioral sciences and chief educational psychologist at the Neuropsychiatric Institute of the University of California, Los Angeles. His research interests focus on the analysis of theory and policy for learning and behavioral disabilities.

REFERENCES

Abeson, A., Burgdorf, R. L., Casey, P. J., Kunz, I. W., & McNeil, W. (1975). Access to opportunity. In N. Hobbs (Ed.), *Issues in the classification of children* (Vol. 2, pp. 270–292) San Francisco: Jossey-Bass.

Albinger, P. (1995) Stones from the resource room: Piano lessons, imaginary illness, and broken-down cars. *Journal of Learning Disabilities, 28,* 615–621.

Alexander, C., & Strain, P. S. (1978). A review of educators' attitudes toward handicapped children and the concept of mainstreaming. *Psychology in the Schools, 15,* 390–396.

Alves, A. J., & Gottlieb, J. (1986). Teacher interactions with mainstreamed handicapped students and their nonhandicapped peers. *Learning Disability Quarterly, 9,* 77–83.

Association for Persons with Severe Handicaps. (1992, July). CEC slips back; ASCD steps forward. *TASH Newsletter, 18,* 1.

Bacon, E. H., & Schulz, J. B. (1991). A survey of mainstreaming practices. *Teacher Education and Special Education, 14,* 144–149.

Bain, A., & Dolbel, S. (1991). Regular and special education principals' perceptions of an integration program for students who are intellectually handicapped. *Education and Training in Mental Retardation, 26,* 33–42.

Baker, J. M., & Zigmond, N. (1990). Are regular education classes equipped to accommodate students with learning disabilities? *Exceptional Children, 56,* 515–526.

Baker, J. M., & Zigmond, N. (1995). The meaning and practices of inclusion for students with learning disabilities: Implications from the five cases. *The Journal of Special Education, 29,* 163–180.

Banerji, M., & Dailey, R. A. (1995). A study of the effects of an inclusion model on students with specific learning disabilities. *Journal of Learning Disabilities, 28,* 511–522.

Barnett, C., & Monda-Amaya, L. E. (1998). Principals' knowledge of and attitudes toward inclusion. *Remedial and Special Education, 19,* 181–192.

Bateman, B., & Chard, D. J. (1995). Legal demands and constraints on placement decisions. In J. M. Kauffman, J. W. Lloyd, P. Hallahan, & T. A. Astuto (Eds.), *Issues in educational placement: Students with emotional and behavioral disorders* (pp. 285–316). Hillsdale, NJ: Erlbaum.

Bauman, Z. (1987). *Legislators and interpreters: Modernity, post-modernity, and intellectuals.* Ithaca, NY: Cornell University Press.

Bear, G. G., Clever, A., & Proctor, W. A. (1991). Self-perceptions of non-handicapped children and children with learning disabilities in integrated classes. *The Journal of Special Education, 24,* 409–429.

Bender, W. N., Vail, C. O., & Scott, K. (1995). Teachers' attitudes toward increased mainstreaming: Implementing effective instruction for students with learning disabilities. *Journal of Learning Disabilities, 28,* 87–94.

Bennett, T., DeLuca, D., & Bruns, D. (1997). Putting inclusion into practice: Perspectives of teachers and parents. *Exceptional Children, 64,* 115–131.

Berryman, J. D. (1989). Attitudes of the public toward educational main-streaming *Remedial and Special Education, 10,* 44–49.

Biklen, D. (Ed.). (1985). *Achieving the complete school: Strategies for effective mainstreaming.* New York: Teachers College Press.

Blanton, L. P., Blanton, W. E., & Cross, L. S. (1994). An exploratory study of how general and special education teachers think and make instructional decisions about students with special needs. *Teacher Education and Special Education, 17,* 62–73.

Borthwick-Duffy, S. A., Palmer, D. S., & Lane, K. L. (1996). One size doesn't fit all: Full inclusion and individual differences. *Journal of Behavioral Education, 6,* 311–329.

Brantlinger, E. (1997). Using ideology: Cases of nonrecognition of the politics of research and practice in special education. *Review of Educational Research, 67,* 425–459.

Brown v. Board of Education, 74 S. Ct. 686. (1954).

Brucker, P. O. (1994). The advantages of inclusion for students with learning disabilities. *Journal of Learning Disabilities, 27,* 581–582.

Bryan, I. H., & Bryan, T. H. (1988). Where's the beef? A review of published research on the Adaptive Learning Environments Model. *Learning Disabilities Focus, 4,* 9–14.

Carlberg, C., & Kavale, K. A. (1980). The efficacy of special versus regular class placement for exceptional children: A meta-analysis. *The Journal of Special Education, 14,* 295–309.

Carlson, E., & Parshall, L. (1996). Academic, social, and behavioral adjustment for students declassified from special education. *Exceptional Children, 63,* 89–100.

Carnine, D. (1997). Bridging the research-to-practice gap. In J. Lloyd, E. Kameenui, & D. Chard (Eds.), *Issues in educating students with disabilities* (pp. 363–373). Mahwah, NJ: Erlbaum.

Carr, M. N. (1993). A mother's thoughts on inclusion. *Journal of Learning Disabilities, 26,* 590–592.

Cartwright, W. J., & Burtis, T. R. (1968). Race and intelligence: Changing opinions in social science. *Social Science Quarterly, 49,* 603–618.

Center, Y., Ward, J., Parmenter, T., & Nash, R. (1985). Principals' attitudes towards the integration of disabled children into regular schools. *The Exceptional Child, 32,* 149–160.

Chow, V. T., & Kasari, C. (1999). Task-related interactions among teachers and exceptional, at-risk, and typical learners in inclusive classrooms. *Remedial and Special Education, 20,* 226–232.

Christopolos, F., & Renz, P. (1969). A critical examination of special education programs. *The Journal of Special Education, 3,* 371–379.

Cline, R. (1981). Principals' attitudes and knowledge about handicapped children. *Exceptional Children, 48,* 172–174.

Coates, R. D. (1989) The regular education initiative and opinions of regular classroom teachers. *Journal of Learning Disabilities, 22,* 532–536.

Cohen, M. (1993). The politics of special ed. *The Special Educator, 8,* 266.

Contas, M. A. (1998). The changing nature of educational research and a critique of postmodernism. *Educational Researcher, 27,* 26–33.

Cook, B. G., Gerber, M. M., & Semmel, M. I. (1997). Are effective school reforms effective for all students? The implications of joint outcome production for school reform. *Exceptionality, 7,* 77–95.

Cook, B. G., & Semmel, M. I. (1999). Peer acceptance of included students with disabilities as a function of severity of disability and classroom composition. *The Journal of Special Education, 33,* 50–61.

Cook, B. G., Semmel, M. I., & Gerber, M. M. (1999). Attitudes of principals and special education teachers toward the inclusion of students with mild disabilities: Critical differences of opinion. *Remedial and Special Education, 20,* 199–207, 243.

Cornoldi, C., Terreni, A., Scruggs, T. E., & Mastropieri, M. A. (1998). Teacher attitudes in Italy after twenty years of inclusion. *Remedial and Special Education, 19*, 350–356.

Council for Exceptional Children. (1993, April). *Statement on inclusive schools and communities.* Reston, VA: Author.

Council of Chief State School Officers. (1992, March). Special education and school restructuring. *Concerns, 35*, 1–7.

Danforth, S. (1997). On what basis hope? Modern progress and postmodern possibilities. *Mental Retardation, 35*, 93–106.

Danforth, S., & Rhodes, W. C. (1997). Deconstructing disability: A philosophy for inclusion. *Remedial and Special Education, 18*, 357–366.

Danielson, L. C., & Bellamy, G. T. (1989). State variation in placement of children with handicaps in segregated environments. *Exceptional Children, 55*, 448–455.

Davis, J. C., & Maheady, L. (1991). The regular education initiative: What do three groups of education professionals think? *Teacher Education and Special Education, 14*, 211–220.

Davis, W. E. (1980). Public schools principals' attitudes toward mainstreaming retarded pupils. *Education and Training of the Mentally Retarded, 15*, 174–178.

de Bettencourt, L. V. (1999). General educators' attitudes toward students with mild disabilities and their use of instructional strategies. *Remedial and Special Education, 20*, 27–35.

Deno, E. (1970). Special education as developmental capital. *Exceptional Children, 37*, 229–237.

Deno, E. (1994). Special education as developmental capital revisited: A quarter-century appraisal of means versus ends. *The Journal of Special Education, 27*, 375–392.

Deno, S. L., Foegen, A. M., Robinson, S., & Espin, C. A. (1996). Commentary: Facing the realities of inclusion: Students with mild disabilities. *The Journal of Special Education, 62*, 497–514.

Deutsch, M. (1969). Happenings on the way back from the forum: Social science, IQ, and race revisited. *Harvard Educational Review, 39*, 523–554.

Donaldson, J. (1980). Changing attitudes toward handicapped persons: A review and analysis of research. *Exceptional Children, 46*, 504–514.

Dorn, S., Fuchs, D., & Fuchs, L. S. (1996). A historical perspective on special education reform. *Theory into Practice, 35*, 12–19.

Downing, J. E., Eichinger, J., & Williams, L. J. (1997). Inclusive education for students with severe disabilities: Comparative views of principals and educators at different levels of implementation. *Remedial and Special Education, 18*, 133–142, 165.

Dunn, L. M. (1968). Special education for the mildly retarded—Is much of it justifiable? *Exceptional Children, 35*, 5–22.

Eagleton, T. (1996). *Illusion of postmodernism.* London: Blackwell.

Education for All Handicapped Children Act of 1975, 20 U.S.C. § 1401 *et seq.*

Ellet, L. (1993). Instructional practices in mainstreamed secondary classrooms. *Journal of Learning Disabilities, 26*, 57–64.

Espin, C. A., Deno, S. L., & Albayrak-Kaymak, D. (1998) Individualized Education Programs in resource and inclusive settings: How "individualized" are they? *The Journal of Special Education, 32,* 164–174.

Esposito, B. G., & Reed, T. M. (1986). The effects of contact with handicapped persons on young children's attitudes. *Exceptional Children, 53,* 224–229.

Evans, I. M., Salisbury, C. L., Palombaro, M. M., Berryman, J., & Hollowood, T. M. (1992). Peer interactions and social competence of elementary-age children with severe disabilities in an inclusive school. *Journal of the Association for Persons with Severe Handicaps, 17,* 205–217.

Eysenck, H. J. (1971). *The IQ argument: Race, intelligence, and education.* New York: Library Press.

Ferguson, D. L. (1996). Is it inclusion yet? Bursting the bubbles. In M. S. Berres, D. L. Ferguson, P. Knoblock, & C. Woods (Eds.), *Creating tomorrow's schools today: Stories of inclusion, change, and renewal* (pp. 16–37). New York: Teachers College Press.

Fisher, J. B., Schumaker, J. B., & Deshler, D. D. (1995). Searching for validated inclusive practices: A review of the literature. *Focus on Exceptional Children, 28,* 1–20.

Fox, N. E., & Ysseldyke, J. E. (1997). Implementing inclusion at the middle school level: Lessons from a negative example. *Exceptional Children, 64,* 81–98.

Fryxell, D., & Kennedy, C. (1995). Placement along the continuum of services and its impact on students' social relationships. *Journal of the Association for Persons with Severe Handicaps, 20,* 259–269.

Fuchs, D., & Fuchs, L. S. (1988). An evaluation of the adaptive learning environments model. *Exceptional Children, 55,* 115–127.

Fuchs, D., & Fuchs, L. S. (1991). Framing the REI debate: Abolitionists versus conservationists. In J. W. Lloyd, A. C. Repp, & N. N. Singh (Eds.), *The regular education initiative: Alternative perspectives on concepts, issues, and models* (pp. 241–255). Sycamore, IL: Sycamore.

Fuchs, D., & Fuchs, L. S. (1994). Inclusive schools movement and the radicalization of special education reform. *Exceptional Children, 60,* 294–309.

Fuchs, D., & Fuchs, L. S. (1995a). Special education can work. In J. M Kauffman, J. W. Lloyd, D. P. Hallahan, & T. A. Astuto (Eds.), *Issues in educational placement: Students with emotional and behavior disorders* (pp. 363–377). Hillsdale, NJ: Erlbaum.

Fuchs, D., & Fuchs, L. S. (1995b). What's "special" about special education? *Phi Delta Kappan, 76,* 22–30.

Fuchs, D., Fuchs, L. S., & Fernstrom, P. (1993). A conservative approach to special education reform: Mainstreaming through transenvironmental programming and curriculum-based measurement. *American Educational Research Journal, 30,* 149–177.

Fuchs, L. S., Fuchs, D., Hamlett, C. L., Phillips, N. B., & Karns, K. (1995). General educators' specialized adaptation for students with learning disabilities. *Exceptional Children, 61,* 440–459.

Gallagher, J. J. (1994). The pull of societal forces on special education. *The Journal of Special Education, 27,* 521–530.

Gans, K. D. (1987). Willingness of regular and special educators to teach students with handicaps. *Exceptional Children, 54,* 41–45.

Gartner, A., & Lipsky, D. K. (1987). Beyond special education: Toward a quality system for all students. *Harvard Educational Review, 57,* 367–390.

Gartner, A., & Lipsky, D. K. (1989). *The yoke of special education: How to break it.* Rochester, NY: National Center on Education and the Economy.

Garvar-Pinhas, A., & Schmelkin, L. P. (1989). Administrators' and teachers' attitudes toward mainstreaming. *Remedial and Special Education, 10,* 38–43.

Gerard, H. B. (1983). School desegregation: The social science role. *American Psychologist, 38,* 869–877.

Gerber, M. M. (1996). Reforming special education: "Beyond inclusion." In C. Christensen & F. Rizvi (Eds.), *Disability and the dilemmas of education and justice* (pp. 156–174). Philadelphia: Open University Press.

Gersten, R., Walker, H., & Darch, C. (1988). Relationships between teachers' effectiveness and their tolerance for handicapped students. *Exceptional Children, 54,* 433–438.

Giangreco, M. F., Dennis, R., Cloninger, C., Edelman, S., & Schattman, R. (1993). "I've counted Jon": Transformational experiences of teachers educating students with disabilities. *Exceptional Children, 59,* 359–372.

Gibb, G. S., Young, J. R., Allred, K. W., Dyches, T. T., Egan, M. W., & Ingram, C. F. (1997). A team-based junior high inclusion program: Parent perceptions and feedback. *Remedial and Special Education, 18,* 243–249, 256.

Glicking, E. E., & Theobald, J. T. (1975). Mainstreaming: Affect or effect? *The Journal of Special Education, 9,* 317–328.

Goldstein, H. (1967). The efficacy of special classes and regular classes in the education of educable mentally retarded children. In J. Zubin & G. A. Jervis (Eds.), *Psychopathology of mental development* (pp. 580–602). New York: Grune & Stratton.

Goldstein, H., Moss, J. W., & Jordan, L. J. (1965). *The efficacy of special class training on the development of mentally retarded children* (U.S. Office of Education, Cooperative Research Project No. 619). Urbana: University of Illinois, Institute for Research on Exceptional Children. (ERIC Document Reproduction Service No. ED 002 907)

Gottlieb, J. (1981). Mainstreaming: Fulfilling the promise? *American Journal of Mental Deficiency, 86,* 115–126.

Gottlieb, J., & Corman, L. (1975). Public attitudes toward mentally retarded children. *American Journal of Mental Deficiency, 80,* 72–80.

Green, S. K., & Shinn, M. R. (1994). Parent attitudes about special education and reintegration: What is the role of student outcomes? *Exceptional Children, 61,* 269–281.

Griffin, D. R. (Ed.). (1988). *The reenchantment of science: Postmodern proposals.* Albany: State University of New York Press.

Gross, P. R., & Levitt, N. (1994). *Higher superstition: The academic left and its quarrels with science.* Baltimore: Johns Hopkins University Press.

Grove, K. A., & Fisher, D. (1999). Entrepreneurs of meaning: Parents and the process of inclusive education. *Remedial and Special Education, 20,* 208–215, 256.

Guskin, S. L., & Spicker, H. H. (1968). Educational research in mental retardation. In N. R. Ellis (Ed.), *International review of research in mental retardation* (Vol. 3, pp. 217–278). New York: Academic Press.

Guterman, B. R. (1995). The validity of categorical learning disabilities services: The consumer's view. *Exceptional Children, 62,* 111–124.

Hall, L. J. (1994). A descriptive assessment of social relationships in integrated classrooms. *Journal of the Association for Persons with Severe Handicaps, 12,* 280–286.

Hallahan, D. P., Keller, C. E., McKinney, J. D., Lloyd, J. W., & Bryan, T. (1988). Examining the research base of the regular education initiative: Efficacy studies and the adaptive learning environments model. *Journal of Learning Disabilities, 21,* 29–35, 55.

Hammill, D. D., & Wiederholt, J. L. (1972). *The resource room: Rationale and implementation.* Philadelphia: JSE Press.

Hannah, M. E., & Pliner, S. (1983). Teacher attitudes toward handicapped children: A review and syntheses. *School Psychology Review, 12,* 12–25.

Harwood, J. (1976). The race–intelligence controversy: A sociological approach I—External factors. *Social Studies of Science, 6,* 369–394.

Harwood, J. (1977). The race–intelligence controversy: A sociological approach II—External factors. *Social Studies of Science, 7,* 1–30.

Heller, K., Holtzman, W., & Messick, S. (1982). *Placing children in special education: A strategy for equity.* Washington, DC: National Academy of Science Press.

Heller, W. H., & Schilit, J. (1987). The regular education initiative: A concerned response. *Focus on Exceptional Children, 20,* 1–6.

Helmstetter, E., Peck, C. A., & Giangreco, M. F. (1994). Outcomes of interactions with peers with moderate or severe disabilities: A state-wide survey of high school students. *Journal of the Association of Persons with Severe Handicaps, 19,* 263–276.

Hendrickson, J. M., Shokoohi-Yekta, M., Hamre-Nietupski, S., & Gable, R. A. (1996). Middle and high school students' perceptions on being friends with peers with severe disabilities. *Exceptional Children, 63,* 19–28.

Hernstein, R. J. (1973). *IQ in the meritocracy.* Boston: Little, Brown.

Hirsch, J. (1975). Jensenism: The bankruptcy of "science" without scholarship. *Educational Theory, 25,* 3–28.

Hirshoren, A., & Burton, T. E. (1979). Willingness of regular teachers to participate in mainstreaming handicapped children. *Journal of Research and Development in Education, 12,* 93–100.

Horne, M. D. (1985). *Attitudes toward handicapped students: Professional, peer, and parent reactions.* Hillsdale, NJ: Erlbaum.

Houck, C. K., & Rogers, C. J. (1994). The special/general education integration initiative for students with specific learning disabilities: A "snapshot" of program change. *Journal of Learning Disabilities, 27,* 58–62.

Hunt, P., & Goetz, L. (1997). Research on inclusive educational programs, practices, and outcomes for students with severe disabilities. *The Journal of Special Education, 31,* 3–29.

Idol, L. (1997). Key questions related to building collaborative and inclusive schools. *Journal of Learning Disabilities, 30,* 384–394.

Individuals with Disabilities Education Act of 1990, 20 U.S.C. §1400 *et seq.*

Individuals with Disabilities Education Act Regulations of 1992, 34 C.F.R, § 300.533.

Individuals with Disabilities Education Act Amendments of 1997, 20 U.S.C. § 1401 *et seq.*

Janney, R. E., Snell, M. E., Beers, M. K., & Raynes, M. (1995). Integrating students with moderate and severe disabilities into general education classes. *Exceptional Children, 61,* 425–439.

Jenkins, J. R., & Heinen, A. (1989). Students' preferences for service delivery: Pull-out, in-class, or integrated models. *Exceptional Children, 60,* 6–16.

Jenkins, J. R., Pious, C. G., & Jewell, M. (1990). Special education and the regular education initiative: Basic assumptions. *Exceptional Children, 56,* 479–491.

Jensen, A. R. (1969). How much can we boost IQ and scholastic achievement? *Harvard Educational Review, 39,* 1–123.

Johnson, G. O. (1962). Special education for the mentally handicapped: A paradox. *Exceptional Children, 19,* 62–69.

Johnson, L. J., & Pugach, M. C. (1990). Classroom teachers' views of intervention strategies for learning and behavior problems: Which are reasonable and how frequently are they used? *The Journal of Special Education, 24,* 69–84.

Jordan, A., Lindsay, L., & Stanovich, P. J. (1997). Classroom teachers' instructional interactions with students who are exceptional, at risk, and typically achieving. *Remedial and Special Education, 18,* 82–93.

Katsiyannis, A., Conderman, G., & Franks, D. J. (1995). State practices on inclusion: A national review. *Remedial and Special Education, 16,* 279–287.

Kauffman, J. M. (1989). The regular education initiative as Reagan–Bush educational policy: A trickle-down theory of education of the hard-to-teach. *The Journal of Special Education, 23,* 256–278.

Kauffman, J. M. (1993). How we might achieve the radical reform of special education. *Exceptional Children, 60,* 6–16.

Kauffman, J. M. (1995). Why we must celebrate a diversity of restrictive environments. *Learning Disabilities Research & Practice, 10,* 225–232.

Kauffman, J. M. (1999). Commentary: Today's special education and its messages for tomorrow. *The Journal of Special Education, 32,* 244–254.

Kauffman, J. M., Gerber, M. M., & Semmel, M. I. (1988). Arguable assumptions underlying the regular education initiative. *Journal of Learning Disabilities, 21,* 6–11.

Kauffman, J. M., & Hallahan, D. P. (Eds.). (1995). *The illusion of full inclusion: A comprehensive critique of a current special education bandwagon.* Austin, TX: PRO-ED.

Kaufman, M. J., Agard, J. A., & Semmel, M. I. (1986). *Mainstreaming: Learners and their environment.* Cambridge, MA: Brookline.

Kavale, K. A., & Forness, S. R. (1999). *Efficacy of special education and related services.* Washington, DC: American Association on Mental Retardation.

Kavale, K. A., & Glass, G. V. (1984). Meta-analysis and policy decisions in special education. In B. K. Keogh (Ed.), *Advances in special education* (Vol. 4, pp. 195–248). Greenwich, CT: JAI Press.

Kearny, C. A., & Durand, V. M. (1992). How prepared are our teachers for mainstreamed classroom settings? A survey of postsecondary schools of education in New York State. *Exceptional Children, 58,* 8–11.

King-Sears, M. E. (1997). Best academic practices for inclusive classrooms. *Focus on Exceptional Children, 29,* 1–22.

King-Sears, M. E., & Cummings, C. S. (1996). Inclusive practices of classroom teachers. *Remedial and Special Education, 17,* 217–225.

Kirk, S. A. (1964). Research in education. In H. A. Stevens & R. Heber (Eds.), *Mental retardation: A review of research* (pp. 57–99). Chicago: University of Chicago Press.

Klingner, J. K., Vaughn, S., Schumm, J. S., Cohen, P., & Forgan, J. W. (1998). Inclusion or pull-out: Which do students prefer? *Journal of Learning Disabilities, 31,* 148–158.

Koertge, N. (Ed.). (1998). *A house built on sand: Exposing postmodernist myths about science.* New York: Oxford University Press.

Korinek, L., McLaughlin, V., & Walther-Thomas, C. S. (1995). Least restrictive environment and collaboration: A bridge over troubled waters. *Preventing School Failure, 39,* 6–12.

Kozleski, E. B., & Jackson, L. (1993). Taylor's story: Full inclusion in her neighborhood elementary school. *Exceptionally, 4,* 153–176.

Kuhn, T. S. (1970). *The structure of scientific revolutions* (2nd ed.). Chicago: University of Chicago Press.

Lakatos, I. (1978). *The methodology of scientific research programs.* Cambridge, England: Cambridge University Press.

Landesman, S., & Butterfield, E. C. (1987). Normalization and deinstitutionalization of mentally retarded individuals: Controversy and facts. *American Psychologist, 42,* 809–816.

Larrivee, B., & Cook, L. (1979). Mainstreaming: A study of the variables affecting teacher attitude. *The Journal of Special Education, 13,* 315–324.

Lazar, A. L., Stodden, R. L., & Sullivan, N. V. (1976). A comparison of attitudes held by male and female future school administrators toward instructional goals, personal adjustment, and the handicapped. *Rehabilitation Literature, 37,* 198–222.

Learning Disabilities Association. (1993, January). Position paper on full inclusion of all students with learning disabilities in the regular education classroom. *LDA Newsbriefs, 28,* 1–2.

Leinhardt, G., & Pallay, A. (1982). Restrictive educational settings: Exile or haven? *Review of Educational Research, 52,* 557–578.

Lewontin, R. C. (1970). Race and intelligence. *Bulletin of the Atomic Scientist, 26,* 2–8.

Lieberman, L. M. (1985). Special education and regular education: A merger made in heaven? *Exceptional Children, 51,* 513–516.

Lieberman, L. M. (1996). Preserving special education for those who need it. In W. Stainback & S. Stainback (Eds.), *Controversial issues confronting special education* (pp. 16–27). Needham Heights, MA: Allyn & Bacon.

Lilly, M. S. (1970). Special education: A teapot in a tempest. *Exceptional Children, 37,* 43–49.

Lilly, M. S. (1988). The regular education initiative: A force for change in general and special education. *Education and Training in Mental Retardation, 23,* 253–260.

Lipsky, D. K., & Gartner, A. (1987). Capable of achievement and worthy of respect: Education for handicapped students as if they were full-fledged human beings. *Exceptional Children, 54,* 69–74.

Lipsky, D. K., & Gartner, A. (Eds.). (1989). *Beyond separate education: Quality education for all.* Baltimore: Brookes.

Lipsky, D. K., & Gartner, A. (1991). Restructuring for quality. In J. W. Lloyd, A. C. Repp, & N. N. Singh (Eds.), *The regular education initiative: Alternative perspectives on concepts, issues, and models* (pp. 43–56). Sycamore, IL: Sycamore.

Lipsky, D. K., & Gartner, A. (1996). Equity requires inclusion: The future for all students with disabilities. In C. Christensen & F. Rizvi (Eds.), *Disability and the dilemmas of education and justice* (pp. 144–155). Philadelphia: Open University Press.

Lipsky, D. K., & Gartner, A. (Eds.). (1997). *Inclusion and school reform: Transforming American classrooms.* Baltimore: Brookes.

Loehlin, J. C., Lindzey, G., & Spuhler, J. N. (1975). *Race differences in intelligence.* San Francisco: Freeman.

Lovitt, T. C., & Cushing, S. (1999). Parents of youth with disabilities: Their perceptions of school programs. *Remedial and Special Education, 20,* 134–142.

Lovitt, T. C., Plavins, M., & Cushing, S. (1999). What do pupils with disabilities have to say about their experience in high school? *Remedial and Special Education, 20,* 67–76, 83.

MacMillan, D. L. (1971). Special education for the mildly retarded: Servant or savant? *Focus on Exceptional Children, 2,* 1–11.

MacMillan, D. L., Gresham, F. M., & Forness, S. R. (1996). Full inclusion: An empirical perspective. *Behavioral Disorders, 21,* 145–159.

MacMillan, D. L., & Hendrick, I. G. (1993). Evolution and legacies. In J. I. Goodlad & T. C. Lovitt (Eds.), *Integrating general and special education* (pp. 23–48). New York: Merrill.

MacMillan, D. L., & Semmel, M. I. (1977). Evaluation of mainstreaming programs. *Focus on Exceptional Children, 9,* 1–14.

MacMillan, D. L., Semmel, M. I., & Gerber, M. M. (1994). The social context of Dunn: Then and now. *The Journal of Special Education, 27,* 466–480.

Madden, N. A., & Slavin, R. E. (1983). Mainstreaming students with mild handicaps: Academic and social outcomes. *Review of Educational Research, 53,* 519–569.

Mamlin, N. (1999). Despite best intentions: When inclusion fails. *The Journal of Special Education, 33,* 36–49.

Mandell, C. J., & Strain, P. S. (1978). An analysis of factors related to the attitudes of regular classroom teachers toward mainstreaming mildly handicapped children. *Contemporary Educational Psychology, 3,* 154–162.

Manset, G., & Semmel, M. I. (1997). Are inclusive programs for students with mild disabilities effective? A comparative review of model programs. *The Journal of Special Education, 31,* 155–180.

Margolis, H., & McGettigan, J. (1988). Managing resistance to instructional modifications in mainstreamed environments. *Remedial and Special Education, 9,* 15–21.

Marston, D. (1996). A comparison of inclusion only, pull-out only, and combined service models for students with mild disabilities. *The Journal of Special Education, 30,* 121–132.

Martin, E. W. (1995). Case studies on inclusion: Worst fears realized. *The Journal of Special Education, 29,* 192–199.

McIntosh, R., Vaughn, S., Schumm, J. S., Haager, D., & Lee, O. (1993). Observations of students with learning disabilities in general education classrooms. *Exceptional Children, 60,* 249–261.

McLesky, J., & Pugach, M. C. (1995). The real sellout: Failing to give inclusion a chance. A response to Roberts and Mather. *Learning Disabilities Research & Practice, 10,* 233–238.

Meredith, B., & Underwood, J. (1995). Irreconcilable differences? Defining the rising conflict between regular and special education. *Journal of Law and Education, 24,* 195–226.

Minke, K. M., Bear, G. G., Deemer, S. A., & Griffin, S. M. (1996). Teachers' experiences with inclusive classrooms: Implications for special education reform. *The Journal of Special Education, 30,* 152–186.

Morsink, C. V., & Lenk, L. L. (1992). The delivery of special education programs and services. *Remedial and Special Education, 13,* 33–43.

Munson, S. M. (1986–1987). Regular education teacher modifications for mainstreamed mildly handicapped students. *The Journal of Special Education, 20,* 490–499.

Myles, B. S., & Simpson, R. L. (1989). Regular educators' modification preferences for mainstreaming mildly handicapped children. *The Journal of Special Education, 22,* 479–489.

Naor, M., & Milgram, R. (1980). Two preservice strategies for preparing regular classroom teachers for mainstreaming. *Exceptional Children, 47,* 126–129.

National Association of State Boards of Education. (1992, October). *Winners all: A call for inclusive schools.* Washington, DC: Author.

National Joint Committee on Learning Disabilities. (1993). A reaction to full inclusion: A reaffirmation of the right of students with learning disabilities to a continuum of services. *Journal of Learning Disabilities, 26,* 596.

O'Neil, J. (1994–1995). Can inclusion work? A conversation with Jim Kauffman and Mara Sapon-Shevin. *Educational Leadership, 52,* 7–11.

Osborne, A. G., & DiMattia, P. (1994). The IDEA's least restrictive environment mandate: Legal implications. *Exceptional Children, 61,* 6–14.

Padeliadu, S., & Zigmond, N. (1996). Perspectives of students with learning disabilities about special education placement. *Learning Disabilities Research & Practice, 11,* 15–23.

Pastore, N. (1949). *The nature–nurture controversy.* New York: King's Crown Press.

Payne, R., & Murray, C. (1974). Principals' attitudes toward integration of the handicapped. *Exceptional Children, 41,* 123–125.

Phillips, L., Sapona, R. H., & Lubic, B. L. (1995). Developing partnerships in inclusive education: One school's approach. *Intervention in School and Clinic, 30,* 262–272.

Pugach, M., & Lilly, M. S. (1984). Reconceptualizing support services for classroom teachers: Implications for teacher education. *Journal of Teacher Education, 35,* 48–55.

Pugach, M., & Sapon-Shevin, M. (1987). New agendas for special education policy: What the regular education reports haven't said. *Exceptional Children, 53,* 295–299.

Putnam, J. W., Spiegel, A. N., & Bruininks, R. N. (1995). Future directions in education and inclusion of students with disabilities: A Delphi investigation. *Exceptional Children, 61,* 553–576.

Reid, D. K., & Button, L. J. (1995). Anna's story: Narratives of personal experience about being labeled learning disabled. *Journal of Learning Disabilities, 28,* 602–614.

Reynolds, M. C. (1962). A framework for considering some issues in special education. *Exceptional Children, 28,* 367–370.

Reynolds, M. C. (1988). A reaction to the JLD: Special series on the regular education initiative. *Journal of Learning Disabilities, 21,* 352–356.

Reynolds, M. C. (1989). An historical perspective: The delivery of special education to mildly disabled and at-risk students. *Remedial and Special Education, 10,* 7–11.

Reynolds, M. C. (1991, December). Progressive inclusion. *Quality Outcomes Driven Education, 1,* 11–14.

Reynolds, M. C. (1992). Students and programs at the school margins: Disorder and needed repairs. *School Psychology Quarterly, 7,* 233–244.

Reynolds, M. C., & Wang, M. C. (1983). Restructuring "special" school programs: A position paper. *Policy Studies Review, 2,* 189–212.

Reynolds, M. C., Wang, M. C., & Walberg, H. J. (1987). The necessary restructuring of special and general education. *Exceptional Children, 53,* 391–398.

Richey, D., & McKinney, J. D. (1978). Classroom behavioral styles of learning disabled children. *Journal of Learning Disabilities, 11,* 297–302.

Ringlaben, R. P., & Price, J. R. (1981). Regular classroom teachers' perceptions of mainstreaming effects. *Exceptional Children, 47,* 302–304.

Roberts, C., & Zubrick, S. (1992). Factors influencing the social status of children with mild academic disabilities in regular classrooms. *Exceptional Children, 59,* 192–202.

Roberts, R., & Mather, N. (1995). The return of students with learning disabilities to regular classrooms: A sellout? *Learning Disabilities Research & Practice, 10,* 46–58.

Rojewski, J. W., & Pollard, R. R. (1993). A multivariate analysis of perceptions held by secondary academic teachers toward students with special needs. *Teacher Education and Special Education, 16,* 330–341.

Rosenau, P. M. (1992). *Post-modernism and the social sciences: Insights, inroads, and intrusions.* Princeton, NJ: Princeton University Press.

Safford, P. L., & Safford, E. J. (1998). Visions of the special class. *Remedial and Special Education, 19,* 229–238.

Sailor, W., & Skrtic, T. M. (1996). School-linked services integration: Crisis and opportunity in the transition to a postmodern society. *Remedial and Special Education, 17,* 271–283.

Sale, P., & Carey, D. M. (1995). The sociometric status of students with disabilities in a full-inclusion school. *Exceptional Children, 62,* 6–19.

Salend, S. J., & Garrick Duhaney, L. M. (1999). The impact of inclusion on students with and without disabilities and their educators, *Remedial and Special Education, 20,* 114–126.

Salend, S. J., Johansen, M., Mumper, J., Chase, A., Pike, K. M., & Dorney, J. A. (1997). Cooperative teaching: The voices of two teachers. *Remedial and Special Education, 18,* 3–11.

Salisbury, C. L., Palombaro, M. M., & Hollowood, T. M. (1993). On the nature and change of an inclusive elementary school. *Journal of the Association for Persons with Severe Handicaps, 18,* 75–84.

Samson, S. B. (1982). *The culture of the school and the problem of change.* Boston: Allyn & Bacon.

Schumm, J. S., & Vaughn, S. (1991). Making adaptations for mainstreamed students: General classroom teachers' perspectives. *Remedial and Special Education, 12,* 18–25.

Schumm, J. S., & Vaughn, S. (1992). Planning for mainstreamed special education students: Perceptions of general classroom teachers. *Exceptionality, 3,* 81–90.

Schumm, J. S., & Vaughn, S. (1995). Getting ready for inclusion: Is the stage set? *Learning Disabilities Research & Practice, 10,* 169–179.

Schumm, J. S., Vaughn, S., Gordon, J., & Rothlein, L. (1994). General education teachers' beliefs, skills, and practices in planning for main-streamed students with learning disabilities. *Teacher Education and Special Education, 17,* 22–37.

Schumm, J. S., Vaughn, S., Haager, D., McDowell, J., Rorhlein, L., & Saumell, L. (1995). General education teacher planning: What can students with learning disabilities expect? *Exceptional Children, 61,* 335–352.

Scott, B. J., Vitale, M. R., & Masten, W. G. (1998). Implementing instructional adaptations for students with disabilities in inclusive classrooms: A literature review. *Remedial and Special Education, 19,* 106–119.

Scruggs, T. E., & Mastropieri, M. A. (1996). Teacher perceptions of mainstreaming/inclusion, 1958–1995: A research synthesis. *Exceptional Children, 63,* 59–74.

Semmel, M. I., Abernathy, T. V., Butera, G., & Lesar, S. (1991). Teacher perceptions of the regular education initiative. *Exceptional Children, 58,* 9–24.

Semmel, M. I., Gerber, M. M., & MacMillan, D. L. (1994). Twenty-five years after Dunn's article: A legacy of policy analysis research in special education. *The Journal of Special Education, 27,* 481–495.

Shadish, W. R. (1984). Policy research: Lessons from the implementation of deinstitutionalization. *American Psychologist, 39,* 725–738.

Shanker, A. (1994, February 6). Inclusion and ideology. *The New York Times,* p. E7.

Shanker, A. (1995). Full inclusion is neither free nor appropriate. *Educational Leadership, 52,* 18–21.

Shattuck, M. (1946). Segregation versus non-segregation of exceptional children. *Journal of Exceptional Children, 12,* 235–240.

Shepard, L. A. (1987). The new push for excellence: Widening the schism between regular and special education. *Exceptional Children, 53,* 327–329.

Shinn, M. R., Powell-Smith, K. A., Good, R. H., & Baker, S. (1997). The effects of reintegration into general education reading instruction for students with mild disabilities. *Exceptional Children, 64,* 59–79.

Shotel, J. R., Iano, R. P., & McGettigan, J. F. (1972). Teacher attitudes associated with the integration of handicapped children. *Exceptional Children, 38,* 677–683.

Simpson, R. G., & Eaves, R. C. (1985). Do we need more qualitative research or more good research? A reaction to Stainback and Stainback. *Exceptional Children, 51,* 325–329.

Skrtic, T. M. (1991). The special education paradox: Equity as the way to excellence. *Harvard Educational Review, 61*, 148–162.

Skrtic, T. M., Sailor, W., & Gee, K. (1996). Voice, collaboration, and inclusion: Democratic themes in educational and social reform initiatives. *Remedial and Special Education, 17*, 142–157.

Smith, S. W. (1990). Comparison of Individualized Education Programs (IEPs) of students with behavioral disorders and learning disabilities. *The Journal of Special Education, 24*, 85–100.

Snell, M. E. (1991). Schools are for all kids: The importance of integration for students with severe disabilities and their peers. In J. W. Lloyd, A. C. Repp, & N. N. Singh (Eds.), *The regular education initiative: Alternative perspectives on concepts, issues, and models* (pp. 133–138). Sycamore, IL: Sycamore.

Sokal, A., & Bricmont, J. (1998). *Fashionable nonsense: Postmodern intellectuals' abuse of science.* New York: St. Martin's Press.

Soodak, L. C., Podell, D. M., & Lehman, L. R. (1998). Teacher, student, and school attributes as predictors of teachers' responses to inclusion. *The Journal of Special Education, 31*, 480–497.

Sowell, T. (1995). *The vision of the anointed: Self-congratulation as a basis for social policy.* New York: Basic Books.

Sowell, T. (1999). *The quest for cosmic justice.* New York: Free Press.

Stainback, S., & Stainback, W. (1984a). Broadening the research perspective in special education. *Exceptional Children, 51*, 400–408.

Stainback, S., & Stainback, W. (1984b). A rationale for the merger of special and regular education. *Exceptional Children, 51*, 102–111.

Stainback, S., & Stainback, W. (1987). Integration versus cooperation: A commentary on "Educating children with learning problems: A shared responsibility" *Exceptional Children, 54*, 66–68.

Stainback, S., & Stainback, W. (1989). Integration of students with mild and moderate handicaps. In D. K. Lipsky & A. Gartner (Eds.), *Beyond separate education: Quality education for all* (pp. 41–52). Baltimore: Brookes.

Stainback, S., & Stainback, W. (1992). *Curriculum considerations in inclusive classrooms: Facilitating learning for all students.* Baltimore: Brookes.

Stainback, S., Stainback, W., & Forest, M. (1989). *Educating all students in the mainstream of regular education.* Baltimore: Brookes.

Stainback, S., Stainback, W., Strathe, M., & Dedrick, C. (1983). Preparing regular classroom teachers for the integration of severely handicapped students: An experimental study. *Education and Training of the Mentally Retarded, 18*, 205–209.

Stainback, W., & Stainback, S. (1991). Rationale for integration and restructuring: A synopsis. In J. W. Lloyd, A. C. Repp, & N. N. Singh (Eds.), *The regular education initiative: Alternative perspectives on concepts, issues, and models* (pp. 225–239). Sycamore, IL: Sycamore Press.

Stephens, T. M., & Braun, B. L. (1980). Measures of regular classroom teachers' attitudes toward handicapped children. *Exceptional Children, 46*, 292–294.

Tapasak, R. C., & Walther-Thomas, C. S. (1999). Evaluation of a first-year inclusion program: Student perceptions and classroom performance. *Remedial and Special Education, 20,* 216–225.

Taylor, B. R. (1994). Inclusion: Time for a change—A response to Margaret N. Carr. *Journal of Learning Disabilities, 27,* 579–580.

Taylor, S. (1988). Caught in the continuum: A critical analysis of the principle of the least restrictive environment. *Journal of the Association for Persons with Severe Handicaps, 13,* 41–53.

Thomas, S. B., & Rapport, M. J. K. (1998). Least restrictive environment: Understanding the direction of the courts. *The Journal of Special Education, 32,* 66–78.

Thompson, R. H., Vitale, P. A., & Jewett, J. P. (1984). Teacher–student interaction patterns in full-inclusion classrooms. *Remedial and Special Education, 5,* 51–61.

Towfighy-Hooshyar, N., & Zingle, H. W. (1984). Regular class students: Attitudes toward integrated multiply handicapped peers. *American Journal of Mental Deficiency, 88,* 630–637.

Turner, B. S. (Ed.). (1990). *Theories of modernity and postmodernity.* Newbury Park, CA: Sage.

U.S. Department of Education. (1997). *Nineteenth annual report to Congress on the implementation of the Individuals with Disabilities Education Act.* Washington, DC: U.S. Government Printing Office.

Urbach, P. (1974a). Progress and degeneration in the "IQ debate"—Part I. *British Journal for the Philosophy of Science, 25,* 99–135.

Urbach, P. (1974b). Progress and degeneration in the "IQ debate"—Part II. *British Journal for the Philosophy of Science, 25,* 235–259.

Vaughn, S., Elbaum, B. E., & Schumm, J. S. (1996). The effects of inclusion on the social functioning of students with learning disabilities. *Journal of Learning Disabilities, 29,* 598–608.

Vaughn, S., & Klingner, J. K. (1998). Students' perceptions of inclusion and resource room settings. *The Journal of Special Education, 32,* 79–88.

Vaughn, S., & Schumm, J. S. (1994). Middle school teachers' planning for students with learning disabilities. *Remedial and Special Education, 15,* 152–161.

Vaughn, S., Schumm, J. S., Jallad, B., Slusher, J., & Saumell, L. (1996). Teachers' views of inclusion. *Learning Disabilities Research & Practice, 11,* 96–106.

Vaughn, S., Schumm, J. S., & Kouzekanani, K. (1993). What do students with learning disabilities think when their general education teachers make adaptations? *Journal of Learning Disabilities, 26,* 545–555.

Vaughn, S., Schumm, J. S., Niharos, F., & Daugherty, T. (1993). What do students think when teachers make adaptations? *Teaching and Teacher Education, 9,* 107–118.

Villa, R., Thousand, J., Stainback, W., & Stainback, S. (Eds.). (1992). *Restructuring for caring and effective education.* Baltimore: Brookes.

Villa, R. A., Thousand, J. S., Meyers, H., & Nevin, A. (1996). Teacher and administrator perceptions of heterogeneous education. *Exceptional Children, 63,* 29–45.

Voeltz, L. (1980). Children's attitudes toward handicapped peers. *American Journal of Mental Deficiency, 84*, 455–464.

Waldron, N. L., & McLeskey, J. (1998). The effects of an inclusive school program on students with mild and severe learning disabilities. *Exceptional Children, 64*, 395–405.

Walther-Thomas, C. S. (1997). Co-teaching experiences: The benefits and problems that teachers and principals report over time. *Journal of Learning Disabilities, 30*, 395–407.

Wang, M. C., & Baker, E. T. (1985–1986). Mainstreaming programs: Design features and effects. *The Journal of Special Education, 19*, 504–521.

Wang, M. C., & Birch, J. W. (1984a). Comparison of a full-time main-streaming program and a resource room approach. *Exceptional Children, 51*, 33–40.

Wang, M. C., & Birch, J. W. (1984b). Effective special education in regular classes. *Exceptional Children, 50*, 391–398.

Wang, M. C., Gennan, P., & Waxman, H. C. (1985). The adaptive learning environments model: Design, implementation, and effects. In M. C. Wang & H. J. Walberg (Eds.), *Adapting: Instruction to individual differences* (pp. 191–235). Berkeley, CA: McCutchan.

Wang, M. C., Peverly, S., & Randolph, R. (1984). An investigation of the implementation and effects of a full-time mainstreaming program. *Remedial and Special Education, 5*, 21–32.

Wang, M. C., Reynolds, M. C., & Walberg, H. J. (1986). Rethinking special education, *Educational Leadership, 44*, 26–31.

Wang, M. C., Reynolds, M. C., & Walberg, H. J. (1988). Integrating children of the second system. *Phi Delta Kappan, 70*, 248–251.

Wang, M. C., & Walberg, H. J. (1988). Four fallacies of segregationism. *Exceptional Children, 55*, 128–137.

Weintraub, F. J., Abeson, A., Ballard, J., & LaVor, M. (Eds.). (1976). *Public policy and the education of exceptional children*. Reston, VA: Council for Exceptional Children.

Welch, M. (1989). A cultural perspective and the second wave of educational reform. *Journal of Learning Disabilities, 22*, 537–540, 560.

Werts, M. G., Wolery, M., Snyder, E. D., Caldwell, N. K., & Salisbury, C. L. (1996). Supports and resources associated with inclusive schooling: Perceptions of elementary school teachers about need and availability. *The Journal of Special Education, 30*, 187–203.

Whinnery, K. W., Fuchs, L. S., & Fuchs, D. (1991). General, special, and remedial teachers' acceptance of behavioral and instructional strategies for mainstreaming students with mild handicaps. *Remedial and Special Education, 12*, 6–17.

Wiederholt, J. L., & Chamberlain, S. P. (1989). A critical analysis of resource programs. *Remedial and Special Education, 10*, 15–37.

Wigle, S. E., & Wilcox, D. J. (1996). Inclusion: Criteria for the preparation of education personnel. *Remedial and Special Education, 17*, 323–328.

Wilczenski, F. (1993). Changes in attitudes toward mainstreaming among undergraduate education students. *Educational Research Quarterly, 17*, 5–17.

Will, M. C. (1986). Educating children with learning problems: A shared responsibility. *Exceptional Children, 52*, 411–416.

Yell, M. L. (1992). School reform and special education: A legal analysis. *Preventing School Failure, 36,* 25–28.

Yell, M. L. (1995). Least restrictive environment, inclusion, and students with disabilities: A legal analysis. *The Journal of Special Education, 28,* 389–404.

York, J., Vandercook, T., MacDonald, C., Heise-Neff, C., & Caughey, E. (1992). Feedback about integrating middle-school students with severe disabilities in general education classes. *Exceptional Children, 58,* 244–258.

Ysseldyke, J. E., Thurlow, M. L., Wotruba, J. W., & Nania, P. A. (1990). Instructional arrangements: Perceptions from general education. *Teaching Exceptional Children, 22,* 4–7.

Yuker, H. E. (Ed.). (1988). *Attitudes toward persons with disabilities.* New York: Springer-Verlag.

Zigmond, N. (1997). Educating students with disabilities: The future of special education. In J. Lloyd, E. Kameenui, & D. Chard (Eds.), *Issues in educating students with disabilities* (pp. 377–390). Mahwah, NJ: Erlbaum.

Zigmond, N., & Baker, J. M. (1994). Is the mainstream a more appropriate educational setting for Randy? A case study of one student with learning disabilities. *Learning Disabilities Research & Practice, 9,* 108–117.

Zigmond, N., Jenkins, J. R., Fuchs, L. S., Deno, S., Fuchs, D., Baker, J. M., et al. (1995). Special education in restructured schools: Findings from three multiyear studies. *Phi Delta Kappan, 76,* 531–541.

Zirkel, P. (1996). Inclusion: Return of the pendulum? *The Special Educator, 12,* 1, 5.

CHAPTER 13

Preparing Teachers for Full Inclusion: Is It Possible?

Devery R. Mock
and James M. Kauffman

Advocates for full inclusion posit that students are more alike than different, and therefore, all students are best instructed in the regular classroom. Preparing teachers for this eventuality would require that they be trained in depth to teach students with specific disabilities effectively and trained in extraordinary breadth as well because they would be required to teach students with many different disabilities. Examples from medicine and other fields illustrate the impossibility of such training under even the most favorable circumstances.

Special education is rife with controversy. Issues range from the serious (e.g., the disproportionate representation of minorities in disability categories; Artiles & Zamora-Duran, 1997) to the inane (e.g., the practice of facilitated communication; Mostert, 2001; Shane, 1994). Such issues stir up considerable fervor and debate. At present, the most controversial of these issues is full inclusion (Crockett & Kauffman, 1999, 2001). Although this issue may have at one time held company with other less plausible forms of quackery, full inclusion is presently a matter of very serious import (see Kauffman, 1999).

Advocates of full inclusion subscribe to the basic tenet that students are more alike than different. Thus, they contend that grouping students by performance on academic tasks or on other performance-related variables (homogeneous grouping) is unnecessary (Lipsky & Gartner, 1987, 1996, 1998; Stainback & Stainback, 1988, 1992). Although proponents of full inclusion have yet to offer empirical evidence for their stance, they have made moral arguments for their position (see Kavale & Forness, 2000). These arguments are based—illogically and inappropriately, we believe—on the landmark school desegregation case of *Brown v. Board of Education of Topeka* (1954). The appeal to this case stirs up memories associated with the horrid practice of legal racial segregation and defines the issue of full inclusion as a matter of civil rights (Gallagher, 1998; Gartner & Lipsky,

1987; Stainback, Stainback, East, & Sapon-Shevin, 1994). Additionally, advocates of full inclusion extend this emotional appeal by likening the current special education system to both apartheid (Lipsky & Gartner, 1987) and slavery (Stainback & Stainback, 1988). This line of argument, one that excludes most observable, measurable data and relies solely on emotional appeal, casts full inclusion as an issue lacking any gray area. Consequently, individuals who oppose full inclusion are cast as those who favor at least the equivalents of apartheid, slavery, and segregation. Proponents of full inclusion have thus very cleverly structured a debate in which inclusion is interpreted as all or nothing (Sasso, 2001).

It is difficult to hold fast to a more objective, scientific view in the face of emotional appeals. After all, appeals such as these convert unbelievers, win elections, and sell cars. The United States is a nation besieged by emotional appeals, and the movement toward full inclusion capitalizes on this apparent predilection for emotion. The support and momentum associated with full inclusion suggest that special education is preparing to buy the full inclusion rhetoric, possibly with disastrous results (Kauffman, 1999–2000). Very few individuals advocating or adopting this change have stopped to consider the full cost of full inclusion. Like the car dealer who requires no down payment and forgets to mention just how much the buyer will pay in interest, advocates for full inclusion have neglected to reveal the fine print. They are advocating a change that has yet to be clearly and concretely defined. The savvy consumer must ask, "What does full inclusion actually mean? What will it cost?" After all, it is children, indeed the nation's most vulnerable children, who will be strapped into this shiny, new vehicle.

If the practice of full inclusion is implemented, all students apparently will be instructed in the regular classroom (Gartner & Lipsky, 1987; Lipsky & Gartner, 1987, 1996, 1998; McGill-Franzen, 1994; Stainback & Stainback, 1992). "All" students seems to suggest each and every student. Thus, this regular classroom will include the student who has profound mental retardation and cannot yet toilet himself, as well as the eighth grader who reads on the early first-grade level and the student with emotional and behavioral disorders that manifest in verbal and physical aggression. These students and others with disabilities of varying severity, ranging from blindness to cerebral palsy to autism, will be instructed in the regular classroom. Currently, 11% of school-aged children are identified and served under the Individuals with Disabilities Education Act (IDEA, 1997; U.S. Department of Education, 2000b). Thus, in a setting of full inclusion, the regular classroom of 25 students would contain 2 or 3 students with disabilities heretofore warranting specialized services. These students would remain with their more able peers for the duration of the school day and would engage in all of the activities that the regular classroom offers.

Proponents of full inclusion focus on placement as the critical issue in special education (Crockett & Kauffman, 1999, 2001). In so doing they argue that all students are best instructed in a single ubiquitous setting. Thus, people have said things like the following:

> *There is nothing pervasively wrong with special education.* What is being questioned is not the interventions and knowledge that have been acquired through special education training and research. Rather, what is being challenged is the location where these supports are being provided to students with disabilities. (Blackman, 1992, p. 29)

What is the logic in such statements? How does merely changing the location of instruction make it effective?

If full inclusion is implemented, all students will receive instruction from the same teacher. Thus, in the words of inclusion advocate Richard Allington (1993), "Michael [wouldn't] go down the hall anymore" for help in the resource room. Instead, he would remain in his regular classroom for all of his academic instruction. What Allington fails to explain is that Michael's classroom teacher would now be responsible for addressing all of Michael's academic needs. Although this classroom teacher may seek the advice of other teachers with special expertise, the burden for all 25 students in the regular classroom falls squarely on one teacher's shoulders. Thus, in the best-case scenario the knowledgeable, experienced classroom teacher is responsible for the education of 25 students: 22 typical students, and 3 additional students with very mild disabilities. In another scenario, and arguably the more probable, the teacher with moderate experience and knowledge specific to general education or a particular subject area (e.g., science, math) is responsible for the education of 25 students of varying abilities and achievements (U.S. Department of Education, 2000a). One of these students is likely to exhibit a learning disability that manifests in academic achievement at least 2 years below that of his or her peers. Another student most likely exhibits speech and language impairments or mental retardation or a serious emotional disorder. Additionally, there is likely a third student in this classroom with a disability that could include one or more of the following: specific learning disability, mental retardation, emotional or behavioral disorder, speech or language impairment, visual impairment, hearing impairment, physical impairment, traumatic brain injury, attention-deficit/hyperactivity disorder, or autism. Furthermore, at least 2 other students in this class exhibit disabilities that school professionals have not identified. One of these students likely has an emotional or behavioral disorder (Kauffman, 2001) and another student likely exhibits behaviors resulting from attention-deficit/hyperactivity disorder (Forness & Kavale, 1998). At least 1 student in this class will have limited English proficiency (U.S. Department of Education, 2000a), 4 will live in poverty, 3 will receive food stamps, 6 will live with only one parent, and 1 will live with neither parent (Children's Defense Fund, 2000). The burden for all of these students, including 3 with very diverse and demanding needs, will fall upon the shoulders of one teacher—a teacher who very likely received no more than 3 credit hours of university training in special education. This scenario assumes a uniform distribution of children with disabilities and teacher capabilities across schools and classrooms. Of course, such uniformity is not the case. In some classes, fewer children with disabilities will be present, but in many classes there will be more. A few teachers in general education will have extensive training in special education; most will have virtually none.

The aims of full inclusion are noble and lofty (see Stainback & Stainback, 1992). Virtually no one objects to the ideals of fairness, equality, and justice presented in appeals for full inclusion, for these principles should be at work in every classroom, regardless of inclusion practices. Proponents of full inclusion believe that fairness, equality, and justice are natural outcomes of educating all students in the same instructional setting—students learn fairness by observing fairness (Stainback & Stainback, 1992; see Kauffman & Pullen, 1996, for an opposing view). Thus, proponents of full inclusion suggest that the classroom teacher who would instruct these students should be prepared to teach every variety of student and to do so in a way that is fair and just. This teacher must be able to meet the needs of the weakest students while also devoting time and concern, in a manner that is fair, to the strongest students. More concretely, this teacher must be able to teach toileting skills to the fourth grader with profound mental retardation while also preparing students to take the state mandated end-of-year assessment in reading, mathematics, social studies, science, and technology, an assessment that will be used to gauge the competence of this particular teacher. Are such expectations reasonable? Is it possible to prepare teachers to be competent in so many domains? With such broad competency demands, is there any hope for a teacher's expertise in all areas? Questions like these clamor for answers and expose the details of the full inclusion image. If educators are to buy the full inclusion package, shouldn't they know what they are buying? Shouldn't they check under the hood, take a test drive, and read the fine print? Shouldn't they make certain that this is a purchase that they can afford?

OUR POSITION

The assumption on which full inclusion is based—that students are more alike than different and, therefore, all students will benefit from the same instructional practices and settings—belies the very reality that gave birth to the field of special education. It also thwarts the progress that the field of special education has made over the last two centuries (Fuchs & Fuchs, 1994; Kauffman, 1981, 1994; Kauffman & Smucker, 1995; Kavale & Forness, 2000). Additionally, this assumption permits advocates of full inclusion to draw a very dangerous conclusion: all teachers can be prepared to instruct all students effectively.

Students Are More Alike Than Different: An Oversimplification

Students are alike in their basic humanity, but they are also very different in what they have learned, can learn, and need to learn. In fact, some students have differences so great that they have instructional and personal needs that differ from those of their peers. Consider how much children with various disabilities differ from each other.

For instance, the child with poor eyesight may need corrective glasses, the child with deafness may need to communicate in sign language, and the child with cerebral palsy may need to use a wheelchair. These are needs that may not be shared by the majority of school-aged children; however, in a just and fair world these are needs that educators meet. It would seem nothing short of barbaric to deny a student glasses, sign language, or a wheelchair simply because his or her peers could see, hear, or move without them. These are differences that are easily identified and accommodated.

But there also differences between students that are not as readily apparent. For example, some students possess IQs in the average range, yet have phonological deficits that prevent them from learning to read (Adams, 1990; Norman, & Zigmond, 1980). If these students are to learn to read, they often require sustained and intensive one-to-one instruction from a teacher trained in interventions such as Direct Instruction or Orton Gillingham language therapy (Adams & Engelmann, 1996; Foorman, Francis, Fletcher, Schatschneider, & Mehta, 1998; Stein, Carnine, & Dixon, 1998; Zigmond, 1997). In the same way that the child with poor vision needs glasses, the child with a learning disability in reading needs specialized instruction; however, this is not a provision of the full inclusion model.

There are also students who may appear average, yet behave in ways that are harmful to both themselves and their peers. These students may need highly structured and controlled environments in which teachers trained in Applied Behavior Analysis and behavior modification can work to reduce inappropriate behaviors and increase appropriate ones (Hallahan & Kauffman, 2000; Kauffman, 2001; Kauffman, Bantz, & McCullough, 2002). Just as children with deafness may need teachers proficient in sign language to learn and progress, children with emotional and behavioral disorders may need specialized settings and instruction. Unfortunately, specialized instructional practices and settings are eliminated in the full inclusion model, and needs such as these are ignored, dismissed, or given inadequate attention. With full inclusion, corrective glasses, sign language, and wheelchairs are permitted; however, intensive instruction in alternative settings is not. Thus, the needs of some students are addressed whereas the needs of others are ignored or given short shrift, which is neither fair nor just.

Students Are More Alike Than Different: The Undoing of Progress

Special education has a rich history in which individuals like Jean-Marc Gaspard Itard, Anne Macy Sullivan, Samuel Gridley Howe, and Thomas Hopkins Gallaudet have worked tirelessly to ameliorate the neglectful and often abusive treatment of individuals with disabilities. Some of these efforts have admittedly been misplaced and harmful. For example, the movement for institutionalization that exploded in the late 19th century was not helpful (Dorn, Fuchs, & Fuchs, 1996), but the preponderance of these efforts have resulted in the improved treatment and education of individuals with disabilities. The sine qua non of these improvements is the Education for All Handicapped Children Act (P.L. 94-142; reauthorized as the Individuals with Disabilities Education Act [IDEA] of 1990), a law that mandated a free and appropriate education for all children with

ut this law, students with disabilities might still be
ublic education and appropriate instruction (Mock,
an, 2003).

two centuries, special education has progressed from
the neglect of most students with disabilities and the exclusion of many
students with disabilities from public education to the entitlement of all students with disabilities to a free education tailored to meet their specific needs
(see Dorn et al., 1996; Hallahan & Kauffman, 2000; Kauffman, 1976, 2001).
The practice of full inclusion would undo a large part of this progress. With
full inclusion, students would be provided a free education as long as that
free education took place in the regular classroom with the regular classroom teacher. The assumption is that this education would be free and appropriate for typical students, but not for all of those with disabilities.

When Teachers Are More Alike Than Different

If all students are to be instructed in the regular classroom, then the regular classroom teacher must be prepared to teach all students. The ideal implementation of full inclusion includes the collaboration of general and
special educators sufficient to meet the needs of all students. However, unless the number of special educators is somehow multiplied, effective collaboration will prove to be logistically impossible, as the number of cases
involved does not allow sufficient time for working together, even if all special educators devote all of their time to collaboration. Even with collaboration, regular classroom teachers would bear most if not all of the responsibility for the instruction of their students. These teachers would
need, at a minimum, competence in both general and special education.
They would need a greater breadth of knowledge than the typical teacher.
Hence, areas of specialization and particular expertise would become less
valuable than general knowledge of great breadth.

Unfortunately, training of great breadth is unlikely to prepare teachers
to meet the needs of all students effectively and competently. Expecting
competent regular education teachers to meet the needs of all students effectively is akin to expecting competent general practitioners to meet all
the medical needs of their patients. Although the majority of patients will
have relatively standard medical needs, there will be patients who need
something beyond that which general practitioners can provide. For example, technological advances have made appendicitus easy to identify and

relatively easy to address by the surgical specialist. However, an appendectomy is not a procedure that most general practitioners are prepared to perform. The need for an organ transplant might escape the eyes of general practitioners and would certainly require surgeons who are specialists. Unfortunately, with the medical equivalent of full inclusion, patients would no longer be referred to specialists. Surgeons and operating rooms would no longer be options. All surgical operations would take place in the general practitioners' offices and would be performed by the proprietors themselves. Certainly there could be collaboration. A surgeon might stop by and lend an opinion, but no matter the procedure, the general practitioners would remain the ones wielding the scalpels. Technological advances would become incidental. Why would practitioners make use of technological advances to identify diseases that they had insufficient knowledge to treat? Advances in the science of medicine would slow if not completely halt. This scenario is, of course, preposterous. It is reminiscent of days when hospitals were scarce, antibiotics undiscovered, and appendicitis fatal.

Few individuals would willingly opt for major surgery performed by a general practitioner in his or her office. Most would elect to go to a hospital and seek out the expertise of a surgeon, a doctor with specialized training and experience. To do otherwise would be to ignore all of the progress that the field of medicine has made. When full inclusionists assert that all students can be effectively instructed by general educators, they are in effect asserting that there is no difference in the instruction offered by the general educator and the special educator. They suggest that good teaching is good teaching—a ubiquitous skill that is easily performed regardless of the student or task to be taught. Likewise, the medical treatment offered by the general practitioner and the surgeon would be equivalent; that is, good medicine is good medicine—a ubiquitous skill that is easily performed. Fortunately this is not the case, nor is it the prevailing belief. Surgeons have training and experience that is more specialized than that of general practitioners, and this difference is widely recognized and valued. So too is the case for general and special educators. Although both have knowledge unique to the students they instruct and expertise that is indispensable, special educators have training and experience that is more specialized than that of general educators. This training and experience can not be approximated or replicated in the training and experience of general educators. Special and general educators are alike in some respects, but special educators need additional and different skills.

The Training of the Specialist

Full inclusionists maintain that because students are more alike than different, training teachers to instruct the majority of students will enable them to instruct all students. In fact some proponents of full inclusion even maintain that educators already know more than is needed to successfully teach all children (Gartner & Lipsky, 1987). Thus, the training needed to instruct students with disabilities is deemed essentially no different from the training needed to instruct nondisabled students. It would seem therefore that specialists are special in name only.

What, then, do we make of specialists such as surgeons—doctors who complete an extended medical residency focusing upon surgical procedures? Do these specialists complete their training having acquired the same knowledge as general practitioners? Of course not! Surgeons receive extensive training in surgery, and general practitioners in general medicine. Therefore, surgeons are not trained to cure allergies, psychiatric disorders, or even hypertension, a most prevalent disease, and general practitioners are not trained to perform appendectomies and organ transplants. The field of medicine has found it implausible to attempt to train physicians in both breadth and depth. Instead the members of this field have opted for some professionals to receive training in breadth and others training in depth. Thus, we have doctors that we can rely upon to treat any number of minor ailments, and we also have specialists with extensive training who can cure our more serious diseases.

We have used medicine as an example of the necessity of specialization, but we could use many other professions as well. In law, in the building trades, in car repair, in flying, and in music making as well as in many other professions and lines of work, specialists are relied upon because they know more about particular problems and techniques than do the dabblers or generalists. They know more about particular problems and techniques because they have had special training and experience in doing a particular type of task over and over. A cardiologist is particularly good at assessing and treating heart disease because he or she specializes in—deals exclusively and repeatedly with—heart problems. The electrician knows electrical problems better than framing or drywall or plumbing problems for the same reason. Supposing that education requires only generalists or that educational disabilities do not require instructional specialists does not add up with anything we know about the lines of work and the value of specialized training and experience.

Contrary to the views expressed by full inclusionists, spe
also receive specialized training. In fact, many states have r.
tion in special education specific to a particular disability category. The
idea being that training to be a "Jack of all trades" leaves one a master of
none. Thus, teachers who are training to be specialists in learning disabilities learn the components of Direct Instruction, the implementation of
peer tutoring, the intricacies of mnemonic training, and strategies for
reading comprehension instruction (for a more complete listing of strategies that work in special education see Forness, Kavale, Blum, & Lloyd,
1997; Lloyd, Forness, & Kavale, 1998). These teachers also learn that the effective instruction of students with learning disabilities must control for
task difficulty, be implemented in small groups of six or less, and make use
of direct response questioning (Vaughn, Gersten, & Chard, 2000). Additionally, these teachers must learn how to perform task analyses, write Individualized Education Plans (IEPs), administer and interpret standardized achievement tests, and communicate to parents about very sensitive
issues. Specialists in learning disabilities receive training that focuses upon
a specific population and very specific instructional practices. In the limited amount of time the university training affords, these future teachers
receive the field's best knowledge about the select group of students with
whom they will soon work.

University students training to be teachers of students with emotional
and behavioral disorders also receive very specialized training. These future teachers learn how to implement precise and explicit behavior change
procedures, perform functional behavior assessment, and understand the
phases of behavioral escalation and the dynamics of reciprocal teacher–
student interactions (Walker, Sprague, Close, & Starlin, 1999–2000). Like
their peers specializing in learning disabilities, these teachers also receive
training in assessment, task analysis, IEPs, and parent communication,
and they learn the instructional components necessary for students with
emotional and behavioral disorders to learn and progress, many of which
are not widely accepted by general educators (Lloyd, Keller, Kauffman, &
Hallahan, 1988). The training that these teachers receive is specific to the
population with which they will work. Special educators are not trained to
be "Jacks of all trades"; instead they are prepared to master one.

How then should teachers be prepared for full inclusion? Should they
be "Jacks of all trades" and hence masters of none? If one teacher is expected and trained to meet the needs of every variety of student, that
teacher will be prepared for everything and competent at nothing. The

medical field knows that individuals cannot realistically be trained for both breadth and depth, for in so doing the level of skill displayed by both the practitioner and the field decreases. General practitioners do not perform surgery because surgeons are trained to do it better. Why then would general educators want to assume responsibility for the instruction of all students with disabilities when special educators are trained to do it better?

THE ADVANTAGE OF SPECIALISTS

There is an advantage to specialization that may not be readily apparent. When physicians become surgical specialists, they see only those patients with surgical concerns. Thus, they interact with a very specific and concentrated population. In so doing they see a greater number of less prevalent cases than would be seen in the general population. This specialization permits surgeons to develop new knowledge and expertise that would not otherwise be possible. In performing numerous appendectomies surgeons were able to develop a less invasive, more efficient laparoscopic procedure. Had these surgeons been practicing as general practitioners, this new knowledge and new tool would have developed more slowly. This type of knowledge advances not only the field of surgery but the entire field of medicine.

Special educators serve a very specific population and in so doing have developed knowledge and tools that have advanced both the field of special education and the field of education as a whole. As a result of the research that special educators have conducted, reliably effective tools such as Direct Instruction, peer mediated learning, and early intervention have become common parlance in educational circles (Forness et al., 1997; Lloyd et al., 1998). Within the past 40 years the knowledge base concerning learning disabilities has increased exponentially (Kavale, Fuchs, & Scruggs, 1994). This increase in knowledge benefits regular and special educators alike. If, as full inclusion advocates propose, all students are educated in a single classroom by a single teacher, the progress of the field of special education as well as the greater field of education will be slowed. In fact, it is difficult to know whether the field would even continue progressing.

CONCLUSION

Full inclusionists have made their sell. They promise fairness, justice, and equity in addition to later happiness (Stainback & Stainback, 1992). It is a very attractive deal, but the cost is rather high. In order to buy fairness teachers must relegate all of their students, even those who need specialized settings and instruction, to the regular classroom. To purchase justice, teachers are required to pretend that students' needs are more alike than different and, therefore, essentially the same. To acquire equity colleges of education must pretend to ensure that all teachers have minimal competence in everything and hence real competence in nothing. And to secure later happiness, teachers are required to halt all progress. The cost of full inclusion is inordinate. It is, frankly, too great a risk. Without proof that this model will actually produce fairness, justice, equity, and happiness, educators are asked to wager students, teachers, and knowledge. The potential for loss is staggering.

What then about teacher preparation? Simply put, there is no way to prepare teachers for the reality of full inclusion. Teachers cannot be prepared to competently instruct every student. Presently, teachers are professionals with specific training and expertise. As such, they are well aware of their strengths and limitations. If full inclusion is implemented, they will be asked to declare competence in areas beyond their training and expertise. If teachers respond affirmatively, they will become nothing more than general practitioners performing surgery in their offices. Their technique will be flawed, their tools outdated, and their patients harmed. They will lose all of their credibility and self-respect. Thus, teachers must hold to what they can do and clearly identify that which they cannot. Educators have a long history of underestimating the difficulty of teaching children well, and special educators share that history. We see the full inclusion movement as another example of grotesquely underestimating the difficulty of the task.

REFERENCES

Adams, M. J. (1990). *Beginning to read: Thinking and learning about print.* Cambridge: MIT Press.

Adams, G. L., & Engelmann, S. E. (1996). *Research on direct instruction: Twenty-five years beyond Distar.* Seattle, WA: Educational Achievement Systems.

Allington, R. L. (1993). Michael doesn't go down the hall anymore. *Reading Teacher, 46,* 602–604.

Artiles, A. J., & Zamora-Duran, G. (Eds.). (1997). *Reducing disproportionate representation of culturally diverse students in special education.* Reston, VA: Council for Exceptional Children.

Blackman, H. P. (1992). Surmounting the disability of isolation. *The School Administrator, 49*(2), 28–29.

Brown v. Board of Education of Topeka, 347 U.S. 483 (1954).

Children's Defense Fund. (2000). *The state of America's children yearbook: 25 key facts about American children.* Washington, DC: Author.

Crockett, J. B., & Kauffman, J. M. (1999). *The least restrictive environment: Its origins and interpretations in special education.* Mahwah, NJ: Erlbaum.

Crockett, J. B., & Kauffman, J. M. (2001). The concept of the least restrictive environment and learning disabilities: Least restrictive of what? Reflections on Cruickshank's 1977 guest editorial for the *Journal of Learning Disabilities.* In D. P. Hallahan & B. K. Keogh (Eds.), *Research and global perspectives in learning disabilities* (pp. 147–166). Mahwah, NJ: Erlbaum.

Dorn, S., Fuchs, D., & Fuchs, L. S. (1996). A historical perspective on special education reform. *Theory into Practice, 35,* 12–19.

Education for All Handicapped Children Act of 1975, 20 U.S.C. § 1400 *et seq.*

Foorman, B. R., Francis, D. J., Fletcher, J. M., Schatschneider, C., & Mehta, P. (1998). The role of instruction in learning to read: Preventing reading failure in at-risk children. *Journal of Educational Psychology, 90,* 37–55.

Forness, S. R., & Kavale, K. A. (1998). Impact of ADHD on school systems. In P. Jensen & J. R. Cooper (Eds.), *NIH consensus conference on ADHD* (pp. 61–68). Bethesda, MD: National Institute of Health.

Forness, S. R., Kavale, K. A., Blum, I. M., & Lloyd, J. W. (1997). What works in special education and related services: Using meta-analysis to guide practice. *Teaching Exceptional Children, 29*(6), 4–9.

Fuchs, D., & Fuchs, L. S. (1994). Inclusive schools movement and the radicalization of special education reform. *Exceptional Children, 60,* 294–309.

Gallagher, D. J. (1998). The scientific knowledge base of special education: Do we know what we think we know? *Exceptional Children, 64,* 493–502.

Gartner, A., & Lipsky, D. K. (1987). Beyond special education: Toward a quality system for all students. *Harvard Educational Review, 57,* 367–390.

Hallahan, D. P., & Kauffman, J. M. (2000). *Exceptional learners: Introduction to special education* (8th ed.). Boston: Allyn & Bacon.

Individuals with Disabilities Education Act (IDEA) of 1990, 20 U.S.C. § 1400 *et seq.*

Kauffman, J. M. (1976). Nineteenth century views of children's behavior disorders: Historical contributions and continuing issues. *The Journal of Special Education, 10,* 335–349.

Kauffman, J. M. (1981). Historical trends and contemporary issues in special education in the United States. In J. M. Kauffman & D. P. Hallahan (Eds.), *Handbook of special education* (pp. 3–23). Englewood Cliffs, NJ: Prentice-Hall.

Kauffman, J. M. (1994). Places of change: Special education's power and identity in an era of educational reform. *Journal of Learning Disabilities, 27,* 610–618.

Kauffman, J. M. (1999). Commentary: Today's special education and its messages for tomorrow. *The Journal of Special Education, 32,* 244–254.

Kauffman, J. M. (1999–2000). The special education story: Obituary, accident report, conversion experience, reincarnation, or none of the above? *Exceptionality, 8*(1), 61–71.

Kauffman, J. M. (2001). *Characteristics of emotional and behavioral disorders of children and youths* (7th ed.). New York: Merrill/Macmillan.

Kauffman, J. M., Bantz, J., & McCullough, J. (2002). Separate and better: A special public school class for students with emotional and behavioral disorders. *Exceptionality, 10,* 149–170.

Kauffman, J. M., & Pullen, P. L. (1996). Eight myths about special education. *Focus on Exceptional Children, 28*(5), 1–12.

Kauffman, J. M., & Smucker, K. (1995). The legacies of placement: A brief history of placement options and issues with commentary on their evolution. In J. M. Kauffman, J. W. Lloyd, D. P. Hallahan, & T. A. Astuto (Eds.), *Issues in educational placement: Students with emotional and behavioral disorders* (pp. 21–44). Hillsdale, NJ: Erlbaum.

Kavale, K. A., & Forness, S. R. (2000). History, rhetoric, and reality: Analysis of the inclusion debate. *Remedial and Special Education, 21,* 279–296.

Kavale, K. A., Fuchs, D., & Scruggs, T. (1994). Setting the record straight on learning disability and low achievement: Implications for policymaking. *Learning Disabilities Research and Practice, 9*(2), 70–77.

Lipsky, D. K., & Gartner, A. (1987). Capable of achievement and worthy of respect: Education for handicapped students as if they were full-fledged human beings. *Exceptional Children, 54,* 69–74.

Lipsky, D. K., & Gartner, A. (1996). Inclusion, school restructuring and the remaking of American society. *Harvard Educational Review, 66,* 762–796.

Lipsky, D. K., & Gartner, A. (1998). Taking inclusion into the future. *Educational Leadership, 56,* 78–81.

Lloyd, J. W., Forness, S. R., & Kavale, K. A. (1998). Some methods are more effective than others. *Intervention in School and Clinic, 33,* 195–200.

Lloyd, J. W., Keller, C. E., Kauffman, J. M., & Hallahan, D. P. (1988, January). *What will the regular education initiative require of general education teachers?* (Report). Washington, DC: Office of Special Programs, U.S. Department of Education.

McGill-Franzen, A. (1994). Compensatory and special education: Is there accountability for learning and belief in children's potential? In E. H. Hiebert & B. M. Taylor (Eds.), *Getting reading right from the start* (pp. 13–35). Boston: Allyn & Bacon.

Mock, D. R., Jakubecy, J. J., & Kauffman, J. M. (2003). Special education, history of. In J. W. Guthrie (Ed.), *Encyclopedia of education* (2nd ed., pp. 2278–2284). New York: Macmillan Reference.

Mostert, M. P. (2001). Facilitated communication since 1995: A review of published studies. *Journal of Autism and Developmental Disorders, 31,* 287–313.

Norman, C. A., & Zigmond, N. (1980). Characteristics of children labeled and served as learning disabled in school systems affiliated with child service demonstration centers. *Journal of Learning Disabilities, 13,* 16–21.

Sasso, G. M. (2001). The retreat from inquiry and knowledge in special education. *The Journal of Special Education, 34,* 178–193.

Shane, H. C. (Ed.). (1994). *Facilitated communication: The clinical and social phenomenon.* San Diego, CA: Singular.

Stainback, S., & Stainback, W. (1988). Letter to the editor. *Journal of Learning Disabilities, 21,* 452–453.

Stainback, S., & Stainback, W. (1992). Including students with severe disabilities in the regular classroom curriculum. *Preventing School Failure, 37,* 26–30.

Stainback, S., Stainback, W., East, K., & Sapon-Shevin, M. (1994). A commentary on inclusion and the development of a positive self-identity by people with disabilities. *Exceptional Children, 60,* 486–490.

Stein, M., Carnine, D., & Dixon, R. (1998). Direct instruction: Integrating curriculum design and effective practice. *Intervention in School and Clinic, 33,* 227–234.

U.S. Department of Education. (2000a). *Digest of educational statistics 2000.* Washington, DC: Author.

U.S. Department of Education. (2000b). *Twenty-second annual report to Congress on implementation of the Individuals with Disabilities Education Act.* Washington, DC: Author.

Vaughn, S., Gersten, R., & Chard, D. J. (2000). The underlying message in LD intervention research: Findings from research syntheses. *Exceptional Children, 67,* 99–114.

Walker, H. M., Sprague, J. R., Close, D. W., & Starlin, C. M. (1999–2000). What is right with behavior disorders: Seminal achievements and contributions of the behavioral disorders field. *Exceptionality, 8,* 13–28.

Zigmond, N. (1997) Educating students with disabilities: The future of special education. In J. W. Lloyd, E. J. Kameenui, & D. Chard (Eds.), *Issues in educating students with disabilities* (pp. 377–390). Mahwah, NJ: Erlbaum.

CHAPTER 14

The Delusion
of Full Inclusion

Devery R. Mock
and James M. Kauffman

This chapter is from "The Delusion of Full Inclusion," by D. R. Mock and J. M. Kauffman, 2005, in *Fads: Dubious and Improbable Treatments for Developmental Disabilities* (pp. 113–128), Mahwah, NJ: Erlbaum. Copyright 2005 by Erlbaum. Reprinted with permission.

The place in which instruction occurs—not instruction itself—has become the central issue in special education (Crockett & Kauffman, 1999). "Place-based education" (Smith, 2002) has been described, although it is not explicitly part of the full inclusion movement (FIM) in special education. "Place-based education" is consistent with the FIM assumption that place either can make or does make instruction effective. Blackman (1992) stated about special education:

> "Place" is the issue.... *There is nothing pervasively wrong with special education.* What is being questioned is not the interventions and knowledge that have been acquired through special education training and research. Rather, what is being challenged is the location where these supports are being provided to students with disabilities. (p. 29, italics in original)

The ideas that place is the paramount issue, that education should be based on one's location, and that changing the place of instruction is the key to improving it are likely among the most fatuous contemporary notions about teaching and learning. The idea that special education will become effective if we merely change its location may be laughable, but the idea has not been proposed as a joke. To be sure, the place of instruction constrains it, since all instruction cannot be offered with equal finesse and effectiveness in the same place and at the same time (Kauffman & Hallahan, 1997; Kauffman & Lloyd, 1995). However, the logic of this observation merely refutes the FIM.

Of greater concern is that we see the FIM as fitting Worrall's (1990) criteria for fraud or quackery: It is contrary to common sense, inconsistent with what we know about disabilities, and lacks credible supporting evidence. Fads, pseudotreatments, slogans, and misleading statements have captured the public imagination and the attention of many professional educators today (Kauffman, 2002). One of the most popular pseudotreatments is changing the place in which teaching is proffered. Another is asserting that whatever is or can be offered in a "mainstream" setting (considered by proponents of the FIM as *the* place to be) is better than what is or can be offered in a separate, special setting. That is, proponents of the FIM assume that the normalizing influence of the general education classroom is more important and powerful than specialized, therapeutic interventions, even in the face of evidence that separate, special environments produce better outcomes for some students (e.g., Carlberg & Kavale, 1980; Kavale & Forness, 2000; Stage & Quiroz, 1997). The FIM is consistent not only with Worrall's (1990) description of quackery but also with Shermer's

(2001) description of pseudoscience. Shermer describes how pseudoscience claims an apparent scientific revolution, but the claim will not withstand careful scrutiny. Pseudoscience portrays science as too conservative, not open to radical new ideas. "But science is conservative. It cannot afford not to be. It makes rigid demands on its participants in order to weed out the bad ideas from the good" (Shermer, 2001, p. 64).

The idea that place or location is prepotent over the details of instruction is a particularly noxious delusion when special education is under attack. The delusion is especially noxious because it distracts attention from important issues and holds out the false hope that the FIM will result in better instruction for students with disabilities while undercutting fiscal support for special education. Some have suggested in popular media that the cost of special education is too high, in part because of expensive placements (e.g., Cottle, 2001; Soifer, 2002). Much of the additional cost of special education is spent on space (separate classes), staff (special teachers), and intensified instruction (lower pupil–teacher ratios). The FIM thus seems to be cost saving, as more students with disabilities could be served in general education classes by regular teachers, thereby saving at least the costs of space and staff, if not instructional costs as well.

ATTACKS ON SPECIAL EDUCATION

Special education is receiving particularly intense scrutiny at the beginning of the 21st century. Legislators are preparing to correct the "problems" plaguing special education, which some say is a waste of money (Cottle, 2001; Fletcher, 2001). Critics contend that special education misidentifies students and provides them with services that are too expensive and of poor quality. Children in special education, they argue, are prevented from achieving their true potential because disabilities are poorly defined, instructional practices are fragmented, teachers have low expectations and poor training, and students are separated from the mainstream (Alexander, Gray, & Lyon, 1993; Lyon & Fletcher, 2001; Gartner & Lipsky, 1987; Lipsky & Gartner, 1996, 1997, 1998; McGill-Franzen, 1994; Slavin, 2001; Slavin & Madden, 2001a, 2001b). Ending separation from the mainstream is the central focus of the advocates of the FIM. Most critics of special education advocate full inclusion and the dissolution of special education as a separate, identifiable entity. Although special education surely needs significant improvement, it is the improvement of instruction itself—not the place in which it is offered—that is critical (Kauffman, 1999a, 2002; Zigmond, 1997).

The FIM has its historical and conceptual roots in Dunn (1968) and Deno (1970). The publication of Dunn's article was a watershed event in special education (MacMillan, Gresham, & Forness, 1996). Dunn suggested that special education of children with mild mental retardation was morally and educationally wrong because homogenous grouping damaged these children's self-esteem and caused their educational disadvantage. He urged educators to stop "segregating" students through special self-contained programs. Deno (1970) echoed Dunn's concerns and argued against categorizing students in special education. She suggested that special education should "work itself out of business" (p. 233) by giving general educators the techniques it had developed.

The sentiments of Dunn and Deno helped shape the regular education initiative (REI) of the 1980s. The REI was based on the assumption that all students are very much alike, eliminating the necessity of special education for at least *many if not most* students and returning responsibility for *many or most* students with disabilities to regular classroom teachers (Kavale & Forness, 2000). The FIM of the 1990s, however, carried integration a step further, advocating the *complete* elimination of special education as a separate entity (see Fuchs & Fuchs, 1994). Proponents of the FIM have called for "a fundamental change of the existing dual, failing, and costly special and general education systems … toward the broader matter of educating students with disabilities in a unitary system that will prepare them to participate in society" (Lipsky & Gartner, 1997, p. 69). The FIM suggests that the current "dual system" of regular (or general) and special education is especially harmful to students with disabilities.

Opponents of the FIM maintain that the dissolution of special education would be especially harmful to students with disabilities (Kauffman & Hallahan, 1995). Many arguments against full inclusion focus on students whose disabilities are severe and hence particularly troublesome to general education teachers. However, Walker and Bullis (1991) noted that the characteristics of students with behavioral disorders "make delivery of specialized intervention services within regular classrooms highly problematic" (p. 84). Kauffman, Lloyd, Baker, and Riedel (1995) concurred.

Crockett and Kauffman (1998, 1999) described how parents of children with severe disabilities found general education to be unhelpful for their children. Regarding the mother of a child with autism they noted, "She observed that so much is counterintuitive in the treatment of autism that her son Daniel's general education teachers often hinder rather than help him learn to cope with his classroom environment" (Crockett & Kauffman, 1999, p. 180). For students with severe disabilities, even the most basic aspects of general education classrooms (e.g. interactions with peers, unpredictable reinforcement schedules, and environments filled with desks, chairs, books, and many other objects) serve as triggers for problematic behavior. Perhaps the greatest parental objection to full inclusion is that effective teaching of their child is delayed or denied by the placement (Crockett & Kauffman, 1999; Palmer, Fuller, Arora, & Nelson, 2001). Teachers simply cannot teach a general education class effectively and at the same time offer the intensive, focused, relentless instruction that many children with disabilities require if they are to make reasonable progress. Palmer et al. (2001) noted the pros and cons of full inclusion and reported a parent's observations on the matter:

> I have two children with disabilities; this survey is about one. He is uncomfortable around other children and in close spaces. He expresses dislikes of normal students. He is also disliked by them and they tell me about his behavior when I'm on campus. Mainstreaming to a large extent would not do anyone service in this case.
>
> My other son has been fully and successfully mainstreamed for years. I know the downfalls, I know the up side. I consider mainstreaming as something that *must be decided on a case-by-case basis.* Like any other fad, it is being evangelized as a cure-all. It isn't. It is terrific in some cases. In others, it is child abuse. (p. 482)

Although arguments such as these make evident the problems inherent in educating *all* students in the general classroom, they do not directly defend a continuum of alternative placements (CAP) for students with less obvious disabilities. The CAP is a wide range of alternative placements, including regular classroom placement, resource rooms, special classes, special day schools, and special residential schools (see Hallahan & Kauffman, 2003, pp. 13–17 for description). Learning disability, for example, is not obvious to the casual observer (Forness, Sinclair, Jura, McCracken, & Cadigan, 2002). The majority of students with learning disabilities (LD) now spend most of their instructional day in the regular classroom (U.S. Department of Education, 2000). These students constitute most of the "gray area" in the inclusion debate, the students whose disabilities can most readily be denied or passed off as minor differences that require little or nothing special or as normal variations that general education teachers can easily accommodate. These students are the pawns in the FIM game plan.

ATTACKS ON THE CONTINUUM OF ALTERNATIVE PLACEMENTS

Sarason (2001) discussed society's initial responses to the virus that causes AIDS. After he noted that science, sociology, psychology, and medicine at first responded ineffectively to both the virus and the illness, Sarason concluded that there were lessons to be learned from the AIDS story.

> First, when a field is confronted with new and puzzling phenomena, the odds are very high that it will seek to understand them in ways that were productive in the past. Second, that understanding will, for varying lengths of time, turn out to be very oversimple. Third, the approach to the problem will markedly downplay the ways the phenomenon has cause and effect transactions with existing social attitudes, different interest groups.... There are correspondences that can be summed up in two statements: The problem is far more complicated than was initially thought. The more you know, the more you need to know. (pp. 58–59)

The FIM, rife with ignorance and irrelevant claims of cause and maltreatment, may parallel Sarason's example of the AIDS story. Attacks on the CAP make use of strategies and tactics that have been discussed elsewhere (e.g., Kauffman, 1999a, 2002; Sasso, 2001): nonsequiturs, oversimplifications, and willful ignorance.

Nonsequiturs

Special education has been based not merely on the applied sciences of medicine and education but also on the idea of social justice (Mock, Jakubecy, & Kauffman, 2003). In many instances, social advocates organized and worked to secure federal policies that provided both protection and opportunity for individuals with disabilities (Hallahan & Mock, 2003). This is a history that should engender pride; however, it is also a history often predicated more on conviction than observable truth. Kavale, Fuchs, and Scruggs warned that "without a properly rendered research base, policy analysis becomes policy advocacy because reason alone and the influence of values goes unchecked" (1994, p. 76; see also Sasso, 2001). Advocates of the FIM argue for policies unchecked by empirical science. As Sasso (2001) observed, argument unaccompanied by reliable scientific evidence is simply propaganda.

Stainback, Stainback, East, and Sapon-Shevin (1994) have proposed that the goal of full inclusion is to "create a world in which all people are knowledgeable and supportive of all other people" (p. 487). In this way, their logic suggests, students learn that all persons are equally valued members of society and that inclusion of all persons is the most important of all goals. In yet more impassioned pleas, proponents of the FIM have likened current special education to racial segregation. These arguments are based on a misapplication of the landmark U.S. Supreme Court case, *Brown v. the Board of Education of Topeka* (see Kauffman, 2002; Kauffman & Lloyd, 1995). They evoke shameful memories of legalized racial segregation and define the issue of full inclusion as a matter of civil rights (Gallagher, 1998; Gartner & Lipsky, 1987; Stainback et al., 1994; Stainback, Stainback, & Stefanich, 1996). Additionally, advocates of full inclusion have intensified this emotional appeal, likening current special education to both apartheid (Lipsky & Gartner, 1987) and slavery (Stainback & Stainback, 1988). Through such nonsequiturs, advocates of full inclusion attempt to rally public opinion against special education practices born of concerns for social justice.

Legalized segregation was a far too monstrous and systematic policy to be likened to education in a resource or special class or special school for students with disabilities or to the CAP. Appealing to *Brown* as justification for the FIM trivializes the experiences of those who lived through or currently live with the repercussions of racial segregation. Racial segregation and special education are built on entirely different legal, moral, and educational premises (see Crockett & Kauffman, 1999; Kauffman, 2002; Kauffman & Lloyd, 1995).

However, even if argument from *Brown* were not a nonsequitur, it would not be convincing. In 1954, the Supreme Court (in *Brown*) ordered the desegregation of all public schools. Almost 50 years later urban schools are more racially segregated than ever before (Sarason, 2001), and citizens in cities like Cincinnati, Ohio, are boycotting hotels, restaurants, and stores in protest of systemic racism (Pierre, 2002). The U.S. Supreme Court decision clearly did not end segregation at the societal or even the school level. Such evidence is clearly disturbing, especially to individuals who had hoped that a simple change in a law or policy would effect immediate social change.

In explaining the naiveté of social scientists who had expected immediate change to accompany the *Brown* ruling, Sarason wrote:

> My own explanation of the unpreparedness of American social science was that it viewed segregation as basically a moral issue and when that moral issue received the appropriate legal–political resolution, implementation would not encounter, except perhaps initially, serious obstacles. (2001, p. 19)

Social scientists distilled the practice of segregation into a single issue of morality. Clearly, they oversimplified a very complex issue. Likewise, when full inclusionists distill criticisms of special education into the single issue of segregation, they also oversimplify a very complex issue in addition to using an argument (segregation) that does not rest on the same premise as special education. They beg the field to solve current problems using tools of the past and tools nor appropriate for the problems, and hence to choose social activism over logical thinking and scientific evaluation.

Oversimplifications

Full inclusionists propose redesigning schools to create environments in which all children are known individually and, consequently, have all of their needs met (Lipsky & Gartner, 1997). This utopian goal, apparently shared by some teachers and administrators but rejected by others, may be in some respects inviting, but it is based upon oversimplified understandings of schools, students, and research (see Crockett & Kauffman, 1999; Hallahan & Kauffman, 2003; Palmer et al., 2001).

Middle schools and high schools are complex environments. They are often characterized as both balkanized and resistant to change (Sarason, 1990, 2001). It is therefore not surprising that the majority of articles about full inclusion focus on elementary schools. Conceptually, full inclusion becomes more difficult to envision in the upper grades. For instance, would *all* students be included in calculus? Would *all* students be included in Spanish IV? How would placement decisions be made so as not to exclude *any* student?

The policy of full inclusion would affect all students with disabilities, more than half of whom receive educational services in middle or high school settings. McIntosh, Vaughn, Schumm, Haager, and Lee (1993) studied the instruction offered to students with LD in mainstreamed high school classes. They found that teachers provided few adaptations, and instruction was generally not differentiated to meet the needs of students with disabilities. Students with LD infrequently asked the teacher for help, seldom volunteered to answer questions, and interacted with both the teacher and peers at a low rate. At present, there is not sufficient empirical evidence to support the full inclusion of students with LD, much less students with other more severe disabilities, at the middle or high school level.

Lipsky and Gartner (1997) suggested that to successfully accomplish full inclusion general educators should use instructional strategies that experienced and qualified teachers use for all children. These strategies included (a) cooperative learning, (b) curricular modifications, and (c) whole language instruction. Each of these recommended strategies will now be examined in the light of relevant empirical data.

In cooperative learning, teachers group students to work together on assigned tasks. These tasks may range from practicing teacher-taught skills to attempting to discover new, student-identified knowledge. Tateyama-Sniezek (1990) reviewed 12 studies in which cooperative learning was the independent variable and academic achievement the dependent variable, finding that the opportunity for students to study together did not guarantee gains in academic achievement. Over 10 years later McMaster and Fuchs (2002) conducted another literature review of cooperative learning. They concluded that the use of empirically supported cooperative elements may be an important, but *not a sufficient,* determinant of cooperative learning's effectiveness, specifically for students with LD. A reasonable person would ask, "Why would we expect classmates to be better at helping LD students learn than professional teachers using an empirically validated curriculum?"

The curricular adaptations that full inclusionists advocate are reminiscent of medicines dispensed to cure all that ails a person, better known as quack remedies (see Worrall, 1990). That is, teachers are urged to dispense weak, palliative treatments in response to problems that are often quite severe. Proponents of full inclusion often fail to specify whether these adaptations (which may range from special seating arrangements to modified assignments) are in fact accommodations or modifications. Additionally, many descriptions are such that it is difficult to ascertain how the adaptation is implemented, let alone how it is to be effective. For example, Stainback et al. (1996) wrote:

For many students an objective for a lesson may be to learn to write letters to friends. But for other students a more appropriate objective might include dictating a letter into a tape recorder.... Developing separate or different objectives for one or a few students can lead to their isolation or segregation within the classroom. (p. 14)

Given such an assumption it is difficult to understand how the decision to adapt a curriculum is to be made. Despite this level of ambiguity, Stainback et al. (1996) assured readers that developing curricular accommodations was relatively easy. Research in both testing and instructional accommodations demonstrates that nothing could be further from the truth (Bielinski, Ysseldyke, Bolt, Friedebach, & Friedebach, 2001; Fuchs & Fuchs, 2001; Johnson, Kimball, & Brown, 2001; Pitoniak & Royer, 2001).

Fuchs, Fuchs, Hamlett, Phillips, and Karns (1995) found that the instructional adaptations that general educators make for students with LD are typically oriented to the group, *not the individual*, and are relatively minor in substance. Additionally, Fuchs et al. (1995) observed that most adaptations were made in a rather indiscriminate manner, thus questioning the very validity of both the adaptation and the instruction. In another study, McIntosh et al. (1993) reported that due to inappropriate adaptation of class work, as well as instruction aimed at the large group, most students with LD were not engaged in the learning process. Instructional adaptations do not appear to have the palliative effect that full inclusionists have described.

Stainback et al. (1996) also encouraged readers to implement constructivist practices such as whole language in full inclusion classrooms. The 1980s' whole-language instructional approach was introduced by reformers who openly and explicitly rejected the value of quantitative evidence of effectiveness and held to the belief that learning to read was as simple as learning to speak (Dudley-Marling & Fine, 1997; Garan, 1994; Goodman, 1992, 1994). Using this philosophy, specific skill instruction was abandoned in favor of a focus on the reading process as a whole—reading as using language rather than reading as decoding written language. After the whole language philosophy had been implemented, the results of the 1992 and 1994 National Assessment of Educational Progress demonstrated that more than 40% of fourth graders instructed using a whole language approach were unable to read grade appropriate texts (Adams, 1997). Researchers have since questioned the way in which whole language was so universally adopted in the absence of any credible evidence of its efficacy (Adams, 1995; Slavin, 2001). The lessons from this example are multiple.

Whole language does not have sufficient evidence to ʼ
students with or without disabilities. Additionally, ʋ
educational practice in the absence of empirical suₚₚₜ
harmful to student progress.

Willful Ignorance

The research we have reviewed to this point illustrates that the FIM is
based on false premises. However, other research and, in addition, misrepresentations of research by proponents of the FIM, also reveal that full inclusion will not withstand careful scrutiny.

Beginning with the REI, supporters of inclusionary practices have used
efficacy studies to question the effectiveness of special education practices
(Kavale & Forness, 2000). Research outcomes that demonstrated a lack
of efficacy for resource room models served as an impetus for the full inclusion movement (Lyon et al., 2001). For example, Lipsky and Gartner
(1997) wrote:

> Outcomes for students who participate in the separate special education
> system are severely limited. This is true across a variety of metrics:
> dropout rates, graduation rates, postsecondary education and training,
> employment, and residential independence. The widespread failures that
> are documented in the special education system provide a strong basis
> for change. (p. 11)

Other studies (Rea, McLaughlin, & Walther-Thomas, 2002; Wallace,
Anderson, Bartholomay, & Hupp, 2002) suggested that students in general
education classrooms achieved better outcomes on some measures than
did their peers in pullout programs. Unfortunately, these studies and others like them violated at least one standard of rigorous empirical research:
random assignment to treatment groups. Thus, the more able students
with LD were served in general education classrooms while their more disabled peers were served in resource rooms. This difference in disability
level accounts for some of the differences in the outcomes.

Additionally, advocates of full inclusion use efficacy studies to suggest
that current special education practices *cause* students with disabilities to
fall further behind their general education peers. Ysseldyke and Bielinski
(2002) found this assertion untenable. In monitoring a group of students
who remained classified as LD over a 5-year period, the researchers found

that the rate of progress for this group remained relatively constant. When this group was modified to account for students placing in and out of the LD category, the mean achievement level dropped and the gap widened. Ysseldyke and Bielinski (2002) explained that students with higher achievement placed out of special education and were then replaced by newly identified students with lower achievement. This change in group membership resulted in lower mean achievement for those receiving special education. Ysseldyke and Bielinski concluded that special education group membership should not be a focus in examining achievement trends. Simmerman and Swanson (2001) found that when researchers failed to (a) control for teacher effects, (b) establish a criterion level of instructional performance, (c) use standardized measures, (d) use the same measures between pretest and posttest, (e) control for sample heterogeneity, and (f) use the correct unit of analysis, they reported inflated or unreliable treatment outcomes. Thus, the efficacy studies used to discredit special education practices are compromised by methodological shortcomings and do not warrant the dissolution of special education's CAP.

Proponents of full inclusion tend to disregard the nature of cause and effect transactions as they pertain to disability. Lipsky and Gartner (1996) wrote: "For students with disabilities, the critical challenge will be how we view and treat difference—as an abnormality or as an aspect of the human condition" (p. 788). The sentiment expressed in that statement is profound; yet, the reality conveyed is overly simplified. Perhaps the critical challenge for an individual will be, as Lipsky and Gartner asserted, to feel included and accepted, but perhaps the critical challenge will be to learn to read or to learn to feed oneself. Additionally, social acceptance of a disability does not cause the disability to vanish. Disability status is not merely a matter of semantics. Perhaps the critical question is whether we assume that all human conditions deserve the same treatment or, if not, treatment in the same location.

Critics of special education often distill disability into an absolute set of measurable constructs. Many researchers guilty of this oversimplification do not define themselves as full inclusionists, yet they propose reforms that would, in all likelihood, result in full inclusion. Lyon and Fletcher (2001) explained the causes of the prevalence of LD in this way:

> We propose that the rise in the incidence of LD is largely the result of three factors. First, remediation is rarely effective after 2nd grade. Second, measurement practices today work against identifying LD children be-

fore 2nd grade. Third, federal policy and the sociology of public educa-tion itself allow ineffective policies to continue unchecked. (p. 2)

Lyon and Fletcher (2001) seem to imply that controlling these three variables will result in the disappearance of the disability. Is the cause and effect relationship really that direct? Oversimplified understandings of cause and effect engender oversimplified solutions to disability. These un-derstandings move critics of special education, be they full inclusionists or individuals advocating inclusionary practices, to propose reforms aimed at erasing disability. Three such reforms proposed by Lyon and Fletcher (2001) focused upon (a) the definition and identification of LD; (b) teacher preparation; and (c) prevention, early intervention, and remediation.

Like Gartner and Lipsky (1987), many researchers have questioned the validity of LD (Lyon & Fletcher, 2001; Lyon et al., 2001; Shaywitz, Escobar, Shaywitz, Fletcher, & Makuch, 1992; Siegel, 1989; Vellutino, Scanlon, & Lyon, 2000; Vellutino, Scanlon, & Tanzman, 1998). They argue that students with LD are not readily distinguishable from students with low achieve-ment. Despite research showing that students with LD demonstrate achievement that is the "lowest of the low" (Kavale et al., 1994), Lyon et al. (2001) proposed that effective intervention can occur without the identi-fication of disability. Lyon (personal communication, March 20, 2002) suggested replacing the term *learning disability* with *learning difference*, as *everyone* demonstrates learning differences. Any label that applies to all rather than a subset of the population perpetuates the incorrect assump-tion that students with a disability (including LD) do not differ signifi-cantly from the general population (Fuchs & Fuchs, 1995; Kauffman, 2002).

Lyon and Fletcher (2001) maintained that highly intensive, systematic instruction can only be accomplished when the number of children with reading difficulties declines. Additionally, asserting that most early reading difficulties are similar regardless whether the student is served in special or compensatory education programs, Lyon et al. (2001) argued for the deliv-ery of services in the regular classroom. Critics of special education have argued that teacher training in special education is inadequate and inef-fective (Alexander et al., 1993; Gartner & Lipsky, 1987; Lipsky & Gartner, 1997, 1998; Lyon & Fletcher, 2001; McGill-Franzen, 1994; Slavin, 1997, 2001; Slavin & Madden, 2001a, 2001b). Assuming that this ineffectiveness results from lack of depth and intensity of training, it is difficult to imag-ine how a general educator could be more effective with even less deep and extensive training. This logic is even worse than that used when making decisions regarding class size. Sarason (2001) wrote: "The assumption is: A teacher who is inadequate or mediocre with a class of 25–30 students will become adequate with a class of 15–20 students" (p. 102). Likewise, individuals advocating inclusionary practices seem to suggest that returning all students to the regular classroom will improve teacher efficacy or that the efficacy of all teachers can be improved to the point at which all children will thrive in regular classrooms. This suggestion ignores both logic and evidence.

The National Reading Panel (2000) concluded that systematic phonics instruction produces significant benefits for students in kindergarten through sixth grade and for students with reading disabilities regardless of socioeconomic status. However, Mather, Bos, and Babur (2001) suggested that teachers are ill-prepared to offer such instruction. Surveying preservice and inservice teachers of grades kindergarten through third grade, Mather et al. found that only 16% of preservice and 47% of inservice teachers were able to match the term *digraph* with its definition. Additionally, only 48% of preservice and 37% of inservice teachers knew that phonics was a reading method that teaches the application of sounds to letters. Once again, cause-and-effect has been drastically oversimplified. Returning students with disabilities to the regular classroom does not ensure that teachers will be equipped to instruct them effectively.

Special education has been criticized for its reliance on a "wait-to-fail" model (Lyon & Fletcher, 2001; Lyon et al., 2001). Thus, proponents of the FIM have advocated a shift from an emphasis on remediation to an emphasis on prevention, wherein regular classroom teachers use effective instructional programs that ensure that most students achieve success the first time they are taught (Slavin & Madden, 2001a). Special education researchers have agreed that primary prevention aimed at averting the manifestation of disabilities represents an important focus for research and funding (Andrews et al., 2000). It is generally agreed that prevention is a good thing, and evidence does suggest that primary prevention is sometimes possible (e.g., Kauffman, 1999b).

Unfortunately, the best prevention we can devise will not eliminate all failure or all disability. The cause-and-effect relationship is just not that simple. Primary prevention, when implemented effectively, reduces the manifestation of dysfunction. The most effective primary prevention programs are comprehensive, sustained across age levels, and based upon empirically validated practices (Coie et al.,1993; Cowen, 1996; Zigler, Taussig, & Black, 1992). Even with such preventative interventions, some individuals manifest dysfunction and require additional intervention—secondary or tertiary prevention after a disorder or "failure" has occurred. When, as Lyon and Fletcher (2001) have suggested, primary prevention is the work of both special and regular education, and when special educators focus on early identification and the implementation of specialized interventions within the regular classroom (Lyon et al., 2001), where will the students who manifest disabilities resistant to primary prevention receive instruction? Additionally, who will instruct these students? And this point must not be lost: Effective prevention requires unequivocally that, at least in the beginning years of implementation, *more students, not fewer, must be served* (Kauffman, 1999b).

Long ago, Kauffman (1989) pointed out how proponents of the REI (now the FIM) ignored or misinterpreted research findings like those of Carlberg and Kavale (1980). Ignorance and misrepresentation of research continue. Perhaps additional statements about instructional research should give pause to those who promote the FIM:

> In reform-based lessons, low achievers face the challenge of becoming part of a community of learners in which students are to construct their own understanding of mathematical concepts through conversations with peers and the teachers. An underlying assumption is that students can exchange ideas and learn from each other (Baxter, Woodward, & Olson, 2001, p. 543).... The assumption that all students will flourish with the challenging mathematics curricula and pedagogy that comprise reform needs to be questioned. (Baxter et al., 2001, p. 545)

CONCLUSION

Kavale et al. (1994) were correct in suggesting that the formulation of LD policy "is a fragile endeavor" complicated by ideology (p. 76). Advocates of full inclusion have adopted an ideology—a delusion, in our judgment—that being in the same place as others is a necessary, if not sufficient condition, for fair treatment of students with disabilities. This delusion includes at least one of the following assumptions, if not all of them: (a) if all students receive instruction in the same setting, they will receive the same opportunities to learn; (b) fair treatment of students with disabilities can be achieved only when these students are in the same place as students without disabilities; and (c) students with disabilities should be treated like all other students (see Ysseldyke, Algozzine, & Thurlow, 2000, p. 67, for a statement of the last assumption).

Special education is by nature paradoxical, in that it is a way of achieving equal opportunities through treatment that is different (and therefore unequal). In attempting to provide students the same access and opportunity afforded to everyone, we treat students with disabilities differently and individually. It is impossible to offer such treatment to all students. In order to maximize equity, we offer *special* education to students with disabilities (see Crockett & Kauffman, 1999; Hockenbury, Kauffman, & Hallahan, 1999–2000). This reality may prove difficult for some to accept, as they see equal treatment as the key to equal opportunity. Students with disabilities benefit from specialized interventions (Foorman, Francis, Fletcher, Schatschneider, & Mehta, 1998; Forness, Kavale, Blum, & Lloyd, 1997; Fuchs, Fuchs, Mathes, & Martinez, 2002; Lloyd, Forness, & Kavale, 1998; Torgesen et al., 2001; Vaughn, Gersten, & Chard, 2000). Without different treatment, unfairness is assured.

Perhaps the FIM is popular because if offers what appears to be a road to quick and easy success. It is much quicker and easier to move bodies than to teach well. If the goal is to move students into mainstream classes, this can be accomplished quickly, with little effort or money, and with virtually certain and easily documented success. People start out in one place and are moved to another. All done! Right? Perhaps not. However, if the goal is to teach students exceedingly well, regardless of their characteristics, then success cannot be claimed as quickly, the task requires great effort and monetary costs, the outcomes are uncertain (especially for students with more severe disabilities of any nature), and success may be difficult to document. The ideology of full inclusion may in our opinion be fairly characterized as delusional because it meets Worrall's (1990) criteria for fraud: It is simply unreasonable based on what we know.

REFERENCES

Adams, M. J. (1995). *Beginning to read: Thinking and learning about print.* Cambridge, MA: MIT Press.

Adams, M. J. (1997). The great debate: Then and now. *Annals of Dyslexia, 47,* 265–276.

Alexander, D., Gray, D. B., & Lyon, G. R. (1993). Conclusions and future directions. In G. R. Lyon, D. B. Gray, J. E. Kavanaugh, & N. A. Krasnegor (Eds.), *Better understanding learning disabilities* (pp. 343–350). Baltimore: Brookes.

Andrews, J. E., Carnine, D. W., Coutinho, M. J., Edgar, E. B., Forness, S. R., Fuchs, L. S., et al. (2000). Bridging the special education divide. *Remedial and Special Education, 21,* 258–260, 267.

Baxter, J. A., Woodward, J., & Olson, D. (2001). Effects of reform-based mathematics instruction on low achievers in five third-grade classrooms. *Elementary School Journal, 101,* 529–547.

Bielinski, J., Ysseldyke, J. E., Bolt, S., Friedebach, M., & Friedebach, J. (2001). Prevalence of accommodations for students with disabilities participating in a statewide testing program. *Assessment for Effective Intervention, 26*(2), 21–28.

Blackman, H. P. (1992). Surmounting the disability of isolation. *The School Administrator, 49*(2), 28–29.

Brown v. Board of Education of Topeka, 347 U.S. 483 (1954).

Carlberg, C., & Kavale, K. (1980). The efficacy of special versus regular class placement for exceptional children: A meta-analysis. *The Journal of Special Education, 29,* 155–162.

Coie, J. D., Watt, N. F., West, S. G., Hawkins, J. D., Asarnow, J. R., Markman, H. J., et al. (1993). The science of prevention: A conceptual framework and some directions for a national research program, *American Psychologist, 48,* 1013–1022.

Cottle, M. (2001, June 18). Jeffords kills special ed. reform school. *The New Republic,* pp. 14–15.

Cowen, E. L. (1996). The ontogenesis of primary prevention: Lengthy strides and stubbed toes. *American Journal of Community Psychology, 24,* 235–249.

Crockett, J. B., & Kauffman, J. M. (1998). Taking inclusion back to its roots. *Educational Leadership, 56,* 74–77.

Crockett, J. B., & Kauffman, J. M. (1999). *The least restrictive environment: Its origins and interpretations in special education.* Mahwah, NJ: Erlbaum.

Deno, E. (1970). Special education as developmental capital. *Exceptional Children, 37,* 229–237.

Dudley-Marling, C., & Fine, E. (1997). Politics of whole language. *Reading and Writing Quarterly: Overcoming Learning Difficulties, 13,* 247–260.

Dunn, L. (1968). Special education for the mildly retarded—Is much of it justifiable. *Exceptional Children, 34,* 5–22.

Fletcher, M. A. (2001, October 5). Overhaul planned for special education. *The Washington Post,* p. A3.

Foorman, B. R., Francis, D. J., Fletcher, J. M., Schatschneider, C., & Mehta, P. (1998). The role of instruction in learning to read: Preventing reading failure in at-risk children. *Journal of Educational Psychology, 90,* 37–55.

Forness, S. R., Kavale, K. A., Blum, I. M., & Lloyd, J. W. (1997). What works in special education and related services: Using meta-analysis to guide practice. *Teaching Exceptional Children, 29*(6), 4–9.

Forness, S. R., Sinclair, E., Jura, M. B., McCracken, J. T., & Cadigan, J. (2002). *Learning disabilities and related disorders.* Los Angeles: Wallis Foundation.

Fuchs, D., & Fuchs, L. S. (1994). Inclusive schools movement and the radicalization of special education reform. *Exceptional Children, 60,* 294–309.

Fuchs, L. S., & Fuchs, D. (1995). What's "special" about special education? *Phi Delta Kappan, 76,* 522–530.

Fuchs, L. S., & Fuchs, D. (2001). Helping teachers formulate sound test accommodation decisions for students with learning disabilities. *Learning Disabilities Research and Practice, 16*(3), 174–181.

Fuchs, L. S., Fuchs, D., Hamlett, C. L., Phillips, N. B., & Karns, K. (1995). General educators' specialized adaptations for students with learning disabilities. *Exceptional Children, 61,* 440–460.

Fuchs, D., Fuchs, L. S., Mathes, P. G., & Martinez, E. (2002). Preliminary evidence on the social standing of students with learning disabilities in PALS and No-PALS classrooms. *Learning Disabilities: Research and Practice, 17,* 205–215.

Gallagher, D. J. (1998). The scientific knowledge base of special education: Do we know what we think we know? *Exceptional Children, 64,* 493–502.

Garan, E. (1994). Who's in control? Is there enough "empowerment" to go around? *Language Arts, 71,* 192–199.

Gartner, A., & Lipsky, D. K. (1987). Beyond special education: Toward a quality system for all students. *Harvard Educational Review, 57,* 367–390.

Goodman, K. S. (1992). I didn't found whole language. *The Reading Teacher, 46,* 188–199.

Goodman, K. S. (1994). Reading, writing, and written texts: A transactional sociopsycholinguistic view. In R. B. Ruddell, M. Rapp Ruddell, & H. Singer (Eds.), *Theoretical models and processes of reading* (4th ed., pp. 1093–1130). Newark, DE: International Reading Association.

Hallahan, D. P., & Kauffman, J. M. (2003). *Exceptional learners: Introduction to special education* (9th ed.). Boston: Allyn & Bacon.

Hallahan, D. P., & Mock, D. R. (2003). A brief history of the field of learning disabilities. In H. L. Swanson, K. Harris, & S. Graham (Eds.), *Handbook of learning disabilities* (pp. 16–29). New York: Guilford.

Hockenbury, J. C., Kauffman, J. M., & Hallahan, D. P. (1999–2000). What's right about special education? *Exceptionality, 8*(1), 3–11.

Johnson, E., Kimball, K., & Brown, S. O. (2001). American Sign Language as an accommodation during standards-based assessments. *Assessment for Effective Intervention, 26*(2), 39–47.

Kauffman, J. M. (1989). The regular education initiative as Reagan–Bush education policy: A trickle-down theory of education of the hard-to-teach. *Journal of Special Education, 23,* 256–278.

Kauffman, J. M. (1999a). Commentary: Today's special education and its messages for tomorrow. *The Journal of Special Education, 32,* 244–254.

Kauffman, J. M. (1999b). How we prevent the prevention of emotional and behavioral disorders. *Exceptional Children, 65,* 448–468.

Kauffman, J. M. (2002). *Education deform: Bright people sometimes say stupid things about education.* Lanham, MD: Scarecrow Education.

Kauffman, J. M., & Hallahan, D. P. (Eds.). (1995). *The illusion of full inclusion: A comprehensive critique of a current special education bandwagon.* Austin, TX: PRO-ED.

Kauffman, J. M., & Hallahan, D. P. (1997). A diversity of restrictive environments: Placement as a problem of social ecology. In J. W. Lloyd, E. J. Kameenui, & D. Chard (Eds.), *Issues in educating students with disabilities* (pp. 325–342). Hillsdale, NJ: Erlbaum.

Kauffman, J. M., & Lloyd, J. W. (1995). A sense of place: The importance of placement issues in contemporary special education. In J. M. Kauffman, J. W. Lloyd, D. P. Hallahan, & T. A. Astuto (Eds.), *Issues in educational placement: Students with emotional and behavioral disorders* (pp. 3–19). Hillsdale, NJ: Erlbaum.

Kauffman, J. M., Lloyd, J. W., Baker, J., & Riedel, T. M. (1995). Inclusion of all students with emotional or behavioral disorders? Let's think again. *Phi Delta Kappan, 76,* 542–546.

Kavale, K. A., & Forness, S. R. (2000). What definitions of learning disability say and don't say: A critical analysis. *Journal of Learning Disabilities, 33,* 239–256.

Kavale, K. A., Fuchs, D., & Scruggs, T. (1994). Setting the record straight on learning disability and low achievement: Implications for policymaking. *Learning Disabilities Research and Practice, 9*(2), 70–77.

Lipsky, D. K., & Gartner, A. (1987). Capable of achievement and worthy of respect: Education for handicapped students as if they were full-fledged human beings. *Exceptional Children, 54,* 69–74.

Lipsky, D. K., & Gartner, A. (1996). Inclusion, school restructuring and the remaking of American society. *Harvard Educational Review, 66,* 762–796.

Lipsky, D. K., & Gartner, A. (1997). *Inclusion and school reform: Transforming America's classrooms.* Baltimore: Brookes.

Lipsky, D. K., & Gartner, A. (1998). Taking inclusion into the future. *Educational Leadership, 56,* 78–81.

Lloyd, J. W., Forness, S. R., & Kavale, K. A. (1998). Some methods are more effective than others. *Intervention in School and Clinic, 33,* 195–200.

Lyon, G. R., & Fletcher, J. M. (2001). Early warning systems. *Education Matters, 1,* 2–29.

Lyon, G. R., Fletcher, J. M., Shaywitz, S. A., Shaywitz, B. A., Torgesen, J. K., Wood, F. B., et al. (2001). Rethinking learning disabilities. In C. E. Finn, A. J. Rothrham, & C. R. Hokanson (Eds.), *Rethinking special education for a new century* (pp. 259–287). Washington, DC: Thomas B. Fordham Foundation.

MacMillan, D. L., Gresham, F. M., & Forness, S. R. (1996). Full inclusion: An empirical perspective. *Behavioral Disorders, 21,* 145–159.

Mather, N., Bos, C., & Babur, N. (2001). Perceptions and knowledge of preservice and inservice teachers about early literacy instruction. *Journal of Learning Disabilities, 34,* 472–482.

McGill-Franzen, A. (1994). Compensatory and special education: Is there accountability for learning and belief in children's potential? In E. H. Hiebert & B. M. Taylor (Eds.), *Getting reading right from the start* (pp. 13–35). Boston: Allyn & Bacon.

McIntosh, R., Vaughn, S., Schumm, J. S., Haager, D., & Lee, O. (1993). Observations of students with learning disabilities in general education classrooms. *Exceptional Children, 60,* 249–262.

McMaster, K. N., & Fuchs, D. (2002). Effects of cooperative learning on the academic achievement of students with learning disabilities: An update of Tateyama-Sniezek's review. *Learning Disabilities Research and Practice, 17,* 107–117.

Mock, D. R., Jakubecy, J. J., & Kauffman, J. M. (2003). Special education: History. In *Encyclopedia of education* (2nd ed., pp. 2278–2284). New York: Macmillan Reference.

National Reading Panel. (2000). *Teaching children to read: An evidence-based assessment of the scientific research literature on reading and its implications for reading instruction.* Washington, DC: National Institute of Child Health and Human Development.

Palmer, D. S., Fuller, K., Arora, T., & Nelson, M. (2001). Taking sides: Parent views on inclusion for their children with severe disabilities. *Exceptional Children, 67,* 467–484.

Pierre, R. E. (2002, April 2). Racial strife flares in Cincinnati over downtown business boycott. *The Washington Post,* p. A3.

Pitoniak, M. J., & Royer, J. M. (2001). Testing accommodations for examinees with disabilities: A review of psychometric, legal, and social policy issues. *Review of Educational Research, 71*(1), 53–104.

Rea, P. J., McLaughlin, V. L., & Walther-Thomas, C. (2002). Outcomes for students with learning disabilities in inclusive and pullout programs. *Exceptional Children, 68,* 203–222.

Sarason, S. B. (1990). *The predictable failure of school reform: Can we change course before it's too late?* San Francisco: Jossey-Bass.

Sarason, S. B. (2001). *American psychology and schools: A critique.* New York: Teachers College Press.

Sasso, G. M. (2001). The retreat from inquiry and knowledge in special education. *The Journal of Special Education, 34,* 178–193.

Shaywitz, S. E., Escobar, M. D., Shaywitz, B. A., Fletcher, J. M., & Makuch, R. (1992). Evidence that dyslexia may represent the lower tail of a normal distribution of reading ability. *The New England Journal of Medicine, 326,* 145–150.

Shermer, M. (2001). *The borderlands of science: Where sense meets nonsense.* New York: Oxford University Press.

Siegel, L. S. (1989). IQ is irrelevant to the definition of learning disabilities. *Journal of Learning Disabilities, 22,* 469–486.

Simmerman, S., & Swanson, H. L. (2001). Treatment outcomes for students with learning disabilities: How important are internal and external validity. *Journal of Learning Disabilities, 34,* 221–236.

Slavin, R. E. (1997). Including inclusion in school reform: Success for all and roots and wings. In D. K. Lipsky & A. Gartner (Eds.), *Inclusion and school reform: Transforming America's classrooms* (pp. 375–388). Baltimore: Brookes.

Slavin, R. E. (2001). Show me the evidence. *American School Board Journal, 188*(3), 26–29.

Slavin, R. E., & Madden, N. A. (2001a). *One million children: Success for all.* Thousand Oaks, CA: Corwin Press.

Slavin, R. E., & Madden, N. A. (2001b). Success for all: An overview. In R. Slavin & N. Madden (Eds.), *Success for all: Research and reform in elementary education* (pp. 3–16). Mahwah, NJ: Erlbaum.

Smith, G. A. (2002). Place-based education: Learning to be where we are. *Phi Delta Kappan, 83*, 584–594.

Soifer, D. (2002, June 23). Benefits, placements, funding and regulations are questionable at best. *Lexington Herald Leader*, p. F2.

Stage, S. A., & Quiroz, D. R. (1997). A meta-analysis of interventions to decrease disruptive classroom behavior in public education settings. *School Psychology Review, 26*, 333–368.

Stainback, S., & Stainback, W. (1988). Letter to the editor. *Journal of Learning Disabilities, 21*, 452–453.

Stainback, S., Stainback, W., East, K., & Sapon-Shevin, M. (1994). A commentary on inclusion and the development of a positive self-identity by people with disabilities. *Exceptional Children, 60*, 486–490.

Stainback, S., Stainback, W., & Stefanich, G. (1996). Learning together in inclusive classrooms: What about the curriculum. *Teaching Exceptional Children, 28*(3), 14–19.

Tateyama-Sniezek, K. M. (1990). Cooperative learning: Does it improve the academic achievement of students with handicaps? *Exceptional Children, 56*, 426–438.

Torgesen, J. K., Alexander, A. W., Wagner, R. K., Rashotte, C. A., Voeller, K. K. S., & Conway, T. (2001). Intensive remedial instruction for children with severe reading disabilities: Immediate and long-term outcomes from two instructional approaches. *Journal of Learning Disabilities, 34*, 33–58, 78.

U.S. Department of Education. (2000). *Twenty-second annual report to Congress on implementation of the Individuals with Disabilities Education Act.* Washington, DC: Author.

Vaughn, S., Gersten, R., & Chard, D. J. (2000). The underlying message in LD intervention research: Findings from research syntheses. *Exceptional Children, 67*, 99–114.

Vellutino, F. R., Scanlon, D. M., & Lyon, G. R. (2000). Differentiating between difficult-to-remediate and readily remediated poor readers: More evidence against the IQ–achievement discrepancy definition of reading disability. *Journal of Learning Disabilities, 33*, 223–238.

Vellutino, F. R., Scanlon, D. M., & Tanzman, M. S. (1998). The case for early intervention in diagnosing specific reading disability. *Journal of School Psychology, 36*, 367–397.

Walker, H. M., & Bullis, M. (1991). Behavior disorders and the social context of regular class integration: A conceptual dilemma? In J. W. Lloyd, M. N. Singh, & A. C. Repp (Eds.), *The regular education initiative: Alternative perspectives on concepts, issues, and models* (pp. 75–93). Sycamore, IL: Sycamore.

Wallace, T., Anderson, A. R., Bartholomay, T., & Hupp, S. (2002). An ecobehavioral examination of high school classrooms that include students with disabilities. *Exceptional Children, 68*, 345–359.

Worrall, R. S. (1990). Detecting health fraud in the field of learning disabilities. *Journal of Learning Disabilities, 23*, 207–212.

Ysseldyke, J. E., Algozzine, B., & Thurlow, M. L. (2000). *Critical issues in special education* (3rd ed.). Boston: Houghton Mifflin.

Ysseldyke, J. E., & Bielinski, J. (2002). Effect of different methods of reporting and reclassification on trends in test scores for students with disabilities. *Exceptional Children, 68*, 189–200.

Zigler, E., Taussig, C., & Black, K. (1992). Early childhood intervention: A promising preventative for juvenile delinquency. *American Psychologist, 1992,* 997–1006.

Zigmond, N. (1997). Educating students with disabilities: The future of special education. In J. W. Lloyd, E. J. Kameenui, & D. Chard (Eds.), *Issues in educating students with disabilities* (pp. 377–390). Mahwah, NJ: Erlbaum.

CHAPTER 15

The Special Education Story: Obituary, Accident Report, Conversion Experience, Reincarnation, or None of the Above?

James M. Kauffman

The future of special education might be captured in a variety of stories, including an obituary, or the report of an accident, a conversion experience, a reincarnation, or some other description not captured by any of these. Alternative story lines are suggested.

Some educators have suggested that the "specialness" of special education should be downplayed and that special and general education should be integrated (e.g., Goodlad & Lovitt, 1993). However, this suggestion is incompatible with viable special education in the light of Goodlad's analysis of teacher education (Kauffman & Hallahan, 1993; see also Goodlad, 1990). Moreover, it is contrary to Meyen's (1998) observation that if restructuring results in a loss of identity for special education, it is a mistake. Trends in education reform and numerous newspaper stories about special education reveal serious problems in current practices and intimate that the future of special education is uncertain.

A case in point was a story in *The Washington Post* on Thursday, May 20: "Janney Principal to Head D.C. Special-Ed Program" (Strauss, 1999). Having read the story on May 20, I posted an e-mail message to colleagues in special education as follows:

> *The Washington Post* this morning has an article about how special education in the District is going to be reformed by the superintendent and a newly appointed director of special education (who is now a school principal). Here's what disappoints me most about the article and what it portends: There is not one word in the article about instruction. It looks as if all of the effort is going into (a) keeping costs down, (b) avoiding legal suits, and (c) keeping kids in neighborhood schools and regular classrooms. Apparently, all sped administrators must resign and reapply, but not sped teachers. Place and structure (compliance issues other than special instruction) seem to be the preoccupation of reformers there, not

improving instruction or outcomes for kids. Of course, I guess someone could argue that instruction in general education will be an improvement over what's offered in special education and that outcomes will necessarily improve if kids are in general education. That's not just a matter of exceedingly ridiculous expectations but also a terrible indictment of the depths to which special education practices have fallen. Concern for effective teaching seems to have been replaced by the objectives of moving bodies, saving money, and keeping a lid on disputes. What forces have brought us to this point?

Readers may be aware of some of my opinions related to this question (e.g., Kauffman, 1993, 1994, 1995, 1997, 1999; Kauffman & Hallahan, 1993, 1997). The e-mail responses of colleagues to my post were varied and interesting, as the following excerpts illustrate. One of the e-mail responses I got was one word: "Lawyers." I think lawyers certainly have made substantial contributions to the current state of special education, whether you think we are in good shape or bad. Another person posted, simply, "Doesn't it always boil down to economics?" Probably, I thought. Money speaks. It is a universal language. Another colleague posted the following e-mail:

> Lately, I have been interviewing potential special education faculty and have noticed a shift away from grounding in the discipline (LD, BD, etc.) in favor of knowledge about delivery (inclusion, class within a class, etc.). At all levels, the trend seems to be development of special educators who can cope with a broad array of demands, but in less depth in areas than in the past. Is this your experience also? If so, should it be surprising about what is happening in D.C. at the classroom level? "We" are putting more students with more and more varied problems in classrooms in which teachers are expected to exhibit more and more varied skills. Should we be worried about the future? What is being done in the name of children? How much is for administrative convenience? It is frustrating because we know we can educate children to achieve at higher levels than ever before. So, why aren't we happier?

In other words, as I interpret this perspective, we have not been minding the store very well when it comes to teacher education. Personnel preparation is one of our biggest concerns, and what has happened in the preparation of teachers and leadership personnel should shock us into unhappiness.

Here is another interesting comment in response to my question, "What forces have brought us to this point?"

ORIGINAL SIN

(In this case, a well-intentioned federal law that has stamped out local responsibility and innovation, spawned highly intrusive legal decisions, created obsession with paper and procedures, and generally exceeded its shelf life.)

This one certainly prompted my thinking about sin and salvation. It started my contemplation of the religious or spiritual "take" on special education's story. Maybe we took the wrong road from the beginning, were beguiled by evil disguised as good.

I do not put much stock in religion or mysticism. Besides, I do not think the person who sent the "original sin" message actually sees the problem in religious terms. I was more amused than anything else by the notion of sin, but it did call to mind something I commented on several years ago, namely Fritz Redl's description of our "implementational sins" (Kauffman, 1994; Redl, 1966). The following e-mail post returns to notions more clearly secular:

> I've kept a slightly jaundiced eye on school reform movement. Mostly, I kept looking for any substance in the clouds of high-minded rhetoric. When the high flying (but well intentioned) verbiage is stripped away most of the "reforms, restructurings, and reorganizations" boil down to trivialities. I remember an author who asked a faculty (enthused over their new restructuring which lengthened the time of classes) to tell him three specific advantages the changes would create. The teachers literally were stumped. The only concrete advantage they could offer was that now kids could see an entire tape in one setting rather than in two settings. People might ask why currently popular instructional methods (e.g., whole language, whole math, brain-based instruction) are being

used. They might ask administrators to justify and explain exactly what instructional methods are used in XYZ school and why they are being used. Unfortunately, I don't think too many administrators could give good answers to those questions. People might wonder why demonstrably effective methods (e.g., direct instruction, strategy instruction, self-management, phonics approaches, mnemonics to name a few) were not systematically used. People might ask why, when classroom behavior problems are such an issue, teachers don't receive rigorous training in behavior modification techniques. People might ask why there's no systematic effort to reduce teacher–student ratios.

Posts like these led to my musings about the special education story and my guessing at how different people might conceptualize it. If you were to write a story about special education today—the enterprise, the profession, the structural component of American public education, not the delivery of special education to a particular student but the overall picture—what would you write? I am suggesting that you could very well write an obituary, given special education as some see it. You might write an accident report. Or you might describe what has happened or is happening to special education as something akin to religious conversion. I suppose you could take an alternative view and write a story of how special education has gone through or is in the midst of reincarnation, a rebirth that some may describe as its reinvention. Maybe, for you, none of these are satisfactory and you would write a story I have not imagined. The point is that all of us carry some sort of story about what has happened and is happening in our field. Furthermore, how we would write the story of special education has a lot to do with what we are going to do in response and how we try to shape the direction of our profession from this point on.

Some of the stories we could write about special education are very pessimistic. Others are optimistic in the extreme. How you would write the story depends, I suppose, on whether you believe special education is in trouble or not. Also, if you think special education today is in bad trouble, how did it get there, and what is the solution? Or if you think special education is not in a bad situation, what has contributed to its vitality and gives you a sense of optimism? Let us consider how some of the story types I mentioned might begin. First, let us suppose special education has died and its death is celebrated as a victory for exceptional children. Remember, the story could be written in a variety of ways. An obituary, for example, can be joyous or mourning.

SPECIAL EDUCATION DIES AS NEW MILLENNIUM IS BORN: THOSE WITH DISABILITIES FREE AT LAST

WASHINGTON, D.C.: Apartheid, the Berlin wall, Jim Crow, and special education. All were once very much a part of our lives and consciousness. But special education today joined the list of structures and policies that once stood for the brutal separation and segregation of others and now are over, thankfully gone forever.

Across the nation, celebrants are rejoicing in a new era in which education is no longer divided into special and general, students need not qualify for so-called special treatment, and all students are provided a common education for a common purpose—to be simply citizens and students with equal rights and responsibilities.

"No more special rules, no more special privileges, and no more labels, that's the one rule we have now," said the U.S. Secretary of Education. She continued, "What is good for one student is good for *all* students, and that is to be treated as an individual who is not like anyone else."

A professor of education, formerly involved in the special education system but now an advocate for all children, said "Students are more alike than they are different. We teach *all* children, not just some, and we prepare teachers to teach *all* children—and *all means all.*"

Signs in large block letters reading "Separate is inherently unequal" were waved on the mall by educators and parents who hailed the end of special education as the beginning of a new era of freedom from children being labeled and funneled into a costly, bloated, and segregating system.

One parent who identified himself as a school board member put it this way: "The Individuals with Disabilities Education Act [IDEA] was a horrible idea that said only *some* kids would get treated in a special way. Now *all* kids are seen as special and they're *all* eligible for anything they need. That's the long and short of it, and that's why we're so happy. Now we can just say and act as if a kid is a kid is a kid."

The process of merging special and general education has been gradual until very recently. People started talking about it in the early 1980s. Now, 20 years later, their dreams have been realized. Special education is no more. Gone are the labels and categories of disabilities. The law and the bureaucracy are gone. So are special appropriations. And most observers feel it's good riddance.

SPECIAL EDUCATION DEAD AT MILLENNIUM'S END: LOSS MOURNED BY DISABILITY COMMUNITY

WASHINGTON, D.C.: Some say it started with the muggings special education suffered at the hands of its severest critics, described in the 1990s by Vanderbilt University Professors Doug and Lynn Fuchs (see Fuchs & Fuchs, 1995a, 1995b). In any case, special education's life was snuffed out today. It joins Aid to Families with Dependent Children (the welfare program known as AFDC) and other social welfare experiments of the 20th century that Congress and many social scientists said had failed. In most places, special education was less than 60 years old. It was a century old in only a very few cities. At the federal level, it is survived only by Title I, another program whose life is limited according to many reformers who want the U.S. Department of Education restructured to eliminate all special programs and entitlements.

Rising resentment of children with special needs, especially the high cost of their special education, is part of the reason special education was cut down, according to some advocates for children with disabilities. Misunderstanding of the role of special education as part of the public system of education in this country is cited by many as another reason for its demise. Still another factor in the death of special education was the ideology of inclusion and the notion that anything separate or different is inherently discriminatory.

Like a seemingly innocuous drug, these ideas proved fatal to special education, which depends on recognizing and labeling differences among children, going to extraordinary lengths to teach them, and providing the money to train and sustain special teachers. One former special education teacher said, "We get the picture, and it's this: Now, nobody—nobody in the administration and nobody in the school—is assigned the specific task of seeing that children with disabilities are given an appropriate education. With nobody in particular attending to this task, we know what happens; kids with disabilities get little or nothing. When special education went down the tubes, these kids went down the tubes too, but a lot of folks see that as justice."

The mood among those witnessing the enactment of legislation effectively snuffing out special education was grim. "Goodbye, IDEA, we hardly knew ye," mumbled one dejected observer, the parent of a child with disabilities. In the 1990s, Professors Fuchs warned their colleagues in an editorial about the implications of so-called "reforms" of the welfare system, an older social experiment that until the 1990s seemed invulnerable. Today, the words of these professors seem prophetic: "Many in the disability community would say that in an ideal world our nation would have the knowledge, desire, and money to provide an appropriate education to all children in mainstream classrooms, where they would learn and play together. What the welfare 'reform' bill has taught us most fundamentally is that we don't live in an ideal world" (Fuchs & Fuchs, 1996, p. 231).

SPECIAL EDUCATION A BAD ACCIDENT: CLEAN-UP BEGUN

WASHINGTON, D.C.: The carnage created by a huge structural, bureaucratic accident is being cleaned up, thanks to sustained efforts on the part of reformers in special and general education.

Special education, a monstrous and debilitating structure created by well-meaning educators, legislators, and parents in the early part of the last century, is finally being cleaned up and rehabilitated. The impenetrable thicket of laws and rules known as IDEA has been cleared out and replaced by a new, more easily understood rule. Simply stated, the new rule is that all children, regardless of their characteristics, will be given an appropriate education.

This levels the playing field for everyone and ends a discriminatory, demeaning system of special privileges. Like the policy accident called "affirmative action," special education is being cleaned up to the dismay of some but the delight of many.

The assistant secretary of education formerly responsible for special education admitted, "The clean-up won't make everybody happy, and it's a bit messy, but in the end we'll have a more equitable system where disability doesn't count. All children are different, and now it doesn't matter *how* they are different or how different they are. Now, they all get the same, good education."

SPECIAL EDUCATION IN BAD
ACCIDENT: SURVIVAL IN DOUBT

WASHINGTON, D.C.: Some say that special education was mugged, others that it was in a train wreck. Some say special education was careless, that its smash-up was a logical consequence of taking the wrong road, driving too fast, and steering as directed by careless thinkers. In any case, it is clearly an enterprise staggering from deep wounds, struggling to stay conscious of its whereabouts and avoid catastrophic collapse. Its wounds have come from a variety of sources.

First, special education's face was smashed by the argument of some special educators themselves, not to mention general educators who long resented special education's unique role, that special education is not, or should not be, truly "special." All education should be special, they argued, so who needs particular training or a special administrative structure and budget to do what should be done for *all* students routinely? After all, they said, special education is just good teaching.

Second, special education was deconstructed—reduced by philosophical inquisition to a pile of rubble. Under the guise of a "paradigm shift," reformers prophesied that general education would be restructured to obviate the need for special education. These reformers claimed that special education had outlived its usefulness as a concept. Unfortunately, they never reconstructed special education, just left it for dead.

Third, special education was slammed by critics' claims that it does not work, that it is too big and too costly, and that it serves many students who are freeloaders, not students with actual disabilities. It serves a disproportionate number of poor children and children of color, they noted. It had become, in the view of some, a system designed to give additional advantage to those already privileged by class or wealth and shunt already underprivileged children into cul de sacs from which they never emerged. Robert Worth (1999), writing in *The Washington Monthly* (1999), said that special education is a scandal that "wastes money and hurts the poor" and that it is "the road to hell" (pp. 34–35).

And as if special education might not have suffered enough, the U.S. Department of Education (1998) in its 20th annual report to Congress on the implementation of IDEA suggested that as a response to the shortage of qualified special education teachers general educators should take over even more of the responsibility for teaching students with disabilities.

Whether special education will pull through with intensive care is not clear at this point. What is clear is that this accident will change special education forever. Its life will never be the same. It may eventually emerge stronger, or it may be permanently disabled if it does survive. It is clearly down, but it may not be out. If it survives, it will need sustained help in recuperation and rehabilitation.

SPECIAL EDUCATION'S CONVERSION EXPERIENCE: ALL THINGS NEW AND WONDERFUL

WASHINGTON, D.C.: A former special education teacher says he has found a new faith and, because of it, he has become a new person. He describes how special education recently went through a total transformation. "It has been born again, converted from a place to a service," as he describes it. The old has passed away, and all things are new, he says. According to his account, special education found redemption by rejecting its old self, which included the evil practices of identifying, labeling, and pigeon-holing children in what was euphemistically described as a "continuum of alternative placements." What he calls the "good news of inclusion" has washed it clean of its past wrong practices.

"I'm not even tempted to think of removing a child from general education anymore," said another teacher. "Actually, we don't talk about special education or general education anymore. We just talk about education, period, and teaching and learning, and it frees us from all our old habits. For me, alternative placements might as well not even exist, and I'm just so happy to be included in what we used to call general education and to have all of our students in the same classrooms that I want to tell everybody I meet how wonderful it is. All of the old barriers and distinctions are down, and all of us just work on the same things in the same place together, because there's really no difference among kids or teachers or classes or schools as far as we're concerned."

Today, a new organization was formed to replace the old—some say tainted—special education advocacy groups. Promise Keepers to Kids (PKK) is described in its literature as "a professional collaborative upholding the promise to educate all kids together, no exceptions."

"We don't label kids or teachers, we just teach them," said a PKK official. Apparently without thinking of the irony of her statement, she went on, "Unlike the special educators of the past, we aren't labelers. We are simply teachers who keep our word to educate every child."

Said another, "It feels so good to know we're doing the right thing, even if the so-called evidence says it isn't working. We don't care that much about test scores and other questionable measures of outcome or progress, because we know what real progress is. *Real* progress is doing the right thing, not separating someone out because they're different."

A member of Congress who has been active in special education's conversion added, "Under the old system, half of the students in our schools were below average, and that's intolerable. It doesn't have to be that way if we're serious about reforming our thinking and doing what's right."

SPECIAL EDUCATION REINCARNATED: NEW TIMES, NEW CREATURE

WASHINGTON, D.C.: Special education has died. That much is clear. Its death was slow and agonizing. But it has been recreated in a new form. Clearly, it wasn't cloned. It is not simply a copy of the special education that usually traced its origins to the late 18th century and experienced its major growth period in the 20th century. Some say it was a snake in its first life, some say a wild boar, some say a tiger. Whatever it was, it is gone. It's too early to say just what it will be called in its new life.

Special education died for a variety of reasons, among them the insistence of 20th century reformers that all children—no exceptions—strive to reach the same level of academic achievement and study the same curriculum in the same place and at the same time. Special education is back as a new creature in part because the standards-based reform movement, combined with the ideology of full inclusion, considered students' placement in anything other than "regular" classrooms and curricula to be "tracking," and therefore unacceptable. These ideas—that any different place or pace or topic of instruction is unacceptable—hit the immovable wall of reality. Special education was recreated to deal with differences among students in more realistic and productive ways than the now defunct policies of universal standards of learning and full inclusion would allow.

The reincarnation of special education seems to have much the same goals and function as its former self. Its new name, which is not to be confused with a short-lived measurement system of 20th century education, is precision teaching (PT). Special education was never politically correct (PC), but PT is PC as well as the reincarnation of specialized instruction. PT is for teachers who already have demonstrated mastery of teaching in general education classrooms and are trained how to make teaching more precise and effective for students who, for whatever reason, do not make satisfactory progress in the typical classroom.

Eligibility for special education was based on a student's classification as having a disability. PT does, in fact, serve mostly students who are known to have disabilities of one kind or another, but eligibility is determined by a students' lack of satisfactory progress in the general education curriculum with the typical adaptations that competent teachers make for those who have some difficulty learning. Most of the time, PT requires grouping students together who are having similar learning difficulties. Sometimes this means assigning students to special classes or schools, but most educators now see this as sensible, normal, and necessary if all students are to have a fair chance to learn what is most important to their futures.

Advocates of PT seem to be ready for objections to their craft, partly because of their understanding of what killed special education. "Of course, deciding who qualifies for PT is judgmental. How could it be otherwise?" one experienced PT administrator said at the second annual international Council for Precision Teaching (CPT) conference here in Washington. "Teaching requires judgment. If we could discriminate who needs PT from who doesn't without human judgment, then schools would truly be factories, not places where we use our judgment and teach kids to use theirs." This administrator understands, apparently, that one of the many fatal blows to special education was the objection that disabilities involve judgment, a human and less than perfect undertaking but an unavoidable task of teachers.

Those who practice PT in the schools are keenly aware of the accusation that most clearly cost special education its first life: that special education is a dead end, particularly when students are placed in special classes or special schools. PT teachers are committed to showing the benefits of PT for students who clearly are not going to thrive in the general education classroom and the general curriculum. What students get in PT classes and schools is intensive, relentless, focused instruction at their level, something special educators knew should be provided but were, for whatever reasons, unable to show was consistently a feature of special education. As a consequence, critics of PT have been put on the defensive by those who ask them to demonstrate how students receiving PT would be better off in classes where they get more typical teaching.

When a government official suggested that *all* students should receive PT, he was quickly asked by a CPT member, "Why? Does every kid need it?" The CPT member went on to say, "Look, if you can get all general educators to provide PT, more power to you. Go to it. Do it! But just don't ask us to believe it will happen before you do it, and don't ask us to stop what we're offering because you want to do it too."

NONE OF THE ABOVE

Any of these stories could be written differently, all could be greatly expanded, but they suggest certain views of special education today and tomorrow. For good reasons, you might not like any of the story beginnings as I have written them. Maybe you would like to rewrite one of them, or perhaps you would really like to write a different story entirely, one I have not dreamed of. For example, Vaughn, Klingner, and Hughes (2000) suggested the following:

> Special education research during the past 2 decades has experienced one of the most significant developments in the history of education…. These developments can be linked to the Individuals with Disabilities Education Act of 1997 and the resulting knowledge about teaching individuals with disabilities. This landmark legislation has not only provided a framework for the provision of educational services to all children with disabilities in the United States, it has also paved the way for dramatically altering the knowledge base about effective instructional practices and services for children and youth with disabilities. Research findings in special education have increased our knowledge and understanding about administrative decision making, assessment practices, service delivery models, instructional practices, positive behavioral supports, inclusion, technology, and practices for working effectively with families …

Equally important, research conducted with students with disabilities has informed general education. Research on cooperative learning, reading, comprehension, instructional grouping procedures, and curriculum-based assessment (to name but a few) have significantly informed practice in general education. Special education research and practice, previously viewed as irrelevant by most members of the general education community, have been increasingly valued. (pp. 163–164)

How you would choose to write the story may depend not only on your philosophical perspective but on whether you take the point of view of someone in K–12 schools, higher education, a parent of a child with a disability, a government department of education, the general public, or some other designated group. For those of us in higher education, another statement of Meyen's (1998) bears repeating: "Don't assume that the logic of inclusion in K–12 translates to higher education. If universities reorganized every time a profession restructured its practice we would have chaos" (p. 11).

Regardless of how the story of special education will be written, I think it is clear that today we who provide leadership training are in pretty deep trouble. We have not been able to provide enough leaders with enough skill and other resources to train teachers in adequate numbers and of adequate quality. As my generation of special education faculty leave the field, there will be insufficient numbers to take our place. It will take substantially increased and sustained support from the U.S. Department of Education to address this need. If the need is not addressed, special education will become more obviously an orphan, dependent on the charity of people of good will. Good will toward special education has been undermined by years of unwarranted criticism from within our profession and from others, deliberate deconstruction, and proposals for reform that are unworkable.

Meyen (1998) advised, "*Resist restructuring that diminishes your special education identity*" (p. 11). Good advice, I think, unless our identity is evil. Now, perhaps, we should start by trying to bring clarity to just who we are. If special education really is an evil empire, the road to hell, a discriminatory second system, a dead end, or any of the other vile things it has been called directly or by intimation, then let it die. No, let us kill it as quickly as we can. However, if special education is not these evil things— if it is really a good idea poorly implemented, a justifiable system with flaws—then let us say so clearly, reject those who urge us to merge with general education, and get on with the job of rebuilding our identity and taking pride in our work.

AUTHOR'S NOTE

An earlier version of this article was presented at the 1999 Council for Exceptional Children/Office of Special Education Programs Leadership Training Director's Conference, Washington, D.C., July 14, 1999.

REFERENCES

Fuchs, D., & Fuchs, L. S. (1995a). Special education can work. In J. M. Kauffman, J. W. Lloyd, D. P. Hallahan, & I. A. Astuto (Eds.), *Issues in educational placement: Students with emotional and behavioral disorders* (pp. 363–377). Hillsdale, NJ: Erlbaum.

Fuchs, D., & Fuchs, L. S. (1995b). What's "special" about special education? *Phi Delta Kappan, 76*, 522–530.

Fuchs, D., & Fuchs, L. S. (1996). Editorial: Lessons from welfare "reform." *The Journal of Special Education, 30*, 229–231.

Goodlad, J. I. (1990). *Teachers for our nation's schools.* San Francisco: Jossey-Bass.

Goodlad, J. I., & Lovitt, T. C. (Eds.). (1993). *Integrating general and special education.* Columbus, OH: Merrill/Macmillan.

Kauffman, J. M. (1993). How we might achieve the radical reform of special education. *Exceptional Children, 60*, 6–16.

Kauffman, J. M. (1994). Places of change: Special education's power and identity in an era of educational reform. *Journal of Learning Disabilities, 27*, 610–618.

Kauffman, J. M. (1995). Why we must celebrate a diversity of restrictive environments. *Learning Disabilities Research & Practice, 10*, 225–232.

Kauffman, J. M. (1997). Guest editorial: Caricature, science, and exceptionality. *Remedial and Special Education, 18*, 130–132.

Kauffman, J. M. (1999). Commentary: Today's special education and its messages for tomorrow. *The Journal of Special Education, 32*, 244–254.

Kauffman, J. M., & Hallahan, D. P. (1993). Toward a comprehensive delivery system for special education. In J. I. Goodlad & I. C. Lovitt (Eds.), *Integrating general and special education* (pp. 73–102). Columbus, OH: Merrill/Macmillan.

Kauffman, J. M., & Hallahan, D. P. (1997). A diversity of restrictive environments: Placement as a problem of social ecology. In J. W. Lloyd, E. J. Kameenui, & D. Chard (Eds.), *Issues in educating students with disabilities* (pp. 325–342). Mahwah, NJ: Erlbaum.

Meyen, E. (1998, July). *Preparing leadership personnel for an increasingly diverse world: From a higher education perspective.* Paper presented at the OSEP/CEC Leadership Training Project Directors Conference, Washington, DC.

Redl, F. (1966). *When we deal with children: Selected writings.* New York: Free Press.

Strauss, V. (1999, May 20). Janney principal to head D.C. special-ed program. *The Washington Post,* pp. B1, B9.

U.S. Department of Education. (1998). *Twentieth annual report to Congress on implementation of the Individuals with Disabilities Education Act.* Washington, DC: Author.

Vaughn, S., Klingner, J., & Hughes, M. (2000). Sustainability of research-based practices. *Exceptional Children, 66,* 163–171.

Worth, R. (1999). The scandal of special ed: It wastes money and hurts the poor. *The Washington Monthly, 31*(6), 34–38.

CHAPTER 16

Where Should Students with Disabilities Receive Special Education Services? Is One Place Better Than Another?

Naomi Zigmond

The question of where special education students should be educated is not new. In this article, the author reviews research studies and research reviews that address this question. She argues that research evidence on the relative efficacy of one special education placement over another is scarce, methodologically flawed, and inconclusive. She also states that "Where should students with disabilities be educated?" is the wrong question to ask, that it is antithetical to the kind of individualized planning that should be embodied in decision making for and with students with disabilities, and that it fails to specify where, for what, and for whom. The author calls for new ways of thinking about the problem and of conducting research so that progress can be made on improving results for students with disabilities.

The question of where special education students should be educated is not new. Lloyd Dunn raised the question in 1968, and response to his article spurred the adoption of resource room services in place of special day classes in the 1970s. The question was raised again in 1975 with the passage of the Education for All Handicapped Children Act, later known as the Individuals with Disabilities Education Act (IDEA), and its balanced support for both a continuum of services and placement in the least restrictive environment. The act required that procedures be established

> to assure that, to the maximum extent appropriate, handicapped children ... are educated with children who are not handicapped and that ... removal of handicapped children from the regular educational environment occurs only when the nature or severity of that handicap is such that education in regular classes with the use of supplemental aids and services cannot be achieved satisfactorily. (Part B, Section 612(5)(B))

The very first annual report to Congress by the U.S. Department of Health, Education and Welfare (1979) provided a succinct summary of this balanced position. The argument went as follows. In 1819, in *McColloch v. Maryland,* the courts maintained that the government's purpose should be served with as little imposition on the individual as possible—if less dramatic means for achieving the same basic purpose could be found, they should be taken. Years later, this court decision was interpreted to mean that children with disabilities should be educated in as mainstream a setting as possible. That interpretation was supported by the wave of civil rights litigation in the late 1960s and early 1970s, most notably *Brown v. Board of Education* (1954) and *Pennsylvania Association for Retarded Children (PARC) v. Commonwealth of Pennsylvania* (1972). *PARC,* and the subsequent *Mills v. Board of Education of the District of Columbia* (1972) case, established the proposition that children with disabilities should be placed in the least drastic, or most normal, setting appropriate, with as little interference and as normal an educational process as possible.

Court cases established the principle of least restrictiveness, but they were only part of the story. State and federal legislation reiterated the principle. Well before the federal legislation became effective, the principle of least restrictiveness embodied in the *PARC* agreement was clearly established in the laws, statutes, or regulations of at least 20 states. In fact, in its first annual report to Congress, the U.S. Department of Health, Education and Welfare (1979) proudly proclaimed that even in 1976–1977, the school year preceding full implementation of the new federal law, "many handicapped children are already receiving their education in a regular classroom setting and appropriate alternative placements are in most cases available to accommodate children with special needs" (p. 39). During the following decades, efforts would be made to move services for students with disabilities out of separate schools and into regular schools, with these students being integrated (mainstreamed) into general education classes for part of the school day and provided with pull-out itinerant, resource, or part-time special education services for the rest of the day.

The question of where students with disabilities should be educated was hotly debated again in the mid-1980s, as essays on the failure of pull-out special education began to proliferate. The theme was consistent: Fundamental changes in the delivery model for special education were needed to increase the accomplishments of students with disabilities. Even Madeline Will, then Assistant Secretary of Education and head of the Office of Special Education Programs, joined the fray: "Although well intentioned, the so-called 'pull out' approach to the educational difficulties of students with learning problems has failed in many instances to meet the educational needs of these students" (1986, p. 413). Will and other advocates of the regular education initiative (e.g., Gartner & Lipsky, 1989; National Association of State Boards of Education, 1992) called for children with learning problems to have completely integrated educational experiences in order to achieve improved educational outcomes.

The 1997 IDEA amendments raised the question of where students with disabilities should be educated with a new urgency. Whereas earlier definitions of *restrictiveness* had focused on access of students with disabilities to nondisabled peers, the new focus defined this in terms of their access to the general education curriculum. With the additional requirement that students with disabilities participate in (and perform respectably on) statewide assessments and accountability procedures, pressures to favor one kind of placement (e.g., inclusion in the general education classroom) over any other (e.g., providing pull-out services in some other place) mounted.

A decade earlier, McKinney and Hocott (1988) had explained that "part of the rationale for totally integrated [as compared to pull-out] programs for mildly handicapped students is based on research that questions the efficacy of special education" (p. 15). How solid is the research evidence indicating that any one particular place, or service-delivery model, can achieve better outcomes for students with disabilities, though? In this article I review research studies and research reviews that address the question of place. I argue, as many others have before me, that research evidence on the relative efficacy of one special education service delivery model over another is scarce, methodologically flawed, and inconclusive. But I will also argue that, in practical terms, the question of where students with disabilities should be educated is misguided. That question is antithetical to the kind of individualized planning that is the hallmark of special education for students with disabilities. I will argue for new ways of thinking about the issue of place and the conduit of research on special education placements before progress can be made on improving results for students with disabilities.

Although I limit myself to the research literature in which students with mild and moderate disabilities are studied, I strongly believe that the arguments I make have merit across the entire range of students with disabilities promoted and protected by IDEA and that these arguments have important implications for the rhetoric of the next IDEA reauthorization.

EFFICACY STUDIES ON PLACE

For more than 3 decades, special education researchers and scholars have conducted research, and synthesized research, on the relative usefulness of one place or another for serving students with disabilities. Dunn (1968) concluded, on the basis of several studies conducted in the 1960s and a review of research published by Kirk (1964), that there was no empirical support for educating students with high-incidence disabilities in special classes: "Retarded pupils make as much or more progress in the regular grades as they do in special education [and] efficacy studies on special day classes for other mildly handicapped children, including the emotionally handicapped, reveal the same results" (p. 8). Although Dunn called for the abandonment of special day classes for students with high-incidence disabilities, he also argued persuasively for part-time pull-out special education services to meet their special educational needs.

Ten years later, in a narrative review of 17 studies, Sindelar and Deno (1978) concluded that resource rooms were more effective than general education classrooms in improving academic achievement of students with learning disabilities (LD). At about the same time, a meta-analysis of efficacy studies completed by Carlberg and Kavale (1980) reported more complex results. Carlberg and Kavale's calculations of effect sizes showed that students with mental retardation in special class placements performed academically as well as those placed in general education classrooms. However, they also concluded that students with learning or behavior disorders in special classes (both self-contained and resource programs) had a modest academic advantage over those remaining in the general education classrooms. Leinhardt and Pallay (1982) also concluded from their research review that resource rooms were better than general education classrooms for students with LD. In addition, 1 year later, Madden and Slavin (1983) reviewed seven studies on the efficacy of part-time resource placements compared to full-time special education classes and full-time placement in the mainstream and concluded that if increased academic achievement is the desired outcome, "the research favors placement in regular classes ... *supplemented by well designed resource programs*" (p. 530, italics added).

Research support for supplemental resource room services was, however, overlooked in the national frenzy to reshape special education that swept the country in the mid-1980s. With the introduction of newer, more inclusive service-delivery models, the early research comparing special pull-out placements with general education placements seemed dated and irrelevant. In those earlier studies, it was easy to draw stark contrasts between general education placements, in which no special services were available to students with disabilities, and pull-out services staffed by trained teachers who provided special instruction. In the newer service-delivery models, particularly the full inclusion models for students with mild/moderate disabilities that employed special education teachers in consulting or co-teaching roles, students with disabilities were supposed to be receiving specially designed instruction or supplemental aids and services right in the general education classroom. Research documenting student progress in these new inclusive settings was needed, and it proliferated.

Some studies showed positive trends when students were integrated into general education classrooms (see Affleck, Madge, Adams, & Lowenbraun, 1988; Baker, Wang, & Walberg, 1995; Deno, Maruyama, Espin, & Cohen, 1990; Schulte, Osborne, & McKinney, 1990; Walther-Thomas, 1997), including that full-time placement in a general education classroom resulted in student academic progress that was just as good as that achieved by students in separate settings in elementary schools (see Banerji & Dailey, 1995; Bear & Proctor, 1990). Others, however, reported disappointing or unsatisfactory academic and social achievement results from inclusion models (see Fox & Ysseldyke, 1997; Saint-Laurent et al., 1998; Sale & Carey, 1995; Vaughn, Elbaum, & Boardman, 2001; Zigmond & Baker, 1990; Zigmond et al., 1995). It should come as no surprise, then, that in a review of research on these newer special education service-delivery models, Hocutt (1996) reported equivocal findings. She concluded that "various program models, implemented in both general and special education, can have moderately positive academic and social impacts for students with disabilities" (p. 77). However, no intervention in the research literature eliminated the impact of having a disability. That is, regardless of the place of the intervention, students with disabilities did not achieve even at the level of low-achieving nondisabled peers, and no model was effective for *all* students with disabilities.

Manset and Semmel (1997) compared eight inclusion models for elementary students with high-incidence disabilities, primarily LD, reported in the research literature between 1984 and 1994. They reiterated Hocutt's conclusions: Inclusive programs can be effective for some, although not all, students with high-incidence disabilities. Waldron and McLeskey (1998) agreed with this conclusion. In their research, students with severe LD made comparable progress in reading and math in pull-out and inclusion settings, although students with mild LD were more likely to make gains commensurate with nondisabled peers when educated in inclusive environments than when receiving special education services in a resource room.

Holloway (2001) reviewed five studies conducted between 1986 and 1996 that compared traditional pull-out services to fully inclusive service-delivery models and models that combined in-class services with pull-out instruction. His conclusions did not offer strong support for the practice of full inclusion. Reading progress in the combined model was significantly better than in either the inclusion-only model or the resource room–only model.

In very recent research, Rea, McLaughlin, and Walther-Thomas (2002) used qualitative and quantitative methods to describe two schools and their special education models, one fully inclusive and one with more traditional supplemental pull-out services. Results showed that compared to students in the more traditional schools with pull-out programs, students served in inclusive schools earned higher grades, achieved higher or comparable scores on standardized tests, committed no more behavioral infractions, and attended more school days.

In a specific review of co-teaching as the inclusive service-delivery model, Zigmond and Magiera (2002) found only four studies that focused on academic achievement gains. In the three elementary studies, co-teaching was just as effective in producing academic gains as was resource room instruction or consultation with the general education teacher; in the high school study, students' quiz and exam grades actually worsened following the co-teaching experiment. Murawski and Swanson (2002), in their meta-analysis of the co-teaching research literature, found six studies from which effect sizes could be calculated; dependent measures were grades, achievement scores, and social and attitudinal outcomes. Murawski and Swanson reported effect sizes for individual studies ranging from low to high, with an average total effect size in the moderate range. Both literature reviews on co-teaching concluded that despite the current and growing popularity of co-teaching as a service-delivery model, further research is needed to determine whether it is an effective service-delivery option for students with disabilities, let alone a preferred one.

CONCLUSIONS DERIVED FROM THE EMPIRICAL RESEARCH BASE

There is no simple and straightforward answer to the question of where students with disabilities should receive their special education instruction. The efficacy research reviewed here, which spans more than 3 decades, provides no compelling research evidence that place is the critical factor in the academic or social progress of students with mild/moderate disabilities. There are probably many reasons for reaching this conclusion, · but I suggest only two. The first has to do with the body of research evidence itself. The second has to do with the appropriateness of the question.

Explanation 1: Research Base Is Insufficient

Despite the fact that the efficacy research literature on the places where special education services are provided spans more than 3 decades and that dozens of studies have been reported in refereed special education journals, Murawski and Swanson (2002) are right to ask where the data are. Studies worthy of consideration in a meta-analysis or narrative literature review, with appropriate controls and appropriate dependent measures, are few and far between. Of course, research on the efficacy of special education placements is very hard to conduct at all, let alone to conduct well. For example, definitions of service-delivery models or settings vary from researcher to researcher, and descriptions of the treatments being implemented in those models or settings are woefully inadequate. Random assignment of students to treatments is seldom an option, and appropriately matched (sufficiently alike) samples of experimental and control students and teachers are rare. As a result, *where* special education occurs is not a phenomenon that lends itself to precise investigation, and funding for research studies and publication of results in refereed journals are difficult to achieve.

Methodologically Flawed Research

Research designs used to explore the effectiveness of different service-delivery models often employ pre–post treatment group designs. The limitations of these research designs for studying the efficacy of special education have been reported in numerous previous research reviews, most notably in Kirk (1964) and Semmel, Gottleib, and Robinson (1979). Some studies use control groups, often samples of students experiencing "traditional" programs (sometimes referred to as "business as usual" programs) in nonexperimental schools. In some studies, the researchers manage to achieve random assignment of students to treatments, but most use intact groups of students assigned to the teacher or the school building who volunteered to participate in the experimental treatment program. Often the experimental treatment is well described, although degree of implementation is not. Descriptions of the control treatment and its degree of implementation (if indeed a control group is used) are rarely provided. Most often, replication is hindered by inadequate descriptions of the treatments and insufficient monitoring of treatment implementation. Thus, even if reliable achievement changes are demonstrated in one research study, difficulty in identifying critical treatment variables makes replicability impossible in virtually all cases. Achievement gains, or lack thereof, cannot be related to replicable interventions, and the fundamental question of whether Place A is better than Place B cannot actually be answered.

Inconclusive Research

The accumulated evidence to date has produced only one unequivocal finding: Languishing in a general education class where nothing changes and no one pays you any attention is not as useful to students with mild/moderate learning and behavior disorders as is getting some help, although it does not seem to matter for students with mild mental retardation. All other evidence on whether students with disabilities learn more, academically or socially, and are happier in one school setting or another is at best inconclusive. Resource programs are more effective for some students with disabilities than are self-contained special education classes or self-contained general education classes, but they are less effective for other students with similar disabilities. Fully inclusive programs are superior for some students with disabilities on some measures of academic or social skills development and inferior for other students or on other measures. The empirical research not only does not identify one best place but also often finds equivalent progress being made by students with disabilities across settings; that is, the research reports nonsignificant differences in outcomes. Interpreting nonsignificant findings can be tricky. Do we conclude that the proverbial cup is half full or half empty? Do we acknowledge that it does not matter where students receive their special education services and allow parents or school personnel wide berth in making choices?

Or do we proclaim that one setting is preferred over another for philosophical or moral reasons with empirical evidence that it "doesn't hurt"?

Explanation 2: Efficacy Studies Have Been Asking the Wrong Question

Failure To Specify "Best for Whom?"

Special education has evolved as a means of providing specialized interventions to students with disabilities based on individual student progress on individualized objectives. The bedrock of special education is instruction focused on *individual* needs. The very concept of "one best place" contradicts this commitment to individualization. Furthermore, results of research on how groups of students respond to treatment settings does not help the researcher or practitioner make an individualized decision for an individual student's plan. A better question to ask, if we dare, is "best for whom?" or best for which individual students with which individual profiles of characteristics and needs? Answering this question requires that we abandon the rhetoric in which we call for *all* students to do this, or *all* students to learn that, or *all* students be educated in a certain place.

Special educators understand about individual differences. Special educators understand that no matter how hard they try or how well they are taught, there are some students who will never be able to learn on the same schedule as most others, who will take so long to learn some things that they will have to forego learning other things, or who will need to be taught curricular content that is not ordinarily taught. Special educators understood this when they fought hard for the legal requirement of the Individualized Educational Program for children with disabilities, to permit formulation of unique programs of instruction to meet unique individual needs. By continuing to ask, "What is the best place?" we are ignoring what we know.

Restating the question as "best for whom?" would also require new research designs and data analysis. A first step in that direction might be to reanalyze group design data at the individual student level. For example, Zigmond et al. (1995) collected achievement test data for 145 students with LD in three full inclusion programs and for many of these students' nondisabled classmates. Rather than reporting average growth of the students with LD, the researchers reported the number and percentage of students with LD who made reliably significant gains (i.e., gains exceeded the standard error of measurement of the reading test) during the experimental year. They also reported on the number and percentage of students with LD whose reading gains matched or exceeded the average gain of their grade-level peers. Finally, they reported on the number and percentage of students with LD whose achievement status (i.e., their relative standing in the grade-level peer group) had improved during the school year. These analytic techniques allowed for exploration of setting effects at an individual level. Waldron and McLeskey (1998) followed this same tactic. Unfortunately, neither group of researchers took the final step of describing individual participants in enough detail to permit generalization of the findings or extrapolation of the findings to the individual case. Nevertheless, this approach seems more promising than the traditional approaches that have been used to date in terms of answering the question "best for whom?"

Failure To Specify "Best for What?"

Different settings offer different opportunities for teaching and learning. The general education classroom provides students with disabilities with access to students who do not have disabilities; access to the curricula and textbooks to which most other students are exposed; access to instruction from a general education teacher whose training and expertise are quite different from those of a special education teacher; access to subject matter content taught by a subject matter specialist; and access to all of the stresses and strains associated with the preparation for, taking of, and passing or failing of the statewide assessments. If the goal is to have students learn content subject information or how to interact with nondisabled peers, the general education setting is the best place.

Pull-out settings allow for smaller teacher–student ratios and flexibility in the selection of texts, choice of curricular objectives, pacing of instruction, scheduling of examinations, and assignment of grades. Special education pull-out settings allow students to learn different content in different ways and on a different schedule. A pull-out special education setting may be most appropriate if students need (a) intensive instruction in basic academic skills well beyond the grade level at which nondisabled peers are learning how to read or do basic mathematics, (b) explicit instruction in controlling behavior or interacting with peers and adults, or (c) to learn anything that is not customarily taught to everyone else.

If educators value education that is different and special and want to preserve that feature of special education, it is legitimate to ask whether the general education classroom can be transformed to support this desire. Or, as Fuchs and Fuchs (1995) asked, "Can general education become special education?" (p. 528). Their experience (and mine) strongly suggests that the answer to this question is "no." Attempts to transport teaching methods that were developed and validated in special education to general education settings have not been successful. Instructional practices that focus on individual decision making for individual students and improve outcomes of students with severe learning problems are not easily transposed into practices that can survive in a general education classroom. General educators will make instructional adaptations in response to students' persistent failure to learn, but the accommodations are typically oriented to the group, not to the individual, and are relatively minor in substance, with little chance for helping students with chronically poor learning histories (Zigmond & Baker, 1995).

Over and over again, researchers and staff development personnel have come to recognize that general education teachers have a different set of assumptions about the form and function of education than do special educators. General educators cannot imagine focusing intensively on individual students to the extent that different instructional activities for different students are being implemented at the same time. This is simply impractical in a classroom of 25 to 35 students. Moreover, special education's most basic article of faith, that instruction must be individualized to be truly effective, is rarely contemplated, let alone observed, in most general education classrooms. Mainstream teachers must consider the good of the group and the extent to which the learning activities they present maintain classroom flow, orderliness, and cooperation. In addition, they generally formulate teaching plans that result in a productive learning environment for 90% or more of their students. General education settings are best for learning what most students need to learn.

For many of the remaining 10% of students, however, a different orientation will probably be needed. These students need to learn something different because they are clearly not learning what everyone else is learning. Interventions that might be effective for this group of students require a considerable investment of time and effort, as well as extensive support. Special education in a pull-out setting, with its emphasis on empirically validated practices and its use of data-based decision making to tailor instruction to the individual students' needs, might be better for teaching these students.

CONCLUSION

As early as 1979, federal monitoring of state programs was put into place to guard against not only too much segregation of students with disabilities but also "inappropriate mainstreaming" (U.S. Department of Health, Education and Welfare, 1979, p. 39). Although most would agree that students with mild and moderate disabilities should spend a large proportion of the school day with peers without disabilities, research does not support the superiority of any one service-delivery model over another. Furthermore, effectiveness depends not only on the characteristics and needs of a particular student but also on the quality of the program's implementation. A poorly run model with limited resources will seldom be superior to a model in which there is a heavy investment of time, energy, and money. Good programs can be developed in any setting, as can bad ones. The setting itself is less important than what is going on in the setting.

Reflecting on the 35 years of efficacy research on the settings in which special education is delivered that I have reviewed in this article, what do we know? We know that what goes on in a place, not the location itself, is what makes a difference. We know that you learn what you spend time on and that most students with disabilities will not learn to read or to write or to calculate if they are not explicitly taught these skills. We know that some instructional practices are easier to implement and more likely to occur in some settings than in others. We know that we need more research that asks better and more focused questions about who learns what best where. In addition, we know that we need to explore new research designs and new data analysis techniques that will help us bridge the gap between efficacy findings and decision making on placements for individual students.

In response to the query of what is special about special education, I can say with some certainty that place is not what makes special education "special" or effective. Effective teaching strategies and an individualized approach are the more critical ingredients in special education, and neither of these is associated solely with one particular environment. Educators must also remember that research has shown that typical general education environments are not supportive places in which to implement what we know to be effective teaching strategies for students with disabilities (e.g., Zigmond, 1996). Considering the research evidence to date, it is clear that placement decisions must continue to be made by determining whether a particular placement option will support the effective instructional practices that are required for a particular child to achieve his or her individual objectives and goals.

The search for the best place in which to receive special education services has tended to be fueled by passion and principle, rather than by reason and rationality. Until educators are ready to say that receiving special education services in a particular setting is good for some students with disabilities but not for others, that different educational environments are more conducive to different forms of teaching and learning, that different students need to learn different things in different ways, and that traditional group research designs may not capture these individual differences in useful ways, we may never get beyond the equivocal findings reported here. We may even fail to realize that, in terms of the best place to receive special education and related services, we have probably been asking the wrong questions.

REFERENCES

Affleck, J., Madge, S., Adams, A., & Lowenbraun, S. (1988). Integrated classroom versus resource model: Academic viability and effectiveness. *Exceptional Children, 54,* 339–348.

Baker, E. T., Wang, M., & Walberg, H. J. (1995). The effects of inclusion on learning. *Educational Leadership, 53*(4), 33–35.

Banerji, M., & Dailey, R. (1995). A study of the effects of an inclusion model on students with specific learning disabilities. *Journal of Learning Disabilities, 28,* 511–522.

Bear, G. G., & Proctor, W. A. (1990). Impact of a full-time integrated program on the achievement of non-handicapped and mildly handicapped children. *Exceptionality, 1,* 227–238.

Brown v. Board of Education of Topeka, 347 U.S. 483 (1954).

Carlberg, C., & Kavale, K. (1980). The efficacy of special versus regular class placement for exceptional children: A meta-analysis. *The Journal of Special Education, 14,* 295–309.

Deno, S., Maruyama, G., Espin, C., & Cohen, C. (1990). Educating students with mild disabilities in general education classrooms: Minnesota alternatives. *Exceptional Children, 57,* 150–161.

Dunn, L. M. (1968). Special education for the mildly retarded—Is much of it justifiable? *Exceptional Children, 35,* 5–22.

Education for All Handicapped Children Act of 1975, 20 U.S.C. § 612(5)(B).

Fox, N. E., & Ysseldyke, J. E. (1997). Implementing inclusion at the middle school level: Lessons from a negative example. *Exceptional Children, 64,* 81–98.

Fuchs, D., & Fuchs, L. (1995). What's "special" about special education? *Phi Delta Kappan,* *76,* 522–530.

Gartner, A., & Lipsky, D. K. (1989). *The yoke of special education: How to break it.* Washington, DC: National Center on Education and the Economy.

Hocutt, A. M. (1996). Effectiveness of special education: Is placement the critical factor? *The Future of Children, 6,* 77–102.

Holloway, J. (2001). Inclusion and students with learning disabilities. *Educational Leadership, 57*(6), 86–88.

Individuals with Disabilities Education Act Amendments of 1997, 20 U.S.C. § 1400 *et seq.*

Kirk, S. A. (1964). Research in education. In H. A. Stevens & R. Heber (Eds.), *Mental retardation: A review of research* (pp. 57–99). Chicago: University of Chicago.

Leinhardt, G., & Pallay, A. (1982). Restrictive educational settings? Exile or haven. *Review of Educational Research, 52,* 557–578.

Madden, N. A., & Slavin, R. E. (1983). Mainstreaming students with mild handicaps: Academic and social outcomes. *Review of Educational Research, 53,* 519–569.

Manset, G., & Semmel, M. I. (1997). Are inclusive programs for students with mild disabilities effective? A comparative review of model programs. *The Journal of Special Education, 31,* 155–180.

McCulloch v. Maryland, 4 Wheat 316, U.S. Ed. 579 (1819).

McKinney, J. D., & Hocutt, A. M. (1988). Policy issues in the evaluation of the regular education initiative. *Learning Disabilities Focus, 4*(1), 15–23.

Mills v. Board of Education of the District of Columbia, 348 F. Supp. 866, 880 (1972).

Murawski, W. W., & Swanson, H. L. (2002). A meta-analysis of co-teaching research: Where are the data? *Remedial and Special Education, 22,* 258–267.

National Association of State Boards of Education. (1992). *Winners all: A call for inclusive schools.* Alexandria, VA: Author.

Pennsylvania Association for Retarded Children v. Commonwealth of Pennsylvania, 343 F. Supp. 279, *consent agreement* (1972).

Rea, P. J., McLaughlin, V. L., & Walther-Thomas, C. (2002). Outcomes for students with learning disabilities in inclusive and pull-out programs. *Exceptional Children, 68,* 203–222.

Saint-Laurent, L., Dionne, J., Glasson, J., Royer, E., Simard, C., & Pierard, B. (1998). Academic achievement effects of an in-class service model on students with and without disabilities. *Exceptional Children, 64,* 239–253.

Sale, P., & Carey, D. M. (1995). The sociometric status of students with disabilities in a full-inclusion school. *Exceptional Children, 62,* 6–19.

Schulte, A. C., Osborne, S. S., & McKinney, J. D. (1990). Academic outcomes for students with learning disabilities in consultation and resource programs. *Exceptional Children, 57,* 162–172.

Semmel, M. I., Gottlieb, J., & Robinson, N. (1979). Mainstreaming: Perspectives in educating handicapped children in the public schools. In D. Berliner (Ed.), *Review of research in education* (pp. 223–279). Itaska, IL: Peacock.

Sindelar, P. T., & Deno, S. L. (1978). The effectiveness of resource programming. *The Journal of Special Education, 12,* 17–28.

U.S. Department of Health, Education and Welfare. (1979). *Progress toward a free appropriate public education: A report to Congress on the implementation of Public Law 94-142, the Education of All Handicapped Children Act.* Washington, DC: U.S. Government Printing Office.

Vaughn, S., Elbaum, B. E., & Boardman, A. G. (2001). The social functioning of students with learning disabilities: Implications for inclusion. *Exceptionality, 9,* 47–65.

Waldron, N. L., & McLeskey, J. (1998). The effects of an inclusive school program on students with mild and severe learning disabilities. *Exceptional Children, 64,* 395–405.

Walther-Thomas, C. (1997). Co-teaching experiences: The benefits and problems that teachers and principals report over time. *Journal of Learning Disabilities, 30,* 395–407.

Will, M. C. (1986). Educating children with learning problems: A shared responsibility. *Exceptional Children, 52,* 411–415.

Zigmond, N. (1996). Organization and management of general education classrooms. In D. Speece & B. Keogh (Eds.), *Research on classroom ecologies: Implications for inclusion of children with learning disabilities* (pp. 163–190). Hillsdale, NJ: Erlbaum.

Zigmond, N., & Baker, J. M. (1990). Mainstreaming experiences for learning disabled students (Project MELD): Preliminary report. *Exceptional Children, 57,* 176–185.

Zigmond, N., & Baker, J. M. (1995). Concluding comments: Current and future practices in inclusive schooling. *The Journal of Special Education, 29,* 245–250.

Zigmond, N., Jenkins, J., Fuchs, L., Deno, S., Fuchs, D., Baker, J. N., et al. (1995). Special education in restructured schools: Findings from three multi-year studies. *Phi Delta Kappan, 76,* 531–540.

Zigmond, N., & Magiera, K. (2002). Co-teaching. *Current Practice Alerts, 6,* 1–4.

PART III

Disability-Specific Issues

As noted by Fuchs and Fuchs (1994), Hocutt, Martin, and McKinney (1991), and Kauffman (1989, 1991), the inclusion movement has been driven at different times in the recent history of special education by the agendas of different constituencies. The advocates for students with severe disabilities, however, have propelled the full inclusion movement into the position that placement must be the primary issue and that placement alternatives must be severely truncated or eliminated altogether for all students. Part III contains essays highlighting the perspectives and concerns expressed by parents and advocates for students with disabilities. The authors of these essays caution that the rigidity of the full inclusion movement's insistence that neighborhood schools and regular classrooms are the appropriate and least restrictive environment for all students is, for some students, both demeaning and debilitating.

The essays in Part III refocus our attention on the necessity of making both programming and placement decisions on an individual basis. Chapter 19 offers a cautionary note about inclusion as the only option for children with visual

impairments and also calls for research to answer important questions about educational environments. We agree that the best-informed moral judgments cannot be made in the absence of reliable evidence about the effects of different environments on children's learning and self-concepts. All of the essays in Part III argue for maintaining a full continuum of alternative placements and for renewing our commitment to making all these alternatives what they should be—places in which students learn critical skills, are treated with kindness and respect for their individuality, and are helped to become productive and fulfilled members of supportive communities.

REFERENCES

Fuchs, D., & Fuchs, L. S. (1994). Inclusive schools movement and the radicalization of special education reform. *Exceptional Children, 60,* 294–309.

Hocutt, A., Martin, E., & McKinney, J. D. (1991). Historical and legal context of mainstreaming. In J. W. Lloyd, N. N. Singh, & A. C. Repp (Eds.), *The regular education initiative: Alternative perspectives on concepts, issues, and methods* (pp. 17–28). Sycamore, IL: Sycamore.

Kauffman, J. M. (1989). The regular education initiative as Reagan–Bush education policy: A trickle-down theory of education of the hard-to-teach. *Journal of Special Education, 23,* 256–278.

Kauffman, J. M. (1991). Restructuring in sociopolitical context: Reservations about the effects of current reform proposals on students with disabilities. In J. W. Lloyd, N. N. Singh, & A. C. Repp (Eds.), *The regular education initiative: Alternative perspectives on concepts, issues, and methods* (pp. 57–66). Sycamore, IL: Sycamore.

CHAPTER 17

A Mother's Thoughts on Inclusion

Margaret N. Carr

This chapter is from "A Mother's Thoughts on Inclusion," by M. N. Carr, 1993, *Journal of Learning Disabilities, 26,* pp. 590–592. Copyright 1993 by PRO-ED, Inc. Reprinted with permission.

The year 1993 may become known as the year individuals with learning disabilities lost special education services in the United States. For the first time since the enactment of P.L. 94-142 there is a strong national movement to place all students, regardless of disability, in the regular classroom. This movement has been "sold" to many advocacy groups as meeting these students' need to learn social skills from "normal" peers.

My son has a learning disability. He went to elementary school in a time before students with learning disabilities (LD) were identified. I remember his coming home from first grade and crying over his reader. He could not decode! The only way he managed to get through first grade was to memorize the readers he brought home. He accomplished this by going over and over them with me. I don't think his teacher was ever aware that he memorized.

The texts in second grade were longer; we had to labor over the stories together many times each night. In the spring of his second year our family was transferred for a short period to New York. My son was accepted at his father's old private school, where he finally learned to read. He read slowly, but he was reading.

Spelling was another matter. Try though he might, he simply could not hear the vowel sounds. They all sounded alike to him. His visual memory was also unreliable. I kept one of the science papers he wrote in second grade. It was all about how "gravy" held people on earth.

Teacher comments were predictable. "He is immature." "He could do it if he would just try." "He's just sloppy because he rushes through his work." "He's just lazy." If they had only been with him night after night as he cried over his homework!

My son was lucky. I continued to work with him. As he grew older, he learned to compensate somewhat. He typically avoided classes that required much writing. I typed and edited most of his papers for him. By his sheer determination he made it through school, college, and eventually law school.

I shudder to think what would have happened had we been unable to go to New York his second year. The children of many of my friends were not so lucky. They became so frustrated with school that their only solution was to drop out.

I became active in the Learning Disabilities Association of America (LDA); there I discovered many youngsters like my son—many of whom *never* learned to read. I began to advocate for those students in order for them to get the specialized instruction they required to make sense of the printed word.

In my past 22 years as a professional educator, I have seen many panaceas for educating students with learning disabilities be discovered, only to be discarded. When I first became a teacher, children with LD were placed in "minimal brain injured" classes, where they were taught to walk on balance beams, trace lines, and the like. Brain-injured children looked like everyone else, but they attended separate classes.

"Resource rooms" began to replace the brain-injured classes. In resource rooms, children with LD, if they had a knowledgeable teacher, could learn those skills that had eluded them in the regular classroom. Many students were in extremely successful resource programs. In those resource rooms where the special education teacher worked and planned with the regular teacher, students experienced success. Many special education teachers realized that students learn to read by reading! They provided assistance, strategies for coping, and methods that would enable the students to make sense from printed text. They worked with the regular classroom teacher to be sure that the students learned science and social studies vocabularies. The special teachers provided regular classroom teachers with taped texts and ways to modify assignments. They informed the regular classroom teachers about the unique needs of their students with LD and taught them ways to teach successfully.

Resource rooms, however, were not the panacea. Not all resource programs were successful. Some resource teachers operated in isolation not only from regular classroom teachers, but also from other special educators. Some resource students might have "sight-say" reading 1 year and "multisensory phonics" the next. As some regular educators learned to refer students who did not fit the "norm" in their classrooms, they divorced themselves from special educators and from students with special needs.

One of the by-products of the resource movement was a lot of talk about teacher preparation, both special and regular. With the enactment of P.L. 94-142, wholesale teacher training was promised in our state. Every teacher was to be trained to work with all special children, to modify curricula, to teach to different modalities, to make all children successful. Alas, like so many promises, this one was never realized.

In recent years there has been a trend toward so-called "content mastery" programs. Content mastery programs save scarce funds by increasing the number of students "serviced" by a single teacher. Although there have apparently been some very successful programs, these are not the panacea, either. Many content mastery classes have provided a setting that supports the practice of the regular education teacher being largely ignored by the student with LD. The student "listens" to the regular classroom teacher give instruction and directions and then goes to another teacher who "explains" what the regular classroom teacher said and did. Many students who have participated in such programs fail to listen or attend at all in the regular classroom; have no skills (skills may not be taught to mastery in the content-mastery class, and the student certainly doesn't acquire skills through osmosis in the regular classroom); and function permanently below grade placement.

In the 1990s, the new panacea for educating students with disabilities has become "inclusion." Inclusion has a number of meanings. For the child with mental retardation who has been on a separate campus, in a separate classroom, away from even the sight of nondisabled peers for 6 hours a day, inclusion may provide a means for modeling normal behavior. For the blind child, inclusion may provide exposure to normal language. For the physically challenged child, inclusion may provide access to friends and neighbors that had been denied in previous educational settings. Normal groupings of physically able youngsters and students who use wheelchairs are common in many neighborhoods and in many schools.

But what of students with learning disabilities? They are usually referred to *special* educators because they are unable to read, write, spell, compute, or comprehend spoken or written language at a level commensurate with their peers or their potential. Students with LD are not visibly discernible, but they may be unable to function in classroom settings with large numbers of students. Despite modifications by the classroom teacher, the legacy of students with learning disabilities may be tears and frustration.

What has changed in education since the time my son was in elementary school that would ensure successful inclusion? The answer is, unfortunately, nothing really. Teachers are still working with students as their teachers worked with them. There is different terminology for describing what teachers do, but nothing has radically changed in most classrooms when the door is closed. There are exceptions of course—schools where teachers have high expectations for all students and provide the educational environments necessary for students to succeed. Unfortunately, these schools are so rare that they are shown on national television programs about schools that "break the molds."

What *has* changed in most schools is that today's teachers and schools are under tremendous pressure regarding achievement on paper-and-pencil assessments. In state after state, assessments are being used to measure pupil progress. Results are reported by the mass media and used as measuring sticks, not for individual students, but for teachers, principals, and schools. Research on schools with such high-stakes testing programs has found that the number of students who are retained and referred to special education is rising. The pressure of high-stakes testing plus the pressures of dealing with today's angry, violent children makes teaching an extremely stressful profession, and having to deal with students with disabilities in the classroom will not make it any easier.

There has been no massive teacher training about effective ways to teach students with disabilities. Efforts to get states to require even 6 college hours of study of the characteristics and needs of students with disabilities have been largely unsuccessful. What, then, will become of these students if inclusion becomes the rule rather than the exception? What will be different between the classrooms of the 1990s and those of when my son attended school? Again, the answer is "Nothing." Students with severe and pervasive learning disabilities will seek their own solutions. I predict that if inclusion becomes a reality, the dropout rate for students with LD will soar to a nationally disgraceful figure. I predict that the number of teenagers turning to drugs or alcohol will soar. I predict that an epidemic of teenage suicides will wrap families in despair and grief. I predict that all of us in LDA who have labored for these many years will realize we have lost not only the battle but also the war. Special education services for youth with learning disabilities will no longer be available anywhere in America's public schools.

Inclusionists counter that services for all students with handicaps will be enhanced in the regular classroom with assistive teachers, aides, and other support. Given the scarcity of funding for education today, does it make sense to assume that a school can provide a trained teacher to work with every regular classroom teacher having a child with a disability in his or her classroom? Does it really make sense, is it real to think, that an Individualized Education Program (IEP) committee would agree that a child with LD is unable to benefit from classroom instruction without the aid of a personal computer or occupational therapy? Adequate support and assistance for students with learning disabilities in the regular classroom would be prohibitive in cost because of the numbers of students involved. Does it make sense that with the growing need for earlier, more comprehensive, appropriate educational services for our poor and minority children, millions would be spent to support students with LD in regular classrooms? Where does that leave children with learning disabilities? Unfortunately, it will leave many children waiting for that temporary transfer to their father's private school … a transfer that, of course, will never come.

CHAPTER 18

Mainstreaming, Schools for the Blind, and Full Inclusion: What Shall the Future of Education for Blind Children Be?

Michael Bina

This chapter is from "Mainstreaming, Schools for the Blind, and Full Inclusion: What Shall the Future of Education for Blind Children Be?" by M. Bina, *The Braille Monitor,* November 1993, pp. 1007–1010. Copyright 1993 by National Federation of the Blind. Reprinted with permission. Note that the original material is from a speech.

Both of the previous excellent speakers spoke about full inclusion, but really the best definition, and the most concise definition, I've heard of full inclusion is by Dr. Jernigan. Dr. Jernigan refers to full inclusion as "mainstreaming with a vengeance." I'd like to ask Dr. Jernigan if I could continue to quote him on that.

Perhaps I will shock some of you today when I say residential schools are a thing of the past. But, before you think I have lost my mind, I also want to add that residential schools are also very much a thing of the present and most definitely a very much needed provision in the future.

As a residential school superintendent nowadays, I have to be very honest; my colleagues and I sometimes feel apologetic. Others would have us think we run second-class operations, things of the past, dinosaurs on the verge of extinction. Rather I contend we are places of distinction, and therefore I make no apology. I am proud that in the past and today and clearly in the future these schools are and will continue to be valid, beneficial, and very necessary for kids. Who can deny the success of our many graduates, like so many of you in the audience today? Please do not consider any of my comments today as anti–public school. I worked in public schools, and I strongly believe that they definitely have their place also.

Residential schools today, though, unfortunately are considered placements of last resort. The presumption under the law is that public schools are considered the first and many times the only option. The playing field needs to be leveled so that residential schools can be viewed in the same positive light the public schools currently enjoy. Residential schools (please listen carefully to this because I feel very strongly about this) also need to be rightfully on the menu so that parents and others who make decisions can fully consider and ultimately choose this option if it is in the child's best interest.

In Indiana, unfortunately, we had the parent choice provision taken away by OSEP (the Office of Special Education Programs) last year at a time when President Bush was calling for parent choice in regular education as a method of reform. Taking choice away from parents of blind kids and giving it to parents of nonhandicapped students is what I call adverse discrimination. [applause] While school for the blind programs have adjusted and changed, many people's attitudes about them have not changed. Today many myths persist which negatively influence decision makers, but most disturbing to me is that many children are being excluded from attending these schools to the point that today only 7% of blind children in our country attend schools for the blind.

I'd like to go over some of these myths that make the playing field unlevel. This first one is that residential schools segregate blind children from society. We are told by others, most of whom have never set foot on a school for the blind campus, that we are segregationists. Well this to me is a very negative and inflammatory word choice. These well-educated experts are advocates for severely handicapped individuals and are not trained in blindness. Yet they are more than very strongly pushing for elimination of residential schools and, as the other speakers have already said, even public school resource rooms. These full-inclusion initiatives are counter to federal law, which mandates a full array of services.

Think of this as an analogy: In medicine it would be gross malpractice if doctors removed any proven reliable treatment or medicine from their arsenal which would have the potential to benefit even one patient and they substituted an unproven drug. I contend we should be widening our options and not in any way reducing them. Education, as well as medicine, would be taking a step backwards by doing so.

Residential schools do not segregate or restrict in a discriminatory manner, but rather positively and purposefully bring together children as do science, math, and music magnet schools, which consolidate students with special interests and aptitudes. And, interestingly, magnet schools are being advanced as a way to improve America's schools. Yet, in spite of schools for the blind's proven track record as very productive places for boosting self-image, confidence, and solid skills for future success, they continue to be underutilized and not given the respect I feel they deserve. Doctors separate people needing medical treatment in hospitals, so is it inappropriate that we at some times, for some students when they need specialized placements, do so in special schools?

I am extremely proud of the Committee on Joint Organizational Effort and the position paper which Dr. Hatlen mentioned. This position paper challenges very strongly the requirement in the law that says, to the maximum extent possible, handicapped children must be educated with non-handicapped students. I feel that blind children shouldn't avoid contact with other blind children and that such contact is clearly beneficial. This requirement just doesn't make sense to me, but I guess the lawmakers are a whole lot smarter than I am.

One parent said it best: "How dare the lawmakers tell me who my child's friends will be! Is my child someone who should be avoided by other children?" I have seen in my experience awfully good friendships and counseling going on between blind students that our PhD psychologists couldn't begin to match. [applause]

A 1991 study showed that 50% of residential school students were integrated in public school programs, where they could have the best of both worlds. We are vastly underutilizing our residential schools. We have some classrooms which are nearly empty at a time when blind children in public schools are not receiving all of the services specified in their IEPs. Both placements should be used to benefit the child. Many would agree that all blind children can clearly benefit from residential school some of the time and that some can benefit from residential schools all of the time.

Meaningful integration is very possible in segregated settings, and just because a child lives at home, attends a neighborhood school, and is in physical proximity to nonhandicapped children, that doesn't necessarily mean that they are truly integrated. [applause] We are all aware of integrated public school students who are isolated islands in the mainstream, but our critics don't call this inappropriate isolation segregation. It is less important to me where children go to school than that, wherever they go, they get what they need when they need it in a positive climate. [applause]

Today we hear calls for full inclusion in schools, but I contend the goal needs to be full inclusion in society. For too long we have been preparing students for graduation when we should have been preparing them with skills for life. [applause] Without this solid foundation like Braille and mobility skills, positive integration into schools now or later in life becomes extremely difficult. Swimming teachers (and I used to be one when I was younger) have long since abandoned throwing their students into the deep end of the pool to teach them to swim without carefully developing prerequisite skills. But our policy makers keep overzealously pushing integration before the regular education staff are trained, attitudes are adjusted, and the blind child has the skills to survive—much less to be successful. The standard must be thriving and purposefully going in a positive forward direction as opposed to just surviving or just keeping your head above water. Integration should never become submerging.

We must admit and also address the fact that we have large numbers of underserved students in many programs throughout our country that are advertised as comprehensive when they are not. Two hours of Braille instruction per week, or worse, per month is clearly an intolerable injustice. [applause] In many cases these students are being shortchanged, and fortunately a strong outcry from parents, consumers, and professionals is increasing in intensity. An Indiana parent summed it up beautifully for me. She said, "We need to decide if we want our kids to be social or to be educated."

There is another myth, that our schools are only for students with multiple disabilities. I've had parents come to our school after many, many years of public education and say we wish we could have sent our son or daughter earlier. You have high functioning students there, and our child could have thrived in your environment, but our local district kept telling us that your school was only for multihandicapped children. There was a study done in 1985 that predicted that by 1991 all residential schools would be primarily for multihandicapped students. Another study done last year showed that over 45% of the students in residential schools are in academic programs and that over 39% of these students went on to college.

Another myth is that residential schools are too expensive. We spend approximately $30,000 per child on a national average, and the public schools spend about $3,000 per child per year. Our per capita costs are high, yes, but we likewise offer more than bare bones service. Using another medical analogy, we don't seem to worry about the cost for medical treatment when we roll our child, our spouse, or ourselves in for life-saving surgery. Why do we keep letting our pocketbooks rather than our consciences drive our educational decisions? I'd rather pay now than have some of our students pay for it later in life.

Quality and intensive programs come with a price tag, and I contend most strongly that not learning to read and write Braille or other skills well, when they should be learned, to me qualifies most clearly as life-threatening. Would you agree? [applause]

Also myth number four: Local programs are better than center-based programs. We don't have a college or university in every city or town across the United States; yet in our field we are trying, even in light of the personnel shortage, to apply the chicken-in-every-pot, car-in-every-garage, vision-program-in-each-public-school-building philosophy. When we centralize like this, I feel we are spreading our services so thinly that we can barely tell that the services exist.

Also myth number five: Residential schools are old-fashioned. To that I want to say, yes, to the extent that we model, require, and encourage old-fashioned basic skills, values, and manners. On solid skills I'd have to say we are old-fashioned.

In conclusion, I want to say that we have made many changes, and I only hope that we succeed in educating the public that we are proud places for children to be educated and also that public attitudes need to be changed so that children can have the benefit of all options for them. Also, as AER President, if I could just add this little plug right here. I am very optimistic about the Committee on Joint Organizational Effort (JOE), and I'm excited about the JOE position paper on inclusion. We are developing another position on categorical services, and I pledge very strong leadership in AER to coming together as a field, consumers and professionals. That is our goal; and, as we have been cooperatively doing recently, I hope that we can continue to make the progress we have been. Thank you very much.

CHAPTER 19

Some Thoughts on Inclusion, Alienation, and Meeting the Needs of Children with Visual Impairments

Sandra Lewis

This chapter is from "Some Thoughts on Inclusion, Alienation, and Meeting the Needs of Children with Visual Impairments," by S. Lewis, 2002, *Re:View, 34*(3), pp. 99–101. Copyright 2002 by Heldref Publications. Reprinted with permission.

n *Planet of the Blind*, Stephen Kuusisto (1999) describes a hostile world, a world where it is not acceptable to be blind, where using alternative methods is not encouraged, and where social isolation is common. As he describes his early experiences, it seems almost as if he, a person with significant low vision, were forced to "fit" into an educational system that was not designed for people like him. As a result, he felt for a long time like an alien in this world.

When I first heard the title of Kuusisto's book, I assumed that the book would describe a planet of the blind—a world where the majority of the inhabitants have significant visual impairments, a world with restaurants, recreation activities, and bureaucracies designed for people who are blind. In my mind, this planet had easily managed mass transportation systems (or maybe even personal vehicles that operated at the command of a voice) and microwave ovens and ATMs that were always accessible.[1]

As an educator, I wondered about the structure of the planet's education programs for children in the primary grades. One of the first differences I assumed would be that the "presumption of vision"[1] would not be the basic philosophy underlying all classroom learning. Examples of students' work would not line classroom walls (who would look there?) but would be in portfolios available for parents, teachers, and other students to explore. Classroom teachers would not assume that all of their students had had the same experiences; instead, they would make sure that experiences that they had created or facilitated would be the basis of all learning.

Field trips and activity centers would be the hallmarks of these classrooms. In the snack center, students would count out crackers, slice cheese, wash baby carrots, and pour drinks for each of their peers. Lunch activities would involve setting the table, preparing the food, or washing the dishes. In an animal-care center, students would learn to care for kittens by opening cans of food, scooping it into the kittens' bowls, refilling the water dishes, and making sure the kittens had clean bedding by washing it frequently in the classroom's washing machine. Teachers would use these activity centers and many others as the foundation for teaching reading, writing, and mathematics skills. The children would meet with veterinarians, pet groomers, and others who make their living through work with animals; they would read stories about cats, and write stories about their experiences with the kittens. In this way, the children would develop meaningful understandings of the activity and how it fits into daily life for themselves and others. They would enhance their counting skills, increase their vocabulary, improve their spelling, advance their social skills, extend their ability to work cooperatively, and develop fine and gross motor skills, as well as master key daily living skills and learn about potential careers. It would be well understood that development and integration of all of these skills would be necessary if these children were to become contributing adult members of society.

Classroom reading centers would be stocked with many volumes of books in Braille. At story time, all of the children would hold a copy of the book that the teacher was reading and would follow along as she read aloud. Braille writers, slates and styluses, and electronic notetakers would be everywhere. Reading instruction would be based on a research-supported program that had been designed for blind students. There would be no question about who should teach reading (a teacher who knows how children with visual impairments learn to read), or whether Grade 1 or Grade 2 Braille should be taught (the use of contractions and their order of introduction would have been carefully researched). No child would be pulled out of class for reading instruction, because reading instruction (like that in math, social skills, travel, career education, motor skill development, daily living skills) would occur throughout the day.

A fantasy? A world filled with Braille street signs, vehicles that do not require vision to operate, accessible books in libraries, and early education instruction geared to how blind children learn. Is it totally outside the range of possibility?

Is it possible to create classrooms that are designed to optimize learning in children who are blind or who have low vision? *Of course it is!* However, as long as the driving force in our education system is inclusion, children with visual impairments are likely to struggle to "fit" into a system that only marginally meets their learning needs. Children with visual impairments need education environments that promote unifying experiences using concrete materials in activities in which they are actively engaged. Considerable valid evidence exists that these students often need specialized instruction that builds skills in the academic, communication, sensory-motor, daily living, social, orientation and mobility, and career domains to make sense of their world. They need these skills to achieve, in the current educational vernacular, "positive educational outcomes," or as we say, to function competently as adults.

As professional educators of children who are visually impaired, we must help others who live and work with these children to understand that these children experience the world differently. Then, we must enlist these individuals to work with us to create education environments that meet their needs. We need to remind others that *lifelong inclusion is the ultimate goal in the education of students with visual impairments, but that classroom inclusion may not necessarily always be the best method to achieve that goal.*

Schroeder (1996) noted that "educators (both teachers and school administrators) have a moral responsibility to consider the effects of their education practices on blind children's perceptions of themselves as whole blind persons or as defective sighted persons" (p. 217). We need research on how best to design local educational programs that instill our students with a sense that they are not "defective sighted persons." We have little scientific basis for what we do. We do not know if itinerant programs are effective. We do not know the most effective ways to teach Braille reading or how the presumption of vision affects children's enthusiasm and desire for learning and their motivation for lifelong involvement in the world.

We need the answers to these and other research questions if we are to progress in our search for the planet where students with visual impairments receive the education to which they are entitled, for a planet on which no one with visual impairment feels like an alien.

ENDNOTE

1. Thanks to Kay Ferrell of the University of Northern Colorado for this description of inclusive classrooms.

REFERENCES

Kuusisto, S. (1999). *Planet of the blind: A memoir*. New York: Dell.

Schroeder, F. K. (1996). Perceptions of Braille usage by legally blind adults. *Journal of Visual Impairment & Blindness, 90*(3), 210–218.

CHAPTER 20

The Education of Deaf Children: Drowning in the Mainstream and the Sidestream

Harlan Lane

This chapter includes excerpts, with changes, from "The Education of Deaf Children: Drowning in the Mainstream and the Sidestream," by H. Lane, 1992, in *The Mask of Benevolence: Disabling the Deaf Community* (pp. 135–143, 272–278), by H. Lane, New York: Knopf. Copyright 1992 by Harlan Lane. Reprinted, with changes, with permission of Alfred A. Knopf, Inc.

Nearly three fourths of an estimated 80,000 deaf schoolchildren in the United States now go to local schools with hearing children, and the specialized schools for deaf children they would have attended are closing or serving new populations, such as multiply handicapped children (Ries, 1986, p. 22; see also Allen & Osborn, 1984; Convention of American Instructors of the Deaf, 1990).

The label "mainstreaming" embraces so wide a range of educational arrangements that, as with the label "total communication," people with divergent beliefs about deaf education can be gulled into endorsing it. In some urban schools, there are classes of deaf children, grouped by grade, without any contact with hearing children, or just the odd shared class in art or sports. Often these "self-contained" classes are only nominally within a public school—they are located in temporary trailers, separate buildings, remote corners of buildings, or basements (Goodstein, 1988). In less densely populated areas, on the other hand, the deaf child may have no one with whom he can communicate; he is left to "make do" in the midst of a hearing class and in the occasional coaching session with a few deaf children of various ages and abilities. Most deaf children are in schools where there are only one or two other deaf children (Siegel, 1991).

An American Sign Language (ASL) interpreter may be provided for the mainstreamed deaf child in some classes; but many of these interpreters are insufficiently skilled to cover the range of academic subjects required, and very few are board certified. Many communities can neither recruit nor afford qualified interpreters. Few schools in America would appoint a nurse, a counselor, or an audiologist without certification; standards are much lower when it comes to finding an ASL interpreter. Then, too, the child who depends on an interpreter relates very little, if at all, to the teacher. Moreover, he must keep his eyes glued on the interpreter for long stretches while classroom events suit his hearing classmates: maps are unfurled, slides are projected, tables of numbers are displayed, and all the while the teacher talks, the interpreter interprets, and the deaf child must never look away from the interpreter (Estes, 1991).

Immersed in a hearing, English-speaking environment, the deaf child frequently drowns in the mainstream.

"I have experienced both, mainstream and deaf school," eighth-grader Jesse Thomas testified to the National Council on Disabilities. He first explained, "I'm not disabled, just deaf," and then gave his reasons for opposing mainstreaming: "Learning through an interpreter is very hard; it's bad socially in the mainstream; you are always outnumbered; you don't feel like it's your school; you never know deaf adults; you don't belong; you don't feel comfortable as a deaf person" (Thomas, 1989). That's the gist of surveys of deaf college students who have attended mainstream high school or elementary school programs. Reports one study: "Almost every informant described their social life in terms of loneliness, rejection, and social isolation" (Foster, 1989, p. 44). In order to cope as best he can in a mainstream class, the deaf child hides his hearing aid, pretends he understands lessons when he does not, copies other pupils' work, rarely asks questions in class or volunteers to answer them, speaks as little as possible to hearing students, or even to other deaf students (Booth, 1988; see also Gaustad & Kluwin, 1991). Writes one child trying to pass in the mainstream: "I hate it if people know I am deaf" (Booth, 1988, p. 113).

Mainstreaming is a part of a wider movement in the United States that has removed large numbers of mentally and physically handicapped children and adults from custodial institutions. "Deinstitutionalization," as the movement was called, was accompanied by the promise of more normal life-styles for all and services in the community for those who needed them. There is a consensus that, overall, the promise was not fulfilled, not least perhaps because one motive for the change in policy was cost containment: It is less expensive to foist a deaf child on the local school, even with an allocation for special services, such as an itinerant special teacher or a resource room, than it is to provide education in a residential setting (Emerson & Pretty, 1987; see also Moores, 1991).

Deaf children were thus swept up in the movement to mainstream indiscriminately nearly all previously "institutionalized" children. The old custodial institutions were not only costly; they embraced many more mentally and physically handicapped children than needed to be there, and they fostered dependency and restricted freedom with no countervailing gain. This was not true of the residential schools for deaf children, however. Yes, the audist staffs of these "sidestream" schools frequently infantilized their charges, could not communicate with them, and were ineffective as teachers. Nonetheless, the residential school offered something of immense value: language—the ability to communicate with other human beings. For most deaf children, who came from hearing, languageless homes, this was a boon indeed, as was the community and the culture they found in the residential school. Although manual language was not used in class—although, indeed, it was often forbidden—still the school was a signing community, where the deaf student could get help after class with coursework, discuss local, national, and international events, obtain counseling, participate in student activities, develop friendships with other deaf students, emulate older students and deaf staff, and acquire self-respect as a deaf person (see Mertens, 1989; Stewart & Stinson, 1991).

None of these advantages is available to the deaf child in an ordinary public school, where ASL, deaf adults, and a deaf community are absent. Moreover, in this setting the deaf child is hampered in learning the "indirect messages" of education: the implied and unintentionally taught beliefs, feelings, attitudes, and social skills. Since only one schoolchild in a thousand is deaf, most school districts have too few deaf children to establish an effective program with properly trained staff, a peer group of reasonable size at each age level, and extracurricular activities. The only plausible alternative to residential schools for deaf children, then, is regional programs, but children in those programs may spend almost as much time in the bus as in class, reducing the time they can devote to extracurricular activities, to homework, and to their families. Moreover, their deaf friends are likely to live out of reach (Kluwin, 1991a, 1991b).

Granted that the conditions in the local public school for the deaf child's social and emotional growth are quite poor. Is the child receiving a better education in the "three Rs" there? Not at all. The first report cards on mainstreamed deaf children show no improvement in their blighted English or mathematics attributable to mainstreaming, even though the first to be mainstreamed were the children with the best speech and hearing, and the academic qualifications of their teachers frequently surpass those in the residential schools (Allen & Karchmer, 1990, p. 55). Indeed, there is some evidence that when achievement scores are corrected statistically for differences in the makeup of the deaf student bodies in residential and mainstream schools, the deaf child in the mainstream is at an academic disadvantage (see Author's Note at the end of this chapter).

The deaf children who do best in school, mainstream or residential, are—note it well—the fortunate 10% who learned ASL as a native language from their deaf parents, the core of this linguistic minority. These native speakers of ASL outperform their deaf classmates from hearing homes in most subjects, including reading and writing English—an achievement that is all the more remarkable when we reflect that they come from poorer homes, generally a disadvantage, and that the schools they attend, whether mainstream or residential, do not capitalize on their native language skills (Mindel & Vernon, 1971; see also Brasel, 1975; Corson, 1973; Geers & Schick, 1988; Israelite, Ewoldt, & Hoffmeister, 1989; Weisel & Reichstein, 1987; Zweibel, 1987). Deaf children arriving at school with a knowledge of ASL are also better adjusted, better socialized, and have more positive attitudes than their counterparts who have been deprived of effective communication (Mindel & Vernon, 1971; see also Harris, 1978; Johnson, Liddell, & Erting, 1989). Similar findings come from other lands. In Israel, deaf children of deaf parents were found more successful than those of hearing parents in reading comprehension, emotional development, self-image, and initiative to communicate; in Greece, they were found superior in expressive and receptive communication and in lip-reading; in Denmark, they communicated more effectively with peers (Hansen & Kjaer-Sorensen, 1967; Kourbetis, 1987; Weisel & Reichstein, 1987).

The superior performance of deaf children from deaf homes highlights the changes that most need to be made in the education of deaf children: namely, a return to manual language, deaf teachers, and deaf administrators directing residential schools—successful practices in the last century, when American deaf children studied all their subjects in their most fluent language, ASL. These changes have long been advocated by the deaf community itself. "How could we ever learn to cope as deaf people, without the shared experiences of other deaf people all around us?" asks a California deaf leader, assailing mainstreaming.

> It guarantees the emergence of a deaf adult with serious doubts about himself. How can a child, probably with a reading problem and almost certainly intimidated by the sometimes hostile and generally distractive atmosphere of a main-streamed classroom, learn comfortably through an interpreter (possibly one with minimal skills) and without direct contact with the teacher? It's puzzling to me that the parent will permit this. (White, 1990, p. 2)

But parents are badly advised by the experts, who, in any event, ride roughshod over their wishes.

A further obstacle to revitalizing and expanding the residential schools and other specialized programs for deaf children is placed in the way by spokesmen for people with disabilities. Now that advocates for people with disabilities have gained their hard-won integration of mentally and physically handicapped children in the public schools, they fear that segregated schooling of deaf children, who belong to a language minority, would set a precedent for backsliding on mainstreaming of disabled children. That is why such advocates mounted a major campaign in 1990 to close the American School for the Deaf in Hartford, Connecticut. Deaf leaders from around the country, outraged at this assault on America's oldest residential school, which had spawned so many others, beat back the attack. Such discord between leaders of the deaf community and of the disability rights movement arises only because neither group has control of its destiny and must persuade a third group, the nondeaf, nondisabled experts, whose incomprehension each fears.

Advocates for children with disabilities are joined in their insistence on mainstreaming for all by those in the audist establishment who believe that education without assimilation is a failure and that assimilation can be achieved by brute force (Conference of Executives of American Schools for the Deaf, 1977; see also National Association of the Deaf, 1986, 1987). This is the counsel many hearing parents want to receive, as they prefer, understandably, to have their child live at home. According to the Commission on the Education of the Deaf (1988), the intent of the law to have all handicapped children placed in the "least restrictive environment" was misinterpreted to mean mainstreaming in the local school for nearly all deaf children—precisely the most restrictive environment for those children, given the communicative and social barriers in the local school. The U.S. Supreme Court has ruled that when Congress passed the Education for All Handicapped Children Act in 1975, it recognized that "regular classrooms simply would not be a suitable setting for the education of many handicapped children" and it provided for alternative placements (see Duncan, 1984). The Code of Federal Regulations implementing the act also requires that educational placement be "appropriate," that potential harmful effects on the child must be considered, and that a child can be removed from "regular" classes when education cannot be achieved satisfactorily (34 C.F.R. 300.550, 300.552, 300.550(b)(2), cited in Siegel, 1991). One judge ruled in 1988 that "mainstreaming that interferes with the acquisition of fundamental language skills is foolishness mistaken for wisdom" (*Visco & Visco v. School District of Pittsburg,* cited in Siegel, 1991, p. 137). But the federal and state departments of education and local school boards, frequently encouraged by the audist establishment, have largely ignored provisions of the act, of federal regulations, and of court rulings when full compliance favors placing a deaf child in a specialized program with other deaf children.

Like many mothers of bright ASL-using children, Jesse Thomas's mother appealed the local school board's insistence on mainstreaming Jesse; she agreed with her son's wish to go to the state residential school for deaf children. (Because she is hearing and could not provide a model of manual language for her son, Mrs. Thomas had made a point of placing Jesse in the company of deaf children and adults since his infancy.) The local experts claimed to know Jesse's best interests better than his mother did, however, and she lost her appeal. Teachers and administrators have their ways of keeping parents at bay, despite the law requiring that the parents participate in deciding the Individualized Educational Plan for their child (Bennett, 1988). These ways include withholding information, presenting major issues as minor ones, limiting the topics on which parents may have a say, authoritatively identifying the source of problems as the child and not the school, and choosing the time, place, manner, and language in which the discussion is conducted. Although the professional's judgment may be based on class differences, on stereotypes, on invalid test results, or on an inability to communicate with the child, many parents are intimidated, the more so if they belong to an ethnic minority. Both parties believe that the parents need the professional more than the converse.

The experts present advice, which is really a demand for confirmation of their judgment; the parent is not invited to form a plan collaboratively but asked to accede to the audist's plan. Moreover, parents are encouraged to be compliant by their fear that protest will have harmful repercussions for their child. Determined and resourceful parents can sometimes outwit the establishment, however. Mrs. Thomas had heard of a county that sent its deaf children exclusively to oral programs. Informed that those programs would not accept pupils who used ASL, the Thomases moved to that very county. As they had hoped, the program administrators would not consider Jesse for admission and saw no alternative but to send him to the state residential school for deaf children.

When Susan Dutton, who is deaf, moved with her deaf son, Mark, to Harveys Lake, Pennsylvania, the boy was placed in a local school, in a special-needs class with children ranging in age from 8 to 18. Mark was fluent in ASL, but neither the teacher nor the other students could sign. There was an "interpreter/aide" present, who had completed one class in sign language. When the school convened a meeting to formulate Mark's Individualized Educational Plan, Mrs. Dutton was not provided with an interpreter and was told that "despite my wishes, despite my right as a parent to decide what is best for my son, Mark would have to remain in the local school and be mainstreamed into fourth grade classes with hearing students 2 years younger than he." Since deaf peers, culture, and role models were utterly lacking in the mainstream and there was little effective communication, Mrs. Dutton refused to sign the IEP. A hearing was convened before the school assistant superintendent: "There was no interpreter present. There was no discussion. The assistant superintendent came into this meeting having already made his decision, and he communicated it to me via note writing. It was, of course, in support of mainstreaming." Mrs. Dutton consulted a lawyer, and

9 nights of hearings ensued before a hearing officer employed by the Pennsylvania State Department of Education (Dutton, 1991; Levitan, 1991). The school district's lawyer argued that the mainstream was the least restrictive environment for Mark Dutton. Susan and Mark's lawyer and several scholars contended that the local school was the most restrictive environment for Mark's education since he could not understand his teachers and peers nor they him, and since the school could not nurture his linguistic and cultural development as a deaf person. The school district prevailed, but the Duttons appealed the hearing officer's decision, and it was overturned by a panel of two lawyers and an educator who affirmed that "communication is the essence of education" and that the hearing officer had misinterpreted the law. Susan and Mark were relieved to see their year-long struggle and expense finally end in success—until they learned that the school district had filed an appeal which as of this writing is before a federal court.

Confronted with the mainstreaming tragedy in Britain, members of the British National Union of the Deaf formally charged their government with a violation of the United Nations Convention on the Prevention and Punishment of the Crime of Genocide. That treaty prohibits inflicting mental harm on the children of an ethnic group, and it prohibits forcibly transferring them to another group. According to this deaf organization, mainstreaming will gravely injure "not only deaf children but deaf children's rightful language and culture." Their published *Charter of the Rights of the Deaf* asserts that "deaf schools are being effectively forced to close and therefore children of one ethnic/linguistic minority group, that is, deaf people, are being forcibly transferred to another group, that is, hearing people," in violation of the U.N. convention (National Union of the Deaf, 1982).

For nearly a century, parents of deaf children were told to place them in specialized programs that would teach them to speak and lip-read; at home, they were to drill their child in speech and never let him make a sign. Then, 15 years ago, most parents were told that individual signs could be used at the same time as speech. Some were told that English expressed on the hands through real and invented signs held out the greatest hope for their child's mastery of English. Ten years ago, parents were told to place their deaf child in the local hearing school. Now they are increasingly told that an ear operation combined with oral drills and no sign is his best hope. If the local school cannot provide sufficient training in speech and hearing, they may need to enroll their child in specialized programs that teach him to speak and lip-read; at home, they are to drill their child in speech and never let him make a sign. So the advice comes full circle. The audists keep changing the rules because they have the power to do so as each version of the audist regime becomes a blatant failure. Moreover, the failure of a stage of forced assimilation, far from undermining the establishment and its normalizing principles, leads to an expansion of its regime. So, too, the prison system is offered as the remedy for its own ills and the failures of applied social science justify more research. The fundamental enterprise is never placed in question; instead, bio-power establishes as the question, how best to implement the fixed, accepted goals.

The deaf community, however, has held unswervingly to a single truth: deaf identity, hence deaf language and culture. "Methods are not acquired naturally like languages," writes deaf linguist M. J. Bienvenu (1990, p. 133), "they are invented by individuals for specific purposes."

AUTHOR'S NOTE

In 1981, Allen and Karchmer examined the reading and mathematics scores on the *Stanford Achievement Test* of a random sample of 330 deaf students in elementary and high school who were deafened because their mothers contracted German measles during pregnancy. Those students who were partially integrated into mainstream settings had higher achievement scores to begin with (as well as lesser hearing losses), so this difference between them and deaf students in specialized programs had to be factored out statistically. When that was done, there was no reliable advantage to mainstreaming. Holt and Allen (1989), as part of a larger study, examined the reading and mathematics achievement of about 60 deaf students in special schools and in mainstream settings for whom prior achievement scores were available. When students were, in effect, matched statistically on this and several other variables, there was no difference in reading scores obtained in the two settings. However, deaf students who were fully integrated with hearing students for mathematics instruction achieve lower mathematics scores than their peers in special schools.

Four studies have been cited by some authors as supporting mainstreaming of deaf children. That conclusion, however, does not withstand close inspection. With an avowedly strong mainstreaming bias, Van der Horst (1971) published a report in the

British journal *The Teacher of the Deaf* (Vol. 69, pp. 398–414) on matched groups of 12 "auditory defectives," enrolled in a special school (DS) or in a local school for hearing children (HS). The groups were matched on average hearing loss, age, sex, and non-verbal IQ; they were not matched with respect to the socioeconomic level of their homes, nor with respect to the training their teachers had received, although both factors are known to influence academic achievement. The two groups did not differ on one verbal IQ test, but they did differ, in favor of the HS pupils, on a second; we are told the difference was statistically significant but we are not told its size. Moreover, three of the five subtests on this second IQ test showed no difference between the groups. A comparison of the two groups on writing tests showed no difference, but the DS pupils showed less improvement from age 8 to age 11 on one writing measure. Using personal records and psychological tests they fail to identify, the authors assigned emotional stability ratings to pupils. These data favor the special school children, who were labeled normal 86% of the time compared with only 54% for the deaf children in the hearing school. Because of its failure to control important variables, and the finding of no difference on the first verbal IQ test and three of the five subtests of the second IQ test, I believe it is inappropriate to cite this study as showing an advantage to mainstreaming.

A 1975 study published by the Toronto Board of Education (Reich, Hambleton, & Klein) found higher raw scores on reading, language, and speech intelligibility from HS students than from DS, but "when hearing loss as well as other differences in background were taken into account, there was little remaining difference between groups to unequivocally attest to the superiority of one method over another.... However, the results do not support the view that integration is *harmful*" [italics in original]. As was evident in the first study mentioned, a problem that bedevils comparisons of the achievement of HS and DS deaf students is the lack of comparability of the students who attend the two kinds of schools.

In 1984, Allen and Osborn made a sophisticated attempt to render comparable by statistical methods noncomparable samples of deaf students taught in HS and DS environments. If one knew the contribution of, say, socioeconomic background to reading achievement in deaf students, and if the HS group on the average came from more upper-class homes, one could lower their average reading scores appropriately in order to render them comparable to the DS students. A problem with this approach arises, however, when the groups differ in several important respects, for it is not obvious that the advantage arising from a wealthier background and that arising from, say, residual hearing are simply additive. This statistical issue would be less critical if a substantial difference remained after the corrections, but in fact "the actual proportion of achievement variance accounted for by integration status alone was very small for all three variables" (a reading test and two math tests; p. 112). The authors go on to point out, moreover, that such differences as remain "cannot be interpreted as representing a causal relationship between integration status and achievement" (p. 112). They also recognize that there were many uncontrolled variables, such as prior academic ability, not imputable to the demographic variables controlled for. Moreover, there may have been differences between the groups compared in math and language aptitude and in the preparation of their teachers—to mention just two more unexamined factors. Since the slight difference in scores could be attributed to the correction procedures or to uncontrolled variables, and cannot be causally attributed to integration status, it is inappropriate to cite this study as supporting mainstreaming.

Kluwin and Moores (1985) studied the effects of mainstreaming on mathematics achievement in a nonrandom sample of 80 deaf students in three high schools. The authors used a different method of post hoc corrections for some but not all of the group differences, leaving a small residual (one third of a standard deviation) advantage for the integrated students. They conclude "that the greatest amount of variance may be accounted for by the fact that regular mathematics teachers are subject matter specialists and have more teaching experience" (p. 159). None of the teachers in the special school, who averaged 6 years experience, were math specialists; all of the teachers in the hearing school had master's degrees in mathematics, except one who had a PhD; they averaged 18 years of experience. The same authors again found only trivial effects of placement on the academic achievements of deaf students in a later study: Kluwin and Moores (1989). Kluwin has concluded: "Mainstreaming per se is not a solution to improving the academic achievement of deaf students" (Kluwin, 1991a, p. 274).

To the best of my knowledge there are no studies that support the premise that a deaf child will fare substantially better in a mainstream school than in a special school for deaf children. One study that compared hearing-impaired students in the mainstream with hearing students in the same classes found that hearing-impaired seniors had "greater academic difficulties, took fewer academic courses, evidenced less school motivation, did even less homework and appeared less goal-oriented ... than their normally hearing peers" (Gregory, Shanahan, & Walberg, 1984, p. 16).

REFERENCES

Allen, T. E., & Karchmer, M. (1981). Influences on academic achievement of hearing-impaired students born during the 1963–1965 rubella epidemic. *Directions, 2,* 40–54.

Allen, T. E., & Karchmer, M. (1990). Communication in classrooms for deaf students: Student, teacher, and program characteristics. In H. Bornstein (Ed.), *Manual communication: Implications for education* (pp. 45–66). Washington, DC: Gallaudet University Press.

Allen, T. E., & Osborn, T. I. (1984). Academic integration of hearing-impaired students: Demographic, handicapping, and achievement factors. *American Annals of the Deaf, 129,* 100–113.

Bennett, A. T. (1988). Gateway to powerless: Incorporating Hispanic deaf children and families into formal schooling. *Disability, Handicap and Society, 3,* 119–151.

Bienvenu, M. J. (1990). Letter to the editor. *Deaf American, 40,* 133.

Booth, T. (1988). Challenging conceptions of integration. In L. Barton (Ed.), *The politics of special educational needs* (pp. 99–122). Philadelphia: Falmer Press.

Brasel, K. E. (1975). *The influence of early language and communication environments on the development of language in deaf children.* Unpublished doctoral dissertation, University of Illinois, Urbana.

Commission on the Education of the Deaf. (1988). *Toward equality, education of the deaf.* Washington, DC: U.S. Government Printing Office.

Conference of Executives of American Schools for the Deaf. (1977). Statement on "least restrictive" placements for deaf students. *American Annals of the Deaf, 122,* 62–69.

Convention of American Instructors of the Deaf. (1990). Schools and classes for the deaf in the United States. *American Annals of the Deaf, 135,* 135.

Corson, H. (1973). *Comparing deaf children of oral deaf parents and deaf parents using manual communication with deaf children of hearing parents on academic, social, and communicative functioning.* Unpublished doctoral dissertation, University of Cincinnati, Cincinnati, OH.

Duncan, J. G. (1984). Recent legislation affecting hearing-impaired persons. *American Annals of the Deaf, 129,* 83–94.

Dutton, S. (1991). Deaf education: Who decides? *The Bicultural Center News, 33,* 1–2.

Emerson, E. B., & Pretty, G. M. H. (1987). Enhancing the social relevance of evaluation practice. *Disability, Handicap, and Society, 2,* 151–162.

Estes, C. (1991, April). Bestest from Estes. *The National Association of the Deaf Broadcaster, 13,* p. 3.

Foster, S. (1989). Reflections of a group of deaf adults on their experiences in mainstream and residential school programs in the United States. *Disability, Handicap and Society, 4,* 37–56.

Gaustad, M. G., & Kluwin, T. (1991). Patterns of communication among deaf and hearing adolescents in public school programs. In T. Kluwin, D. F. Moores, & M. G. Gaustad, *Defining the effective public school program for deaf students* (pp. 124–146). Unpublished manuscript, Gallaudet University, Washington, DC.

Geers, A. E., & Schick, B. (1988). Acquisition of spoken and signed English by hearing-impaired children of hearing-impaired or hearing parents. *Journal of Speech and Hearing Disorders, 53,* 136–143.

Goodstein, H. (1988). *What is mainstreaming?* Paper prepared for the Gallaudet Research Institute Roundtable on Mainstreaming, Gallaudet University, Washington, DC.

Gregory, J. F., Shanahan, T., & Walberg, H. J. (1984). Mainstreamed hearing-impaired high school seniors: A reanalysis of a national survey. *American Annals of the Deaf, 129,* 11–16.

Hansen. B., & Kjaer-Sorensen, R. (1967). *The sign language of deaf children in Denmark.* Copenhagen, Denmark: The School for the Deaf.

Harris, R. (1978). Impulse control in deaf children. In L. Liben (Ed.), *Deaf children: Developmental perspectives.* New York: Academic Press.

Holt, J., & Allen, T. (1989). The effects of schools and their curricula on the reading and mathematics achievement of hearing-impaired students. *International Journal of Educational Research, 13,* 547–562.

Israelite, N., Ewoldt, C., & Hoffmeister, R. (1989). *A review of the literature on effective use of native sign language on the acquisition of a majority language by hearing-impaired students.* Unpublished report, Boston University Center for the Study of Communication and Deafness.

Johnson, R. E., Liddell, S. K., & Erting, C. J. (1989). Unlocking the curriculum: Principles for achieving access in deaf education. *Gallaudet Research Institute Working Papers,* p. 10.

Kluwin, T. (1991a). Some reflections on defining the effective program. In T. Kluwin, D. F. Moores, & M. G. Gaustad, *Defining the effective public school program for deaf students* (pp. 272–282). Unpublished manuscript, Gallaudet University, Washington, DC.

Kluwin, T. (1991b). What does "local public school program" mean? In T. Kluwin, D. F. Moores, & M. G. Gaustad, *Defining the effective public school program for deaf students* (pp. 35–55). Unpublished manuscript, Gallaudet University, Washington, DC.

Kluwin, T., & Moores, D. (1985). The effects of integration on mathematics achievement of hearing-impaired adolescents. *Exceptional Children, 52,* pp. 153–161.

Kluwin, T., & Moores, D. (1989). Mathematics achievements of hearing-impaired adolescents in different placements. *Exceptional Children, 55,* 327–335.

Kourbetis, V. (1987). *Deaf children of deaf parents and deaf children of hearing parents in Greece: A comparative study.* Unpublished doctoral dissertation, Boston University.

Levitan, L. (1991, December). Mark Dutton: An educational tragedy. *Deaf Life,* pp. 10–17.

Mertens, D. (1989). Social experiences of hearing-impaired high school youth. *American Annals of the Deaf, 134,* 15–19.

Mindel, E. D., & Vernon, M. (1971). *They grow in silence.* Silver Spring, MD: National Association of the Deaf.

Moores, D. (1991). An historical perspective on school placement of deaf students. In T. Kluwin, D. F. Moores, & M. G. Gaustad, *Defining the effective public school program for deaf students* (pp. 7–34). Unpublished manuscript, Gallaudet University, Washington, DC.

National Association of the Deaf. (1986). Public Law 94–142 and the least restrictive environment: A position paper of the National Association of the Deaf. *NAD Broadcaster, 8,* 1.

National Association of the Deaf. (1987). NAD recommends to the Commission on Education of the Deaf. *NAD Broadcaster, 9,* 1–8.

National Union of the Deaf. (1982). *Charter of the rights of the deaf.* Bedfort, Middlesex, England: Author.

Reich, C., Hambleton, R., & Klein, R. (1975). *The integration of hearing-impaired children in regular classrooms.* Toronto, Canada: Toronto Board of Education.

Ries, P. (1986). Characteristics of hearing-impaired youth in the general population and of students in special education programs for the hearing-impaired. In A. N. Schildroth & M. A. Karchmer (Eds.), *Deaf children in America* (pp. 1–32). San Diego, CA: College Hill.

Siegel, L. (1991). The least restrictive environment? *Deaf American, 41,* 135–139.

Stewart, D. A., & Stinson, M. S. (1991). The role of sport and extracurricular activities in shaping the socialization patterns of deaf and hard of hearing students. In T. Kluwin, D. F. Moores, & M. G. Gaustad, *Defining the effective public school program for deaf students* (pp. 147–170). Unpublished manuscript, Gallaudet University, Washington, DC.

Thomas, J. (1989, June 8). Testimony before the National Council on Disabilities. Special Schools.

Weisel, A., & Reichstein, J. (1987). Parental hearing status, reading comprehension skills, and socio-emotional adjustment. In R. Ojala (Ed.), *Proceedings of the Tenth World Congress of the World Federation of the Deaf.* Helsinki, Finland: Finnish Association of the Deaf.

White, B. (1990, January). Deaf education: A game people play. *DCARA News,* p. 2.

Zweibel, A. (1987). More on the effects of early manual communication on the cognitive development of deaf children. *American Annals of the Deaf, 132,* 16–20.

CHAPTER 21

Inclusion of All Students with Emotional or Behavioral Disorders? Let's Think Again

James M. Kauffman, John Wills Lloyd,
John Baker, and Teresa M. Riedel

Nearly all teachers have at least one student who fits the current federal definition of being "seriously emotionally disturbed"— or, in today's preferred terminology, having an "emotional or behavioral disorder."[1] Such students may be severely antisocial, aggressive, and disruptive; they may be socially rejected, isolated, withdrawn, and nonresponsive; they may show signs of severe anxiety or depression or exhibit psychotic behavior; they may vacillate between extremes of withdrawal and aggression; and they nearly always have serious academic problems in addition to their social and emotional difficulties. These students' problems are severe, pervasive, and chronic—not minor, situational, or transitory.

In many appeals for the restructuring or reform of special education, the call is for inclusion of all students with disabilities, and no attempt is made to disaggregate the population (see Gartner & Lipsky, 1989; National Association of State Boards of Education, 1992; Stainback & Stainback, 1991). Consequently, we must consider the nature and extent of the problems we will face if inclusion of all students with emotional or behavioral disorders in regular schools and classes becomes a reality.

Current national statistics show that less than 1% of public school students are identified as having emotional or behavioral disorders, and the majority of these students are now served in separate classes or facilities (U.S. Department of Education, 1994). Clearly, then, regular classroom teachers will need to be prepared to teach and manage not only those students with emotional or behavioral problems whom they are already teaching, but also additional students who present even more difficult challenges to pedagogy and behavior management. Although we hope that general education will become more accommodating to students with disabilities, we doubt that regular schools and classrooms will ever be able to provide an appropriate education for all students with emotional or behavioral disorders.

NATURE AND EXTENT
OF THE PROBLEM

Study after study over the past 3 decades has indicated that some 6% to 10% of children and youths have emotional or behavioral problems that seriously impede their development and require treatment if these students are to function adequately in school and in the larger society (Brandenberg, Friedman, & Silver, 1990; Institute of Medicine, 1989).[2] Federal data suggest that 70% to 80% of children needing mental health services do not receive appropriate care (U.S. Congress, Office of Technology Assessment, 1986). Other reports indicate that many children do not receive any mental health services until their problems become so extreme as to require residential treatment (Knitzer, 1982; National Mental Health Association, 1989).

Many students with serious emotional or behavioral disorders remain in regular classes and receive little or no special help of any kind. They are unlikely to be identified for special education unless their problems are severe, complex, and global—so severe that they require comprehensive and intensive intervention (see Mattison & Gamble, 1992). Thus only those with the worst emotional or behavioral disorders have been removed from regular classes, and their return would undoubtedly tax the most competent of classroom teachers. The following brief descriptions of two children, provided to us by teachers of our acquaintance, illustrate the severity of problems faced by many regular classroom teachers before children are even identified for special education.

> Tom, a third-grade boy with serious academic deficits, has exhibited severe behavior problems with every teacher he has had. In first grade, he frequently urinated in the classroom and other inappropriate places and picked fights with other children. Now, not only is he highly aggressive, but also he frequently steals from the teacher and his classmates and is labeled a thief by his peers. His mother does not see his stealing as a serious problem; his father is in jail. Neither Tom nor his mother is receiving any counseling or mental health services. The school's pre-referral team has found no strategy to control his aggressive behavior. In the middle of his third-grade year, Tom was placed with an exceptionally strong male teacher, who finds it impossible to control Tom's behavior and to teach the rest of his class at the same time. This teacher wants Tom to be evaluated for special education.

> Pat, a fifth-grade girl, is at or above grade level in all academic areas but has been highly oppositional and defiant of all teachers since kindergarten. Large for her age and strong, she pushes, hits, and threatens her peers, who are fearful of her and will not initiate any interaction with her.

She sometimes bangs her head on her desk or the floor, shouting, "I'm no good" or "I want to die." Pat was evaluated for special education only after terrorizing her classmates and a substitute teacher by tying the cord of a classroom window blind around her neck and jumping from a table, bringing the blinds crashing down with her in an apparent suicide attempt.

In anticipation of the demands of dealing with an influx of more challenging students, we might ask two questions. First, what are the strategies that research and experience have shown to be most effective in working with these students? Second, what is the likelihood that these strategies can be employed consistently and effectively in regular schools and classrooms?

STRATEGIES THAT WORK

Programs for students with emotional or behavioral disorders have been accused of overemphasizing external control of behavior (Knitzer, Steinberg, & Fleisch, 1990). However, programs that do not establish control of disruptive behavior give teachers no opportunity to teach academic and social skills. Effective programs for students with emotional or behavioral disorders provide the necessary control of aggressive and disruptive behavior, but they also offer a rich curriculum that helps students learn self-control, attain academic competence, and acquire employment-related attitudes and skills that will improve their chances of living happily and successfully in their communities.

Special education and mental health services for students with emotional and behavioral disorders have a substantial history, and a variety of programs have produced significant benefits (e.g., Epstein et al., 1993; Fecser, 1993; Peacock Hill Working Group, 1991). Regardless of their differences in philosophy or conceptual orientation, the most effective programs share the following characteristics.

• *Systematic, data-based interventions.* Intervention strategies are chosen on the basis of the best available data regarding their effectiveness with the specific problems exhibited by individual students, and these strategies are implemented with a high degree of fidelity.

• *Continuous assessment and monitoring of progress.* Each student's progress is monitored frequently, usually daily. Decisions about changes in intervention strategies are based on the measurement of progress, and the student often monitors his or her own progress in addition to having it monitored by program staff.

• *Treatment matched carefully and specifically to the nature and severity of students' problems.* One program is not assumed to be appropriate for all who are categorized as having emotional or behavioral disorders. Rather, each student's specific problems are assessed, and the intervention plan is based on the emotional or behavioral characteristics he or she exhibits. Program personnel understand that many kinds of interventions are required to address the diversity of students' problems.

• *Multi-component treatment.* The program includes a combination of services to address all aspects of the problem, including academic and social skills, social and family services, counseling or psychological therapy, and pharmacological treatment as necessary. Services are not provided piecemeal or in isolation. Rather, services are coordinated and mutually supportive.

• *Provision for frequent guided practice of academic and social skills.* It is not assumed that emotional, behavioral, or academic skills are to be learned merely by talking about them. Rather, teachers give students frequent practice and coach them in actually using the skills. Teaching and practice may begin in "safe" settings in which success is virtually guaranteed, and then problems or lessons of graduated difficulty are provided to ensure continued success. Teachers design instruction carefully, so as to avoid those situations in which failure to use the skills has serious negative consequences.

• *Programming for transfer and maintenance.* Intervention across environments or settings is programmed as necessary to produce generalized improvement and maintain gains. Improvement is not assumed to be permanent or self-sustaining, and improvement in one situation is not assumed to produce automatic improvement in another. Program personnel give extraordinary attention to the specific conditions under which the student who has acquired social and academic skills will be expected to use them.

• *Commitment to sustained intervention.* "One-shot" interventions assumed to be "cures" are avoided. Program personnel understand that most severe emotional or behavioral disorders are developmental disabilities, not transient problems, and that most students with these disorders may require prolonged, if not lifelong, support services. (Peacock Hill Working Group, 1991)

REGULAR SCHOOL AND CLASSROOM IMPLEMENTATION

Few if any of the strategies that are successful with students who have emotional or behavioral disorders are unique; many of the same techniques are appropriate in some form for other students. It is not so much particular features that set successful programs apart, but the precision, duration, and intensity of those features. As we have noted, many students with emotional or behavioral disorders are not now identified for special education; they (along with some of those who *have* been identified) are maintained in regular classrooms, albeit marginally and with poor results. Some of these students would probably benefit from regular classrooms in which some of the program features we have discussed were implemented, and in all likelihood some of the students now served in special classes or schools could be appropriately served in regular classes, were adequate strategies employed.

Nevertheless, observational studies suggest that most regular classrooms are not characterized by the strategies known to be effective with these students (Shores et al., 1993; Strain, Lambert, Kerr, Stagg, & Lenkner, 1983). Very significant changes in what teachers know and do will be required before a majority of regular classroom teachers are prepared to create the minimum conditions necessary for the success of students with behavioral and emotional disorders while also providing an appropriate program for the nondisabled students (Lloyd & Kauffman, 1995).

Knowing what is needed to help students is not the same as being able to provide it. Many teachers, administrators, and mental health workers are frustrated because they do not have the resources to do what they know needs to be done. The resources that are lacking are most often human resources—enough properly trained personnel to allow the time and concentration necessary to address students' problems effectively. There is also a lack of appropriate settings in which intensive, sustained, and often highly personal services can be provided.

In our current research on placement, we have interviewed teachers, administrators, and mental health personnel who provide special programs for students with emotional and behavioral disorders. They have described to us the conditions necessary for helping these students: (a) a critical mass of trained, experienced, and mutually supportive personnel located in close physical proximity to one another and (b) a very low pupil/staff ratio (approximately 5:1 for students in day or residential treatment and 1:1 for the most severely disabled students). Not only are these conditions seldom met, but we suspect that very few school systems, let alone regular classroom teachers, will ever be prepared or willing to accept some students with emotional or behavioral disorders. Consider the difficulty of teaching a regular class while simultaneously addressing the needs of the students described in the following vignettes, which are drawn from our own classroom experience.

> Johnny, a child with emotional and behavioral disorders, is included in a regular second-grade class. He begins the school day by kicking apart the puzzle a girl is assembling on the floor. He then takes another boy's paper and runs around the room tearing it up and laughing, ignoring the teacher's instructions to stop. Told to go to the time-out area, he drops to the floor, kicking, pounding the floor with his fists, and crying loudly. When he refuses to stop this behavior the teacher instructs her other 22 students to follow "Plan A"—stop their activities and return immediately to their desks to read or write independently. The teacher then asks a neighboring teacher to supervise her class while she escorts Johnny to the office. Johnny refuses to leave the classroom, so the teacher summons the principal. Johnny ignores the principal's instruction to follow him to the office, so the teacher and principal physically remove him, screaming, kicking, and crying.

> Matt, a seventh-grader, attends a modified self-contained classroom for students with "serious emotional disturbance" but is included in a regular homeroom and goes to lunch with his regular classroom peers. When in his regular homeroom, Matt is prone to jump onto a desk and, when asked to get down, to leap from desk to desk proclaiming loudly, "You can't catch me!" until flinging himself upon a student below. On one occasion he rigged the wiring of his homeroom's overhead projector so that someone touching the metal casing would receive an electrical shock (his prank was reported to the teacher by another student before anyone was hurt). Matt has torn down the entire ceiling of the rest room, destroyed fixtures, and started fires in the rest room, although he is escorted there and back by a female aide. His inability to handle unstructured time in his homeroom and unsupervised activities elsewhere in the school is a contrast to his successes in the highly structured special class.

Given what we know about effective programming for students with emotional or behavioral disorders, the outlook for public schools' resources in the foreseeable future, and the movement to include all students with disabilities in regular schools and classes, we need to assess the probability that inclusion will produce the results we want. Studies of the inclusion of students with emotional and behavioral disorders indicate that it is indeed an arduous task and that a careful case-by-case approach is the only responsible course of action (Fuchs, Fuchs, Fernstrom, & Hohn, 1991).

At the outset, if we are seriously to consider the placement in regular schools and classes of all students with emotional or behavioral disorders, we must have answers to at least the following questions.

1. How will nondisabled students be affected by the modifications of the regular classroom that are necessary to manage and teach students with emotional and behavioral disorders? Especially, how will the educational and social development of students who need far less classroom control and structure be affected?

2. How will schools justify to parents the placement in regular classrooms of students known to be highly volatile, disruptive, and perhaps violent? Will the physical and psychological safety of other students and the benefits of an orderly learning environment be jeopardized? What are the legal liabilities of school personnel involved in the inclusion of these students?

3. As special schools and classes are eliminated as placement options, what alternatives are most likely to be used for these students? If school personnel are forced to choose between keeping students with emotional and behavioral disorders in regular schools and classes or simply not identifying them for special education so that they can be suspended and expelled, how will these students be guaranteed an appropriate education?

4. What will be the benefits to students with emotional or behavioral disorders of being included in regular classrooms? If they have not previously imitated appropriate peer models or benefited from the instructional program in the regular classroom, what assurances can be given that they will now imitate positive models and benefit from instruction?

5. What training would be sufficient to allow regular classroom teachers to deal with these students? What training will regular classroom teachers be given, when, and by whom?

6. Which teachers will be asked to include more students with emotional and behavioral disorders in their classrooms? Will the most capable teachers be asked to assume a disproportionate share of the responsibility for these students?
7. What additional support services will be provided to regular classroom teachers? Will the necessary number of trained personnel be available before these students are included?
8. How will the success of inclusionary programs be assessed? What criteria will be used to ascertain that inclusion is having positive effects on both nondisabled students and those with emotional and behavioral disorders? What will be done if such criteria are not met?

AN ALTERNATIVE DEFINITION OF INCLUSION

A narrow, highly restrictive definition of inclusion requires that all individuals occupy a common space, regardless of whether that space has the features appropriate for their needs; it assumes that every place can be structured to serve every individual's needs. A more adaptive and humane definition of an inclusive school system is one that allows for a variety of placements that offer the conditions under which every individual feels safe, accepted, and valued and is helped to develop his or her affective and intellectual capacities. Such a definition recognizes that in some cases there will have to be different placements for different individuals.

This is not a new idea but is merely a reiteration of the mandate of the Individuals with Disabilities Education Act of 1990—a law with features that some seem to have ignored (see Bateman & Chard, 1995). Research, the history of human services to people with emotional and behavioral disorders, and personal experience suggest that regular schools and regular classrooms are not now and are extremely unlikely ever to be places in which all students with disabilities experience the conditions described above. The demands on regular classroom teachers' time, the lack of concentrated support personnel, and the severity of children's problems preclude the effective education of some students in regular schools and classrooms (Idstein, 1993). On the other hand, we know that special schools and classes can be made safe, accepting, valuing, and productive environments for these students.

A century ago, overenthusiasm for the institution as the sole placement option for people with disabilities resulted in great injustices and the needless exclusion of many individuals from regular schools and communities. Perhaps overenthusiasm for the regular school and the regular classroom as the sole placement options for students with disabilities has the potential for creating an equal tyranny. While we attempt to make regular schools and classrooms inclusive in the best sense for as many students as possible, we should not be guided by overgeneralizations or become detached from the realities of classroom teaching.

ENDNOTES

1. The terminology "emotional or behavioral disorder" is preferred by the National Mental Health and Special Education Coalition. For discussion, see Forness and Knitzer (1992).
2. For a review and discussion of prevalence studies, see Kauffman (1993).

REFERENCES

Bateman, B. D., & Chard, D. J. (1995). Legal demands and constraints on placement decisions. In J. M. Kauffman, J. W. Lloyd, D. P. Hallahan, & T. A. Astuto (Eds.), *Issues in the educational placement of pupils with emotional or behavioral disorders* (pp. 285–316). Hillsdale, NJ: Erlbaum.

Brandenberg, N. A., Friedman, R. M., & Silver, S. E. (1990). The epidemiology of childhood psychiatric disorders: Prevalence findings from recent studies. *Journal of the American Academy of Child and Adolescent Psychiatry, 29,* 76–83.

Epstein, M. H., Kauffman, J. M., Lloyd, J. W., Cook, L., Cullinan, D., Forness, S. R., et al. (1993). Improving services for students with serious emotional disturbance: Recommended strategies for the 1990s. *NASSP Bulletin, 76*(549), 46–51.

Fecser, F. A. (1993). A model Re-ED classroom for troubled students. *Journal of Emotional and Behavioral Problems, 1,* 15–20.

Forness, S. R., & Knitzer, J. (1992). A new proposed definition and terminology to replace "serious emotional disturbance" in Individuals with Disabilities Education Act. *School Psychology Review, 21*, 12–20.

Fuchs, D., Fuchs, L. S., Fernstrom, P., & Hohn, M. (1991). Toward a possible reintegration of behaviorally disordered students. *Behavioral Disorders, 16*, 133–147.

Gartner, A., & Lipsky, D. K. (1989). *The yoke of special education: How to break it.* Rochester, NY: National Center on Education and the Economy.

Idstein, P. (1993). Swimming against the mainstream. *Phi Delta Kappan, 75*, 336–340.

Institute of Medicine. (1989). *Research on children and adolescents with mental, behavioral and developmental disorders: Mobilizing a national initiative.* Washington, DC: National Academy Press.

Kauffman, J. M. (1993). *Characteristics of emotional and behavioral disorders of children and youth* (5th ed.). Columbus, OH: Merrill/Macmillan.

Knitzer, J. (1982). *Unclaimed children: The failure of public responsibility to children and adolescents in need of mental health services.* Washington, DC: Children's Defense Fund.

Knitzer, J., Steinberg, Z., & Fleisch, B. (1990). *At the schoolhouse door: An examination of programs and policies for children with behavioral and emotional problems.* New York: Bank Street College of Education.

Lloyd, J. W., & Kauffman, J. M. (1995). What less restrictive placements require of teachers. In J. M. Kauffman, J. W. Lloyd, T. A. Astuto, & D. P. Hallahan (Eds.), *Issues in the educational placement of pupils with emotional or behavioral disorders* (pp. 317–334). Hillsdale, NJ: Erlbaum.

Mattison, R. E., & Gamble, A. D. (1992). Seventy socially and emotionally disturbed boys' dysfunction at school and home: Comparison with psychiatric and general population boys. *Behavioral Disorders, 17*, 219–224.

National Association of State Boards of Education (NASBE). (1992, October). *Winners all: A call for inclusive schools.* Alexandria, VA: Author.

National Mental Health Association. (1989). *Final report and recommendations of the Invisible Children Project.* Alexandria, VA: Author.

Peacock Hill Working Group. (1991). Problems and promises in special education and related services for children and youth with emotional or behavioral disorders. *Behavioral Disorders, 16*, 299–313.

Shores, R. E., Jack, S. L., Gunter, P. L., Ellis, D. N., DeBriere, T. J., & Wehby, J. H. (1993). Classroom interactions of children with behavior disorders. *Journal of Emotional and Behavioral Disorders, 1*, 27–39.

Stainback, W., & Stainback, S. (1991). A rationale for integration and restructuring: A synopsis. In J. W. Lloyd, N. N. Singh, & A. C. Repp (Eds.), *The regular education initiative alternative: Perspectives on concepts, issues, and models* (pp. 226–239). Sycamore, IL: Sycamore.

Strain, P. S., Lambert, D. L., Kerr, M. M., Stagg, V., & Lenkner, D. A. (1983). Naturalistic assessment of children's compliance to teachers' requests and consequences for compliance. *Journal of Applied Behavior Analysis, 16*, 243–249.

U.S. Congress, Office of Technology Assessment. (1986, December). *Children's mental health: Problems and services—A background paper* (OTA-BP-H-33). Washington, DC: U.S. Government Printing Office.

U.S. Department of Education. (1994). *To assure the free appropriate public education of all children with disabilities, sixteenth annual report to Congress on the implementation of the Individuals with Disabilities Education Act.* Washington, DC: U.S. Government Printing Office.

CHAPTER 22

Separate and Better: A Special Public School Class for Students with Emotional and Behavioral Disorders

James M. Kauffman, Jeanmarie Bantz, and Jenn McCullough

This chapter is from "Separate and Better: A Special Public School Class for Students with Emotional and Behavioral Disorders," by J. M. Kauffman, J. Bantz, and J. McCullough, 2002, *Exceptionality, 10,* pp. 149–170. Copyright 2002 by Erlbaum. Reprinted with permission.

A current controversy is whether special education is basically sound and needs incremental improvement in practices or needs radical restructuring for inclusion. The rationale for inclusion is summarized. Subsequently, the conceptual orientation underlying a special class for students with emotional or behavioral disorders is articulated, and the implementation of this philosophy in a special class is described. The separate, special class was structured to meet the special needs of students whose behavior made them unwelcome in general education classes. Interviews with school personnel suggested that the class provided an invaluable service that could not be provided in more inclusive arrangements.

A current controversy about special education is whether it is best improved through radical restructuring or incremental improvement of its practices (Andrews et al., 2000). The first point of view typically includes the recommendation that children with disabilities be fully included in general education. The second point of view typically includes the reaffirmation of the wisdom of a full continuum of placement options. Both points of view have typically been presented without clear descriptions of actual classroom practices. Our purpose is to contrast the two ideas and then illustrate our own view—that special education is basically a sound idea that needs incremental improvement—by describing one special class for students with emotional and behavioral disorders.

SPECIAL EDUCATION IS DEEPLY FLAWED AND NEEDS RADICAL RESTRUCTURING

One point of view, which we detail in this section, is that special education is defective in concept and structure (for elaboration, see Danforth & Rhodes, 1997; Gartner & Lipsky, 1987, 1989; Lipsky & Gartner, 1987, 1989,

1991, 1996, 1997; Skrtic, Sailor, & Gee, 1996; S. Stainback & W. Stainback, 1984, 1987, 1992; S. Stainback, W. Stainback, & Forest, 1989; W. Stainback & S. Stainback, 1991). It is defective in concept for this reason: Because it is seen as "special" or "different," it inevitably results in identifying and stigmatizing children and segregating them from their peers without disabilities. It is defective in structure because it is a separate system. As a separate system, it can deliver only second-class services and inferior status to students. The solution to special education's inherent defects is to reconceptualize and restructure it in radical ways.

First, special education needs to be reconceptualized as a service, not a place, and as an integral part of a flexible, supple, responsive part of general education that does not require singling children out for special services. All children should be entitled to whatever services they need, and this kind of education should not require highlighting children's differences. Children must be seen as more alike than different, all entitled to the same high-quality education. What we now see as difference or special must become routine, accepted as part of the normal such that the stigmatization and separation of children is avoided. The needs of all children should be met through the collaboration of general and special education teachers and administrative staff so that there is no need for separate programs for "exceptional" children.

Second, the radical restructuring of special education must result in the fusion of general and special education so that they become a single entity. This fusion will obviate the need for separate, special schools and separate classes. All students will become the responsibility of the regular classroom teacher, and all students will be included in all the aspects and activities of the school community, regardless of their characteristics. Because separate structures and programs are inherently unequal, the only way to guarantee equality for children with disabilities is to include them in the same structures, programs, schools, and classes as those used by children without disabilities.

The rationale for restructuring for inclusion is based on moral values, not research data showing that one model is superior to another in outcomes. Inclusion is motivated by the observation that an equitable society demands equal access—including the equal access of children with disabilities to schools, classrooms, and curricula. This equal access can be achieved only when all children, including those with disabilities, are included in neighborhood schools and regular classes, taking their rightful places alongside their neighbors and peers who have not been identified as having disabilities.

SPECIAL EDUCATION IS BASICALLY SOUND BUT NEEDS INCREMENTAL IMPROVEMENT OF ITS PRACTICES

An alternative view, and that from which we have written the remainder of this article, is that special education does not need to be radically restructured or reconceptualized, but its basic structure and concepts need to be reaffirmed if it is to become what it should be for students with disabilities (for elaboration, see Crockett & Kauffman, 1999, 2001; D. Fuchs & L. S. Fuchs, 1994; Hockenbury, Kauffman, & Hallahan, 1999–2000; Kauffman, 1989, 1993, 1994, 1999a, 1999b, 1999c, 2001; Kauffman & Hallahan, 1993, 1997; Kavale & Forness, 2000; MacMillan, Gresham, & Forness, 1996). The success of special education in providing appropriate schooling for students with disabilities is not as dependent on the collaboration of general and special educators as it is on incremental improvement of the quality of academic and social instruction provided by special educators (i.e., on better implementation of special instruction, such that students with disabilities are exposed to more competent, intensive, and sustained instruction). At the heart of the current controversy about special education is the observation and interpretation of human differences, and special educators must understand the meanings and appropriate responses to these differences. Our contention is that some children's differences require distinctive (and, therefore, separate) places for instruction if their educational needs are to be met and, consequently, that separate placements can be superior to inclusive placements for these children. Thus, we begin by addressing issues of difference and our responses to it. Subsequently, we describe a special education program in which our views of difference were implemented.

The Nature and Meanings of Differences Among Children

The basic question posed by science and other forms of inquiry is the question of difference. With regard to children's exceptionalities and the consequences of what we do about them, the observation of, meaning of, and responses to difference are the substance of special education and related disciplines. Understanding the meaning of difference is the first requirement of our science and our advocacy as special educators, as Hungerford (1950) noted long ago. Science and advocacy are both related to culture. Consequently, we preface further remarks about exceptionality with a statement about cultural contexts.

Anyone who responds to questions about children's exceptionalities does so from a point of view grounded in a cultural context. These viewpoints may be called *biases,* but judgments or values cannot be made without them. We recognize that our biases or views will not be shared by all persons, and we understand that we may sometimes need to revise some of our views. Again, we assume that this is true of all people, regardless of their culture. Our "we" is not inclusive of every individual, although our "we" might be taken to represent the opinions of many, or perhaps even most, people in some cases. We see the danger in being blunt about our views. Nevertheless, the failure to be straightforward for fear of offending others is often the beginning of the end of communication. We hope to be clear but not offensive or needlessly contentious in communicating our views.

Cultural differences are important, and they are exhibited in great variety. Our American society has come to understand the value of many types of cultural differences and the necessity of honoring many cultural traditions if our society is to be truly free and humane. Thus, many cultural differences that were previously rejected, prohibited, or treated with contempt by some members of our society are now recognized as not just harmless or tolerable, but helpful, honorable, and worthy of perpetuation. Many of these cultural differences are associated with ethnicity, national origin, religion, sexual orientation, or multiculturalism. What has come to be known as *cultural competence* demands that these differences be honored.

Nevertheless, the fact that something is "cultural" does not justify or sanctify it. Every culture has its flaws, its dark side, its ways of treating others that are unacceptable in or inimical to a just and free society. After all, human slavery and the social rules or traditions known as *Jim Crow* were claimed as cultural traditions, as have been many other degradations of human beings based on their ethnicity, tribal affiliation, gender, color, national origin, religion, sexual orientation, or other characteristics. Moreover, behavior that is "cultural" is sometimes confused with behavior that represents a disorder; cultural difference is sometimes mistakenly identified as a disorder, and vice versa. Therefore, it is critically important to recognize that cultural identification and justification taken to the extreme become destructive ideologies and that "there are actions between nations, as between individuals, which cannot be tolerated" (Conquest, 2000, p. 68; see also Shattuck, 1999).

The Nature of Differences Called "Emotional or Behavioral Disorders"

We have chosen to focus on emotional or behavioral disorders because our task is to explain how the theory, philosophy, or principles we embrace might be implemented in an educational program for children with these disorders. Rather than dealing only in generalities about exceptionality, difference, and special education, we include specifics of how a special class was organized and taught in ways that illustrate best practices within our framework of thinking about broader theoretical, philosophical issues. For elaboration of that framework, see the works by Kauffman or Kauffman and colleagues cited previously (much of this introductory discussion of difference follows the ideas of Kauffman, 1999c).

To us, some of the views expressed about the differences called *emotional or behavioral disorders* are disquieting. The idea that these differences should be viewed as normal or tolerable, if not completely acceptable, strikes us as disingenuous at best and incompatible with prevention and encouraging of social maladjustment at worst (see Kauffman, 1999b). Behavior that is a disorder cannot be tolerated without serious risk, either to others in the environment, to the child himself or herself, or to both. Emotional or behavioral disorders are differences that threaten or foreclose the child's options for self-fulfillment, including the establishment of mutually positive relationships with others.

Sometimes our efforts to help students with emotional or behavioral disorders fall short of our intentions and hopes. Our failures are often extremely discouraging. Perhaps it is predictable that some people would rather ignore such disorders or explain them away than persist in confronting them for what they are and take preventive action. At present— and we believe this will be true for a long time to come—we have imperfect understanding and limited ability to change children whose behavior is persistently problematic. The problems of these children convince some people that we should abandon questions about how such children differ behaviorally from what is normal and how we can change them. Yet, recognizing the psychosocial characteristics of these children as abnormal and changing these characteristics is our business. We recognize that we need to change both the children and their environments, but if our efforts produce no changes in the children we serve, then we will not be successful. We understand also that we do not want to change everything about these children, but whenever we can, we want to change the characteristics that limit the child's options in life.

Changing children's behavioral characteristics is now seen as trivial or inappropriate by some educators. Some deny the reality or significance of behavioral differences. The denial that behavioral differences are real and important may be expressed by the opinion that the child with an emotional or a behavioral disorder is just another kid or that similarities among children are more important than differences (see W. Stainback & S. Stainback, 1991). Some persons also note that emotional and behavioral disorders are social constructs, as if this fact destroys the reality or importance of these disorders (see Biklen, 1989; Danforth & Rhodes, 1997). Never mind that all virtues, vices, arts, and languages—even childhood itself—are social constructions and that children are now often tried and imprisoned as adults, in part because the concept of childhood itself is questioned as a social construction (see Talbot, 2000).

Other educators suggest that all behavioral differences are enriching and enlivening, as if all such differences are of equal value, none to be desired over another and none to be avoided or eliminated, even if doing so is possible (see Council for Exceptional Children, 1997). Still other persons maintain that no behavioral difference should be seen as a deficit, that such differences should be welcomed as bonuses, that we should speak not of the risk of failure but only of the promise of development. These individuals may complain of "deficit thinking." The implication seems to be that behavioral deficiencies can be turned into strengths simply by refusing to think of differences as deficiencies or by altering the social policies in which certain differences are defined as deficits (see Valencia, 1997).

The people who deny difference seem to value it without discrimination. Some of these people urge us to see difference as ordinary, to assume that exceptionality is the rule (e.g., Biklen, 1989). However, thinking about difference in this way is either self-contradictory or an expression of equal value for all differences. Some people reject the idea that emotional or behavioral disorders exist in individuals and support "a philosophy that opposes and subverts the disability construct" (Danforth & Rhodes, 1997, p. 357), as if deconstruction eliminates disability. Their assumption seems to be that reality can be constructed in nearly any way we want. To us, these ideas are associated with helplessness and hopelessness, resignation and depression. If we adopt this view, then we see little reason to do anything but ignore emotional or behavioral disorders, deny them, or, because they are only in the eye of the beholder, just "get over" them. At best, we will begin to view ourselves as the problem rather than recognizing that the child's behavior is the problem, which does not augur well for the child. This view suggests that data do not matter (Landrum, 1997), that they are merely a pretext for any convenient narrative, or that truth is no better apprehended by scientific investigation than by any other means, and that education cannot be based on reliable scientific evidence (see Carnine, 2000; Koertge, 1998; Sagan, 1996). Deconstructivism and related "postmodern" philosophies may appear to promote equality among ideas, but ultimately they create intolerance and tribalism by pitting individuals and groups against each other because there are no universal truths that grant power—except, ironically, the absence of universal truth (see Kauffman, 1999a; Koertge, 1998; Shattuck, 1999; Sokal & Bricmont, 1998). Thus, what may be dissembled is not merely the construct of disability but the possibility of tolerance of differences that cannot be changed and of effective treatment of emotional and behavioral differences that are debilitating.

Some people have suggested that a disability is a gift or a blessing (Council for Exceptional Children, 1997). One Virginia gubernatorial candidate referred in his political campaign to "my sister Kathy, who is blessed with a mental retardation disability" (Beyer, 1997, p. 1). Such language may be mere gibberish, or it could be used to justify bestowing the "blessings" or "gifts" of disabilities on others or to justify failure to offer effective intervention in disabilities when doing so is possible. In any case, we find referral to disabilities as "gifts" or "blessings" a chilling use of language, especially in light of Gelernter's (1997) statement that "When you are trying to figure out how a society thinks and feels, words are the surest route to the truth" (p. 10).

To us, there is a profound difference between seeing a *person* with a disability as a gift or a blessing and seeing his or her *disability* as a blessing. We are reminded of the scripture "What man is there of you, whom if his son ask bread, will he give him a stone? Or if he ask a fish, will he give him a serpent?" (Matthew 7:9–10; King James Version). Some people seem to confuse good things and bad, seem to be willing to let others eat stones and pretend they are bread. We do not want to be so confused that we would as soon celebrate the gift of disability as give the gift of teaching. We want to see clearly the difference between the stone of "being there" and the bread of learning critical skills. Failure to make the distinction is a moral catastrophe.

We start with this proposition: Special educators are in the business of measuring and then changing children. This means enhancing their development. If we do not measure and change the children we serve, then we are truly derelict in our duty. We realize that some special educators may reject this premise, perhaps suggesting that to measure children is to label and categorize them, that we do not want to change children but social ecologies, especially our own view of disabilities as undesirable differences. However, the idea that we can change children without changing ourselves is as simpleminded as the view that changing the social ecology does not change the children.

To be successful in educating children with emotional and behavioral disorders, we have to change two things at once: ourselves and the children with whom we work. We ourselves must become more competent in instruction and more understanding of the lives of children in and out of school. We must also become more tolerant of undesirable differences that cannot be changed and more nurturing of children's culture and uniqueness, so long as these characteristics do not shorten children's developmental horizons. We want the children we work with to become more typical, more normal in their social behavior and their academic abilities. Otherwise, we consign our students to greater handicaps.

Eventually, we have to question why we value human beings. Clearly, we do not want a child's worth to be measured only by what he or she can do, but neither is what a child can do a trivial matter. In a just and humane society, people are not valued for what they can do, but their ability to do certain things is valued. After all, if we do not value what people can do, then we have no reason to teach anyone anything. We value what people can do because of what accomplishment does for them, the additional opportunities it brings them. Being able to do certain things does not make our students better people, but it does make them people who are better off.

At the dawn of the 21st century, our society is infatuated with diversity, unwilling to tell the difference between what matters and what does not for a particular social purpose (see Gelernter, 1997; Glazer, 1997). Although as a consequence of our views we may reap the scorn or hostility of some people, we who work with children who have emotional or behavioral disorders must not tolerate all differences gladly. We hope to make a difference in the lives of children and their families in ways that contradict the conventional wisdom of many of our contemporaries, who claim to value diversity indiscriminately and reject as false or trivial the normative measures and expectations of behavior that is adaptive in the broader American culture. We suggest that teachers should love and foster some differences, but not all differences. Some differences teachers should not be concerned about; still others they should try to reduce or eliminate. They should value children's acquiring the skills that typical children acquire, the social and academic abilities that make children with emotional or behavioral disorders less easily distinguishable from the norm. This is to say that teachers should value students' learning adaptive behavior and the reduction of maladaptive behavior. Teachers should value faster positive changes, more than slower growth, in adaptive behavior and academic skills.

Of course, the question for practice is this: How can these ideas be put into practice? In the next section, we provide an example of one special class in which these foundational ideas were put into practice. We do not claim that this one example is a full and complete explanation of all the philosophical positions that we have articulated. However, the operation of the class is consistent with what we have said to this point.

An ongoing debate in special education has revolved around the "least restrictive environment" provisions of the Individuals with Disabilities Education Act (IDEA). The law requires school districts to educate students with disabilities as closely as possible with students without disabilities (Yell, 1998b). From this requirement has emerged the philosophy of *inclusion,* which is essentially considered a movement to merge general and special education, so that all students are taught in general education classrooms (Turnbull, Turnbull, Shank, & Leal, 1995). Proponents of full inclusion assert that the least restrictive environment for all children must be the general education classroom within the neighborhood school (e.g., Lipsky & Gartner, 1987; W. Stainback & S. Stainback, 1991; Wang, Reynolds, & Walberg, 1988) and that separate placements—ranging from part-time "pullout" programs to self-contained classes and separate schools—are clearly unjust, if not illegal. Often, the ideological basis for this argument stems from the comparison of educational grouping on any basis to the morally repudiated and long-outlawed American policy of segregation by race in public schooling. As Kauffman and Hallahan (1993) noted, the idea that separate education is inherently unequal is used "to justify [wrongly] the conclusion that grouping children for instruction based on their performance is ... inherently unequal, particularly when children differing in performance are instructed in different classrooms" (p. 79).

Indeed, "the educational rights of exceptional children and those of ethnic minorities rest on the same foundation, namely, that children's characteristics must not be used as justification for unfair treatment" (Kauffman & Hallahan, 1993, p. 79). However, the difference between these two types of segregation lies in the fact that ethnicity (a group identity) is a variable presumably irrelevant to the instructional needs of a student, whereas academic ability and performance are variables directly related to the selection and delivery of appropriate instruction (Kauffman, 1989). Educational decision making for students with disabilities must be based on the principles of individualization and appropriateness, not on group identity (Yell, 1998b). Moreover, full inclusion is indefensible conceptually and legally (IDEA; Crockett & Kauffman, 1999). According to Yell (1998b), "To make a placement decision that all students will be in the general education classroom is just as illegal as placing all students with disabilities in special schools" (p. 73).

In fact, separate education may be unequal in some sense, but the education offered in a separate setting may address the needs of students with disabilities better than any that can be offered in general education (see Carpenter & Bovair, 1996; Milloy, 2001; and Chapter 8 of this book). General education—not the place of education—is by definition inappropriate and inferior for some students with disabilities, even on a legal basis (Dupre, 1997). Special education, to which students with disabilities are entitled by law, can sometimes but not always be delivered in the context of a general education classroom. Indeed, the question of which educational services are required must precede questions of where they should be required (Crockett & Kauffman, 1999; Yell, 1998a).

A CASE IN POINT

We next describe a program designed for a self-contained special education classroom for students with emotional and behavioral disorders. The second author developed this program during her 12 years of teaching and adapted it, with the help of the third author, for use in this setting. We explain how and why this classroom was not merely a separate place but a better place for these students, for whom general education had failed. First, we describe in detail the major operational features of the program and their empirical basis. Second, we provide student outcome information and interview data indicative of the program's benefits to the students. We conclude with reflections on some of the contextual factors that facilitated the program's success, as well as goals for improving and enhancing the program in the future.

Description of the Program

Students and Teachers

Students in the self-contained special education classroom for the 1997–1998 school year were fifth and sixth graders ranging in age from 10 years, 10 months to 13 years, 4 months. The school in which the class was housed was a public upper elementary school (fifth and sixth grades only) in a medium-sized town in the southeastern United States. Most of these students had been receiving special education services from very early in their school careers, and all the students participated in the free-lunch program, which typically indicates low socioeconomic status. Three students had been diagnosed as having attention-deficit/hyperactivity disorder (ADHD) and used medication (Ritalin). Student achievement levels varied widely as indicated by standardized test scores. Of the 12 students, 9 were African American and 3 were White. Student demographic information is summarized in Table 22.1.

For the second consecutive year, the previously separate fifth- and sixth-grade self-contained special education teachers had agreed to combine their classes and implement a team-teaching model for instruction. The special self-contained class would therefore consist of 12 students taught by two special education teachers with the help of two educational assistants, an adult-per-child ratio that is not typical but may be required to provide the education such children need. This arrangement allowed greater flexibility for instructional grouping, readily available adult assistance in crisis situations, opportunities for observation and discussion of one another's instructional and behavior management decisions, sharing of classroom facilities and resources, and the ability to foster a sense of group cohesiveness.

Program Philosophy of Lead Teacher

The lead teacher was strongly influenced during her early years of teaching by the philosophy of Nicholas Hobbs (e.g., Hobbs, 1982). Hobbs's emphasis on five factors—the adult–child relationship; the importance of success and competence for children; the powerful influence of the group; the necessity of order, routine, and ceremony; and the value of joy in the classroom—inspired her to incorporate these elements into her personal teaching philosophy. In addition, her powerful stance against violence and for compassion toward all living things has influenced her teaching. In an effort to teach students the foundation on which the classroom was built and to involve them in formulating some of the rules, routines, and policies

TABLE 22.1
Student Characteristics

ID No.	Gender	Ethnicity	Age[a]	Grade	Identified Disability	Entered Sp. Ed.[b]	WIAT Standard Scores		
							Reading	Writing	Math
1	M	W	10, 10	5	SED	K	117	92	119
2	F	AA	11, 5	5	SED	Pre-K	89	86	91
3	F	AA	11, 6	5	SED	4	75	85	93
4	F	AA	11, 10	6	OHI	Pre-K	82	71	84
5	M	AA	11, 10	6	SED/LD	1	99	94	95
6	F	AA	12, 1	6	SED/SLI	5	78	79	71
7	M	W	12, 1	6	SED	Pre-K	66	82	84
8	M	AA	12, 8	6	SED	4	99	108	84
9	M	AA	12, 10	6	LD/SLI	1	78	92	78
10	M	AA	12, 10	6	OHI	Pre-K	60	60	78
11	F	AA	13, 4	6	SED	3	70	70	76
12	M	W	13, 4	6	OHI	K	84	75	85

Note. WIAT = Wechsler Individual Achievement Test; Sp. Ed. = special education; W = White; AA = African American; SED = seriously emotionally disturbed; OHI = other health impaired; LD = learning disabled; SLI = speech/language impaired.

[a]Age as of 1998 (years, months).

[b]Grade in which student was first identified as eligible for special education services.

that would allow building on that foundation, the teachers started each school year by developing a *class creed* expressing a shared vision of the ideal classroom environment. Recent authors who have done extensive research in classrooms have supported this idea (e.g., Curwin & Mendler, 2000; Van Acker, 2000). Depending on the age and maturity of the students, the teachers either developed the creed with the students or presented it to stimulate discussion of the principles it expressed. In the upper elementary school where the lead teacher taught in 1997–1998, her self-contained room's class creed was eventually adopted by the entire school and taught in all classrooms. The class creed that year read as follows:

> As a member of this class, I promise to respect all people, even though they may be different from me, to take learning seriously, and to allow others to learn; to solve problems without violence; to be honest and to earn the trust of others; to accept responsibility for the choices that I make. When I do these things, I will help to make our classroom a place where people feel safe, respected, and challenged to learn.

This statement was not only displayed prominently in the classroom but also actively taught—through having discussions, modeling, presenting examples and nonexamples, using role playing, engaging in cooperative activities, and implementing strategy instruction—and used as a common language in mediation and problem solving and as the basis for establishing new rules and classroom policies. The use of direct-teaching, practice, and generalization activities such as these is strongly supported in the social skills training literature (e.g., Goldstein, 1988; McGinnis & Goldstein, 1984; Walker et al., 1983; Walker, Todis, Holmes, & Horton, 1988).

For example, in efforts to create a nonviolent environment, the teachers established the policy that violence, even in its mildest forms, would not be permitted. Therefore, talking, drawing, or writing about guns, fights, violent movies or games, killing (even as it pertained to animals), violent sports (like professional wrestling), or anything else that contained elements of violence were not permitted at school. The teachers did not tolerate nonverbal threats, such as "bucking up" (jutting chin, chest thrust forward) or tones of voice suggesting intimidation, even if the verbal content was acceptable (e.g., "What did you say?" spoken in an intimidating way). Even seemingly innocuous cartoon decals on T-shirts were banned if the message could be considered potentially threatening (e.g., a Sylvester and Tweety shirt with the wording "You better get out of my face, or else!"). Recently, early intervention and elimination of low-level violence has gained increasing attention in response to the highly publicized school shootings in this country (e.g., Goldstein, 2000; Johns, 2000). According to Johns, "Within our classroom and our school we can no longer turn a blind eye to *any* form of aggression ... [Therefore], we must model a no-tolerance approach for aggression, eliminating violence in its earliest stages" (p. 30).

Instruction

According to Kauffman, Mostert, Trent, and Hallahan (1998), when a teacher is experiencing behavior problems in the classroom, the first question he or she should ask in an attempt to find the source of the problem is, "Could this problem be a result of inappropriate curriculum or teaching strategies?" (p. 5). Well aware of the importance of using empirically based methods like teacher-directed instruction (Engelmann & Carnine, 1991; Nelson, Johnson, & Marchand-Martella, 1996; Porter & Brophy, 1988; Wehby, Symons, Canale, & Go, 1998; White, 1988) and cognitive strategy instruction (Deshler, Ellis, & Lenz, 1996; Wood, Woloshyn, & Willoughby, 1995), the teachers employed these methods consistently in all subject areas. The team-teaching arrangement allowed as many as four instructional groups to be operating simultaneously under the direction of one of the adults. Independent worksheet activities were kept to a minimum and used only as a means for practicing already-learned skills, as suggested by the literature (see Gunter, Hummel, & Conroy, 1998). In addition, hard-to-measure qualities like teacher energy, enthusiasm, affect, sense of humor, and creativity in creating lessons undoubtedly enhanced the academic engagement and investment of the students. The atmosphere in the room was one of serious learning, just as the class creed emphasized. Indeed, to the best of their abilities, the teachers provided instruction that was "more urgent, more intensive, more relentless, more precisely delivered, more highly structured and direct, and more carefully monitored for procedural fidelity and effects" (Kauffman, 1996, p. 206) than that which would have been available to these students in general education.

Classroom Management

The keys to the success of the management systems used in the classroom were (a) the abundance of positive interactions and opportunities that far outweighed the need for reprimands or punishment, (b) the "catch-it-early" approach that facilitated the prevention of problem behaviors before they escalated, and (c) the teachers' efforts to address not only inappropriate behavior but also the context and culture that serves to maintain it (see Kauffman, 1999b; Manno, Bantz, & Kauffman, 2000, for elaboration).

No individual can complete a teacher preparation program or attend a professional conference without hearing about the importance of positive reinforcement in the classroom. Yet, research suggests that most teachers use far more reprimands and reductive strategies than praise and positive procedures (Gunter, Denny, Jack, Shores, & Nelson, 1993; Gunter, Jack, DePaepe, Reed, & Harrison, 1994; Jack et al., 1996; Shores et al., 1993; Wehby et al., 1998). The effective instruction literature recommends that positive teacher–student interactions outnumber those that are negative by a ratio of at least 3:1 (see Gunter et al., 1998). In the special classroom, students were given frequent opportunities for correct academic responding, appropriate behavior was consistently recognized, and students were engaged in numerous enjoyable activities that precluded the need for escape, avoidance, and acting-out behaviors.

Reductive procedures such as time-out or disciplinary referrals to the office are necessarily predicated on the fact that the classroom is a reinforcing place to be; thus, removal from it is unpleasant. The area in which most teachers fall short in trying to use these techniques is in creating a positive classroom environment that causes students to want to be there. Students in the self-contained class frequently told the teachers that they loved coming to school, and parents often reported noticing significant changes in their children's attitudes toward school. One parent noted that for years she had battled her son every morning about going to school, but for the first time, he left the house willingly and came home to report enthusiastically on the day's events. Comments and perceptions such as these indicated that the special class was a positive environment.

In a global sense, schools in this country have established and maintained a reactive and punitive approach to discipline problems. Office referrals, suspension, and expulsion remain the predominant means of dealing with serious misbehavior (Bear, 1998), even though these strategies may actually exacerbate the problem and increase student misbehavior (Lewis & Garrison-Harrell, 1999; Mayer, 1995; Skiba & Peterson, 2000). The teachers knew that their students needed to be at school—away from the environment that, more often than not, contributed to their antisocial behavior—and immersed in a supportive and carefully monitored environment, where the skills they needed to avoid repeating problem behaviors were actively being taught, modeled, practiced, and reinforced. Therefore, the teachers did not use office referrals or suspensions as consequences for misbehavior; instead, they chose to handle behavior problems within the classroom, where they could administer appropriate and meaningful consequences, engage the student in problem solving and reflection, and teach replacement behaviors to avoid recurrences. Furthermore, because the strength of the school social bond is an important factor in avoiding delinquency, the teachers' goal was to reinforce this bond and steer clear of exclusionary practices that would serve only to weaken it (Jenkins, 1997).

Another key to the smooth operation of the special classroom was the teachers' commitment to catching misbehavior at its earliest stages, avoiding escalation, and reducing the need for more intrusive interventions. Research suggests that a systematic response to low levels of misbehavior can effectively reduce coercive interactions and maintain appropriate behavior by intervening early in the chain of events (see Cypress Group, 1996; Kauffman, 1999b; Nelson, 1996). The teachers' three-tiered cooldown system (see Table 22.2) was consistent with this model. The lowest level, or green cooldown, was used liberally as a means of interrupting a behavior chain that could potentially escalate. Students were taught to initiate green cooldowns themselves when they were able to recognize their own agitation or anticipate a problem in the making. Cooldown was presented as a tool that even adults use when they need to remove themselves from a stressful situation. A green cooldown consisted of 2 minutes at a desk away from the group, where the student was still able to observe classroom activities. The higher levels of cooldown, yellow and red, were used when a green cooldown was not successful. Cooldowns always (with one exception, to be explained in the next paragraph) began at the green level and increased in length, degree of separation from the group, and significance of the consequence that followed as the level increased from green to yellow to red. In other words, students had much to gain by resolving their problem immediately, without argument, and before their misbehavior became serious. Again, because the students wanted to be a part of the class and were motivated to participate in group activities, removal from the group was sufficiently unpleasant to serve as a deterrent to misbehavior. Often, students would encourage another student to take a hassle-free cooldown and would remind him or her that he or she would be able to return more quickly if he or she cooperated.

The only exception to the progressive nature of the cooldown system was when the misbehavior was considered a serious offense. Serious offenses, which resulted in an automatic red cooldown, included being physically aggressive, making threats, destroying property, and leaving the

TABLE 22.2

Procedures for Cooldown

Level	Length	Requirements	Consequences
Green	2 min.	Self- or teacher-directed. Taken at cooldown desk. May return to group immediately.	Self-directed = no point loss; teacher-directed = −1 point
Yellow	5 min.	Teacher-directed if green is unsuccessful. Taken at cooldown desk. Automatic yellow after two greens in the same period. May return to group with permission.	−2 points
Red	10 min.	Teacher-directed if yellow is unsuccessful. Taken in cooldown room. Automatic red after two yellows in the same period. Automatic red for a serious offense. May return to group after medication.	Minus all 5 points for period. Must make reparations if needed. Must make up all work missed.

classroom without permission. These behaviors were clearly defined, with very distinct lines drawn between occurrence and nonoccurrence. For example, physical aggression included hitting, pushing and shoving, throwing an object (even a pencil), and more intense displays of aggressive behavior. Threats could be verbal (e.g., "How about if I show you what I mean?") or gestural (e.g., "bucking up" or punching the air). Destruction of property included any attempt to damage or destroy (e.g., intentionally knocking over a chair or kicking a wall). These very concrete definitions for potentially serious misbehaviors allowed the teachers to avoid arguing over details, as well as to "catch [aggression] low to prevent it high" (Goldstein, 2000). Most red cooldowns resulted in 10 minutes away from the group and a substantial point or privilege loss for the student, but did not escalate further. Although there were times when the teachers were unable to intervene early enough or to de-escalate student behavior, the frequency of such events requiring more intrusive interventions decreased steadily throughout the school year.

Although the proactive cooldown procedures were especially effective in reducing classroom behavior problems and in increasing students' use of prosocial problem-solving strategies, they were by no means the only class-room management strategies used. Classroom management is referred to as a *system* because the combination of and interaction among various re-search-supported practices and procedures are essential to their effective-ness. For. example, use of the Premack principle (Premack, 1959) to design the class schedule, a response-cost point system (Rhode, Jenson, & Reavis, 1992) to determine access to privileges, and a classroom level system (Kerr & Nelson, 1998) to monitor long-term progress each played a role in the success of the program. However, it is beyond the scope of this article to explain in detail the application of all these principles and approaches.

An important point to note is that none of the strategies discussed pre-viously would have been effective if implemented haphazardly. Ongoing training, continuous communication and evaluation of decisions, and consistent adherence to the management systems by all members of the team were essential. Furthermore, because students were able to learn and to understand the procedures used, they were better able to anticipate the consequences (positive or negative) of their actions—a necessary condi-tion for teaching students self-control and responsible decision making.

Context and Culture

For many years, professionals who work with antisocial youth believed that most of these students experienced peer rejection because of their deviant behaviors. However, recent research into the social dynamics of classrooms and schools suggests that many of these students tend to associate with sim-ilarly deviant peers, who help support and maintain one another's antisocial tendencies (see Farmer, Farmer, & Gut, 1999; Kamps, Kravits, Stolze, & Swaggart, 1999). Therefore, intervention efforts with these youth require attention not only to specific problem behaviors but also to the social context of these behaviors, which may be supporting them (Kauffman & Burbach, 1997). For many students with behavior problems, their acting-out behav-iors may be the mechanisms through which they gain power and status, especially among their deviant peers (Farmer et al., 1999). A self-contained classroom for students with emotional and behavioral problems, then, is particularly at risk for becoming a microculture in which inappropriate behavior is reinforced; alternatively, a special, separate environment can be structured, as Hobbs (1982) suggested, to support positive behavioral change. One of the most difficult but, at the same time, most important tasks the teachers faced was finding ways to alter the beliefs and values of the entire classroom social context so that problem behavior was not val-ued and so that students who engaged in it did not hold high status.

Dismantling the existing social context of the classroom and transforming it into one that values and maintains prosocial behavior required a tremendous amount of effort. First, the teachers focused on creating a richly reinforcing environment where students saw and learned that appropriate behavior consistently brought desirable outcomes for them. The students learned that life was good when they behaved appropriately. Recognition of appropriate behavior and hard work was an important part of many of the classroom ceremonies, such as advancement on the level system or daily "positives" time, when students and teachers exchanged positive comments about themselves and other members of the group.

Second, by using a catch-it-early philosophy to stop teasing, put-downs, and other disrespectful behavior instantly, the teachers consistently conveyed the message that these behaviors would be actively addressed in the classroom, not simply ignored by adults and reinforced by peers, as is typically the case in general education settings. This tactic had the additional effect of creating an environment where students truly felt safe and were more likely to take good risks and to experiment with newly learned prosocial behaviors. Simultaneously, the teachers invested a great deal of time and energy into teaching children to ignore a student (in cooldown) who was not acting appropriately and not to join in and contribute to the problem. Teachers were always prepared with backup lessons that were flexible enough to allow relocating or combining smaller instructional groups to allow instruction to continue despite serious disruption from another student.

Third, the teachers incorporated into their program a wide array of alternative sources of reinforcement to counter the reinforcement that the students were accustomed to receiving by engaging in antisocial activities. Mattaini, Twyman, Chin, and Lee (1996) noted that without rich alternative sources of reinforcement for productive behavior, an intervention designed to reduce misbehavior is likely to fail. The lives of many students outside school provided few, if any, opportunities to gain reinforcement from activities other than antisocial or violent behavior, which in turn increased the value of the only reinforcement available. Therefore, a vital component of the program was providing these alternative sources, both in and out of school. For example, the teachers planned monthly field trips for the entire class, as well as after-school outings, which were accessible to only higher level students. Outings consisted of social and recreational activities, like bowling, swimming, go-cart racing, and college basketball games. In the spring, the teachers established a class running club, members of which had the opportunity to run (or walk) 1 mile before school started every morning. As students accumulated miles with time, they earned items like water bottles, personal hygiene kits, team T-shirts, and individual trophies. In addition, the group went "camping" together twice each year. The first "trip" was actually an overnight stay at school. The teachers and students cooked and served their own meals, set up tents in the classroom, and participated in various activities, some of which included guest appearances by teachers and school administrators or other members of the community. An end-of-year camping trip was held at the lead teacher's house, which was situated on the side of a mountain. It began with a hike in the Blue Ridge Mountains, a pretend campfire, and a variety of cooperative games. The event culminated the next morning with swimming at a nearby lake. After each special event, each student received several photographs to be kept in an album of school memories. All these activities represent only a sample of the numerous ways the teachers attempted to enrich students' lives and expose them to alternative sources of enjoyment and reinforcement for positive behaviors and hard work.

Student Outcomes

An overwhelming challenge the teachers faced while they were implementing and maintaining this intense intervention program was the accurate collection of academic and behavioral data. Although the staff kept consistent records for each student on (a) attendance, (b) daily points earned, (c) advancement on the level system, (d) frequencies of red cooldowns and serious offenses, and (e) formal and informal academic assessments, they were never able to compile these data and analyze them regularly in a meaningful way. However, certain apparent trends are worth mentioning.

First, and probably foremost, all students in the special class maintained school attendance either at a high level or a significantly improved level. A major factor in improving attendance outcomes was that the teachers did not use office referrals as a consequence for misbehavior; therefore, students in the class were not suspended or otherwise excluded from school for behaviors that occurred in the classroom. In fact, the small number of disciplinary referrals that the students in the special class did receive (six for the entire year) were the result of behavior on the bus or possession of weapons, for which the school administration believed that a more publicly visible consequence was necessary.

Second, students' use of the cooldown system was evident by a tendency for red cooldowns and serious incidents to decrease with time. This finding suggests that students were using the lower tiers of the cooldown system to interrupt their acting-out behavior before it escalated to the level of a serious offense.

Third, the level system appeared to provide a strong incentive for the students to maintain appropriate and responsible behavior with time, because all students in the class advanced steadily, if not quickly, through the levels. Because greater freedom and improved privileges awaited students at the higher levels, the level system helped create a status system in the classroom—one that afforded benefits to students who engaged in prosocial behavior and strived for academic improvement.

Perceptions of School Personnel

Because the teachers had a very different kind of class within a regular public school, they were also interested in how others viewed the program and its value to the school and to the students. With the help of a graduate student from the University of Virginia, the teachers obtained interviews from school personnel—other teachers, administrators, and support staff—to obtain their perceptions. Twelve members of the school volunteered to participate in the semistructured interviews that lasted an average of 20 minutes and were tape-recorded. The interviews contained open-ended, exploratory questions and a few categorical questions.

The transcriptions were analyzed by first identifying categories by using a method of qualitative analysis suggested by Erikson (1986). The categories emerged from the participants' responses and typically used participant language. After each interview was coded for categories, assertions were developed and verified by systematically checking for disconfirming evidence. In some cases, not all the participants specifically addressed the assertion, but they did not provide conflicting statements, either, so these assertions were considered valid. A summary of the interviewees' responses is provided in Table 22.3.

Contextual Factors

As we reflect on the special class program at this particular school, we realize that the context in which the teachers worked contributed greatly to its success. The support that the teachers received from both the building-level and the district-level administrations enabled them to carry out their

TABLE 22.3

Summary of Interviews with School Personnel

1. All participants noted anger management or lack of self-control as the differentiating factor between students in this class and the general education population.

2. All participants were familiar with the program. One third of the participants were very familiar.

3. The participants stated that the self-contained environment allowed the teachers to provide a highly structured, individualized education that addressed the unusual needs of the students. In addition, the participants believed that the self-contained setting provided an internal support system for the teachers and staff.

4. Most respondents thought that without this placement these students would not be able to learn nor would their specific emotional and behavioral needs be met. Further, the amount of time, energy, and resources these students demanded would place an excessive burden on the general educator and ultimately affect the education of students in the mainstream classes.

5. None of the respondents thought that these students could be served in the general education setting. Seven of 12 believed that the students would end up in an alternative setting. The other 5 believed that even if the students were placed in a general education setting, they would spend their time out of the classroom or not learning. About half the respondents stated that the learning that occurs in the self-contained class could not be replicated in another setting.

6. When questioned about their perceptions of the academic abilities of these students, none of the respondents assumed the students would necessarily be having great academic difficulty. Those who were familiar with the students believed there was a wide range of reading and math ability levels in the class. More of the respondents believed that writing was especially difficult for these students. However, behavioral needs were not assumed by the general education teachers to be related to academic needs.

7. Although most respondents thought that these students had a lot of trouble getting along with others—a typical characteristic of students with emotional and behavioral disorders—a few believed that the intense focus in this class on remediating those deficits left the students better equipped to deal with others.

8. Most respondents indicated that "taking care of themselves" was difficult for these students. However, some of the respondents believed that because of the challenging home environments of many of the students, they were often "forced" to take on more responsibilities than those taken on by children of the same age without emotional and behavioral disorders.

9. The respondents overwhelmingly identified consistency, structure, individualization, and strong educational practices (both academic and behavioral) as the backbone of this successful class. In addition, they noted that the unique dynamic of the teachers and paraprofessionals enhanced the effectiveness of these characteristics.

Note. The 12 participants consisted of 6 general and 2 special education teachers who interacted with these students regularly, the school principal, the school's curriculum coordinator, the school librarian, and the clinical psychologist who provided services to the students identified as having emotional and behavioral disorders.

program as they had conceptualized it. At the building level, administrators remained open to the use of alternatives to suspension and expulsion as disciplinary procedures. In addition, they offered flexibility in student scheduling and in carrying out important school practices. For example, the building administration allowed the teachers to substitute periodic home visits for parent conferences at school, which thereby increased parental participation. At the district level, administrators also facilitated the success of the program by modifying physical facilities to meet needs (e.g., building a safe time-out room, providing an outside telephone line in the classroom) and by recognizing the need for training support staff (educational assistants, counselors and psychologists, nearby teachers) to deal effectively with students, especially in crisis situations. Moreover, taking into consideration the intensity of the behavior and learning problems of the students placed in the class, the special education administration made every effort to maintain small class sizes well below state maximums. Without this administrative confidence in the program—combined with a willingness to invest time and money into it—the teachers would surely have been less successful.

Many parents of students in the program had become accustomed to associating school with failure, often for themselves as well as for their children. Perhaps for this reason, many remained extremely reluctant to become involved with the school. Even though the teachers made significant efforts to establish positive working relationships with all the parents of their students, teachers were only minimally successful in this area. Before school began, the teachers sent postcards to incoming or returning students and brief letters of welcome to every parent or guardian. If possible, they arranged a home visit during the weeks just before school started to allow parents to meet them personally and to ask questions. As school events occurred throughout the year, the teachers conveyed a great deal of enthusiasm to the students and made efforts to ensure that every student would be represented by some important adult in his or her life at these important school functions. The teachers offered transportation, babysitting, and refreshments whenever possible to remove some of the barriers often encountered by parents who want to become involved in their child's school life. For the first half of the school year, the teachers also held monthly parent group meetings to create a support system for parents and to gain insight into what the parents needed from the school. Nevertheless, parent attendance at school events rarely exceeded 50%, and the teachers grew frustrated with the minimal returns from their efforts. Perhaps it is important to request assistance from other school personnel (administrators, counselors, psychologists) and possibly other community agencies (social services, parent–teacher associations) to find and carry out ways of increasing parental involvement at school.

Another aspect of the program that could be improved is the use of ongoing academic assessments. Having learned a great deal in graduate studies about formative assessments like curriculum-based measurement (L. S. Fuchs & D. Fuchs, 1996; Overton, 2000), the teachers were anxious to add this component to the program. In addition to providing the teachers with accurate data to inform instructional decision making, this approach allows for students to take an active role in charting their progress and setting goals for academic achievement. As we suggested previously, teachers must foster change, and the only way to know that children have changed is to assess their behavior carefully and frequently.

CONCLUSION

The special class described in this article bolsters the argument for preservation of the continuum of alternative placements available to students with disabilities, including separate classes and special schools. If our goal as a society is to provide equal access to an appropriate education, then some students with disabilities may truly need something that is unequal to the general education classroom—a more supportive, more individualized, and more carefully monitored classroom environment (Brigham & Kauffman, 1998). The differences we know as emotional or behavioral disorders are particularly likely to require special environments to meet students' needs.

We caution that a special class or a special school is not better than general education simply because it is separate. Separate can be worse than not separate. Separation from general education is never sufficient in itself to make an environment better. The program's components—teaching, providing emotional support, providing structure, and offering systematic rewards—make a place better than an alternative. However, we believe that separation from the mainstream of education is sometimes necessary for educators to develop and maintain the nature and intensity of instruction and support needed by some students.

ACKNOWLEDGMENT

This article was prepared while James M. Kauffman was associated with the Shaklee Institute for the Improvement of Special Education as a Shaklee Scholar. The co-authors were co-recipients of the Shaklee Teacher Award in 1998.

REFERENCES

Andrews, J. E., Carnine, D. W., Coturnho, M. J., Edgar, E. G., Forness, S. R., Fuchs. L. S., et al. (2000). Bridging the special education divide. *Remedial and Special Education, 21,* 258–260.

Bear, G. G. (1998). School discipline in the United States: Prevention, correction, and long-term social development. *School Psychology Review, 27,* 14–32.

Beyer, D. S. (1997, October). *Strengthening Virginia's communities—Everyone can do something.* [Position statement by Lt. Governor Donald S. Beyer, Jr. on community support for people with disabilities]. Richmond, VA: Office of the Lieutenant Governor.

Biklen, D. (1989). Making difference ordinary. In S. Stainback, W. Stainback, & M. Forest (Eds.), *Educating all students in the mainstream of regular education* (pp. 235–248). Baltimore: Brookes.

Brigham, F. J., & Kauffman, J. M. (1998). Creating supportive environments for students with emotional or behavioral disorders. *Effective School Practices, 17*(2), 25–35.

Carnine, D. (2000). *Why education experts resist effective practices (and what it would take to make education more like medicine).* Washington, DC: Fordham Foundation.

Carpenter, B., & Bovair, K. (1996). Learning with dignity: Educational opportunities for students with emotional and behavioral difficulties. *Canadian Journal of Special Education, 11*(1), 6–16.

Conquest, R. (2000). *Reflections on a ravaged century.* New York: Norton.

Council for Exceptional Children. (1997). A disability or a gift? *CEC Today, 4*(3), 7.

Crockett, J. B., & Kauffman, J. M. (1999). *The least restrictive environment: Its origins and interpretations in special education.* Mahwah, NJ: Erlbaum.

Crockett, J. B., & Kauffman, J. M. (2001). The concept of the least restrictive environment and learning disabilities: Least restrictive of what? Reflections on Cruickshank's 1977 guest editorial for the *Journal of Learning Disabilities.* In D. P. Hallahan & B. K. Keogh (Eds.), *Research and global perspectives in learning disabilities: Essays in honor of William M. Cruickshank* (pp. 1–20). Mahwah, NJ: Erlbaum.

Curwin, R., & Mendler, A. (2000). Six strategies for helping youth move from rage to responsibility. *Reaching Today's Youth, 4*(2), 17–20.

Cypress Group. (1996). *The think time strategy for schools: Bringing order to the classroom* [Video and workbook]. Spokane, WA: Author.

Danforth, S., & Rhodes, W. C. (1997). Deconstructing disability: A philosophy for inclusion. *Remedial and Special Education, 18,* 357–366.

Deshler, D. D., Ellis, E. S., & Lenz, B. K. (1996). *Teaching adolescents with learning disabilities: Strategies and methods* (2nd ed.). Denver, CO: Love.

Dupre, A. P. (1997). Disability and the public schools: The case against "inclusion." *Washington Law Review, 72*(3), 775–858.

Engelmann, S., & Carnine, D. (1991). *Theory of instruction and mastery: Principles and applications* (2nd ed.). Eugene, OR: Association for Direct Instruction.

Erikson, F. (1986). Qualitative methods in research on teaching. In M. C. Wittrock (Ed.), *Handbook of research in teaching* (3rd ed., pp. 119–161). New York: Macmillan.

Farmer, T. W., Farmer, E. M., & Gut, D. (1999). Implications of social development research for school-based interventions for aggressive youth with emotional and behavioral disorders. *Journal of Emotional and Behavioral Disorders, 7,* 130–136.

Fuchs, D., & Fuchs, L. S. (1994). Inclusive schools movement and the radicalization of special education reform. *Exceptional Children, 60,* 294–309.

Fuchs, L. S., & Fuchs, D. (1996). Combining performance assessment and curriculum-based measurement to strengthen instructional planning. *Learning Disabilities Research and Practice, 11,* 183–192.

Gartner, A., & Lipsky, D. K. (1987). Beyond special education: Toward a quality system for all students. *Harvard Educational Review, 57,* 367–390.

Gartner, A., & Lipsky, D. K. (1989). *The yoke of special education: How to break it.* Rochester, NY: National Center on Education and the Economy.

Gelernter, D. (1997). *Drawing life: Surviving the Unabomber.* New York: Free Press.

Glazer, N. (1997). *We are all multiculturalists now.* Cambridge, MA: Harvard University Press.

Goldstein, A. P. (1988). *The prepare curriculum.* Champaign, IL: Research Press.

Goldstein, A. P. (2000). Catch it low to prevent it high: Countering low-level verbal abuse. *Reaching Today's Youth, 4*(2), 10–16.

Gunter, P. L., Denny, R. K., Jack, S. L., Shores, R. E., & Nelson, C. M. (1993). Aversive stimuli in academic interactions between students with serious emotional disturbance and their teachers. *Behavioral Disorders, 18,* 265–274.

Gunter, P. L., Hummel, J. H., & Conroy, M. A. (1998). Increasing correct academic responding: An effective intervention strategy to decrease problem behavior. *Effective School Practices, 17*(2), 55–63.

Gunter, P. L., Jack, S. L., DePaepe, P., Reed, T. M., & Harrison, J. (1994). Effects of challenging behaviors of students with EBD on teacher instructional behavior. *Preventing School Failure, 38*(3), 35–39.

Hobbs, N. (1982). *The troubled and troubling child.* San Francisco: Jossey-Bass.

Hockenbury, J. C., Kauffman, J. M., & Hallahan, D. P. (1999–2000). What's right about special education. *Exceptionality, 8*(1), 3–11.

Hungerford, R. H. (1950). On locusts. *American Journal of Mental Deficiency, 54,* 415–418.

Individuals with Disabilities Education Act of 1990, 20 U.S.C. § 1400 *et seq.*

Jack, S. L., Shores, R. E., Denny, R. K., Gunter, P. L., De Briere, T., & De Paepe, P. (1996). An analysis of the relationship between teachers' reported use of classroom management strategies on types of classroom interactions. *Journal of Behavioral Education, 6,* 67–87.

Jenkins, P. H. (1997). School delinquency and the school social bond. *Journal of Research in Crime and Delinquency, 34,* 337–367.

Johns, B. H. (2000). The peace-filled classroom: Creating a non-aggressive classroom environment. *Reaching Today's Youth, 4*(2), 27–31.

Kamps, D., Kravits, T., Stolze, J., & Swaggart, B. (1999). Preventive strategies for students at risk and students with EBD in urban elementary school settings. *Journal of Emotional and Behavioral Disorders, 7,* 178–188.

Kauffman, J. M. (1989). The regular education initiative as Reagan–Bush education policy: A trickle-down theory of education of the hard-to-teach. *Journal of Special Education, 23,* 256–278.

Kauffman, J. M. (1993). How we might achieve the radical reform of special education. *Exceptional Children, 60,* 6–16.

Kauffman, J. M. (1994). Places of change: Special education's power and identity in an era of educational reform. *Journal of Learning Disabilities, 27,* 610–618.

Kauffman, J. M. (1996). The challenge of nihilism. *Teacher Education and Special Education, 19,* 205–206.

Kauffman, J. M. (1999a). Commentary: Today's special education and its messages for tomorrow. *The Journal of Special Education, 32,* 244–254.

Kauffman, J. M. (1999b). How we prevent the prevention of emotional and behavioral disorders. *Exceptional Children, 65,* 448–468.

Kauffman, J. M. (1999c). What we make of difference and the difference we make [Foreword]. In V. L. Schwean & D. H. Saklofske (Eds.), *Handbook of psychosocial characteristics of exceptional children* (pp. ix–xiii). New York: Plenum.

Kauffman, J. M. (2001). *Characteristics of emotional and behavioral disorders of children and youth* (7th ed.). Upper Saddle River, NJ: Prentice Hall.

Kauffman, J. M., & Burbach, H. J. (1997). On creating a climate of classroom civility. *Phi Delta Kappan, 79,* 320–325.

Kauffman, J. M., & Hallahan, D. P. (1993). Toward a comprehensive delivery system for special education. In J. I. Goodlad & T. C. Lovitt (Eds.), *Integrating general and special education* (pp. 73–102). New York: Merrill.

Kauffman, J. M., & Hallahan, D. P. (1997). A diversity of restrictive environments: Placement as a problem of social ecology. In J. W. Lloyd, E. J. Kameenui, & D. Chard (Eds.), *Issues in educating students with disabilities* (pp. 325–342). Hillsdale, NJ: Erlbaum.

Kauffman, J. M., Mostert, M. P., Trent, S. C., & Hallahan, D. P. (1998). *Managing classroom behavior: A reflective case-based approach.* Boston: Allyn & Bacon.

Kavale, K. A., & Forness, S. R. (2000). History, rhetoric, and reality: Analysis of the inclusion debate. *Remedial and Special Education, 21,* 279–296.

Kerr, M. M., & Nelson, C. M. (1998). *Strategies for managing behavior problems in the classroom* (2nd ed.). Columbus, OH: Merrill.

Koertge, N. (Ed.). (1998). *A house built on sand: Exposing postmodern myths about science.* New York: Oxford University Press.

Landrum, T. J. (1997). Why data don't matter. *Journal of Behavioral Education, 7,* 123–129.

Lewis, T. J., & Garrison-Harrell, L. (1999). Effective behavioral support: Designing setting-specific interventions. *Effective School Practices, 17*(4), 38–46.

Lipsky, D. K., & Gartner, A. (1987). Capable of achievement and worthy of respect: Education for handicapped students as if they were full-fledged human beings. *Exceptional Children, 54,* 69–74.

Lipsky, D. K., & Gartner, A. (Eds.). (1989). *Beyond separate education: Quality education for all students.* Baltimore: Brookes.

Lipsky, D. K., & Gartner, A. (1991). Restructuring for quality. In J. W. Lloyd, N. N. Singh, & A. C. Repp (Eds.), *The regular education initiative: Alternative perspectives on concepts, issues, and models* (pp. 43–57). Sycamore, IL: Sycamore.

Lipsky, D. K., & Gartner, A. (1996). Equity requires inclusion: The future for all students with disabilities. In C. Christensen & F. Rizvi (Eds.), *Disability and the dilemmas of education and justice* (pp. 144–155). Philadelphia: Open University Press.

Lipsky, D. K., & Gartner, A. (Eds.). (1997). *Inclusion and school reform: Transforming American classrooms.* Baltimore: Brookes.

MacMillan, D. R., Gresham, F. M., & Forness, S. R. (1996). Full inclusion: An empirical perspective. *Behavioral Disorders, 21,* 145–159.

Manno, C. J., Bantz, J., & Kauffman, J. M. (2000). Cultural causes of rage and violence in children and youth. *Reaching Today's Youth, 4*(2), 54–59.

Mattaini, M. A., Twyman, J. S., Chin, W., & Lee, K. N. (1996). Youth violence. In M. A. Mattaini & B. A. Thyer (Eds), *Finding solutions to social problems: Behavioral strategies for change* (pp. 75–111). Washington, DC: American Psychological Association.

Mayer, G. R. (1995). Preventing anti-social behavior in the schools. *Journal of Applied Behavioral Analysis, 28,* 467–478.

McGinnis, E., & Goldstein, A. P. (1984). *Skillstreaming the elementary school child: A guide for teaching prosocial skills.* Champaign, IL: Research Press.

Milloy, C. (2001, March 7). Students thrive at a supportive special school. *The Washington Post,* p. B1.

Nelson, J. R. (1996). Designing schools to meet the needs of students who exhibit disruptive behavior. *Journal of Emotional and Behavioral Disorders, 6,* 147–161.

Nelson, J. R., Johnson, A., & Marchand-Martella, N. (1996). Effects of direct instruction, cooperative learning, and independent learning practices on the classroom behavior of students with behavioral disorders: A comparative analysis. *Journal of Emotional and Behavioral Disorders, 4,* 53–62.

Overton, T. (2000). *Assessment in special education: An applied approach* (3rd ed.). Upper Saddle River, NJ: Merrill.

Porter, A. C., & Brophy, J. (1988). Synthesis of research on good teaching: Insights from the work of the Institute for Research on Teaching. *Educational Leadership, 45*(8), 74–85.

Premack, D. (1959). Toward empirical behavior laws I: Positive reinforcement. *Psychological Review, 66,* 219–233.

Rhode, G., Jenson, W. R., & Reavis, H. K. (1992). *The tough kid book: Practical classroom management strategies.* Longmont, CO: Sopris West.

Sagan, C. (1996). Does truth matter? Science, pseudoscience, and civilization. *Skeptical Inquirer, 20*(3), 28–33.

Shattuck, R. (1999). *Candor and perversion: Literature, education, and the arts.* New York: Norton.

Shores, R. E., Jack, S. L., Gunter, P. L., Ellis, D. N., De Briere, T. J., & Wehby, J. H. (1993). Classroom interactions of children with behavioral disorders. *Journal of Emotional and Behavioral Disorders, 1,* 27–39.

Skiba, R. J., & Peterson, R. L. (2000). School discipline at a crossroads: From zero tolerance to early response. *Exceptional Children, 66,* 335–347.

Skrtic, T. M., Sailor, W., & Gee, K. (1996). Voice, collaboration, and inclusion: Democratic themes in education and social reform. *Remedial and Special Education, 17,* 142–157.

Sokal, A., & Bricmont, J. (1998). *Fashionable nonsense: Postmodern intellectuals' abuse of science.* New York: Picador.

Stainback, S., & Stainback, W. (1984). A rationale for the merger of special and regular education. *Exceptional Children, 51,* 102–111.

Stainback, S., & Stainback, W. (1987). Integration versus cooperation: A commentary on "Educating children with learning problems: A shared responsibility." *Exceptional Children, 54,* 66–68.

Stainback, S., & Stainback, W. (1992). *Curriculum considerations in inclusive classrooms: Facilitating learning for all students.* Baltimore: Brookes.

Stainback, S., Stainback, W., & Forest, M. (1989). *Educating all students in the mainstream of regular education.* Baltimore: Brookes.

Stainback, W., & Stainback, S. (1991). A rationale for integrating and restructuring: A synopsis. In J. W. Lloyd, N. N. Singh, & A. C. Repp (Eds.), *The regular education initiative: Alternative perspectives on concepts, issues, and models* (pp. 226–239). Sycamore, IL: Sycamore.

Talbot, M. (2000, September 10). The maximum security adolescent. *The New York Times Magazine,* 41–47, 58–59, 88, 96.

Turnbull, A. P., Turnbull, H. R., Shank, M., & Leal, D. (1995). *Exceptional lives: Special education in today's schools.* Upper Saddle River, NJ: Merrill.

Valencia, R. R. (1997). Conceptualizing the notion of deficit thinking. In R. R. Valencia (Ed.), *The evolution of deficit thinking: Educational thought and practice* (pp. 1–12). London: Falmer.

Van Acker, R. (2000). From enraged to engaged: School-based strategies to address aggression and violence. *Reaching Today's Youth, 4*(2), 32–39.

Walker, H. M., McConnell, S., Holmes, D., Todis, B.,Walker, J., & Golden, N. (1983). *The Walker social skills curriculum: The ACCEPTS program.* Austin, TX: PRO-ED.

Walker, H. M., Todis, J., Holmes, D., & Horton, D. (1988). *Adolescent coping curriculum for effective social skills (ACCESS).* Austin, TX: PRO-ED.

Wang, M. C., Reynolds, M. C., & Walberg, H. J. (1988). Integrating the children of the second system. *Phi Delta Kappan, 70,* 248–251.

Wehby, J. H., Symons, F. J., Canale, J. A., & Go, F. J. (1998). Teaching practices for students with emotional and behavioral disorders: Discrepancies between recommendations and observations. *Behavioral Disorders, 24*, 51–56.

White, W. A. (1988). A meta-analysis of the effects of direct instruction in special education. *Education and Treatment of Children, 11*, 364–374.

Wood, E., Woloshyn, V., & Willoughby, T. (1995). *Cognitive strategy instruction for middle and high schools.* Cambridge, MA: Brookline.

Yell, M. L. (1998a). *The law and special education.* Upper Saddle River, NJ: Merrill.

Yell, M. L. (1998b). The legal basis of inclusion. *Educational Leadership, 56*(2), 70–73.

CHAPTER 23

Inclusive Education: Right for *Some*

Bernard Rimland

s there the parent of an autistic child who wouldn't be delighted beyond words if the child would simply blend smoothly into a regular classroom? That is a dream we all share. For a few, the dream becomes a reality. Over the years, I have heard from a number of parents who have shared with us their joy, their pride, and their good fortune: "Billy has been included in a regular classroom! He is having a hard time adjusting, but he is making it!" But, for every parent whose child "makes it," there are many more who are not so fortunate.

Much as my wife and I would like to have our autistic son Mark be able to cope successfully in a normal school, it is very clear to us that he could not have done so. He has come along much farther than we ever dared hope, and we are quite confident it is because he was always in special classes, taught by experienced, skilled, caring teachers, exhibiting monumental patience, who had gone to great lengths to train themselves in methods that would help Mark and children like him achieve their full potential.

If a child can be effectively "included," he probably should be. Lovaas got excellent results by mainstreaming the most successful of his early intervention group, but only after intensive training. But there is a difference between inclusion and over-inclusion.

If your child functions far below the normal child intellectually, academically, and socially, does it make sense to insist that he or she be "included" in a regular classroom? Certainly not, in my view, and in the view of many, if not the vast majority, of parents of autistic children.

Today, special schools and special classes for autistic children are under heavy attack by people promoting "full inclusion." What is full inclusion? Full inclusion means abolishing the special education provisions that are vitally important to autistic children.

Unfortunately, many professionals and parents have adopted the ideology that full inclusion is the *only* option that should be made available for any child, irrespective of how inappropriate it may be for that child, and irrespective of the wishes of the parents of that child. What is worse, these people have managed to sway legislative and educational policy so that other options are prohibited. A quarter of a century ago, those of us who pioneered public education for autistic children struggled long and hard to compel the educational system to provide things that we knew were necessary to the appropriate education of our children. This included, first and foremost, teachers who were trained in the techniques of behavior modification and who understood the peculiarities of autistic children.

In the last issue of the ARRI [*Austism Research Review International*] we published a small article titled "Full Inclusion: The Right Choice?" Our article was based on a report by Simpson and Sasso in which they noted that there was no empirical evidence showing that full inclusion was beneficial to autistic children. That short article brought a surprisingly strong response from our readers. It seems that the full inclusion movement has been so quickly bought by the educational establishment that those who believe that a full range of options should be available have not had time to organize any meaningful opposition. We received many letters and calls of thanks from parents who were pleased to see that we were addressing this issue.

Several years ago I received an urgent plea for help from a group of parents in Michigan whose children attended the Burger Center for Autistic Children. I was invited to speak there and made a tour of the facility. I was impressed. The staff were obviously very much involved with autism, the teaching of autistic children, and all the details of autism. They communicated with each other with ideas and suggestions and enthusiasm that won my admiration. They certainly had the support of the parent group. The problem was that full inclusion was being heavily promoted in Michigan, and rational and efficient programs like the Burger School program for autism were in dire threat of being closed down.

I have no quarrel with inclusionists if they are content to insist upon inclusion for their children, or for children of other parents who feel that it is optimum for their children. But when they try to force me and other unwilling parents to dance to their tune, I find it highly objectionable and quite intolerable. Parents need *options.*

If there are no objective data showing that full inclusion works better than giving people several options, why is it being promoted so avidly? Douglas Biklen attempts to answer that question solely on ideological grounds. In his book, *Achieving the Complete School,* he says of mainstreaming, "To ask, Does it work? is to ask the wrong question." He believes that full inclusion and mainstreaming should be the only choice available to us because it is the right choice, the *right thing to do.* He makes an analogy with slavery. Slavery, he says, was abolished because it was morally wrong, not because it didn't work. He also asserts that objective scientific data are irrelevant because the issue is a moral one.

I disagree strongly with Biklen on both counts. Biklen has the slavery analogy exactly backward: Making full inclusion the only option does not resemble the *abolition* of slavery, but instead the *imposition* of slavery. Like slavery, full inclusion rejects the idea that people should be free to choose for themselves the options they desire, and compels them to accede to the wishes of others. And as for Biklen's rejection of scientific data, I want my children educated in ways that will assure the best outcome, as learned from scientific studies, not in ways that accord with someone's theory, or ideology, or the educational fad of the year.

Special education consultant Laurence Lieberman is one of the very few educators with the courage to speak out and tell the compulsory full inclusionists that they are wrong. Recently the National Association of State Boards of Education endorsed the principle of full inclusion of students with disabilities. Lieberman's insightful response, published as a letter to the editor in *Education Week* for December 16, 1992, is a classic, and is reprinted here in part:

> People involved in education cannot agree on school choice, promotion policies, achievement testing, curricula, teaching approaches, or the distribution of condoms. But all the state boards of education can agree on full inclusion for all disabled students?
>
> This is obviously a money issue, pure and simple. The key may be found in the paragraph in your story that says a new report from NASBE proposes that funds be provided on the basis of instructional need, not head counts. That need seems to have been already predetermined by the organization: full inclusion in regular classrooms for all disabled students.
>
> The article—and quite possibly the report—refuses to deal with the real nature of some children, which might require that they not be in a regular classroom.
>
> Some educators would place the issue of full inclusion solely in the realm of morality. Anything separate is evil. There may be a higher immorality than separateness: lack of progress, lack of achievement, lack of skills, and splintered learning of meaningless academic trivia.
>
> There is the issue that special education hasn't been effective. Where, and for whom and why? Because it has been too separate? Unlikely. The regular classroom is not separate by definition. Has it worked? Sometimes, but not all the time. Placing severely disabled students in regular classrooms presupposes a level of individualization that does not exist.
>
> Some educators believe that disabled children will be much more accepted, and society as a whole will show much greater compassion for the disabled, if all children are in regular classrooms—Knowledge does not necessarily lead to compassion.

There is a common belief that when disabled children are in physical proximity to normal children they will tend to adopt more normal behavior patterns. This is obviously not the case with many autistic children, who generally begin life surrounded by normal families.

Full inclusion is not *the* right thing to do. It is one right thing to do, sometimes.

Any organization … that endorses full inclusion is taking an extremist position that has no place in an educational system and a society that prides itself on its choices and multiple ways to achieve a desired quality of life.

I agree with Lieberman. If special education for autism is destroyed, it will be lost for at least one generation, and perhaps several.

Author Index

Subject Index

About the Editors

James M. Kauffman is Professor Emeritus in the Curry School of Education at the University of Virginia (UVA), where he has been a faculty member since 1970. He held the Charles S. Robb and William Clay Parrish, Jr., professorships and served as chair of the Department of Special Education and as Associate Dean for Research at UVA. He has taught in both general elementary and special education classrooms. He received his EdD in special education from the University of Kansas in 1969. Kauffman is a past president of the Council for Exceptional Children's (CEC's) Council for Children with Behavioral Disorders (CCBD) and served for 3 years as co-editor of *Behavioral Disorders*. He received the 2002 Outstanding Leadership Award from CCBD, the 1991 Award for Outstanding Service from the Midwest Symposium for Leadership in Behavior Disorders, the 1994 CEC Research Award, and a 1995 Special Kuhn Barnett Award from the Virginia Federation of the Council for Exceptional Children.

Daniel P. Hallahan received his PhD in education and psychology from the University of Michigan and has been a member of the faculty of the Curry School of Education at the University of Virginia since 1971. He is currently chair of the Department of Curriculum, Instruction, and Special Education. Hallahan has held the Virgil S. Ward endowed professorship and the Cavaliers' Distinguished Teaching Chair at UVA. He was the inaugural editor of *Exceptionality* and serves on the editorial boards of *Learning Disabilities Research and Practice, Learning Disability Quarterly, The Journal of Special Education,* and *Exceptionality.* Hallahan is a past president of CEC's Division for Learning Disabilities and received the University of Virginia Outstanding Teaching Award in 1998, the 2000 CEC Research Award, and a State Council of Higher Education for Virginia Outstanding Faculty Award in 2003.